YANK

THE STORY OF WORLD WAR II
AS WRITTEN BY THE SOLDIERS

YANK

THE STORY OF WORLD WAR II
AS WRITTEN BY THE SOLDIERS

by the editors of *Yank*,
the Army Weekly

With a new Foreword by Franklin S. Forsberg,
former Commanding Officer of *Yank*

GREENWICH HOUSE
Distributed by Crown Publishers, Inc.
New York

A Lou Reda Book.
Compilation Copyright © 1984 by Yank Productions, Inc.
All rights reserved.

This 1984 edition is published by Greenwich House, a division of
Arlington House, Inc. distributed by Crown Publishers, Inc.
by arrangement with Lou Reda.

Manufactured in the United States of America
The material in this book was previously in *Yank—The GI Story of the War,* and
The Best From *Yank the Army Weekly.*

ISBN: 0-517-436221
h g f e d c b a

PHOTO CREDITS

CONTENTS

FOREWORD

Yank, the Army weekly, was the most unique publication in the annals of publishing history. *Yank* was, in every sense of the work, a medium "by and for the enlisted man." Those of us officers who had the privilege of being associated with *Yank* never contributed to the editorial content. We merely did the administrative chores. Much credit is due to the intrepid, enterprising, courageous and hard-working G.I. writers, editors, artists, photographers, production, circulation and administrative staff.

Yank was a global publication with twenty-one editions produced weekly and printed in seventeen locations. It truly was the pioneer in world-wide publishing and will remain a monument to genuine freedom of the press.

I salute all those who worked on and for *Yank* and all those G.I. readers who knew it was "their" publication.

FRANKLIN S. FORSBERG
FORMERLY COLONEL IN THE ARMY
OF THE UNITED STATES
AND COMMANDING OFFICER OF *YANK*

The GI

THE CIVILIAN went before the Army doctors, took off his clothes, feeling silly; jigged, stooped, squatted, wet into a bottle; became a soldier.

He learned how to sleep in the mud, tie a knot, kill a man.

He learned the ache of loneliness, the ache of exhaustion, the kinship of misery. From the beginning he wanted to go home. He learned that men make the same queasy noises in the morning, feel the same longings at night; that every man is alike and that each man is different.

Maybe he was white or black or yellow or red, and if he was on the line it didn't make much difference, because a soldier on the line was so dirty you couldn't tell his color anyway.

Maybe he huddled at night in a hole dug in jagged coral or clammy sand and prayed: "God, let me get hit tomorrow but not bad, so I can get out of this." Maybe he didn't fight at all. Maybe he built latrines in Mississippi or cranked a mimeograph machine in Manila, taking chicken, knowing that you can't kill the enemy with a shovel or book at more than ten paces, still wanting to go home.

He was often bored; he wasn't always brave; most times he was scared.

Maybe he was young, like 20-year-old Ed Halpin, who landed at Normandy, H-Hour, D-Day, crawled on his belly up the beach and said: "Goddammit, no matter what place the Army picks to put soldiers, it always picks a place that looks like Oklahoma." Or maybe he wasn't so young, like Jake Privett, a 37-year-old pfc, who

was killed in the Battle of Luxembourg and left a wife and five kids back in Blytheville, Arkansas.

Maybe he's just a memory in a photo album now, or a dogtag stuck on a cross of wood near a tiny town whose name you can't pronounce. Or maybe half his face was torn away and he's ashamed to walk down the streets any more because other people are whole and he's not. Maybe he broke his neck slipping on an orange peel in front of a whorehouse in Algiers.

Or maybe he made it. Maybe he came through all right. Maybe no one ever shot at him. Maybe he wonders why he was in the Army—what he did. There was John Padgett, a rifleman from the blue hills behind Chattanooga, who squirted tobacco juice on a bunker of the Siegfried Line and said: "Beats hell out of me what I'm doing here except I always did kinda have an itch to pat my behind at that feller Hitler."

Maybe he didn't know what fascism was—maybe he did. The GI did not destroy fascism. But he helped defeat the fascists and he took away their guns.

He was part of an army that left its bootprints on three continents, a hundred islands—deep in history. With his allies he saved the world; and hoped to God he'd never have to do it again.

He had learned the ache of loneliness, the ache of exhaustion, the kinship of misery. He had learned how to sleep in the mud, tie a knot, kill a man.

And having learned all this, if he got through all right the soldier came home and took off his clothes, feeling silly; jigged, stooped, squatted, wet into a bottle; became a civilian.

—SGT. DEBS MYERS

Here are their faces————

Nobody knows the trouble they've seen

THE INFANTRY, free from the claustrophobia of the Huertgen Forest, went on, but behind them they left their dead, and the forest will stink with deadness long after the last body is removed. The forest will bear the scars of our advance long after our own scars have healed, and the Infantry has scars that will never heal.

For Huertgen was agony, and there was no glory in it except the glory of courageous men —the MP whose testicles were hit by shrapnel and who said, "Okay, doc, I can take it"; the man who walked forward firing Tommy guns with both hands until an arm was blown off and then kept on firing the other Tommy gun until he disappeared in a mortar burst.

—SGT. MACK MORRISS

————————

It had been such a long day. All day and all night riding in trucks with the same old K rations to eat, sleeping in your clothes as usual, a single blanket maybe to cut off the night wind. Just some sniper fire and a few isolated machine-guns to wipe out. Nothing much.

Two buddies stretched out together off the road.

"You know, Willie, I'm scared. I'm so goddam scared . . ."

"Are you nuts? The way we're going now, the whole thing will blow over in a couple of weeks. Then you can go back to your wife and make babies and tell all your kids about what a wonderful hero you were."

"That's what I'm scared about, Willie. It's almost over and I'm almost home and I'm scared that maybe just a lucky shot will get me. And I don't want to die now, Willie, not when it's almost over. I don't want to die now. Do you know what I mean?"

"I know what you mean . . ."

—SGT. RALPH G. MARTIN

————————

It is strange the way some people still think of war as all shooting and Commando raids, when as a matter of fact it is nine-tenths grind with no excitement and a great deal of unpleasantness. Sometimes there is excitement, but mostly it is the loose-bowled kind that you would just as soon be without. Sometimes, of course, there is more than excitement; there is the good feeling that comes from being with men you trust and doing a job you believe in.

But, most of the time, for the men who are really up there, the war in Italy is a tough and dirty life, without immediate compensation. It is cold nights and no sleep, the beard matted on your face and the sores coming out on your feet, the clothes stiffening and the dirt caking on your body.

It is digging and crawling and sweating out the 88s, inching forward over rocks and through

New Georgia

Africa

rivers to mountains that no one in his right mind would ever want. It is doing the same filthy job day after day with a kind of purposeless insanity; and dreaming all the time of warm beds with clean sheets and a steak the size of your arm; and pushing, always pushing.

—SGT. WALTER BERNSTEIN

Actor Brian Aherne had been touring Italy, France, and Holland portraying Robert Browning in The Barretts of Wimpole Street. *He was standing backstage in Florence when a little dough came up and asked Aherne for his autograph. The dough mentioned he had met Aherne once before at Camp Wheeler in Georgia.*

"Ah, yes, I remember that day at Camp Wheeler," said Aherne. "I went out on the range with you fellows there. And I remember one of your colonels telling me, 'We are making it very hard for these men, but when they get overseas they'll look back and thank us for it.' And you are thanking him for it now, aren't you?"

The little dough, who had come out of a rough sector of the 85th Division's line that morning and was going back into it that night, just glanced up at Aherne, lit a cigarette, and walked away.

—SGT. JOE MCCARTHY

The big U.S. battleship was covered with her own wreckage, but she kept on rolling and she kept on firing at the Jap ships. Robertson, a quartermaster third-class, came through the opening from the catwalk and said, "I've lost my shoe, help me find my shoe." He stood there holding one bare foot off the hot deck, groping in the dark. Everyone helped him, even two commanders. The shoe was not found until next morning—under a body on the catwalk.

An officer came into the compartment. He walked to the quartermaster and said in a strained voice, "Feel my arm. It's been hit and I can't tell if it's still there. Go ahead, tell me." The quartermaster, still standing without his shoe, timidly reached for the officer's shoulder but then decided to find out the other way. He groped his way up the officer's leg until he came to his hip, then reached out for his hand. Finding it still there, he ran his hand up the officer's arm until he came to a gaping shrapnel wound in the officer's shoulder. He reported what he had found, and the officer said, "Thanks," and walked out.

During the entire action a lookout standing by a slot kept repeating in a low voice: "Lord, I'm scared. Nobody has any idea how scared I am. How could anyone be this scared? My God. I'm scared."

—ROBERT L. SCHWARTZ Y2c

There was so much violation of the non-fraternization ruling that the GIs in Germany compared it with prohibition. A staff sergeant in the 30th Infantry Division said there was one big difference between non-fraternization and prohibition—in the old days a guy could hide a bottle inside his coat for days at a time, but it was hard to keep a German girl quiet there for more than a couple of hours.

A tanker said: "Fraternization? Yeh, I suppose it's all right. Anyway, I've been doing it right along. But every now and then I wake up in a cold sweat.

"What do I dream about? I dream that we are at war again, and the German bastards I'm fighting this time are my own."

—SGT. ALLAN B. ECKER

At night before a big airborne operation you crawl deeper in your sack, but you can't get away from the noise. Over the roar of engines somebody is shouting a bunch of names: Andrews . . . Burger . . . Edwards . . . Fairbanks . . . Jones, Jack Jones . . . and on down the roster.

Attu

Italy

C Company is falling out to fit their 'chutes.

Tomorrow there will be an early breakfast—0400, the order said. Then we will climb into our parachutes as dawn breaks. We will trudge out to the planes and climb in, not saying much of anything about anything. The men will know where they are going and what they are going to do. Some have done it before; for others this is the first time. But they all know that this jump across the Rhine will be the end of the krauts.

They'll sweat a bit, as any paratrooper sweats before making a parachute jump. They will get the same old butterflies. But they'll jump.

—CPL. BOB KRELL

(Cpl. Krell was killed in action twelve hours after he wrote this.)

When the Bushmasters—the 158th Regimental Combat Team—landed at Sarmi they encountered more Japs than anyone had figured. A big hump covered with a thick strand of trees and undergrowth rose along the shore. A good part of the time the Japs and the Bushmasters were on top of each other without knowing it.

When the word came for the Bushmasters to pull back, Pfc. Dan French, an Indian BAR man in Company F, didn't hear the order. He stayed there and killed Japs until he lost count of how many he had killed. Maybe it was 30, or maybe it was 40.

The Bushmasters later retook the hill. The brass and everybody else pounded French on the back until it hurt.

But later on whenever French got drunk he'd wail and moan and beat his chest and feel bad because no one had had the common courtesy to tell him to get the hell off that hill.

—SGT. DALE KRAMER

That night in New Georgia the Jap worked by familiar formula, throwing in his little grenades which exploded with much noise and little effect, tossing in his knee-mortar shells, pouring

in his fast-firing, brittle-sounding automatic fire.

Three times during the night the Jap attacked in what would amount to platoon strength, and each time the attack was cut to pieces. In the morning the air-cooled light machineguns looked as if they'd been in a fire, with their barrels burnt orange and flaking. But they kept on firing.

In the jungle the first light of dawn always brings heavy fire, and this time it was heavy.

Once a man was gut-shot, and two medics picked him up and walked him, one on either side, through the fire to safety. Another man was shot and as he raised up he said, "I'm hit." As he fell forward he said, "I'm dead." He was.

—SGT. MACK MORRISS

Rest periods in the ETO may have been short, but on occasion they gave a soldier a chance to get completely away from traditional Army life. No matter how wretched and dirty an Italian town happened to be, at least it was a change. In the Pacific there are no civilian cities to visit or hot spots to gather in.

And these Pacific battlefields are of little interest to the average American. There seems to be a greater incentive to fight for Paris than to slug one's way toward Garapan, the capital of Saipan. Even fighting for the dirty North Africa towns had more personal meaning to the GI.

There is yet to be a case in the Pacific equal to the first hours at Salerno, where in the midst of flying shells a man ran up to the beachmaster and cried, "Where's the pro station?"

—CPL. JUSTIN GRAY

Sgt. Rafferty of the 101st Airborne sat at the Eagle's Nest overlooking Berchtesgaden and said that he wanted, more than anything else, to be home by Christmas. He said he had spent last Christmas at a place in Belgium called Bastogne.

"We were cut off there," the sergeant said,

Leyte

Belgium

Saipan

"and it was cold and there was snow on the ground. I was lying in the snow in a gully when I saw a German officer and six other krauts start running from one side of a field to the other side about two hundred yards in front of me. I had the officer in the sights of my M1 just as he started climbing over a fence.

"I squeezed the trigger and this kraut officer just kind of folded across the fence, pressing his hands against his belly and screaming, real high-pitched, like a hurt rabbit. I stood that for about five minutes, then I shot him again. He quit yelling. I got to thinking about it later.

"You know, that was the first time I ever had killed a man on Christmas day."

—SGT. DEBS MYERS

Manila was burning. The whole downtown section was smothered in roaring black billows of smoke. The Jap shells were coming in. A sprawling wooden structure across the street got a direct hit. A Filipino girl stood beside us shaking her head. She said her father and baby brother were inside the burning house.

A pretty, light-skinned woman, dressed in a kimono, was standing across the street. She scolded a little boy, who was pulling at her kimono. She pushed the child and yelled: "Get away from me, you little Jap bastard!"

The Japs threw in more shells. An MP said: "That goddam piece ain't a quarter mile from here! Why don't them spotters get on the ball?"

A middle-aged Filipino wearing a straw hat came up to a GI whose hands were trembling violently and said: "Have you heard any news about the war in Europe?" The GI dropped the cigarette he was trying to get into his mouth. "What the hell about that?" the GI asked, talking to himself. "The man asks me if I've heard any news about the war in Europe, and for three days and nights I haven't been able to find any news about fighting four blocks in front of me."

—SGT. H. N. OLIPHANT

"Sure, there were lots of bodies we never identified," said T/Sgt. Donald Haguall of the 48th Quartermaster Graves Registration. "You know what a direct hit by a shell does to a guy. Or a mine, or a solid hit with a grenade, even. Sometimes all we have is a leg or a hunk of arm.

"The ones that stink the worst are the guys who got internal wounds and are dead about three weeks with the blood staying inside and rotting, and when you move the body the blood comes out of the nose and mouth. Then some of them bloat up in the sun, they bloat up so big that they bust the buttons and then they get blue and the skin peels. They don't all get blue, some of them get black.

"But they all stink. There's only one stink and that's it. You never get used to it, either. As long as you live, you never get used to it. And after a while, the stink gets in your clothes and you can taste it in your mouth.

"You know what I think? I think maybe if every civilian in the world could smell that stink, then maybe we wouldn't have any more wars."

—SGT. RALPH G. MARTIN

Germany

They had come a long way to lie in the sand . . .

To the beaches of New Guinea

THE RIFLEMAN presses the trigger, and the bullet passes through the helmet, scalp, skull, small blood vessels, membrane, into the soft sponginess of the brain.

Then a man is either paralyzed or he's blind or he can't smell anything or he's an idiot with his memory gone, or he's dead.

If a medic picks up a man quickly enough there's a surgeon who can pick out the bullet, tie up the blood vessels, cover up the hole in a man's head with a metal plate. Then, sometimes, a man can learn things all over again, whether it's talking, walking, or smelling.

But if the bullet ripped through the medulla region in the back of a man's head, or if it tore through a big blood vessel in the man's brain, then he's had it.

In Sicily or on New Guinea, it all depends on how a man was holding his head when the bullet hit.

When American troops went into New Guinea, most people, including most of the guys who landed there, didn't know much about the place, except that there were a lot of jungle swamps along the coast and a lot of mountains behind the jungle swamps. The New Guinea campaign didn't get much space in the newspapers at home. It was a long, slogging, bellying-ahead kind of campaign. And, anyway, a man can't show his newspaper clippings to a rifle bullet. It depends on how he was holding his head.

Quite a few Americans didn't get past the beaches in New Guinea.

An army sergeant named Charles E. Butler wrote a poem called "Lullaby" about it:

Was it evening, with a slow wind falling
Upon the gray and broken stillness in the leaves,
The birds calling in terror, and the sky
Broken with wings, and on the drifting shore
The slow tide curling inward, curving and rippling,

Fold upon foam-edged fold, folding at last
Upon you in the sand? Was it evening then,
And quiet, falling to sleep in the silence,
You, with your cheek soft on the ultimate pillow
And your outstretched hand reaching no more
    for the gun,
Or love, or the things of life, sleeping there,
    sleeping?

You have come a long way to lie on the sand,
Forgetful of the motion of
The slow, incessant waves
Curving and falling, the white foam lifting
The white sand drifting
Over your face, your outflung hand,
Drifting and creeping,
Slow and incessant and cool. . . .
You have come a long way, a world away, to
    sleep.

The page will remember a little while;
You are a warning now; a message,
Sleeping like children on the rippled shore,
Forgetful now forever of the slow
Whispers of the curling water
Sifting the sand around you with its long
Reiterant falling and lifting whispering
    music. . . .
You are a message now, forgetful, sleeping;
The idiot print of Time on the wave-washed
    shore. . . .

Sleep now, forgetful of the drifting sand,
The strange cries of birds in the green forest;
Sleep, cold on the sand, immortal on the fading
    page,
Emphatic, grim, forgetful. . . . Sleep, sleep. . . .
Silence will shield the shrieking of the birds,
The wild, quick beating of their wings against
    the tree fronds;
The storm will pass. . . . Silence will cover it;
    Sleep. . . .

Jap run-out at Kiska

IN A JAP ACK-ACK emplacement on South Head, Kiska, Yanks found a copy of Margaret Mitchell's "Gone With the Wind," with the title in English on the rear cover and the entire 614 pages of text in Japanese.

A partly destroyed hut yielded Jap popular song sheets, together with pictures of geisha girls, phonograph records, and the face masks and wooden rifles used in *kendo*, a form of bayonet practice.

Deep in the mud of a cavern were several cases of Suntory whiskey ("First Born in Nippon"), and near the cave was the wreckage of an American P-40, with a Jap-inscribed plaque in English: "Sleeping here a brave hero who lost youth and happiness for his motherland, July 25."

A prize trophy was a panel at Kiska Harbor, lettered in hand-high characters: "WE SHALL COME AGAIN AND KILL OUT SEPARATELY YANKI-JOKER."

But if any Japs dared to come back to Kiska today they would be blown out of the bay or blasted out of the sky with their own guns. Less than a week after Yanks and Canadians foreclosed on Hirohito's abandoned homestead in the Aleutians, Kiska was as strongly defended —with our own and with enemy equipment— as it had been at any time during the 14 months of Jap occupation.

The plain fact is that the Nips were pot-poor retreaters. The bulk of the Japanese troops were probably shuttled out over a period of several weeks, with only a skeleton garrison left behind to defend demolition crews in case we arrived sooner than expected. Though these crews laid a great many mines, they pulled out in such a rush that the major plans for destroying Jap installations and camp areas were botched up.

Big four-and-a-half and six-inch coastal cannon and three-inch dual-purpose guns were left intact, except for missing breech locks. Trained on American invasion parties fighting their way up the cliff walls, these guns might have massacred great numbers of our forces.

Cached away near the abandoned guns was plenty of ammunition, enough for us to have fought off a month-long counterseige, using only the enemy's fortifications. Dozens of six-inch shell casings had been stuffed with explosives by the Japs and cemented at the mouth, but fuses intended to blow them up fizzled out less than a foot from the charges.

Small arms and ammunition, construction materials, piles of blankets, and heavy coats with dog-fur lining and sea-otter collars and cuffs were scattered around for the taking—further evidence that the Jap demolition crews had muffed the ball.

But most of the installations of the Jap Army garrison at Gertrude Cove were "wired for sound," as were almost all the major Jap Navy and Marine installations at Kiska Harbor.

Advance elements, exploring half-buried Jap

huts at the Gertrude Cove beaches, picked up boots and blankets from the floor and exposed booby traps. Dark shafts into the mountainsides, almost as complicated as a Pennsylvania coal mine, had to be scouted as possible hiding places for Japs.

Even after the Allied invasion forces had swarmed over the island, a number of Americans and Canadians fell dead and wounded as a result of enemy mines. Unlike Attu, where American soldiers on the hunt for souvenirs pawed through tents and dugouts almost without mishap, the pickings on Kiska were dangerous.

All these details we had no way of knowing as we boarded the invasion ships, our faces painted green and gray. At midnight we breakfasted on grilled steak and potatoes and a couple of soft-boiled eggs—standard invasion fare. As the men stood at their mess racks to eat, the chaplain's voice came over the ship's loudspeaker: "And now we commit ourselves, our bodies, and our souls unto Thy keeping." Some of the boys did not finish their breakfast.

By a kind of poetic justice, the first four American soldiers to set foot on Kiska were Alaskans. They were part of an advance patrol of scouts from the Alaska Combat Intelligence Platoon, known as "Castner's Cutthroats."

From offshore a brisk chill wind was blowing in their faces as they left the big ship in bobbing rubber boats and paddled through the dangerous rocky passage toward Quisling Cove on the west side of the island. It was 0230, and the jagged skyline of Kiska was silhouetted in the moonlight 500 yards abeam.

Sgt. Clyde Peterson, a 22-year-old fisherman from Sitka, Alaska, was first ashore. Clambering out of the fragile rubber dory right on the heels of Peterson's shoepacs were Pvts. Stanley Dayo, from the interior Alaska mining hamlet of Livengood; Chuck O'Leary of Nome, and Billy Buck, half-Eskimo from King Cove.

While Peterson's squad of scouts, headed by Lt. Earl Acuff, paced hand-picked troops up the knife-edge ridges rising from Quisling Cove, S/Sgt. Edgar M. Walker, a few miles to the north, was guiding a spearhead party of 16 under S/Sgt. Dan Green of Swift Current, Saskatchewan, onto Lilly Beach. Behind their two rubber boats on a towline was a third air-inflated craft with one and a half tons of dynamite aboard.

One hundred yards from the surf, the deploying patrol crawled into the barbed-wire entanglements. They crept beyond, through the wet morning darkness, until they were within grenade range of Jap machinegun dens burrowed into the cliff faces commanding the entire shore.

Satisfied that this area was clear of Japs, Sgt. Walker and his men gingerly shifted the cases of dynamite ashore and planted them among the reefs blocking the passageway to Lilly Beach. Promptly at 0530 they touched off the charge.

For the troops still churning the bay in landing boats, that explosion was a heartening signal. It meant that everything was proceeding according to plan. An hour later the barges were lining up to disgorge men, guns, ammunition, and tractors on the beach.

We crouched low across the rocky beach and scrambled up the mossy cheek of the mountain on our hands and knees. By daybreak the first objective, Link Hill, had been reached. Wind cupped under our tin hats and almost snapped our heads off. Fog pressed against our bodies, shouldering us onward like an invisible wet net. We could hear the voices of the men in our patrol, but we couldn't see them.

Already tiers of empty enemy gun slots, deep interlaced trenchworks, and one observation post sunk into the hilltop had been passed. By noon, after trailing a thin yellow strand of Jap communications wire over the moss bogs, we had cautiously explored the deep, awesome caverns of Lazy Creek.

As darkness fell, we trudged through the dismal desolation of Gertrude Cove on the southeast side of the island, where steam and stench rose in smoky plumes from the sodden earth. Warily we bedded down for the night in a long, low hutment, half-buried in the ground, shattered by some of the 4,000,000 pounds of bombs dropped by the Eleventh Air Force since Jan. 1.

Before morning we were cursing the Air Force for its marksmanship. Rain roared down and poured through the splintered roof onto the raised wooden platform where we were huddled, rolled up in damp, musty Jap blankets.

At dawn our patrol was on the march again. We stumbled up the steep, twisting road that the Japs, with dynamite and tamping blocks and little wicker baskets full of dirt, had scratched out of the rocky promontory separating Gertrude Cove from Kiska Harbor. Along the road were abandoned Jap heavy-gun emplacements.

Ahead of us, in the murky dusk of the first day ashore, two Yank dogfaces, supported only by each other, had invaded the main camp area at Kiska Harbor. Like a pair of hobos sneaking into a chickenyard, Pvt. Francis Heston of Council Bluffs, Ia., and Sgt. Gerald Roach of Wilkes-Barre, Penna., had crept along the road.

Now, with fog and sweat begriming our faces, we followed their path to the summit of Magic Mountain. And while we paused, panting, for a break, the haze blew out to sea for an instant.

Below us, gray and ashen and still, lay Kiska Harbor, the main camp area of the Japs. And now we knew for certain they were gone. At first disappointment rippled hotly over us. "Dirty bastards," we muttered. And then we remembered the first day at Attu, and the way litter bearers had shuffled past with their limp loads. And our disappointment passed, even if we had waited 14 months.

Veterans of Attu among the American invasion forces found it hard to believe that the Japs had chickened out. Though we had been repelled by the methods, we had respected the singleness of purpose of an army whose men committed suicide by grenade rather than surrender, who shoot or bayonet their seriously wounded fellow soldiers before relinquishing the ground where they fell. That respect was gone now.

Japs, we learned at Kiska, are only human after all.

—SGT. GEORG N. MEYERS

Invasion of Italy

ITALY WAS wet and cold. "The Germans counterattacked early one morning," said Platoon Sgt. Dave Haliburton of the 36th Infantry Division, "and my men came up to me and said their rifles were frozen tighter than a by-God.

"They asked me what to do. 'Hell,' I said, 'urinate on the sonsuvbitches.' It didn't smell so good after firing a couple of hours, but it saved our lives."

Italy wasn't what the travel posters had cracked it up to be, all blue skies and crowds of pretty girls coming down the streets singing opera. It rained and kept on raining until the weather got too cold for rain, and then it snowed. There was mud and slush everywhere, and men went around in the mud up to the top of their leggings and sometimes up to their belly-buttons.

It was so bad that the men got to thinking how good they'd had it in the training camps back home, and they wished they were somewhere else—anywhere else, in Mississippi or even New Guinea.

Now and then the GIs heard how the Russians were sweeping ahead, recapturing Kharkov, Bryansk, and Smolensk, liberating an area 700 miles long and 180 miles wide. They heard of the mop-up of the Americans on Guadalcanal, the six-week conquest of Munda, and the steady, painful progress in the Pacific.

It was good news, but it didn't help the Allies in Italy. Things had started out fine. But now, with the winter winds whistling, the Allies were bogged down, and any man in his right mind knew that the toughest part was still ahead. Particularly the mountains. There were always mountains.

At first everything had looked dandy. Italy had thrown in the sponge in secret negotiations, and a week later the announcement of the unconditional capitulation was made public. On Sept. 3 the British had invaded Italy from Sicily, converted into a jumping-off base after its 38-day conquest.

The Italian Navy surrendered to the Allies. German parachutists rescued Benito Mussolini from confinement. The Germans disarmed Italian soldiers and occupied Italy.

On Sept. 9, the American Fifth Army, chosen to make the major assault on the Italian mainland, landed at Salerno and ran into savage German opposition. The Germans almost threw an armored wedge through to the beaches. The battle lasted in fury for nine days.

It was near Salerno that a pfc from Pittsburgh knelt in the window of a building and burned out four automatic rifles killing 35 Germans. When the fourth gun got so hot that it started to fall apart, the pfc threw 60mm. mortar shells at the Germans. Later the pfc said: "I don't think there is a man in the Army who isn't scared in every battle' after his first one." His name was Charles Edward Kelly. The newspapers called him Commando Kelly. The guys in his outfit called him Chuck.

On Sept. 18 the Germans began to withdraw from Salerno, with both the Fifth and Eighth Armies in pursuit. The Fifth Army, aided by a civilian uprising, occupied Naples on Oct. 7. Naples was thick with snipers. Cpl. Joseph Toporski, a paratrooper from Milwaukee, shot two snipers and was looking for a third when an Italian girl named Marissa tapped him on the shoulder as he peered around a building and asked him if he would like to go to her apartment and listen to American phonograph

. . . there were no blue skies or crowds of pretty girls singing opera.

records. Cpl. Toporski took an hour off for recreation. He got the third sniper on the way back to his unit.

The Allied push was still on. On Oct. 14, under heavy fire, the Americans crossed the Volturno.

Then the Allies came probing into the German winter line. They were still probing when winter came.

The men went around in mud up to the tops of their leggings and sometimes up to their belly buttons.

It was wet and cold.

Anzio was still ahead.

Nightmare job at Anzio

IT WAS NOW 0720. Just five hours ago I was sweating out this invasion in the first landing boat of the first wave with the Rangers, the tough, commando-trained, and experienced outfit that spearheaded the attack on Anzio.

We disembarked before midnight from a proud British ship, a former English Channel ferry that has seen them all—Lofoten, Dunkirk, Dieppe, Africa, Sicily, Salerno. As planned, we lay off shore in invasion barges awaiting H-Hour.

We had been briefed on the town until, as Pfc. Henry J. Corven of Ridgewood, N. J., put it, "I could pick out the town bootlegger's home."

It was perfect invasion weather, neither too bright nor too dark, with a calm sea glistening in the silver moonlight. Cramped in the only available space in the rear of the barge, I listened to the Rangers.

"Did you ever hear of Zip Koons?" asked Lt. Tom Magee of Springfield, Ill. "He was the Ranger who got credit for killing 66 Germans at Dieppe. He went wrong—he's a lieutenant now, you know. We had a lot of fun with him in Sicily when he was my first sergeant. *Superman* magazine made him the Superman of the Month, so the fellows went around shouting: 'Let me be Koons today. You were Koons yesterday. After all, it's my gun!'"

"I wish to hell we would get going," came a voice from the darkness, expressing the awful nervous impatience all of us felt.

"Koons told me to watch out on my third, seventh, and thirteenth invasions," said Sgt. Samuel Cooperstein of Malden, Mass., who got the Silver Star for gallantry in action in Sicily and was twice awarded the Purple Heart for wounds suffered elsewhere. "This is my third."

"What worries me is those 300 yards of shallow water we have to wade through," said another voice through the darkness. "Funny thing about beaches. The boat pulls in until it can't move any more, and then you step out and it is only one foot deep. Then you move farther in and—*plop*—you're over your head. I hit that kind of a beach in Sicily. Damn near drowned and took my radio equipment with me."

"My feet are cold," complained Pfc. Edward Daley of New York City. "I'm going to take my time when I hit the beach—sit down and change into dry socks. May even shave."

It was now 0150; H-Hour was 0200. All was quiet except for the lapping of water against the barge. With no air interception or sign of the enemy, it seemed too good to be true.

Then at 0151 came the ear-splitting wave of sounds we were waiting for. The briefing officers had told us that a British ship would fire its guns at the coast at exactly 0151, and we were glad now to have that promise confirmed.

It was suddenly silent and black again as the guns halted and the steel barges crept in at three miles an hour toward the beachhead. I disobeyed SOP and peered over the side to see the beachfront. Typical white marble and stucco Italian buildings loomed up on the terraced hillside behind the beach.

We knew roughly what we were getting into. The beach, we had been told, was probably mined. Behind it was a barrier of "three to seven feet," a sea wall with barbed wire on top. There were also several gun positions, but these were believed to be unoccupied. Another version had it that seven batteries of artillery had recently been moved into the vicinity.

We were all thinking of Salerno, and we

thanked God for the relatively flat land, which didn't make the beach easy to defend.

The barge pulled up by the sand at the proper place and the proper minute. Almost the last man out of the boat because of my position in the rear, I followed gingerly while a score of others in squad column sloshed through several hundred yards of knee-deep water toward shore. I had one hand on my helmet, ready to dig for quick cover if machineguns or artillery opened up. The others ran up that beach so fast I was almost alone. But, even though side-stepping driftwood that might be mines, I soon caught up.

Fortunately the sea wall was only three feet, and the barbed wire was easily cut. I crossed the main highway, nicknamed "Hitler Road" in the briefing, and joined a squad searching one of the large resort-type homes.

Except for less than a score of German soldiers who were quickly taken care of, our immediate front had been hastily deserted.

Writing this story, I have dived dozens of times for shelter from Jerry bombers hitting the beaches, but our air force is also much in evidence. Outside is a sign pointing to Rome.

—SGT. BURTT EVANS

_____

THIS LITTLE ALLIED COLONY on the shinbone of the Italian boot is only a few weeks old, but it is rapidly become one of the hottest corners of this struggling earth.

It measures only about 12 miles in length along the shore and averages about seven miles penetration inland, or about 84 square miles in area—every foot of it vulnerable to bombs, shells, and machinegun and small-arms fire.

There is no relatively safe rear area as in most operations. One place is about as bad as another, inside or out. Men working on the ships and on the beaches are targets for artillery and bombs; men working in the front lines are exposed to shells and small arms; those in the middle frequently get a mixture of all three.

The invasion area is humming with activity day and night. Kraut dive bombers filter through the air cover and ack-ack regularly and lay their eggs along the beach. They do damage, but the work of landing supplies goes on. In fact. Pvt. Maxwell Remmick of Cincinnati, O., member of an Army beach party, wasn't even interrupted; he stayed by his telephone even though his shoulder was dislocated by the concussion of a nearby bomb blast.

Men on the long pontons, who direct vehicles and men coming ashore, have to stick by their posts when the bombers come over because there's no place to go. At night the men who guide the traffic over the pontons use blackout flashlights and keep hoping they won't see the terrible sight of flares in the sky. On shore the MPs take over, directing the vehicles to assembly areas. From there they are routed to their designated locations.

It is almost unbelievable that the great amount of men and materiel now beyond the beaches could have been unloaded in the few days since D-Day. The Quartermaster and Signal Corps, Engineers, and Medics are set up and operating as if they had been here for months.

The hospitals were set up the day after D-Day. One hospital is doing business—a lot of it—in spite of Jerry shells flying regularly overhead. One afternoon the doctors and medics performed an appendectomy with 88s swishing just above the ridgepole of the operating tent.

From the debris littering the beach, it's quite evident that Anzio and Nettuno were in days past the resort towns the guidebooks make them out to be. The Tyrrhenian Sea's mild surf tosses up strips of faded canvas and broken sticks that once were bright beach chairs; on the sand are battered hulls of runabouts and sailboats; the bathing beaches are littered with Italian suntan lotion bottles.

But more and more the sea washes up equipment that wasn't made for peacetime pleasure but for war. And sometimes what looked like a piece of driftwood turns out to be a corpse.

—SGT. BURGESS H. SCOTT

Death battle at Tarawa

EVEN THE DEAD MARINES were determined to reach Tarawa's shore.

As one Higgins landing boat roared toward the dry sand, you could see a hand clutching its side. It was the hand of a marine, frozen in the grip of death.

The 2d Marine Division took this island because its men were willing to die. They kept on coming in the face of a heavy Jap defense, and though they paid the stiffest price in human life per square yard that was ever paid in the history of the Marine Corps, they won this main Jap base in the Gilbert Islands in 76 hours.

Out of two battalions—2,000 to 3,000 men— thrown onto the beach in the first assault at 0830, only a few hundred escaped death or injury. Officer casualties were heavy. And still the marines kept coming.

Before dawn of the first day of the invasion, the Navy opened up with a tremendous bombardment. Carrier planes dropped 800 tons of bombs, while battleships, cruisers, and destroyers hurled 2,000 tons of shells on an area two and a quarter miles long and at no point more than 800 yards wide. This was Betio, the fortified airstrip that is the main island of 26 comprising the Tarawa atoll.

The marines were to hit the sandy beach immediately after these softening-up operations ceased, and everybody on the boats was happy because it seemed like very effective fire, the kind of intense blasting that would make the Japs "bomb happy." But that wasn't the way it worked out.

The Japs were too well dug in. Their blockhouses were of concrete five feet thick, with palm-tree trunks 18 inches in diameter superimposed on the concrete. And superimposed on the trees were angle irons, made of railroad steel. On top of these were 10 to 12 feet of sand and coral rock. Only a direct hit by a 2,000-pound bomb would cave in or destroy such blockhouses.

The Jap pillboxes were built out of sandfilled oil drums, buttressed by heavy coconut logs and then sandbags. Air-raid shelters were constructed from coconut-tree trunks, piled high in two walls, with coral sand filling the space in between. Our heavy machineguns and 75s couldn't penetrate these emplacements or knock out the enemy eight-inch shore batteries and machineguns that were awaiting our assault waves.

Daylight had been chosen for the assault because it permitted naval gunfire and aviation as support, and because a night attack might have caused the boats to miss the beaches. But there was another important reason:

It was flood tide. At low tide the coral shelf that forms Betio and the rest of Tarawa atoll is practically dry; at high tide there are four and a half feet of water at the shore line, and it gets deeper farther out. The assault was timed to take advantage of the flood tide.

Then the unexpected happened. A sudden shift of wind swept the water back from the beaches. Many of the Higgins boats piled up on a treacherous table reef of coral, barely submerged in the water. The marines were forced to debark and wade in the rest of the way— some 500 to 800 yards—in the face of murderous Japanese fire, with no protection.

Those few hundred yards seemed like a million miles. Even before the boats went aground on the reef, the Japs opened up with rifles, machineguns, heavy mortars, 75mm. and 90mm. guns. But the marines kept coming on, across the corpses of other marines whose lifeless heads were bobbing in the water.

The assault was made against three designated beaches by three battalion landing teams. One of the teams was so powerfully opposed that only two companies could land. Many casualties were the result of a Jap trick. Snipers, hidden in the hulk of a wrecked Jap sailing vessel on the reef, let the marines move in beyond the hulk and then shot them down from behind.

Just after noon a reinforcing wave of Higgins boats was sent in. Five-inch automatic Jap weapons on the flank blew two of the boats out of the water. Several companies were shifted against the Jap flanking position to protect the passage of new reinforcements.

Then the Hellcat fighters, TBFs, and dive-bombers worked over the area for about an hour from 1430 to 1530, flying sometimes only 60 feet off the water. No point on Betio was much more than 10 feet above sea level except where the Japs had built up their emplacements.

After the planes, two U. S. minesweepers went in and tried to trade punches with the shore batteries. Then two destroyers pushed into the lagoon and fired at close range, 700 to 900 yards; then more planes. We had absolute aerial supremacy; the greatest number of Jap planes seen at Betio at any one time was six.

Meanwhile the blood-and-guts landing operation was continuing. Ten or 15 feet from the high-tide mark on Betio's narrow beaches the Japs had constructed walls of coconut logs as a barrier to tanks. Marines rushed the beaches and scaled the chin-high walls in the face of Jap machineguns.

Behind the barricade the island was ringed with about 500 pillboxes, so arranged that when you fought your way past one pillbox you were moving into two inner pillboxes' crossfire.

In the shallows, on the beaches, and before the Jap emplacements marines died by squads.

In less than 100 yards on the beach and within 20 yards of machinegun emplacements 105 marines were killed. But others kept advancing until at last they took the emplacements and wiped out the Jap gunners.

By the end of the first day, the three battalion landing teams and reinforcements had secured little more than a toehold—three small beachheads from 70 to 150 yards in depth. The men dug in and held on there through the night. They established all-around security with orders to shoot anything that moved. There were local efforts at counterattacking. During the night some artillery was brought ashore.

The second day the marines began widening their beachheads and improving their positions. The center battalion pushed ahead until it was stymied by pillboxes and blockhouses. This same day reinforcements, including some light and medium tanks, were landed on the comparatively lightly defended west end of the island, and they pushed east down the airstrip, which forms a diagonal line across the island, to the point where the advance marines were being held up by the pillboxes. The Hellcats were called in again to strafe the area while the battleships and cruisers pounded from offshore. Then Marine infantry and tanks advanced.

After the second day the battalion was able to penetrate to the opposite shore of Betio, bypassing or destroying the stubborn pillboxes and blockhouses, and by this time the critical period was past. But the fighting was not "officially" over until 76 hours had passed from the time of the assault, and even then there was still a handful of Jap snipers, in trees and dugouts, that had to be picked off.

In all, an enemy force of about 4,500 defenders was wiped out, including about 3,500 Imperial Marines and 1,000 laborers. Fewer than 200 of the defenders, most of them laborers, surrendered. Tarawa was taken by less than a division of U. S. Marines. We suffered the loss of 1,026 men killed and 2,557 wounded.

—SGT. JOHN BUSHEMI

It looked easy: There was still no sign of Japs. ▶

Mission's end in the Marshalls

THE AERIAL BOMBARDMENT began soon after morning chow, which included fresh eggs because this was the day of battle.

From our troopships only a few hundred yards offshore, the entire island of Eniwetok seemed on fire. Red, yellow, and black smoke clung to the shattered trees and bushes. At dawn our destroyers moved closer, almost hugging the beach.

By the time our assault boats had gathered in the rendezvous area, coconuts and huge palm fronds were floating out from the beach.

Suddenly the bombardment ceased; for a single, incredible minute there was silence. That silence seemed to underline the question all of us were asking ourselves: Where were the Japs?

At no time had the enemy answered the Navy's surface and air bombardments. None of our observers had sighted a single Jap on the island—or any other living thing. Some of the men of the 106th Infantry wondered out loud whether Eniwetok was another Kiska, whether the Japs had fled without a fight.

There was nothing to make the infantrymen change their minds as the first two assault waves piled out of amphibious tractors and threw themselves over the steep fire trench that ran along the entire beach, then stood upright and moved inland. There was still no sign of Japs.

As troops under Lt. Col. Harold I. (Hi) Mizony of Spokane, Wash., moved north and troops under Lt. Col. Winslow Cornett of White Plains, N. Y., moved south, the guns of the destroyer force shifted their fire ahead of the moving troops to clear the way north and south.

By this time the fourth wave had hit the beach. Sgt. John A. Bushemi of Gary, Ind., YANK staff photographer, and I landed in this wave.

There was still no resistance. The only sounds were the sounds of our BAR and rifle fire, spraying every tree that might contain a sniper and every exposed shell crater.

Sgt. Mat Toper of New York City lay flat on his back on the fire trench and lit the first of 20 cigars he'd managed to keep dry through the landing operation. Pfc. Albert Lee, a Chinese-American tank gunner from Los Angeles, Calif., grinned and said: "This is the easiest one yet." Lee had made three previous assault landings.

Our rear elements, preceded by tanks, were moving up to the front. At 1010 a cooling rain began to fall, and in a few minutes you couldn't see more than a few feet ahead.

It was then that the Japs decided to let us know they were present and ready to fight. The high-pitched ring of Jap rifle fire sounded on all sides, our first warning that there were nearly as many Japs behind as in front of our own lines. Knee-mortar shells, from positions on both ends of the island, began to sprinkle the landing beach, just short of the incoming boats. A few shells hit the troops south of the beach party, killing six men and wounding eight.

As 1st Lt. John Hetherington of Mt. Vernon, N. Y., transportation officer, headed back for the beach in search of his motor sergeant, he saw some engineers blasting away at what looked like a small pile of mangrove leaves, evidently knocked down from a tree by a Navy blast.

Just ahead were some communications men,

cleaning their rifles and sharing a D-ration chocolate bar. As the engineers moved out, Lt. Hetherington saw a Jap rise up from under the leaves, knife in one hand, grenade in the other. The lieutenant fired his carbine once and squeezed the trigger for a second shot. The carbine jammed but that didn't matter; his first shot had plugged the Jap in the head. Under the palm fronds and dried leaves, Hetherington found a neatly dug square hole, four feet deep. Inside were three other dead Japs.

He saw hundreds of similar holes later on; we all did. Some were spider trenches, connected by carefully covered underground passages, a few with corrugated tin under the fronds and mangrove leaves. Many of the trenches had been built for a single Jap, others for two or three or four men. None of the holes was large enough to accommodate more than six Japs.

Sgt. Chris Hagen of Fairmont, Minn., a squad leader, and eight riflemen became separated from their platoon in the landing. Just as they walked over the fire trench, in the area through which almost the whole battalion had passed without encountering resistance, scattered Jap rifle fire came from their rear, barely clearing their heads. They dropped to the ground.

"Underground!" shouted Hagen. "The sons-uvbitches are underground!" This squad began throwing grenades into every pile of fronds. Three Japs darted out of one hole and ran for the beach. Hagen fired once and hit the first one before he'd gone 15 yards. He hit the other two a few yards farther on. In the next 20 minutes, Hagen killed 12 Japs by pitching grenades into a dozen holes. Pfc. Joseph Tucker, a rifleman from Live Oak, Fla., accounted for at least nine more, and the entire outfit cleaned out about 50 in some 20 unconnected holes, all dug underground in an area about 40 yards square.

As Col. Mizony moved up with 18 of his enlisted men, including battalion CP personnel, Capt. Carl Stoltz of Binghamton, N. Y., commander of a heavy-weapons company, yelled: "Look out, Hi!" The colonel hit the ground,

and Stoltz, a former Binghamton cop, got the underground sniper with a carbine. He found four others in a tin-and-palm-covered trench on the beach. As he started to walk over it, the captain stopped, looked down, and noticed a movement inside. He killed two Japs with the carbine and the other two with grenades.

When the company commanded by Capt. Charles Hallden of Brooklyn, N. Y., reached a native village and the smoking ruins of some Jap concrete installations, a young native stuck his head up from a hole and shouted, "Friend!" The advance halted while the native guided First Sgt. Louis Pawlinga of Utica, N. Y., and a search party to other holes, where they found 33 natives—four men, 12 women, and 17 children—only three injured. They were taken to the beachhead.

Just before noon the troops circled south, although there were some Japs still alive on the western side of the island. As 1st Lt. George Johnson of Sikeston, Mo., moved up with his company, the leader of the second squad, Sgt. Earl Bodiford of Pocahontas, Tenn., fired at a covered foxhole. The muzzle of a rifle moved in the shadows. Bodiford raced forward, grabbed the gun from a dazed Jap, and hurled it as far as he could. He killed the Jap and moved on.

By early afternoon we had run up against concentrated underground defenses and were held up by knee-mortar fire. Shells were falling on every side, in and around the CP and ahead and just behind the front lines. Col. Cornett ordered the line held and called for reinforcements.

The sun was shining again and the atmosphere was hot and muggy as hell. Black flies covered everything — guns, clothes, faces, and hands. Knee-mortar fire was falling throughout the area, no spot was safe from snipers, and there was Jap heavy-machinegun fire up ahead. Col. Mizony called for some Navy Avengers.

Johnny Bushemi and I crouched behind a medium tank with some other men to smoke our first cigarettes in several hours and tell one another what had happened since we'd become separated that morning. When the short, concentrated aerial strafing was completed, five of us, including Johnny Bushemi, started forward to take a look at the damage.

Just beyond the fire trench on the lagoon side of the beach, perhaps 75 yards behind the front lines, we stopped to examine a bullet-ridden chest filled with Marshallese books. That area had been under sporadic knee-mortar fire throughout the morning, but for two hours none of the 60mm. grenades had fallen there.

Then, suddenly, the first shell landed in our midst. I ducked into an exposed hole, just below the chest of books, and the others threw themselves on the open ground. Shells burst all around us, pinning us in a diminishing circle of fire.

Each explosion kicked up dirt and sand as it landed; we thought each shell would be our last. No one knows how many bursts there were in all—probably five or six—but after two or three interminable minutes the explosions stopped. Johnny had been hit and was bleeding profusely. Three of us ran 300 yards down the beach to get the medics.

By the time we returned to the shallow crater where Bushemi lay, Johnny had already lost a tremendous amount of blood from shrapnel wounds in his left cheek and neck and in his left leg. But he was still conscious, and as we returned through the sniper-infested area inland from the lagoon beach, he asked for his two cameras. He carried both of them until we reached the advanced aid station in a demolished coconut-log emplacement. There he was given more sulfanilamide and two plasma applications.

Johnny was conscious, joking with all of us, until after he had reached our transport. He died at 1750, a little less than three hours after he was wounded, while Navy surgeons were tying the arteries in his neck. His last words were: "Be sure to get those pictures back to the office."

During the night the advance continued on Eniwetok, the marines pushing seaward on the eastern end and the soldiers continuing northward. They moved barely 15 yards at a time, tanks leading the way, flanked on each side by infantrymen—BAR men spraying every foot and riflemen throwing grenades into each mound.

There was no organized counterattack by the enemy, and only two attempts at resistance. At about 2000, an hour after the advance began, a dozen Japs tried to swim through the lagoon to reach the rear. Spotted by a destroyer searchlight, they were wiped out when they reached the beach.

The second attempt came at 0100, when 40 Japs leaped from their holes about 30 yards from the Marine lines and raced forward. Brandishing sabers, hurling grenades, and screaming, "Banzai! the f - - - - - - marines will die!" they leaped into the Marine foxholes. There was hand-to-hand combat, jujitsu, knifing, and bayonetting. In less than 20 minutes, 40 Japs and 20 marines were killed on a line not more than 30 yards long.

Then the entire battalion was ordered back 300 yards to mop up the southern, lagoon side of the island for the second time. They found almost as many live Japs hiding under their feet this time as during the first advance.

Dead Japs were being piled up on the beach, but many still remained where they had fought and died—underground. At almost any spot on the island there were still some Japs alive, and occasionally rifle fire broke out around the aid station. Several times mop-up squads came back to clean out all the holes they could find. Then, after they had left, the fire would break out again in another spot. A few Japs, not many, were taken prisoner. There had been a steady stream of American casualties flowing back to the aid stations the first day, but our casualties were lighter now.

By late afternoon of the third day, Eniwetok, last stronghold of the enemy in the Marshalls, was secured.

—Sgt. Merle Miller

Battle above the Solomons

WE'RE OUT ON an armed reconnaissance in a B-24, droning over the Solomons Sea toward New Britain, New Ireland, and points east, flying deep into Jap territory all by ourselves, looking for trouble.

We reach the coast of New Britain and skirt it for about an hour, meanwhile downing a lunch of oranges, canned tomato juice, cheese, and dog biscuits. As we swing over St. George's Channel near Rabaul, we spot a tiny dot in the water off the cape.

Lt. F. E. Haag, our pilot, a former Rutgers University student from Pelham, N.Y., changes course and descends to identify the vessel. It's a 4,500-ton Jap freighter-transport heading north. Now Lt. William H. Spencer Jr., ex-telephone man from Roanoke, Va., takes over command of the bomber from his bombardier's perch. We make a bomb run at medium altitude.

Two bright yellow demolition bombs tumble out of the bomb racks. Beside me S/Sgt. Mike Nesevitch, former coal operator from Olyphant, Penna., keeps his aerial camera clicking. The bombs describe a graceful, lazy curve as the ship below swerves sharply to the right.

The bombs hit the water about 100 yards from the freighter. Lt. Spencer had figured the ship would turn the other way.

"Let's try it again," Lt. Spencer hollers over the interphone. We wheel over the cape lighthouse to make another run. Only now do we notice white puffs of ack-ack blossoming all around us. And only now do we spot another freighter, just as big, going south in the channel. Up from the second ship come two floatplanes, a biplane and a Zero with pontons.

A hand grabs my shoulder. I turn to find S/Sgt. R. D. Brown, former cleaner and presser from Rusk, Tex., our assistant radioman, pointing out the left waist window. There, slightly below and to our left, are eight Jap planes with flaming circles on their dirty tan wings. Four of them are Zeros, the others twin-engined bombers. Evidently they are returning from a bombing mission in the Solomons.

Lt. Haag guns the four motors on our big plane and banks it southward, toward a far-off cloud bank. The bombers and floatplanes disappear. But the Zeros climb toward us. Everyone clambers to his machinegun.

Back in the rear turret S/Sgt. A. F. Weisberger, ex-sawmill worker from Rio Linda, Calif., gets in the opening burst. Soon most of the guns on our big bomber are chattering away. The Zeros split up and close in from two sides. They dart as swiftly and effortlessly as dragonflies.

Nesevitch yells at me above the din, motioning me to his side at the right waist window. His cartridge belt has jumped its guide, silencing the gun. He yells for me to pull the end of the belt through the receiver slot as he works the belt entirely clear of the guide.

There's a Zero riding alongside us—ready to

wing over and make a pass. We manage to fix the gun. Nesevitch blazes away at the Jap, who noses up to escape the tracers.

Then the Zero rolls over and curves in toward our nose. It races toward our bomber at 12 o'clock—a head-on pass. Pfc. Don Bellmore, former factory worker from Clinton, Mich., draws a bead from his nose turret and squeezes the trigger for a long burst. At the same time S/Sgt. Edgar F. Dow, ex-rayon maker from Lumberton, N.C., draws a bead from the top turret.

Tracers from their guns converge on the hurtling Zero. It falters a split second, then dives under our right wing to vanish in clouds below.

Now there's one Zero to the right of us, just beyond range, and two to the left. They ride along beside us for several minutes, eying us like three hungry hawks ready to pounce on a plump chicken. Short bursts of our guns keep them at a safe distance.

"Don't waste bullets, fellas," drawls Lt. D. P. Johnston, the co-pilot, over the interphone. He used to be an ornamental-iron designer in Memphis, Tenn. "This heah looks like it's gonna be a long fight."

Suddenly tracer bullets streak by from in front of our plane. A second Zero is making a one o'clock pass—coming in from almost dead ahead. Dow and Bellmore in the top and nose turrets blaze away. The Zero rolls off to the right through the Japs during this maneuver. The plane dives out of range, wriggling queerly. Before we can see whether it ever comes out of that dive, the Zero passes into a fleecy cloud. We score a probable.

"Look out—10 o'clock pass!" yells Lt. Haag over the interphone. A third Zero flicks in with smoking guns from slightly below and in front of us. None of our guns can follow its lightning-quick course. But the Zero never reaches our level, diving away instead. I pull the belly-gun triggers. It zips right through the tracers.

The last Zero flips up in a tight Immelmann turn and leaves us without attempting a pass. Now everything is silent except for the roar of our four engines. We are at last alone in the sunny, cloud-flecked sky. The running fight has lasted 12 minutes.

Over the interphone comes Lt. Johnston's Memphis drawl: "Anybody hurt?" Nobody is. "I think we took a few bullets in the nose," he says. We light up cigarettes, grin at each other, and trade comments on the fight.

We fly 500 miles down to the Huon Gulf. There is a sunken freighter seaward of Lae's airstrip, and Salamaua lies bomb-pocked along the narrow neck of a fat peninsula. We come in for a bombing run as the bomb-bay doors grind open. Black puffs of ack-ack surround us, and some of the stuff hits. It sounds like pebbles being thrown against a tin roof. The plane lurches and reels. Our last yellow bombs angle down toward some buildings near Salamaua's ruined air strip.

We plunge into big storm clouds and thread our way through the towering Owen Stanley peaks. It is dusk as we set down gently on our home field. In the nine hours we've been away we've covered more than 1,500 miles.

Now the crew admits this was the first time they've been jumped by the Japs in their 11 bombing missions.

—SGT. DAVE RICHARDSON

Mission over France

SOMEBODY ought to write a story about a briefing room, with the lights going on and off and the experts stepping up one by one to give you the dope on the mission. The lights go off and the maps appear on the screen. The voices go on. Here is the weather, here is the formation, this is where your plane will be. Nobody says much. The job is set, is definite. You even know the figures on the antiaircraft that will be down below blowing up those black puffballs of hot iron at you. And here is your mission—St. Nazaire, the myth, the Paul Bunyan place where you're supposed to be able to walk across the flak. St. Nazaire is where you're bound for today.

And today the sun is spread everywhere over the English countryside as you go down the road to the line and break down your guns. Rub that oil off, for the stuff will freeze in the guns at altitude. Check oxygen, radio, bomb fuses; check a thousand damn things and still you haven't checked them all. Around you are the boys on your crew, Clanton and Petro and Lt. Brady, the pilot: the men who will go with you through the living myth of St. Nazaire. Time runs and take-off time will not wait, for the timing is spread through a dozen airfields, and up in the sky over England the armada will form. Take-off time waits for no man. Gangwer, the ball-turret operator, can't find his flying boots and electrically heated shoes. To hell with them.

You're in the radio room—"Saul's bird cage," somebody names it. Please, buddy, remember your signals for enemy aircraft or in case that old devil sea gets you on the way back. Remember to turn on the detonator so, just in case you land in Jerry's Europe, the secret equipment will be blown to hell. Remember this, remember that.

And that's all you have to do as you climb up there and circle in the sun, sweating out that bombing run—your very first real mission. Back in the waist Clanton and Petro, the waist gunners, are leaning out of the open hatches, checking the formation. You smoke cigarette after cigarette because after altitude you won't be able to smoke any. The signals are beating through the static into your headset.

Now the water down below. Good-bye, England. Over the interphone, the navigator says, "An hour and a half to the target." Now you go to your gun and swing her through her circle. "How about test firing?" asks the ball turret. "Okay," says the pilot. The caliber .50s sing through the air. Petro, the gun expert at the waist, asks through the interphone about all guns. "All guns okay." Down in the ball, that lonely ball turret below the belly, Gangwer's feet are beginning to get cold. The cold is knifing through the metal. An electric suit doesn't quite do the trick for toes and fingertips.

You are at altitude now, and soon there is France below. The enemy is down there in his Fortress Europe, and his St. Nazaire submarine-building plant is buried under 14-foot roofs. But maybe your bombs can rip up some of the works. You swing your gun through her circle.

You are over St. Nazaire. The planes go in one by one. Don't ask what you think about because you don't think. You just stretch taut. The bomb doors go down. There are minutes now, maybe seconds. There's an uprush of cold air that cuts your ears and fingers into little pieces, and with one dead finger—by God, you did remember it—you press the camera button. Hold it for two minutes. And now the bomb doors close. You get a glimpse of innocent-looking puffs of smoke. There's a sharp crack like a pistol shot somewhere in the ship, it seems up forward.

Over the interphone: "Let's get away from here in a hurry." That's Lt. Hamilton, the bombardier from Kansas, speaking from the nose.

You are riding away from France now. And eastward there's a line of smoke climbing into the sky. You open the radio-room door to the bomb bay, and there is one flak hole. Just one. You look around to find more. That single piece of hot iron ripped through the bay and went somewhere. But just where? Clanton comes up and points, and you follow his finger around to where that little hunk of iron went—in the wall a foot from your head.

The coast of France and that line of smoke seem to hang on to us, won't let go. Why aren't you moving? Can't you get out of here? The interphone is silent for a minute. You suppose everybody is holding his little hunk of life in his hands and looking it over tenderly. And that damn coast of France and that smoke hanging on.

A voice out of the cockpit: "Is everybody okay?"

Gangwer from the ball turret: "My feet are frozen. I can't take this much longer."

"Just a little longer," says the pilot.

"How much longer on oxygen?" asks Blum, the engineer.

"Just a little longer," says the pilot.

"My oxygen line is screwed up," says Blum.

"We're descending gradually," says the pilot.

"We should be seeing fighters just about here," says Lt. Crosby, the navigator.

"I've got to get out of here," says Gangwer. "My feet are gone."

Petro, the waist gunner, steps up and opens the ball turret. Clanton comes over, too. They lift Gangwer out and lay him out in the waist.

Just what do you do for frostbite? You forget. Your mind isn't good at 20,000 feet; it's kind of slow and frozen. Frostbite, and you're the first-aid man: That's the radioman's job. What did they tell you about frostbite? Your mom used to take your shoes off when you were a kid and rub your feet until they were warm and stinging. You pull off Gangwer's shoes and wrap his feet in blankets. Under the oxygen mask his eyes are yelling at you to do something.

"Fighters at three o'clock level," says the co-pilot.

Petro is now in the turret, and you and Clanton are at the waist guns. You see them sweep wide and around to the rear. "Eighteen of them," says McCusker, the tail gunner. Your guns circle, waiting. The fighters hang back of you. One of your ships fall back; maybe flak in an engine, maybe this, maybe that.

Now you're below oxygen level. You rip the things off your face. You go up to the radio room, give Gangwer a cigarette. Life is back in his feet. His eyes are better. Signaling England now about enemy aircraft and no answer. The radio picks its own damn time to get coy.

The fighters disappear below the horizon, but one of your planes is going down. She lands and the planes circle her like a flock of birds as she settles in the sea, with her crew tumbling efficiently into their dinghies. They go in right, just the way they've been told a thousand times in lectures about those dinghies and how to get into them, and all the radios are at work summoning help.

You're over England now. England, I love you. Everybody is chattering, including brother Frostbite, now that the big thing is over.

And that's all there is to your first mission, just that and no more.

—SGT. SAUL LEVITT

The general briefed his men for the assault, and the President led the people in prayer.

"Grant us faith. . . . Let us march"

FRANKLIN D. ROOSEVELT'S D-DAY PRAYER:

"God of the Free, we pledge our hearts and lives today to the cause of all free mankind. Grant us victory over the tyrants who would enslave all free men of nations. Grant us faith and understanding to cherish all those who fight for freedom as if they were our brothers. Grant us brotherhood in hope and union, not only for the space of this bitter war but for the days to come which shall and must unite all the children of earth. Our earth is but a small star in the great universe—yet of it we can make, if we choose, a planet unvexed by war, untroubled by hunger or fear, undivided by senseless distinctions of race, color, or theory.

"Grant us that courage and foreseeing to begin this task today, that our children and our children's children may be proud of the name of Man. The spirit of man has awakened and the soul of man has come forth. Grant us the wisdom and the vision to comprehend the greatness of man's spirit that suffers and endures so hugely for a goal beyond his own brief span. Grant us honor for our dead who died in the faith, honor for our living who work and strive for the faith, redemption and security for all captive lands and peoples. Grant us patience with the deluded and pity for the betrayed, and grant us the skill and valor that so cleansed the world of oppression and the old base doctrine that the strong must eat the weak because they are strong. Yet, most of all, grant us brotherhood, not only for this day but for all our years, a brotherhood not of words, but of acts and deeds. We are all of us children of earth—grant us that simple knowledge. If our brothers are oppressed, then we are oppressed. If they hunger, we hunger. If their freedom is taken away, our freedom is not secure. Grant us a common faith that man shall know bread and peace, that he shall know justice and righteousness, freedom and security, an equal opportunity and an equal chance to do his best, not only in our own lands but throughout the world, and in that faith let us march toward the clean world our hands can make. Amen."

This was D-Day

WHEN *Pvt. Charles Schmelze of Pittsburgh, Penna., stationed in England, had finished servicing a big troop-carrying glider of the Ninth Air Force, he was pretty well pooped. So he climbed aboard a glider, picked himself a comfortable corner, and went to sleep.*

The glider, towed by a plane piloted by F/O E. G. Borgmeyer of St. Louis, Mo., was next seen landing in France in a zone of heavy fighting. Pvt. Schmelze had slept his way into the greatest military operation in history.

• • •

Most of the plans were neatly filed in a fat-folder labeled "Operation Neptune." Everything had been figured out, on paper. There would be so many personnel and vehicles on so many boats, so much ammo, so many rations, so many stretchers. Each truck would have its gas tank full, carry enough extra for a 150-mile trip, and each soldier would carry a K and a D ration. All officers would send their trunk-lockers to storage.

There had been dry run after dry run, with soldiers seldom sure whether or not it was the real thing. There had been a final date set, and changed, postponed a day because of bad weather. It all depended on weather, tide, and what the moon looked like.

This was the plan:

Simultaneous landing on two main beaches. V Corps would hit near St. Laurent-sur-Mer, on the northern coast of Calvados, with a regimental combat team of the 29th Division on the right and an RCT of the 1st Division on the left. Meanwhile, at the southern part of the east coast of the Cotentin Peninsula, the VII Corps would land near Varreville with the 4th Division making the assault by sea and two airborne divisions, the 82d and 101st, dropping inland the night before in the area around Ste. Mere-Eglise. The British and the Canadians would come in north of Caen near Le Havre.

There would also be a one-hour air bombardment and continuous naval bombardment of the 16 German coastal guns and the myriad of six-foot-thick concrete pillboxes, things the Nazis called *Widerstandsnets*. And there would be three companies of Rangers going in to destroy a battery of 155mm. guns at Pointe du Hoc, which commanded both beaches. And there would be Engineer special brigades with the big job of blowing gaps in the thick concrete wall lining the beach, cutting through the rows of barbed wire, bulldozing roads out of nothing, and sweeping the mines.

According to COSSAC (Chiefs of Staff, Supreme Allied Command), there would be a maximum of five German infantry divisions and one panzer division along our whole front on D-Day.

It was there in the folder, everything you could think of. Somebody had even sat down with a pencil and paper and figured out that by D-plus-10 we would have had 43,586 casualties.

• • •

An invasion ship is a lonely ship. Downstairs in an LST you sit and sweat and nobody says anything because there is nothing to say. You look around and you wonder who will be dead soon. Will it be that tall, tough-looking sergeant who is busy double-checking his M1; or the guy stretched out in his upper bunk who keeps praying aloud all the time; or the kid sitting next to you who wet his pants? Who will be dead soon?

Then the thought comes, swelling inside of you, a huge fist of fear socking at your gut, ham-

June 6th: "If you want to live, keep moving."

mering and hammering. . . . "Maybe it's me. Maybe I'll be dead soon . . ."

•   •   •

COMMUNIQUE No. 1, Tuesday, June 6, 1944:

"Under the command of General Eisenhower, Allied naval forces, supported by strong air forces, began landing Allied armies this morning on the northern coast of France."

•   •   •

The sea was choppy and Omaha Beach was a long seven miles away when the first wave of the 1st and 29th Division soldiers lowered into their assault boats. Coming in, there was naval gunfire bursting all along the beaches; large, medium, and fighter bombers swooping down by the dozens, dropping their loads on gun positions, troop concentrations, coastal batteries, bridges, highways, railroads.

With so much air-navy pounding, everything looked easier. Somebody even thought that it might be a walk-in.

But nobody walked. They came in running fast, falling flat, getting up again, crouching, running fast, falling flat, hunting for a big rock, a shellhole, anything. Then digging in, because the Germans still had plenty of guns and ammo and defense positions behind the bluffs.

From these 100-foot-high bluffs, their guns not only commanded the beach strip of 7,900 yards but also the five small valleys reaching out into the beach. These five valleys were the keys to the tactical situation, because they were the only exits through which all our troops and supplies would have to pass. If the Germans could keep these exits closed and pin down our troops and shoot up our ships and vehicles, the show would soon be over. But if we could force the exits, then our troops could fan out behind the hill defenses, neutralizing them and consolidating the beachhead.

We would be able to do that because the German defense was not in depth. They were concentrating their strength along the beaches.

It looked bad at first. When the 2d Battalion of the 16th RCT landed on the billiard-table beach, near the mouth of the Ruquet River, they were supposed to get off the beaches in a hurry, but they couldn't go anywhere. The Germans were pouring in enfilading fire from 57-mms. and 75mms. in concrete pillboxes in addition to mortars and 88s. They had been practicing anti-invasion maneuvers just two days before.

After a half hour, elements of the 16th and 116th Regiments supported by 16 Army-Navy assault teams had succeeded in establishing a ragged line on some sectors of the beach.

Everything was confusion. Units were mixed up, many of them leaderless, most of them not being where they were supposed to be. Shells were coming in all the time; boats burning; vehicles with nowhere to go bogging down, getting hit; supplies getting wet; boats trying to come in all the time, some hitting mines, exploding; more than 30 tanks never reaching shore because of the high seas or because the Germans' guns picked them off on their way in; only six out of 16 tankdozers reaching the beach; everything jammed together like a junkyard.

Soon, though, scattered units got assembled; one of the valley exits was forced open, and trucks started moving off the beach. Some gaps were blown through the wire and concrete, and troops began pushing southward across the high ground, into a position near Colleville-sur-Mer. Landing farther to the left, the 164th RCT's 3d Battalion fought inland, up a deep draw, moving eastward on the Anglo-American boundary.

"If you want to live, keep moving," everybody said.

•   •   •

When the British ship pulled slowly into port, all the newspapermen crowded inside because it was the first boat back from the beach. The boat was loaded with dead and wounded. One of the wounded talked quickly, excitedly.

He told how he got soaking wet wading ashore

with a load of explosives on his back. He was part of a demolition team of 28 who were supposed to blow gaps in the concrete wall.

"I was just coming out of the water when this guy exploded right in front of me. There just wasn't anything left of him except some of his skin which splattered all over my arm. I remember dipping my arm in the water to wash it off. I guess I was too excited to be scared."

· · ·

Farther up, on the same Omaha Beach, at the same time, the 116th RCT swept in north of Vierville-sur-Mer with two battalions in the assault wave. They had Rangers with them to help clear the beach through one of the planned exits. The 1st Battalion swung west along the enemy defenses occupying the western edge of Vierville while the 2d Battalion pushed into the western outskirts of St. Laurent-sur-Mer just before darkness. The 3d Battalion had to fight through snipers and strong points that had been bypassed by the other two battalions.

It was expensive for them, too. Dead were scattered liberally—on the sand exposed by the low tide, in the fields below the bluff, on the bluff itself, and in the sea.

Still, an exit had been cut into the valley.

The Infantry kept coming. At 0850, right on schedule, the 18th RCT was working its way across the beach, up the bluff to the edge of Colleville, cutting the Vierville-Colleville road, finally digging in on the high ground. Right after the 18th came the 26th RCT, getting into position to the right of the 18th, commanding the road between St. Laurent and Formigny. The major part of St. Laurent was soon occupied by the 115th RCT, which landed at 1045, battling its way to the south.

Twelve hours after H-Hour only one of the planned exits was in operation. Most of our artillery was under water, but by 1600 the 7th Field Artillery had five howitzers just off the beach, supporting the 16th RCT. Two hours later there were 10 more howitzers of the 33d FA, backing up the 18th RCT.

During all this, the naval shore fire control parties, who had come in with the doughboys, were talking to their big gray ships telling them what to bomb with how much.

By midnight, the tired, dirty assault forces of V Corps were spread out on a strip of free France about 10,000 yards wide, straddling the coastal road, with their deepest inland penetration estimated at 3,000 yards and their forward positions sitting on the high ground which divided the sea from the Aure River.

· · ·

The two DUKWs floundered around in the rough waves, and shells kept plopping close. The big ships seemed far away, and the 15 guys in the two DUKWs kept working on their SCR-300 radio sets. At H-plus-15 they finally got through. "Testing . . . one, two, three, four, can you hear me . . . Over. . . ."

There were four SCR-300s going into Utah. Two had been put in waterproofed jeeps which were knocked out long before they got onto the beach. The other two were in the DUKWs. If they got knocked out too, then the distance from shore to ships would be a million miles and a million years apart.

At H-plus-Three, the two DUKWs wobbled for shore, tried to race up the beach behind cover. One was smacked square; one guy was killed, several others were wounded, the radio was smashed. For 15 hours the single SCR-300 did the job of four, filling one hot-priority order after another: change of fire direction, more boats for the wounded, more this, more that, more everything.

For 15 hours, "Can you hear me . . . can you hear me . . . . Over. . . ."

· · ·

They started dropping by the light of the full moon at 0130, five hours before the first waves of infantry hit Utah Beach. They started dropping from 800 invasion-decorated planes (black and white stripes) on six predetermined zones. Twenty planes never got back.

Of the two airborne divisions, the 101st was

widely dispersed because of thick flak and fog. Even as late as June 8, the 101st still had only 2,100 combat effectives under unified control. But that didn't stop them from storming Pouppeville, a tiny town which was important because it blocked the causeway entrance from Utah Beach. Before glider reinforcements arrived the next night, they had also taken stubbornly defended Varreville, pushing down Purple Heart Lane toward Carentan, to link up Omaha and Utah. Purple Heart Lane went through canals, swamplands, and across the Douve River. To get out of the swamps, they used bayonets for the first time in France.

Meanwhile, paratroopers of the 82d Division landed mostly west of the main Carentan-Cherbourg road, west of Ste. Mere-Eglise, which the troopers promptly walked into, cleaned out, and took over. That was the first town taken in France, and the Germans shoved in several tank attacks trying to get it back. There were two bazooka teams who took care of five tanks all by themselves. Finally the Germans pulled out. But they still tried to retake or knock out the paratroop-held bridge over the Merderet River, which the 82d was holding for the 4th Division. They called it Kellams Bridge, after a major who was killed there, and they held it intact. Before the day was over, 500 planes and 500 gliders were on their way with more troopers.

They had done their job—elbowing enemy reinforcements away from the beaches.

Now they were waiting for the Infantry.

• • •

"*Just before we pulled out, the CO read us this message from Eisenhower about how we were all crusaders and all that and it made us feel pretty good," said Sgt. Robert Miller of the 502d Regiment, who was in the sixteenth plane over France.*

"*It seemed like a long trip, but it was only two hours. It was a long two hours though, because it was so hot in the plane, and with all that 120 pounds of stuff on us, most of the guys got a little sick.*

"*You don't talk much. I didn't say a damn word. And don't ask me what I was thinking because I don't remember. I guess I was thinking a little about everything.*

"*And don't ask me what I saw when the 'chute opened, because I don't remember that either. But I remember everything after I hit the ground. Seeing a guy burning in the air. Things like that.*

"*The most terrible thing is when you hit the ground and you don't see anybody and you don't hear anything and you're all alone. Being lonely like that is the worst feeling in the world."*

• • •

The landing at Utah was smooth and quick compared with Omaha. That's because Utah was a mistake. With the 8th RCT spearheading, the 4th Division landed 1,500 yards southeast of the beaches at which they were supposed to land. They still got plenty of fire, almost continuous from some German battery in nearby Fontenay, but this was only a small sprinkling of the stuff they would have got if they had landed where they had intended to.

Here it was so smooth that 30 amphibious tanks of the 70th Tank Battalion, launched 5,000 yards ashore in two waves, came in with the loss of only one tank. Together with other regiments of the 4th came a 90th Division RTC.

Soon after five forts were cleared around the beaches, the 4th crossed some of the flooded area, the 12th RCT pushing through to Pouppeville to relieve the 101st Airborne, and the 8th RCT heading for Ste. Mere-Eglise to do the same for the 82d. By midnight, they had cleared an arc-shaped area four to seven miles inland.

The expected Luftwaffe show of strength never materialized. Instead of an estimated 1,800 Nazi sorties over the beaches on D-Day, the ack-ack crews spotted several single planes which didn't stay around long enough to be shot at. The first ack-ack crew moved in at H-plus-17; the first barrage balloon was floating in the breeze at H-plus-225 minutes.

Even our artillery came in early, delivering supporting fire as quickly as H-plus-90.

But despite the smoothness and quickness of everything, there were still plenty of red crosses scattered along the beach (832 wounded were evacuated from France that first day, the others were stretched out behind cover somewhere). As for the dead, they lay where they fell. There was no time to bury the dead that first day.

• • •

This was his fourth D-Day, he said—Arzew in Africa, Gela in Sicily, Salerno in Italy, and now this one. He was a medic with the 3052d Combat Engineers, Pfc. Stanley Borok of Center Moriches, L. I.

"If you're shooting dice," he said, "how many lucky sevens can you roll before you crap out? I figured that this time maybe I was gonna crap out and I didn't want to crap out. But it was rough; it was sure rough."

The waves slapping and banging and the LCVP floating around in circles for two hours before H-Hour and everybody sits with a helmet between his knees puking his guts out, so sick that he doesn't care what happens to him. But suddenly the boat starts moving in and somehow you stand up and swallow what you've got in your mouth and forget you're sick.

"I took five steps and this 88 lands about 30 feet to my left. Then I run to the right and bang! another 88, and this time my buddy is staring at his hand because his thumb is shot off. Then two more, just like that, and I found some backbone and ribs and the back of a skull with the whole face cleaned out, all of it right near the pack next to me."

His first patient was a guy who had his front tooth knocked out by a piece of shrapnel. His second was in a foxhole, buried up to his thighs.

"I didn't even notice it at first but the blood was spurting from his chest. Two big holes. You can't plug up a guy's lungs, brother. We did all we could, though. I spotted this bottle of blood plasma we were giving some other guys and then I noticed this other one was dead, so I just took out the needle and put it in this guy's

arm. But it didn't do much good. *He died in my arms.*"

• • •

The British were having it tough those first few days. They had landed near Bayeux, two British divisions and one Canadian. Their foothold near Caen was the hinge of the whole beachhead. Three German armored divisions were hammering away at them, throwing in attack after attack. The Germans rightly figured that if they could crack through the British-Canadian position with tanks they could race down the beaches, cut off our supplies, surround us, separate us, and chop us up.

The Germans were also particularly sensitive about our threat to Carentan and the possible link-up of the two beaches into a firm front. To keep the two beachheads separated, they threw in a single extra paratroop division, which was like adding meat to a grinder, because our build-up was steady, with more and more troops pouring over the beaches (the 2d Division on D-plus-One).

But as late as June 9 the beaches still weren't completely secure. There were still plenty of sniper nests fringed all along the full length of the beach. A whole battalion got the job of housecleaning the area.

That same day, advance units of the 747th Tank Battalion rumbled into Isigny, following a terrific bombardment by artillery, tanks, and naval guns. Behind the tanks came the doughfeet of the 29th Division, with the dirty job of erasing the several hundred stubborn snipers who were scattered among the rubbled buildings.

At Isigny, divers of the 1055th Engineer Port Construction and Repair Group were the first to go below the surface of France, opening the canal locks to relieve the flooded countryside where our troops were fighting.

It was the continued pressure west of the Merderet River that temporarily cracked the Nazi line of resistance, and V Corps started fanning out, with the 1st and 2d Divisions securing

the high ground between the Aure and Tor-
tonne Rivers, putting the beaches almost beyond
artillery range. It was near Agy that the 1st Division contacted the British on June 10.

Meanwhile, part of the 29th Division was securing the right bank of the Vire River, and
troops of the 115th RCT began the slow crossing of the Aure. For almost two miles they
waded through water three feet deep before they
finally got onto the high ground on the southern side of the marshland.

·   ·   ·

*"I'll never forget that swamp," said Pfc. Vito
Dziengielewski of Company G, 2d Battalion of
the 115th Regiment of the 29th. "It was stinking, scummy, gray-looking water and it came up
to our knees. I'll never forget that stink. It just
made you kinda sick. As if a lot of things had
died there. Then there were millions of bugs
buzzing around, biting the hell out of you
and you were too tired to even shoo them away.
You were so tired that you just wanted to fall
down in the swamp and stretch out for a while.
Some of the guys did slip and fall. If you didn't
see a guy fall, it was hard to spot him because
the weeds were so high and thick, just like Sea
Breeze Bay in Rochester."*

*But even when you crossed the swamp, there
was no time to sit down and take off your shoes
and wipe your feet and wiggle your toes in the
sun and change your socks. You could feel the
wet socks sucking down in your shoes with each
step, wet socks heavy with mud and scum. Some
of the Joes threw their leggings away and rolled
up their pants so that their legs would dry a
little quicker. But nobody had a chance to
change his socks for three days. Some of them
didn't have to.*

·   ·   ·

Back on the VII Corps front, our troops were
sitting on the high ground looking down into
the German flats, at the same time holding a
line along the Merderet and Douve Rivers.
Somewhere between Carentan and Isigny, at the
Auville Bridge, a paratrooper from the 101st

shook hands with a dough of the 29th, and newspapers back home headlined the fact that Utah
and Omaha were now one solid front.

But they weren't. Temporarily, the junction
was thin because troops on both beaches were
heading away from each other, trying to swell
out and make some elbow room for maneuvers.
Besides, the Germans still held the high ground,
which meant that they could throw artillery fire
any time they wanted to on both the Isigny-
Carentan highway and the vital Carentan
bridge. It was the bridge we were particularly
worried about, because if the Germans got the
bright idea of breaking through in strength to
retake it, it would have sliced an unhappy wedge
into our supply line. For insurance the Engineers built another bridge 2,000 yards downstream.

Troops and supplies were still flowing over
the beaches in a steady stream (the 9th and 90th
Divisions), and one of the forgotten units with
a private headache was the Traffic Headquarters
Subsection of G-4.

·   ·   ·

*"There was one vehicle for every six men in
the invasion force, so you figure it out," said Sgt.
Francis Scanlon, who used to be an accountant
in West Medford, Mass.*

*"Our phone used to ring all day and all night
long, and people wanted to know where their
unit was and which was the best way to get there
and which roads were open."*

He remembered something and smiled.

*"The last question was the easiest to answer,
because there were so few roads open to anywhere."*

*They had to make records of every vehicle
hitting the beach, which unit, and where it was
going. They did this 24 hours a day.*

*At certain critical sections of the road there
was an hourly flow of more than 1,700 vehicles.*

*"And there were only 17 men in our sec-
tion," said the sergeant. Then he remembered
something else.*

"I'm the only one who's alive now," he said.

—SGT. RALPH G. MARTIN

Fall of Rome

ON THE ROAD outside Rome three infantrymen were talking to an Italian civilian carrying a jug of wine. One of the infantrymen took a big slug out of the bottle. There was a rifle shot, and the GI holding the bottle fell into the road, the wine spilling onto his boots.

The civilian ran into a field, and two of the soldiers jumped into a ditch. The third rifleman—a little dark guy—bent over the fallen man for just a second and then ran into the ditch on the opposite side of the road.

"Is he hurt bad?" yelled one of the infantrymen to the little dark guy. "No," said the little dark guy. "He ain't hurt—he's dead."

The tanks came, and the infantrymen moved on down the road. Everyone felt uneasy. Men kept nudging closer to the tanks. Pretty soon the riflemen and the tanks passed two long rows of apartment houses where the Appian way ends and the city of Rome begins.

All of a sudden a big crowd of Italians came surging out of the houses and up the streets, some of them singing and laughing and some of them crying. An old lady with white hair ran up and kissed a tank. A girl stuck a rose behind an infantryman's ear. The tanks could barely move without killing somebody. The tankers and infantrymen started drinking wine out of bottles. Almost everyone had a bottle. A tall thin-faced captain kept pacing up and down the road.

"These crazy people don't know it," he said, "but they're holding up the war."

Pretty soon the crowd thinned out. The tanks and infantrymen moved on through the streets of Rome. It had been a long way to come, and there were mountains and Germans ahead. Silent now, they kept on moving toward the front and the Tiber.

—SGT. JAMES P. O'NEILL

The islands were full of jungles, and there was always another island ahead.

The jungles were lousy with Japs

AMERICAN NEWSPAPERS celebrated the landings in Normandy, and GIs celebrated in Rome. There was no celebrating in the Pacific. There was always another island ahead, and the islands were full of jungles and lousy with Japs.

One night, while Pvt. LeRoy Fessenden of Binghamton, N. Y., crouched in a hole dug in a swamp, with guns roaring all around him, something flew through the air and hit him be-tween the eyes. Fessenden rolled out of the hole, figuring the missle was a Jap grenade. When the missile didn't explode, he went back to investi-gate. His hand touched something soft, warm and wet. "It was the lower jaw of a Jap," Fessen-den said, "teeth on one side and straggly, black whiskers on the other."

One week after D-Day in Normandy, Amer-icans landed on Saipan.

Mission over the North Pacific

THE BOMBS went *snap-snap-snap* as they left. We could look down into the night underfoot, and we strained to hear the splash in the sea.

When the bomb bay banged shut, T/Sgt. David Viers went past me, headed for the tail of the plane. He grabbed an upright and swung out around me. I tried to make myself small on the catwalk.

"What a night!" Viers yelled. "You picked a hell of a mission!"

Viers shook his head at the thought of dropping the bombs, but in a way it was appropriate that we bombed the sea. That was our enemy. We were losing altitude 300 feet a minute, four hours away from a friendly land. Every man on the plane could feel the cold North Pacific lapping at the seat of his pants.

Up here, on the run from the Aleutians to Paramushiru, longest over-water bombing run in this war, you fight the sea and distance and weather and your plane, and incidentally you fight Japs.

"Open the doors!" Viers was beside me again on the catwalk, shouting close into my ear. I passed the message to the man ahead.

The bomb-bay doors banged open and the icy wind rushed up. Viers lifted a belt of .50-caliber ammunition level with his chest and dropped it straight down into the dirty gray darkness. Somebody behind kept handing him more, and he kept dropping it out chest high.

Now that I knew we were losing altitude, I imagined I could feel the plane drop. When we hit an air pocket and wavered for an instant, my stomach told me we had lost 300 feet.

"I hate this standing around and waiting," one of the crew had said while we were messing around outside the plane, waiting for take-off

time. The only thing anyone had worried about then was what we would eat on the long monotonous grind to Paramushiru.

"Paramoosh," they all called it, not Paramushiru. They spoke of it almost affectionately during the briefing.

When we got in the plane the waist gunner told me, "On the take-off lean against the bulkhead and brace yourself and relax." I leaned against the bulkhead and braced myself.

We rolled down the steel-matted runway, the bumps smoothing out as we started to fly. But suddenly my stomach found out we were in the air; it caught up, with a long loop, and settled down. They brought out candy and cheese and chewing gum. On the interphone the conversations were full of "Roger!" and occasionally a Georgia voice broke in with "Rawjah!" The tail gunner stretched out across the camera hatch and closed his eyes. The rest of us looked out the gun hatches at the clouds that stretched below us like mountains, turning blue and purple in the gathering darkness.

Viers waved and yelled that things were going good and the weather was holding up. I found out he was from Tampa, Fla., and that he was the flight engineer and that we should be over Paramushiru in three hours, at about 0130.

Now, at midnight, he was back on the catwalk in the freezing, roaring, pitch-dark bomb bay.

"Open the doors again!" he yelled, and I passed it along. Viers dropped out something that looked like cloth but sounded like metal as it whooshed down and into the slipstream and vanished.

"What was that?" I yelled.

"Flak suits. We're unloadin'. She's flyin' tail-heavy, losin' power and mushin' down. We're at 4,000 now." Once again he disappeared toward the tail.

It was my last question. Others in the crew packed in the bomb bay with me seemed to prefer not to know what went on. We had all been cut off from the interphone ever since the pilot had said, "Everybody forward, out of that waist and up on the flight deck!" There wasn't room there, so the overflow was lined along the bomb-bay catwalk.

"Move up!" Viers yelled from behind me. I shoved the man in front and we all moved up. Finally I found a corner to crawl into under the flight deck, alongside the big nose wheel. I wondered what was going out next. It occurred to me that I was the least useful man aboard.

Viers dragged a machinegun in and laid it by me, and two others followed it. Then he lay on top of the guns to get close to my ear.

"We're shiftin' all weight forward," he yelled. "We turned around a while ago. We're headin' home!" I nodded. After that I lay beside the guns, watching Viers fling himself on and off the flight deck, back and forth on the catwalk, checking gauges, throwing switches, changing hoses, flashing his light all over the plane.

About 0300 he shined his light on me and yelled, "Thank God for the rain!"

"Is it raining?" I asked, but he couldn't hear me, and the question was too silly to repeat at a shout. He said, "We had trouble with the one, two, and four motors. Cylinder-head temperatures way too high. We were losin' power and our tail was draggin' and we were mushin' down fast. After we dumped and turned back we hit rain and cooled the motors."

I nodded, but he shook his head. "If we get through this night," he said, "I'm goin' to chapel Sunday."

Later Viers came back and shook my foot.

"Get out of here," he shouted. I got out, back on the catwalk, and Viers slid over the guns and down beside the nose wheel.

He poked my leg and yelled "Okay?" and I shouted "Okay!" up to the flight deck. I passed a dozen messages back and forth in the dark, without knowing what was going on. At last I figured out we were over our home island, circling for a landing, and the nose wheel wouldn't come down.

Viers was fighting the nose wheel by flashlight. Kelso Barnett, from Glendale, Calif., the other engineer, shoved past me to help Viers.

The wheel jerked part way as the hatch opened to receive it, letting a blast of cold air roar through the plane. Then the wheel twitched and froze.

Viers threw his hands before his face. They were dripping red, and the wrench he held was red and his face was red, from hydraulic fluid blowing wildly in the blast from the open hatch. The wheel went up, over, down into place.

Aleutian fog, in one of its frequent whims, had closed in on the field while we were circling. We had to fly up the chain to another island base. Viers was rubbing red hydraulic fluid off his face with his handkerchief and checking gas gauges with his flashlight.

"We bled the damn line," Barnett said. "Viers got a faceful." We were back in the waist, braced against the bulkhead. "I only hope she holds when we hit," Barnett said. The plane dragged suddenly as the flaps went down. She hit hard, bounced, and settled down. We had been in the air almost nine hours.

At the transient hut most of us hit our sacks right away. Two men horsed around, mauling each other, until they overturned a bed. Someone found a deck of cards. Two men were heating bouillon on the stove. They were singing, "Send some beer to the boys over here," to the tune of "Say a Prayer for the Boys Over There."

Viers was writing up his report of the mission, and when he finished he read it out loud. "We let down," he concluded, at "at 0545 and made the field without further trouble."

"And at 0645," somebody added, "we finished washing out our underdrawers."

—SGT. RAY DUNCAN

They hated the hedgerows the way men in the Pacific hated the jungle.

Every field a battlefield

INFANTRYMEN IN FRANCE hated the hedgerows that lined the fields of Normandy the way infantrymen in the Pacific hated the jungle. Pfc. Bob Sloane of Detroit, Mich., said, "Every goddam field in this hedgerow country is a battlefield."

The infantrymen ribbed each other about being students at Hedgerow High. It was wonderful country for snipers. All a man had to do was to stick his head above the hedgerows and he could get a Purple Heart, although sometimes his kinfolk got it for him.

Sgt. Frank Kwiatek had 19 notches on his rifle for killing snipers, and he was always telling the men in his platoon to keep their heads down. Once when one of Kwiatek's men stuck his head above a Normandy hedgerow, a sniper got him dead center. "His brains splattered all over my face," Kwiatek said. "I never was so sick in all my life."

Battle of the hedgerows

THE WAR OF THE HEDGEROWS is a strangely limited kind of war. Hedgerows are tall, thick breastworks lining almost every road and every field. They are not new emplacements but ancient demarcation lines, and they have been packed down into a cement-like hardness by the pressure of centuries. Sometimes when 88s and 105s score direct hits on hedgerows, they blast holes barely large enough for two men to squeeze through.

Fighting is from field to field and from hedgerow to hedgerow. Frequently you don't know whether the field next to yours is occupied by friend or foe.

Sometimes you man the four hedgerows bordering a field and hold it as you would a tiny fort surrounded by the enemy.

You rarely speak of advancing a mile in a single day; you say, instead, "We advanced 11 fields." Normally no-man's-land is the width of a single field, but sometimes it's the width of a single hedgerow. That happens after a long period of fighting and firing, when both sides are too tired to move, and you can hear Jerries talking a few feet away on the other side of the hedge.

Sometimes you hold one end of a field and the enemy holds the other, and you maneuver around in two- or three-man patrols until either you or the enemy is thrown out.

This kind of war is paradise for the sniper, the rifleman, the automatic-weapons man, the bazookaman. Conversely, it's death on tanks and armored cars.

As Lt. Jack Shea put it: "Give me 10 infantrymen in this terrain with the proper combination of small arms, and we will hold up a battalion for 24 hours."

The man on the ground is the important joe here, and he isn't fighting by the books. An outstanding example of improvising is the use of the rifle grenade as a substitute for mortar fire. The rifle is fired from the ground with the butt down, giving the grenade a high angle of elevation.

The projectile travels about 200 feet in a high arc and then, at the end of its five-second fuse, explodes in the air. The fragmentation usually kills any Germans who may be caught beneath the airburst.

Patrols go out from both sides at night in search of information, and counterpatrols are sent to fight them. In the darkness, strange things sometimes happen. At one advanced CP, bars of pink all-purpose GI soap were found with tooth marks in them. Jerries who had been there the night before evidently thought the soap was candy.

Throughout the fighting, French farmers and their families live in holes dug into their cellars while the farmhouses are destroyed over their heads.

When the fighting passes or a lull begins, the children come out to play and their parents bring eggs and butter to the GIs.

These lulls are necessary in hedgerow warfare. After hours spent advancing through fields, both sides are so worn out that they must stop to rest, regroup, and gather up the dead and wounded.

Lull, of course, is a misnomer. Snipers keep working, mortar and artillery shells plop down, and patrols go out at night. But it's like Sunday in the park back home compared with what went on before.

—SGT. BILL DAVIDSON

Summer on the Riviera

WE TOOK CARE of the Germans; sat on our dead hams, spat out skins of juicy grapes, and admired the view we had of the Riviera. To our right was a small, pleasant valley with orange-roofed farm houses, and back of the valley were green pine hills. All around us were thick vineyards and cane fields. A short time before, Sgt. Frank Moran had caught three Jerries in one of those cane fields.

"I was demining through this field," explained Moran, "when I saw an artillery officer and some German prisoners in the back of a jeep He had found those prisoners in the woods a mile away. The only weapon I had was a sickle I'd picked up in a French house I had gone through looking for booby traps.

" 'This country is alive with Jerries,' the officer told me. 'You'd better go back and get yourself a weapon.' So I was on my way to the bivouac for my carbine when these three Jerries jumped out of the cane brush. They were riflemen. I made a lunge for them with my sickle, and all they did was put their hands up. I took them down the road a piece, and there was that artillery officer. I turned the Jerries over to him. Then I went back to the cane field. This is my fourth invasion," Moran added as he hoisted the deminer over his shoulder, "but I've never seen anything as soft as this one. More like a picnic than an invasion. For us fellows anyway."

It hadn't been much different ever since our LST set sail with the convoy that left on the afternoon of Aug. 12. The weather was bright and sunny, the Mediterranean was calm, and there wasn't a Jerry plane or sub to be seen or heard during the entire trip up to the time we anchored half a mile off the coast of southern France in the morning of the 15th, two hours before H-Hour.

There wasn't much to do after the novelty of counting the crisp, new French money wore off, or after skimming through the French language guidebooks, or wearing the new American-flag armbands. Some of the men read, others played cards. Many simply lay out in the sun and stared up into the sky or out across the sea with the blank stare of "two-year men."

T-5 Kenneth Anthony, a photographer who had been overseas 27 months, explained that look: "It doesn't mean we're dreaming of home or our girls or anything," he said. "We're past that stage. We're just looking, that's all. Looking and waiting."

There was also, of course, a great deal of sweating out lines for the GIs aboard; lines for chow, for the latrine, for washing, for water. There were three toilet bowls for the more than 400 men on the ship, so sweating out the toilet lines took up a lot of slack time. The latrines were next to the boiler room and you got the additional benefit of a Turkish bath.

When we climbed out of our sacks at dawn of D-Day, our ship already lay at anchor. All about us, as far as the eye could reach, were row upon row af Allied ships: LSTs, minesweepers, Liberty ships, destroyers and destroyer escorts, cruisers and giant battlewagons. Two hours before H-Hour the warships opened fire on the German positions in the hills behind the beachhead. First the battlewagons shook the sea with the thunder of their 16-inch guns; then came the flat, dull pounding of the cruisers' eight-inchers, followed by the sharp, angry barks of the destroyers' five-inch pieces.

Even then, while the entire Mediterranean seemed to tremble from the terrific gunfire of the Allied fleet, and our LST shook from stem to stern with each blasting of the battleships, it was like watching a football game from a choice 40-yard-line seat.

Minesweepers patrolled up and down the coast shoreline. LSTs all around us were opening their broad bows and pouring out LCIs and LCVTs loaded with combat infantrymen and tanks speeding toward the beachhead. Far overhead groups of Thunderbolts and Spitfies and Lightnings swept across the pale blue sky looking in vain for Jerry planes. Flocks of Liberators, looking like giant silver birds, swung majestically toward the hills beyond the beachhead, and from the hills we could hear the faint but clear reverberations of their bombs.

At H-plus-Five an LCVP swung along our ship and a GI yelled up, "It's all over but the shoutin'! We walked right in." That was the only news we had of the progress our doughfeet were making on the beachhead until late in the afternoon, when another LCVP came by to report that our troops were eight miles inland, though the Jerries were putting up a rough rear-guard action. We sat around, still lining the top rails, waiting for some official announcement of the invasion's progress, but the announcement never came.

Throughout the afternoon the gunfire from our warships increased in intensity. Great clouds of smoke billowed over the hills on the coast. We listened for the return fire from the Jerry guns. There was none. "Jerry's getting it this time," said one GI grimly. "It sure was different at Salerno."

At H-plus-10 our LST made its way around the peninsula to our designated landing point.

We were ordered to pack and prepare to disembark. We crowded our way into the hot, stuffy tank deck. The ship's door swung open, and through the giant tunnels we could see flame-colored splashes of sunset.

We waited for more than half an hour without any order to disembark, and the RAF men started to sing, "Oh, why are we waiting, Oh, why are we waiting, Oh why, Oh why, Oh why?" with profane variations, and followed it up with "There'll be no promotions this side of the ocean, so cheer up, my lads, f - - - 'em all, f - - - 'em all!" They were filling the tank with the sentimental refrain of "Annie Laurie" when an ear-splitting staccato of ack-ack suddenly burst from the top deck. We ran for the life belts, which we had already tossed aside, and the bow doors swiftly closed. "Army personnel," came a voice from the loudspeaker, "will return to their former positions and will remain on ship until further advice."

When we returned to our top deck corner, we were told that a Jerry ME-109 had been shot down while making a recon over the convoy.

On H-plus-20 we finally got orders to disembark. We walked through the open doors of our LST, across the narrow ponton strips, and onto the short, sandy beach. The early morning air was damp, cold, and full of mist. Two hours later the sun broke through the mist, the air became bright and warm, and, as we trudged up the road from the beach to the wooded slope that was to be our bivouac area, we felt the cool breeze coming from the hills.

The invasion of southern France was scarcely one-day old when T/Sgt. Murray Johnson of Boston, Mass, sauntered into the bivouac area, bringing with him a pretty French girl walking her bicycle, and a gnarled French farmer with a jug of wine. We pulled out our canteen cups. The wine was bright red, clear, and dry.

"He's been saving it for us," explained Johnson. "He's been saving it for us a helluva long time."

—SGT. HARRY SIONS

Fall of Paris

WE WEREN'T supposed to go into Paris. We were supposed to outflank it.

But we hadn't counted on the FFI. Highly organized, spread out all over the city, the FFI started their own sniping-street-fighting on a big scale on Aug. 19. For the Germans in Paris the situation got so serious that Gen. von Choltitz arranged a verbal agreement. If the sniping would stop, he would permit food convoys to come into Paris. The FFI agreed not only because their food situation was critical but because they had an acute shortage of ammo and couldn't fire for much longer.

As soon as they learned all this, 12th Army Group Headquarters, under Gen. Omar Bradley, decided to enter Paris as soon as the armistice ended at noon, Aug. 23.

Selected for the entry was the 4th Division of the First Army's VII Corps and the 2d French Armored Division, detached from the Third Army. Both entered Paris at 0700 Aug. 25.

With the 4th occupying the part of Paris north of the Seine and the 2d French Armored in the southern sections and the FFI everywhere else, Gen. von Choltitz formally surrendered shortly after noon.

The Germans resisted only in a group of buildings east of Vincennes, shooting down both the German and American officers who walked toward them with a white flag. It wasn't until the next morning that the 4th reduced this strong point and it wasn't until the day after that that all street fighting and sniping completely stopped and Paris was formally returned to the French.

When the rest of the V Corps started moving northeast, the 28th Division was paraded through Paris enroute to the front.

"We didn't have a damn thing to do with the taking of Paris," said Pfc. Verner Odegard of Gonvick, Minn., a rifleman with Baker Company of the 1st Battalion of the 19th Regiment of the 82th Division. "We just came in a couple of days later when somebody got the bright idea of having the parade and we just happened to be there and that's all there was to it. What can you do, though—that's just the way it goes. And after all, we did a helluva lot of things that we didn't get credit for.

"As long as I live I don't guess I'll ever see a parade like that. Most of us slept in pup tents in the Bois de Boulogne the night before, and it rained like hell and we were pretty dirty, so they picked out the cleanest guys to stand up in front and on the outside. I had a bright new shiny patch, so they put me on the outside. It was a good place to be, too, because every guy marching on the outside had at least one girl on his arm kissing him and hugging him.

"We were marching 24 abreast right down the Champs Elysees and we had a helluva time trying to march, because the whole street was jammed with people laughing and yelling and crying and singing. They were throwing flowers at us and bringing us big bottles of wine.

"The first regiment never did get through. The crowd just gobbled them up. They just broke in and grabbed the guys and lifted some of them on their shoulders and carried them into cafes and bars and their homes and wouldn't let them go. I hear it was a helluva job trying to round them all up later."

—SGT. RALPH G. MARTIN

◄ *"I don't guess I'll ever see a parade like that."*

On island after island, Japs were flushed out of caves.

Island after island

By THE END of August 1944 Allied armies in France had killed or wounded 200,000 Germans, captured 200,000 more. In the Pacific the Japs still fought fanatically, seldom surrendered. On island after island it was a job of flushing the Japs out of caves with grenades, machineguns, flamethrowers. The GIs told a story about an American who trapped a Jap in a cave and demanded: "Come out and surrender!" In English the Jap answered: "Come and get me, you souvenir-hunting sonuvabitch!"

GIs in the Pacific moved on, faster now, towards the Philippines and the final push on Japan.

PTs in the Philippines

A CAT CAN look at a king, and a PT boat can challenge a battleship. Ask the men of the *Lakacookie.*

A heavy haze lay over the water as the *Lakacookie,* flanked by two other PT boats, cruised slowly through the darkness of Surigao Strait. Aboard the *Lakacookie,* Lt. Weston C. Pullens Jr. of Lyme, Conn., tactical officer in command of the three PTs, chatted in low tones with the skipper, Lt. (jg) J. A. Eddins of Rosedale, Miss.

Otherwise there was little talk as the men huddled in their battle positions, kapok life jackets pulled close around their necks to insure all possible protection against fragments. Gun trainers, from force of habit, slowly maneuvered their pieces through the prescribed arcs of fire. Loaders tightened and relaxed their grips on waiting canisters. Torpedomen went nervously through the motions that would cast their 'fish into the sea. The men were relatively green, and none had ever dropped a fish in earnest.

Throughout the New Guinea and New Britain campaigns it had been a slow but useful grind for the PTs. Prowling nightly past jungle-choked shores, risking coral reefs and enemy shore batteries, they had worked hand-in-glove with the Army Air Forces, seeking out and destroying the Japs' barge hide-outs and traffic.

Lacking targets, torpedomen had fumed at serving as gunners or cooks while their tin fish lay unused. There had been few attacks from the air, for the armament of the PTs had been built up, and by experience the Japs had learned.

But this night everybody, torpedomen included, had reason to be tense. Shortly before, a strong Jap naval force had headed through Surigao Strait toward Leyte Gulf.

Aboard the command ship the skippers had received their last-minute instructions at dusk. The PTs' job was to throw a cordon across the strait, patrolling in groups to cover every possible approach of the Jap force. Their first and main job was to locate and identify the force and report its position, strength, and speed so that our heavy naval units would know what they were up against. Having reported, the PTs were on their own to harrass and confuse the enemy in any way they could.

At 2300 hours the curtain of mist lifted as neatly as if some stagehand had pulled a rope. What the men of the *Lakacookie* saw on the other side of the curtain struck them dumb for a moment. Frank Miller QM3c of Aberdeen, Md., was the first to find his voice. "Skipper," he shouted to the conning tower, "there they are."

Eddins couldn't quite believe what he saw through his glasses. "It was a battlewagon all right," he said afterward. "But I just couldn't make myself say so when I turned in my report that morning. I didn't trust myself to list it as more than a heavy cruiser."

The *Lakacookie* and two other PTs were half-way between the forward screen of Jap destroyers and the main body of cruisers and the battleship.

As Lt. Pullens gave orders to close for torpedo attack, Jim Dempster RM3c broke radio silence. "I have an urgent message for you," he called. That much and that much only was received aboard the command tender. Heavy static and Japanese jamming of channels prevented the tender from hearing the PT as Dempster again and again reported that part of the enemy force had been sighted.

As the PTs surged forward with wide-open engines, the Japs opened fire. It was careful, deliberate fire—as dead on the button as only radio directional finders could make it. Fred Vislosky GM2c of Shenandoah, Penna., saw one shell cast up a geyser 20 yards astern. The next salvo lifted the stern out of the water. Vislosky was thrown against his gun, and his loader, C. W. Patterson S1c of Dade City, Fla., was knocked off the gun mount and thrown against the ready box.

The Japs were too far away to make it worthwhile for the PT to launch those long-unused torpedoes, and it would have been suicidal to try to press the attack. Anyway, the primary mission of the PTs was to spot the force and get the message through. So Lt. Pullens ordered the PTs out of there. Fast.

Even as the PTs swung around, Jap shells scored. A direct hit exploded the magazine of the bow gun. Fragments ripped the deck and hull. Flames licked at the painted plywood, while mattresses in the crew's quarters below decks smoldered and caught fire. The heavy spray from shells hitting the water soaked everybody aboard but helped the crew to quench the fire. With each flash from the warships, Lt. Pullens ordered a sharp change in course, and the *Lakacookie* weaved like a halfback.

The other PTs were not coming through so well. No. 2 boat under Lt. Brian Malcolm of Bar Harbor, Me., was hit by an eight-inch shell that grooved its imprint along the warhead of a torpedo. The detonator was left hanging in the air, but the fish didn't explode. The shell ripped up 10 feet of deck planking, tore through sea bags below decks and passed out through the side of the hull.

It wasn't dark any more. The Japs were throwing up star shells to illuminate the PTs and give their gunners even better aim. Appar-

ently thrown off balance by three PTs, the whole Jap force of battleship, cruisers, and destroyers turned from its course and began chasing the little group of PT boats. That was something for the PT men to boast about later, but at the time nobody made remarks about having unnerved the Japs.

There was more interest aboard the *Lakacookie* in smoke cylinders that refused to work and blot out the PT from Jap sight, and an engine that for one long minute and a half refused to work. The brief loss of speed from the cranky engine gave one of the Jap destroyers a chance to close within a mile and a half. It snapped a searchlight square on the *Lakacookie*. Every gun that was still working on the PT blasted at the light. It wavered, turned, and went out.

Forty-five minutes after it had started, the firing stopped. In that time the PTs had managed to put seven miles between themselves and the Japs. All the while Dempster kept sending out his message, but he was sure it wasn't getting through because he could hear the other boats, now out of sight, reporting the *Lakacookie* as lost. "If you think that's a pleasant feeling, you ought to try it some time," Dempster said.

The *Lakacookie* was the first boat to Sogod Bay, where the command tender was anchored. The PT gave Sogod Bay a surprise and got one in return. A quarter of a mile out, Dempster established radio contact and reported that the *Lakacookie* wasn't at the bottom of the sea.

This time it was Dempster who was surprised. The message he'd tapped out so often had gotten through after all. Lt. Malcolm of the No. 2 boat had contacted another PT patrol, which relayed the message in. That message provided our fleet with the last vital link in the chain of information it need to find and then conquer the Jap fleet.

The PTs had challenged a battleship and held their own.

—Sgt. Ralph Boyce

An assault wave hits the beach at Leyte . . .

. . . and General MacArthur comes ashore.

"I have returned . . ."

How the Jap soldier thought

THE STOCKADE was set in a large rectangular clearing near the edge of a grove of coconut palms and guava trees. Off to the right was a mangrove swamp and beyond that a swollen, clay-covered river that wound like a dirty, twisted ribbon through tangles of Philippine fronds and water weeds.

We went for several yards along a narrow passage formed by barbed wire until we came to the main yard, a cleared square about the size of a baseball diamond with OD tents and little nipa-thatched huts lining three of its four sides. "Jitter," the staff-sergeant interpreter with me, stopped for a minute and pointed to the yard where the Japs were and said: "There they are, more than 200 of the filthy bastards. You ought to be able to get a cross-section of the Jap soldier's mind from them."

He explained the procedure we were to follow. I was to put my questions to him in English; he would translate them to the Japs. If it proved necessary, he would carry out the interrogation further himself to get as complete and revealing answers as possible. When he was satisfied with an answer, he would sum it up for me in English.

"Before we go in," he said, "there are some things you ought to know. The Japs you'll see and talk to will fall into two broad types. There will be those who surrendered voluntarily because they couldn't take it, and those taken against their wills because of wounds or shock.

"The first are mostly stupid animal-slaves who have been drilled and drilled until they know how to handle a piece or wield a knife and kill. Otherwise they know absolutely nothing about anything. They have no minds of their own and act only when a superior presses a button.

"The second type is something else again. They are fantastic, shrewd, and possessed of an amazing singleness of purpose that is the direct result of just one thing—their sheep-like subservience to their superiors and to the Emperor. They're slick and well-trained and live only to obey their superiors' orders to kill as many guys as possible. Otherwise they're just like the first type—mindless automatons who move when the button is pressed.

"There is a third type, too, but you won't see many of them in any prison camp because they're almost never captured. They're the killers who fight like madmen until they're wiped out. You can realize how many of these bastards there are when you consider the small number of prisoners we've taken compared with Jap casualties. They're the type who tortured captured marines on Guadalcanal and engineered the March of Death on Bataan."

Jitter led the way over to a tent.

"Here's one who's as good to start with as any," he said. "He's a sergeant, with those paratroops the Japs tried to land on Leyte the other night. His transport was shot down off the coast, and everyone in it was killed except him. He managed to get ashore but he ran into a bunch of guerrillas. You can imagine what a going-over they gave him. He falls into the second type I mentioned. He was captured against his will, and now he thinks he's disgraced forever; says he'll commit suicide the first chance he gets."

When we ducked under the tent flaps, the Jap, sitting Buddha-fashion with one foot under

his buttocks and the other pulled up on the opposite thigh, looked up with a startled expression. Then he stood abruptly and bowed up and down, his arms spread wide, a cringing, crinkled smile on his face. He was big for a Jap, with broad shoulders and a clean-shaven bullet-shaped head. There were Band-Aids on his chin and under his jaw, apparently mementos of his session with the guerrillas, and there were thin, uneven gold edges on his protruding teeth. Jitter asked him to sit down and told him what we wanted to talk about. Then the questioning began. Every time the prisoner spoke, a nervous tic twitched above his right eye.

Q. Where is your home town?

A. Osaka.

Q. How long have you been in the Army?

A. Five years.

Q. Did you take your basic training in Japan?

A. Some of it.

Q. While you were training did your officers ever talk to you about the United States or tell you that Americans were bad and were a threat to the peace of Japan?

A. No. All they talked about was how to shoot guns, how to fight.

Q. Did you volunteer or were you conscripted?

A. I volunteered.

Q. Why did you volunteer?

A. Because I like army life; it makes you feel like a man.

Q. When you were captured, how did you think you would be treated? [The tic above the Jap's eye twitched three or four times in rapid succession. He didn't say anything. Jitter repeated the question with an addition.]

Q. Did you think you would be tortured or killed?

A. Yes.

Q. Has anyone in this camp hurt you in any way?

A. No. Every one has been kind. Plenty of food. Nobody has hurt me.

Q. Do you think you will be hurt or killed?

A. I don't know. [The Jap's tic twitched more violently.] I have asked MPs to kill me. I have asked MPs to let me kill myself.

Q. Why do you want to kill yourself?

A. Because I am disgraced. I could never go back.

Q. Do you have a family?

A. A mother and sister.

Q. Friends? Schoolmates?

A. Yes.

Q. Wouldn't they understand and forgive you? [The prisoner was suddenly a blank again, as if he didn't know what the question meant. Jitter asked it again.]

A. I don't know if they'd understand. It wouldn't make any difference if they did.

Q. Would you be afraid to go home?

A. Yes; afraid, ashamed.

Q. If you were able to escape back to your lines, would you fight and try to kill as hard as you did before you were captured?

A. Harder.

Q. Why? for what? [The Jap, his tic still twitching, started picking at a big scab on his ankle. Once more he didn't understand the meaning of a question.]

Q. Why were you fighting in the first place?

A. For the Emperor. [When he said the word Emperor, the Jap sergeant made a quick, slight, almost imperceptible movement, snapping his spine straight. Jitter turned to me and said, "They all do that."]

Q. Are you fighting for anything else but the Emperor? [At the sound of the word, the Jap's spine snapped straight again.]

A. No.

Q. Why do you think Japan should rule the world?

A. Because Japan is greater than any other country.

Q. What makes you think that?

A. Japan has everything. Japan is powerful and right.

Q. Did you hear or read much about the United States?

Jap prisoner: fantastic, shrewd, and purposeful.

A. No.

Q. Do you think America is powerful?

A. I don't know.

Q. Do you think America is right?

A. I don't know. Japan is right.

Q. Why do you think Japan is right? Can't anyone possibly be right but Japan? [The prisoner looked blank again.]

Q. Is Japan right because only Japan has the Emperor?

A. [The Jap's spine snapped straight and he answered quickly as if from memory, like a high-school elocutionist, speaking the words fast and without expression.] The Emperor is God. The Emperor is God for the whole world. [Jitter looked at me, shrugging his shoulders as if to say, "See what I mean?" He went on.]

Q. When were you last in Japan?

A. I was in Miyazaki Dec. 4, 1944.

Q. Did the people there have enough to eat?

A. Yes.

Q. Were they concerned or scared about the war?

A. They were afraid.

Q. Do they think Japan will win the war?

A. Every Japanese thinks that Japan will win the war.

Q. Did you ever hear of Midway, Guadalcanal, Tarawa, Eniwetok, Saipan, Hollandia, Morotai?

A. Yes. They have told us about them.

Q. Do you know you've been kicked out of those places and that now you're being kicked out of the Philippines?

A. I don't know. All places so far are just battles. You maybe win battles. Japan will win the war.

Jitter got up, sighed and said: "There's no point talking to this one any longer. Let's go in the next tent."

The next tent was larger. It had a long bamboo pole in the center, and over the ground the prisoners had spread layers of palm leaves. There were 16 Japs in the tent, and all of them were squatting on the floor tying palm leaves together with strands of rattan. They were naked except for jock-strap arrangements of white cloth.

When we came in the prisoners stood up immediately. Jitter told them to sit down. Then he picked out two who could answer for the others. One of them, a pfc in the Infantry, was very young and rather frail-looking. His cheek bones weren't as high as those of most of his race and his skin had a certain unhealthy pallor. The two characteristics combined to make him look less Japanese. He had no expression at all when he talked, but when he bowed he had the usual insipid, crinkled grin.

The other prisoner was a seaman second-class who had been fished out of Surigao Strait after his ship was blasted in the now-famous battle of the night Oct. 24-25. He was pudgy-faced, remarkably slant-eyed and fat, with a clean-shaven, abnormally large head.

Jitter turned to the young pfc first.

Q. Where's your home?

A. In the prefecture of Kagawa.

Q. When did you get in the Army?

A. In October 1943.

Q. What did you do before you were in the Army?

A. Worked on my father's farm.

Q. Did you have plenty to eat?

A. We had enough.

Q. Did the Japanese Government get any of your food?

A. Some of it.

Q. After you got into the Army were you told anything about the war, what you were fighting for and so forth?

A. They told us we were fighting for Eternal Peace.

Q. When you were in school before the war did you ever read or study much about the United States?

A. No.

Q. Do you hate Americans?

A. I don't know.

Q. Do you hate America?

A. I don't know.

Q. Then why did you fight and try to kill Americans? [The young pfc's eyes darted back and forth nervously over the tent wall. One of the other prisoners, a thin, demented-looking Jap, stopped grinning and waited, his mouth hanging open and his eyes fixed on the pfc.]

Q. Why did you fight and kill Americans?

A. Because of the Emperor. [Every back in the semicircle of listening prisoners straightened up when the word was spoken. The thin prisoner was a few seconds late, but he finally jerked to attention, his idiot grin restored.]

Q. Do you believe that the Emperor is God?

A. Yes. [Jitter put the same question to all of the others and each one in his turn nodded and said "Haee," the sound Japs make when they answer yes to their superiors.]

Then Jitter asked, "Why do you think the Emperor is God?" and the pfc said that every Japanese knew the Emperor was God. They knew it, he said, because it was the only truth, the only thing that meant anything to them.

Jitter looked at me helplessly. "What can you do?" he said.

Then he turned to the pudgy-faced sailor.

Q. Do you think Japan will win the war?

A. [The Jap sailor grinned smugly.] Of course Japan will win the war.

Q. Why?

A. Japan can beat anybody. [The others were listening intently, hanging on to each word.]

Q. What makes you think Japan will win?

A. Japan never lost a war. She cannot be beaten. All of Japan is one mind.

Q. What do you mean, "Japan is one mind?"

[In his answer the prisoner used a phrase that I had heard frequently throughout the questioning. It was "Yamato Damashi." When I asked what it meant, Jitter said: "The phrase is hard to translate. There is no American word or phrase which means quite the same thing. The closest I can come to it is 'fighting spirit,' but to these people, it means much more than that. If you think of a willpower that no force

on earth could discourage, short of killing its possessor, and add to that the stubborn, cold belief of a bigot you might get a little closer to its meaning." He went on with his questioning.]

Q. Do you think Japan can beat America at anything—sports, for example?

A. Yes.

Q. How about baseball? Didn't the Americans beat your pants off at baseball a few years ago?

A. They got the highest score, yes.

Q. You mean that America didn't beat you?

A. Yes. Japan won. [Jitter looked at me with the expression of exaggerated patience, tapping his fingers on the ground like Oliver Hardy used to do when Stan Laurel tripped him into a trough of white plaster.]

Q. Look. First you said that the Americans got the high score and now you say that Japan won. What exactly do you mean by that?

A. Yamato Damashi. You got high score, but there are more important things. It's the way Japan plays the game. [Then the sailor burst into a flood of wild hissing chatter that lasted a good two minutes. When he finished, Jitter translated.] You come over to play in a big baseball tournament. You hit the ball plenty. You make runs, but your players are not honorable. They were crude. They didn't bow and talk properly to people, and while they played they paid no attention to anything but the game. Also, they show no Yamato Damashi. They wear uniforms with no American flag on them. Every Japanese player wears a uniform with the Rising Sun on it.

Jitter stood up. "I expect," he said, "that gives you a pretty good picture of how his brain works. Let's go out and get some fresh air."

Outside the sun was trying to break through the clouds, but there was a dismal drizzle and the yard was deserted except for one prisoner who was filling a canteen from the Lister bag that hung in the center of the compound.

"That joe over there is a Navy pilot," Jitter said. "Let's talk to him."

The pilot was about 25 years old. He had a sparse, stringy mustache and some hairs on his chin that passed for a goatee. There was a purple-streaked swelling over his left eye, and one of his front teeth was missing. He had been shot down in San Pedro Bay on A-plus-Four and picked up by one of our Navy boats.

Though he had been cocky around the other Japs, when he saw Jitter approaching he became all smiles and bows. Jitter told him I would like him to answer a few questions, and he nodded so agreeably that you would have thought answering my questions was his life's ambition.

Q. Where is your home?

A. Osaka.

Q. How long have you been in the Navy?

A. Six years.

Q. How long have you been a fighter pilot?

A. I graduated from Kasugamuira four months ago.

Q. Ever in combat before Leyte?

A. No.

Q. Do you feel any disgrace because you were picked up alive?

A. Yes, I do.

Q. Why did you let them pick you up out of the bay?

A. I was very sick.

Q. Why didn't you kill yourself then? You had a gun, didn't you?

A. Yes, but it was rusty.

Q. How did you think you would be treated as a prisoner?

A. I didn't know. International law protects officers.

Q. Did you ever hear of Jimmy Doolittle's raid on Tokyo?

A. Yes.

Q. Do you know what happened to the American pilots who were captured there?

A. No.

Q. Did you know that their heads were cut off?

A. No.

Q. Well, they were. Do you believe it?

A. No. [Jitter shrugged and offered a cigarette to the Jap pilot, who took it greedily, but only after he had executed a short, quick bow.]

Q. Have you heard about the B-29 raids on Tokyo?

A. Yes. They have told us about them.

Q. Did they tell you that the raids caused any appreciable damage?

A. They told us there was not much damage.

Q. Do you think the B-29s can wreck Japan?

A. They cannot hurt Japan.

Q. Why?

A. Japan has too much antiaircraft, too much defense, too many fighter planes.

Q. What do you think of American pilots?

A. Some good, some bad.

Q. Are they any better than Japanese pilots?

A. We have some good, some bad, too.

Q. Who do you think has the better, stronger air force?

A. [The pilot looked blank for a moment, attempted to formulate an answer, tried a few broken phrases and gave up.]

Q. When you went out to attack an American troopship or vessel, what did you think about?

A. Hitting the target.

Q. Anything else? [No answer.]

Q. Why did you do it?

A. For the Emperor. [The Jap pilot snapped straight.]

Q. Why do you think the Emperor is making Japan fight?

A. Japan is fighting for Eternal Peace.

Q. Do you think Japan will win?

A. Yes.

As the interrogation progressed we had been walking slowly over to the far corner of the compound where the pilot's tent was. We were in front of the tent now, and the pilot bowed us in. On a GI cot at the rear of the tent squatted a little wizened Jap with horn-rimmed spectacles. He was about 40 years old and, as Jitter explained, a doctor with more than three years' Army service. When we entered, he was reading what appeared to be a Japanese medical journal. There were illustrations showing blood-transfusing equipment, operating techniques, and other medical procedures.

Jitter questioned the doctor. While the questioning went on, the pilot, like the silent prisoners in the other tent, sat very still, listening intently.

Q. Doctor, you've read widely in medicine. Do you think that America's contribution to world medicine has been important?

A. I think it has been extremely important.

Q. You have heard, of course, of Johns Hopkins, the Mayo Clinic, and other American medical centers?

A. Yes. Their work has been of the utmost importance to the general advance of medicine.

Q. How do you think Japan's medicine, its doctors, its operating equipment, and so on compare with those of America?

A. Japan is first rate in everything.

Q. Tell me, Doctor, who do *you* think will win the war?

A. Japan will win.

Q. Are you aware of how many places your Army and Navy have lost in the last two years during America's steady march into the Far East?

A. Yes. They tell us of the progress of the war.

Q. Why are you being beaten so steadily?

A. We are not being beaten. We will strike when the time comes.

Q. When do you think the war will end?

A. They do not tell us that.

Q. [Jitter looked at me and said: "The doctor doesn't understand English but, as you see, he's a pretty well educated professional man. Now watch what happens when I begin to question him on another track."] Doctor, have you read America's Bill of Rights?

A. Yes.

Q. Do you believe, as that document states, that all people have a right to worship God according to their own conscience, without dictation from anyone?

A. [At this question the doctor's face sagged and his eyes glazed. His blank look recalled the uncomprehending Osaka sergeant of the first interview.] I don't understand.

Q. [Jitter put his hand out in an appealing gesture.] Look. You have read the Bill of Rights. You know that it sets forth certain freedoms, certain protections for the securities of God-fearing peoples. Do you think that document is a good sensible, right doctrine?

A. I do not know.

Q. What is a right doctrine for decent human living?

A. The Emperor's doctrine. [The doctor's spine straightened.]

Q. Would you do anything the Emperor commanded you to do?

A. Certainly.

Q. Doctor, you consider yourself an honorable man and you believe that the Japanese are an honorable people. Do you think your leaders are truthful, honest, and above-board?

A. Yes.

Q. Did you ever hear of Pearl Harbor?

A. I have heard of Pearl Harbor.

Q. Did you know that the Japanese sneaked up on Pearl Harbor and stabbed America in the back? Did you know that, at that very moment, two of your most celebrated statesmen were in Washington pleading for Eternal Peace?

A. No.

Q. Do you believe it?

A. No.

Jitter looked at the doctor for a few seconds, smiled wearily, and nodded his head as if admitting that the whole thing was futile. Then he turned to me and said, "Had enough?" I said I had, and we went out of the tent.

As we left the camp, just as we turned through the gate, we caught a glimpse of the sergeant from Osaka. He was squatting under a tent flap, picking the scab on his ankle. Every now and then the tic above his right eye would twitch convulsively.

—SGT. H. N. OLIPHANT

How the Japanese-American fought

THERE ARE THREE outfits that will remember the little Tuscany town of Belvedere for a long while to come. One of them is a German SS battalion, the remnants of which continued on from Belvedere, spearheading a drive towards Naples and the nearest PW camp. The other two are the American 100th Infantry Battalion and the 442d Combat Team, both of them composed of Americans of Japanese ancestry.

The 442d was a recent arrival, but the 100th had been in Italy a long, long time. The men of the 100th went in at Salerno and had since fought through almost every major action from the Volturno to Rome. In a battalion of 1,300 men they had more than 1,000 Purple Hearts.

The story of Belvedere really began after Rome fell, when the 100th was pulled out of the line and sent to bivouac in the pleasant countryside just north of the city. There it joined the 442d. It was a happy day for both outfits; most of the 100th's younger brothers, cousins, and friends were in the 442d, and they hadn't seen each other since shortly after Pearl Harbor, when the 100th left Hawaii, the home of many of its members, for training in the U.S.

For three days the brass hats left the two outfits alone. The kids of the 442d plied their older brothers with questions of war. The older brothers, like all combat men, dodged these questions and asked questions of their own about Hawaii and their families and girls. Together the outfits visited Rome, buying souvenirs and baffling the Romans, who decided they must be Japanese prisoners.

American soldier: Pvt. Henry (Slim) Nakamora ▶

After the three days, the two outfits went to work. For 14 days the men of the 100th drilled the 442d, sweating with the kids from morning to night, cursing and pushing and ridiculing and encouraging them, giving the final polish that makes a man as much of a combat soldier as he can be before combat. And in the evenings they would sit around together and drink *vino* and sing their soft Hawaiian songs.

Then on the seventeenth day after the fall of Rome the 100th Infantry Battalion and the 442d Combat Team were pulled into the line, and two days later they headed for the beautiful little hilltop of Belvedere.

The 100th was the first to go into the line. Its objective was a small town about seven miles below Belvedere. The German strategy since Rome had been to fight in pockets on each sector of the front, and the mission of the 100th was to clean up one of these rearguard pockets. The men of the 100th did it in two days, chasing the Germans up the inland road toward Florence and meeting little resistance until they neared the valley directly before Belvedere. There they were stopped by four 155mm. cannon and by several self-propelled guns. The German artillery was also holding up a battalion to the right of the 100th. This battalion was trying to use a crossroad, but the Germans had it zeroed in. Division sent orders for the 100th to stop while division artillery tried to clear out the Germans. When the barrage was over, the 100th was pulled out and the 442d was sent in to assault the German positions.

It didn't work. The 442d made an initial breakthrough, but that was all. The Germans counterattacked against the 442d's left flank, throwing in a mess of mortars. They pushed the 442d out of the valley and pinned the outfit down in an exposed and highly uncomfortable position in a wheat field. Meanwhile the German artillery had moved back and was still stopping the battle on the right of the 442d.

Back in their bivouac areas, the men of the 100th heard what was happening to the 442d

and began to get itchy. The enlisted men began to clean and oil their guns; the officers brought out their maps and began to think. And then, finally, the 100th had orders and a mission.

The mission was simple. All the battalion had to do was to infiltrate the German positions in the valley, the hill that Belvedere was on, and the town itself; to encircle and capture the town and cut off the main road out of Belvedere that runs north to Sasseta and Florence. That was all. Division intelligence said the position was being held by an *SS* battalion which had an OP in the town directing artillery and mortar fire on the 442d and the battalion on its right.

A and B Companies of the 100th were assigned to assault positions, with the rest of the battalion in reserve. The jump-off was at 1200 hours. By 1300 both companies had infiltrated completely around Belvedere and were behind the town at a farm called Po Pino. The rest of the battalion dug in among the olive groves at the edge of the valley. B Company was to initiate the attack, while A Company was to rendezvous at Po Pino.

Commanding B Company was Capt. Sakae Takahashi. He planned the attack this way: The 1st Platoon under S/Sgt. Yeki Kobashagawa was to take the town; the 2d Platoon under Lt. James Boodry, a former Regular Army dogface from Boston, was to move on the main road leading out of town and cut it off; the 3d Platoon under Lt. Walter Johnston of New York was to cover the northern position of the company. The heavy-weapons platoon was to move with the 2d Platoon and cover the road north to Sasseta.

Sgt. Kobashagawa broke his 1st Platoon into three squads, two of which encircled Belvedere on each side while the sergeant led his squad into town. On the outskirts Kobashagawa's squad located the Jerry OP wires, which were cut by one of the point men, Pfc. Seikichi Nakayama. Then the squad moved cautiously into town. It was quiet, and the men were almost up to the modern three-story Fascist headquarters when two German machine pistols opened up on them. They ducked behind some houses and settled down to work.

Kobashagawa and two men, loaded with grenades, moved toward the big building under cover of the others. The machine pistols were located in a doctor's office on the first floor. One of the men was hit, but the sergeant and the other man got to the house next door. They tossed four grenades in the window, and the machine pistols were through. Four Germans came out of the building, and the covering fire killed three and wounded one.

That left about 20 Germans in the building. They started to retreat the back way and out of town toward the valley. They fought from house to house and then ducked over a ravine and down into the valley. The two squads encircling the town caught some of these Germans coming out of the ravine.

When Kobashagawa's platoon assembled again at the edge of town, it ran into machine-gun fire from a German half-track located in front of one of the valley farmhouses. The platoon could also hear the noise of a battle opening up to the right. Kobashagawa decided to dig in and call for mortar support before jumping the farmhouse.

The mortar support didn't come. The heavy-weapons platoon had discovered a nice reverse slope and set up there to cover the road to Sasseta. The platoon was about to open up on some Germans trying to make a get-away when the point squad of the 2d Platoon, preceding the weapons platoon, arrived at the edge of the hill and practically ran into the four German 155s that had been firing on the 442d and its flank battalion. The Germans had just moved into this position and were preparing to fire.

They never did. Lt. Boodry, commanding the platoon, had Cpl. Hidenobu Hiyane, communications man, get the weapons platoon on the radio. Cpl. Hiyane contacted T/Sgt. M. Nakahara and gave him the essential data. Their conversation must have sounded terrifying if any

Germans were listening—it was conducted in a personal code, combining Hawaiian dialect with Japanese and American slang.

The plan worked all right. While Lt. Boodry and his platoon moved in on the German battery with carbines and M1s, the weapons platoon cut loose with its mortars. In five minutes 18 Germans had been killed and all four of the 155s were out of action.

The Germans knew they were encircled now and tried to make a break up the main road toward Sasseta. Capt. Takahashi ordered the 3d Platoon to move up and cover the flank of the 2d Platoon. He told both rifle platoons and the weapons platoon to hold their fire until the Germans made a break, which sooner or later they had to do. And they did.

Seventeen of their amphibious jeeps loaded with Jerries swung out of an olive grove and headed hell-bent for Sasseta. The three platoons let them get onto the road and then let them have it. All 17 jeeps were knocked out. Two light machineguns manned by Sgt. K. Yoshimoto and Sgt. Nakahara accounted for most of the damage, and the riflemen picked off the Germans as they ran from the jeeps.

Right after that, four German trucks filled with men broke from the olive grove and tried to swing around the knocked-out jeeps. The first two made it, but the other two were stopped. Lt. Boodry picked out one driver with his carbine and one of his riflemen got the other. The trucks piled up in the middle of the road, blocking it effectively and preventing any further German escape. "The next half-hour," said Pvt. Henry (Slim) Nakamora, a bazookaman of the 2d Platoon, "that valley was like a big box of chocolates and us not knowing which piece to take first."

The rest of the Germans retreated to the grove and dug in. Sgt. Kobashagawa's platoon on top of the hill picked off a few of them. The sergeant was good and sore about not getting his mortar support and kept calling for it, but the mortars were needed somewhere else. Capt.

Takahashi had decided to make a frontal attack on the farmhouse with the 3d Platoon. The 1st Platoon was assigned to keep the Germans busy in the grove, while the 2d Platoon was to knock off any snipers on the platoon's flank.

When the Germans in the farmhouse saw the 3d Platoon moving toward them, they opened fire. The 3d returned the fire, aided by elements of the 1st and 2d Platoons, and moved in and around the farmhouse. There was a German half-track there, with two Germans working its machinegun. Cpl. Toshio Mizuzawa, who had plopped a rifle grenade into the back seat of a jeep earlier in the day, scored another basket when he dropped one into the half-track and rendered it highly ineffective.

This was enough for the occupants of the farmhouse. They came out with their hands up.

Sgt. Kobashagawa had seen the Germans reforming in the olive grove and had spotted a PzKW IV tank there. He relayed this information to Capt. Takahashi, who didn't exactly relish the idea of running into a tank with so little ammo. The captain sent an urgent call for A Company and ordered the 3d Platoon back to the reverse slope to join the weapons platoon, leaving a patrol to scout the area. The patrol consisted of Sgt. A. Governagaji and Pfc. Teneyshi Nakana, working as a BAR team, and Pvt. Nakamora with his bazooka. Snipers tried to get them but were silenced by Lt. Boodry and a squad from his platoon.

Then the German counterattack started. The tank rolled out of the olive grove and started up the slope. It was followed by a half-track, and behind that were some soldiers with two light machineguns and what was left of a rifle company. Sgt. Governagaji of the patrol crawled over to Pvt. Nakamora and asked him if he wanted to take a crack at the tank with his bazooka.

"Yeah," said Pvt. Nakamora, who is a man of few words.

Sgt. Governagaji nodded and started to crawl back to his position. On the way he was hit by a slug from the tank. Then the tank bounced into view about 15 yards from Nakamora. He aimed, fired, and hit the tank right in the belly. He reloaded and hit it in the same place. The tank moved about 10 yards and blew up. The concussion knocked out Nakamora and killed Sgt. Governagaji, who was lying about 10 feet away. Two Germans started out of the tank, but Pfc. Nakana, working the BAR alone, got both before they were half out of the turret.

The weapons platoon on the slope took care of the half-track, knocking off its tread. The 2d Platoon had run out of ammunition and withdrawn; the weapons platoon had one box of machinegun ammo left. Now the German rifle company with the two machineguns started up the hill. The dogfaces didn't know what they were going to do, but they hadn't counted on Nakana with his BAR. Nakana waited until the Germans were within 50 yards, then knocked out the four Jerries carrying the two machineguns. The rest of the rifle company hightailed it back to the olive grove. The counterattack was over.

After that the 100th mopped up. B Company called it a day; A Company moved through and chased the retreating Germans among the olive groves and up and down the ravines. When B Company took stock they found they had one box of ammo left. It was now 1660 hours.

In the valley of Belvedere lay 84 dead Germans; headed for the rear were 32 prisoners and 29 wounded Jerries. By 1900 hours A Company had accounted for 26 more German dead, 18 prisoners, and nine wounded. The box score of Jerry equipment was: 13 motorcycles, 19 jeeps, seven trucks, two half-tracks, one PzKW IV tank, one SP gun, two antitank guns, four 155mms., one radio CP, and one battalion CP with 20 telephones.

The 100th lost one man and had eight wounded. The next morning the outfit was relieved. It bivouacked that day with the 442d.

After a couple of days both of them went back into the line.

—SGT. JAMES P. O'NEILL

Aachen was heroism and death and the dust of buildings.

One more winter

In the mountains behind Rome, the Germans had holed up tight, and the GIs in Italy knew they were in for another winter of the awful cold that leaves a man numb and freezes the leak from his nose and eyes onto his whiskers. Everywhere casualties were mounting.

In Germany, where the Americans were battering Aachen, a little private whose face was covered with German dirt walked through the door of a battalian aid station and sat on a davenport. Another soldier lit a cigarette and put the cigarette in the mouth of the little private. The private said, "Thanks." His right arm had been severed at the elbow and the stump of his arm dripped blood through a battle com-

press. He sat up straight on the davenport so the bloody bandage didn't touch the cushioned seat.

"I could stretch out here and sleep a week," he said. Lt. Ralph Weiber of Chicago, assistant to the battalion surgeon, had treated the little private just after he was hit. The lieutenant told about it.

"This little guy came over and said: 'Hey, Doc, would you mind cutting this off? It's not doing me much good any more.'

"So I cut two ligaments that were holding his lower arm and hand and put on the bandage."

"One of our medics hid the hand under the rug so the other patients wouldn't see it."

How Aachen died

THE INFANTRY OUTFIT had lost its platoon sergeant that morning. He went down the hill into the town a little way and didn't come back. The boys who did come back told the lieutenant about it. The lieutenant said quietly, "After months of this stuff without a scratch he has to get himself killed by a sniper." Then he added, "Those sonsuvbitches!"

After the outfit heard about its platoon sergeant, it went back to its outposts, OPs, and machineguns and waited. Nothing happened. Down below Aachen lay in the sunlight, motionless except for smoke that drifted up from old fires or boiled up from new ones. There were Germans in Aachen, but the city lay there quietly letting itself be mauled. The Infantry sat back on its haunches, watching the buildings burn and the artillery working on targets of opportunity. Those were the outfit's orders and there was a reason for them.

The Infantry was taking no chances of being knocked off. Aachen wasn't worth it. The first German city to lie in its path, Aachen wasn't important to anybody except the Germans. To them it was a symbol. To us it was nothing more than a place to be encircled, then mopped up.

The real fight wasn't in the city but in the country that lay beyond it, where panzer outfits and *SS* units tried desperately to form for counterattack. Aachen would fall in time—there was no hurry for the Infantry, no desperate need for dying.

So the Infantry took no chances. While artillery and air forces pounded away, the Infantry moving in begrudged every man lost to the German garrison, which had not only refused the ultimatum but had ignored it. The Germans fought well, but the doughboys moved slowly and inexorably into the city and started mopping up. The Infantry hated the Germans because war in a city is quite another thing from war in the countryside. As a small-town boy mistrusts the city and suspects it of dishonesty and pitfalls, so the Infantry mistrusted Aachen.

War in the open is as clean as war can manage to be, but in the city it's a nasty thing of strange death in familiar places—of Schmeisser fire behind a gravestone or a mortar blast in front of a barber shop.

A soldier stood easily in a doorway. A sniper two blocks away put a bullet through his head. The boy fell and lay quietly for a while. Then he bled from his mouth, groaned, and died. His blood covered the doorway. It was the door that led out the back way to the urinal.

The Infantry had to be watchful because there was nothing to prevent infiltration into our positions by night. The Germans knew their streets in the dark.

There weren't always power-phone communications between men on the first floor of a house and men on the third. But there was communication of a sort. Pfc. Charles Mateer of Mount Joy, Penna., was part of a guard that worked out its own method. "When it's dark," he said, "the man on the top floor ties a string to his arm, and the other end is lowered out the window to the ground and tied to the man down there. If the man on top throws a grenade, the string jerks so the man below can duck away from the window. That way we don't telegraph any punches and none of us gets hurt."

The Infantry was cautious, but only because there was no reason to be spectacular. Its phaselines were street corners. It cleaned out blocks up to its phaselines, then waited for the next orders to move on. It used a heavy hand—tank destroyers—to discourage stubborn strong points.

Self-propelled artillery skip-shelled cellars. First they fired armor-piercing stuff so that it ricocheted off the sidewalk, then they fired high-explosive rounds through the holes the AP had made.

When the people of Aachen, the civilians, had had all they could stand they came out of their shelters and gave up. The Infantry was glad to see them—glad to have them out of the way—but they were a nuisance. Perhaps they were more of a nuisance because the Infantry had soft hearts.

"Damn it," said an infantryman, "these people come out and you want to get them out of the way so you can go on. Then some old lady 80 years old will remember that she left her kerchief behind. Of course, she'll want to go back and get it. Or some little girl of six will have run off without her coat and her mother will want to go back to the house and get it. Damn, that's a nuisance when you're fighting a war."

Considering the size of the town, the Infantry hadn't got very far by the third day. But it didn't matter. Aachen could die slowly as well as any other way, and then not so many of our own people would die. As a city, Aachen was doomed. To the OPs on the hills it didn't seem chewed up except when you looked through a pair of binoculars, but when you walked down the streets you had to pick your way through debris and you learned the full power of shellfire and bomb blast. Aachen was not yet utterly destroyed as our ultimatum had promised, but the job was well under way.

There's a certain shock in seeing any town that has felt war. You were shocked that way when you entered Aachen, and you were shocked again to see a gasoline station with prewar pumps marked "Esso" and the familiar Coca-Cola bottle sign. It seemed more normal to join the Infantry in the graveyard, because that at least you remembered from "All Quiet on the Western Front"—the scene where German infantrymen died under shellfire in a French cemetery. In Aachen an American company commander died in a German cemetery as old graves were unearthed around him by mortars and artillery of both sides.

The war had moved on a few feet. To follow it you walked through the cemetery until you reached a wall. The top of the wall had been partly blown away so you crawled over it, dropped down on the other side, moved over to an outhouse, then dashed across an open space to the doorway of a building. Here the Infantry was laying siege to a huge concrete air-raid shelter or pillbox, perhaps, since Aachen is itself part of the Siegfried Line.

A bearded sergeant on the second floor plugged away at its two entrances with rifle grenades. As he fired, the sound of the launching was much louder inside the building than the sound of the grenade exploding a few hundred feet away.

After the grenades stopped, the Infantry lost interest for a moment. Then a man ran up the stairs and asked eagerly: "Did you see that guy go in over there?" Nobody had. The man balanced himself on the railing back of the window and watched the entrances of the shelter. He sat poised and anxious, rifle held lightly in both hands. He was grinning with a queer intensity. "I'll plug that joker if he comes out," he said.

Two blocks away, another Infantry group stood near the end of a cleaned-out block. Halfway up the street was a pile of debris. The Infantry, which had reached its phaseline the night before, was waiting for the jump-off time of another attack. Through the debris of the street corner which had been their previous phaseline, three men wheeled unsteadily on bicycles they had discovered in the hallways of houses on their street. In a few minutes they would leave the bikes and attack toward another phaseline, another corner two streets away. The Infantry was taking Aachen in its own good time.   —SGT. MACK MORRISS

Battle of the Bulge

IN THE FIRST frantic days of mid-December, the newspapers called it Von Rundstedt's Breakthrough in the Ardennes. Then, as the American line stiffened and held from Elsenborn to Bastogne, it became known as the Battle of the Bulge. In between that time it was probably the most frightening, unbelievable experience of the war.

At Corregidor and Bataan it was a lack of men and equipment. At Kasserine Pass it was inexperienced leadership. At Anzio and Omaha Beach it was the natural advantage of the defense over the offense. But in the Ardennes there was no alibi. The odds were all in our favor, yet we were being pushed back.

It was a nightmare of bewilderment for the first few days. Everybody knew we had superiority in men and equipment. There was no questioning the leadership on the grounds of experience. The Germans here were not exploiting fixed defenses.

What was it, then? Why were we falling back? Had the First Army leaders really been caught with their pants down? Were the Germans really turning the tide? Would they reach Liege, cutting off supply lines to the Ninth Army along the Roer?

Everybody asked himself those questions. And nobody knew the answers until the 2d Division held at Bulligen, the 30th plugged the gap at Stavelot, and the 101st Airborne stayed put at Bastogne. The answers finally came from the people such answers always come from, the guys in the line.

In most cases the fighting, the holding, and the winning were done by regular infantrymen and tankmen. But the Breakthrough also made infantrymen out of cooks and clerks and MPs.

They gave a few answers to another question, the one about "rear-echelon commandos." More than one Belgian town in those days owed its continued freedom to Americans who never got a Combat Infantry Badge.

• • •

In the middle of December the people of the town of Hotton, Belgium, heard frightening news. The Boche had driven the Americans from St. Vith and were rolling along relentlessly toward Hotton, just as they had done in the fearful days of 1940. Holiday spirits, bubbling over at the prospect of the first free Noel since 1939, quickly died down. The Boche was coming back for Christmas.

But new hope came to Hotton the week before Christmas when American tanks and armored vehicles rumbled across the village bridge. Most of them continued north toward the approaching Germans, but some half-tracks and trucks and a hundred-odd U. S. soldiers stopped in the village. The burgomeister quickly gave permission for the Americans to occupy any buildings they might need.

The people of Hotton went to bed that night confident that the Americans had come back to protect their village from the Boche. They didn't know that the handful of U. S. troops were only rear-echelon men who are not rated as combat soldiers. They were Headquarters Company cooks and clerks, Signal Corps radio operators and linemen, Armored Engineer demolition men and mechanics, and half a dozen MPs from the division Provost Marshal's Office. They had been left behind in this safe spot when Maj. Gen. Maurice Rose took the rest of the 3d Armored Division forward to meet the Germans.

Headquarters Company was eating chow in

the schoolhouse at 0730 the next morning when eight rounds of mortar fire exploded 40 yards away in the schoolyard. That was Hotton's first warning that elements of a panzer grenadier division had rolled in from the east to take the main highway at Hotton running north to Liege.

Quick reconnaissance disclosed Jerry infantry and four Mark V tanks in the woods east of the village. Capt. William L. Rodman, of Philadelphia, Penna., Headquarters Company CO, ordered a firing line built up along the hedgerows running from the school to the sawmill at the north end of the main street. Then he told T-4 Paul H. Copeland of Columbus, O., Special Services noncom, to take three men and a half-track and set up an outpost at the north end of town to protect that flank. Copeland grabbed a .50-caliber and a .30-caliber machinegun and asked for three volunteers to help him man the buildings on the north edge of the village. The first volunteer was his buddy, Cpl. D. A. Henrich of Antigo, Wis., followed by T-5 Peter Brokus, of Shamokin, Penna., half-track driver, and Pvt. Carl Hinz of Chicago, Ill. Meanwhile the Armored Engineers under Maj. Jack Fickessen of Waco, Tex., had set up a defense of the southwest section of the village.

Following the heavy burst of mortar fire which ripped off part of the schoolhouse roof and wounded five Yank soldiers, two of the Mark Vs started moving on the village, supported by a small infantry force which stayed a safe distance behind the vehicles. One tank came down the ridge road on the east toward the Engineers' CP; the other headed along the railroad tracks which bisected the village just north of the schoolhouse. A partly disabled American M4 tank, which had been left in Hotton for repairs, went out to meet the Jerry tank coming down the ridge road. They met directly in front of the Engineers' CP. The U. S. tank threw the first punch and missed. It didn't get another. The heavier enemy tank knocked it out.

The other Mark V bulled through a stone wall and edged out on the village main street.

Waiting for it, game but overmatched, was a U. S. light tank which had stopped in the town the night before. The uneven battle was over in a matter of seconds. Rumbling on, the Mark V stuck its nose up to the window of a house where two Yank bazookamen were firing at it. Firing point-blank, it wrecked the house, but the two bazookamen miraculously escaped injury. One of them, T-5 John Swancik of Melvin, Ill., was scorched slightly by exploding powder which went off practically under his nose.

As the Mark V backed up, it was jumped from behind by two Headquarters Company bazookamen, T-4 Philip Popp of Lincoln, Neb., and Pfc. Carl Nelson of Arcadia, Neb. They scored a hit on the turret, and the tank was abandoned by the Jerry crew.

While the tank battles were going on, Maj. Fickessen notified Headquarters by radio that there were German forces trying to move into Hotton. He asked for instructions. He got them. They were: Hold the village at all costs until a relief force arrives.

Hotton, the sleepy little crossroads village, had become an important military objective. Control of it meant control of the road net running west to Belgium's important cities and vital U. S. supply installations. Until combat troops could reach the village, its defense depended upon rear-echelon men who'd been left behind while their troops went off to fight.

Loss of the patrol tanks discouraged the Jerries. Instead of following through with an infantry assault, as the outnumbered Americans expected, the Germans started building their own firing line on a ridge that overlooked the village. That gave the Americans time to organize their forces. Maj. Fickessen, senior officer in the village, took over the defense set-up and started posting his men—the cooks, clerks, mechanics, and radio operators—in strategic locations. He established strongholds in the school-

. . . they infiltrated through gaps in the Jerry lines. ▶

house, in the sawmill, in the Hotel de la Paix, and in the buildings which commanded the road branching off to the east where enemy armored attacks might be expected.

Meanwhile the people of Hotton readied themselves for a siege of their village. With the men unable to work in the sawmill and the children unable to go to school, whole families moved into cellars to sit out the war that had come back.

The Germans continued pouring massed mortars into the village during the afternoon, scoring hits on the theater, where the treatment station was located, and severely damaging several other buildings and homes. The Yanks defending the sawmill area had to take shelter behind piles of lumber to escape the intense mortar fire. The other defenders of the outposts around the village traded small-arms fire with the enemy. But the attack which the Americans expected momentarily failed to develop. It was learned later from PWs that the Germans had sent back a hurried call for reinforcements when their four tanks and company of infantry failed to overrun the hundred-odd American rear-echelon men. When they finally made their big bid for Hotton the next night, they had a full battalion of infantry plus 14 tanks and supporting artillery.

Next morning the village defenders were reinforced by a platoon of 81mm. mortars and four medium tanks which came in from the division forward CP. The tanks set up roadblocks on a road east of the village, the most likely route for a German armored attack.

During the night, the Signal Corps had laid a wire net to all the strongholds for constant intradefense communications. A mortar OP was set up in the schoolhouse under the direction of 1st Lt. Clarence M. McDonald of Long Beach, N. Y., who happened to be around only because he was in the treatment station suffering from a mild case of pneumonia when the Jerries first struck. He didn't stay in bed long.

The mortar platoon had only 150 rounds, and the men had to make every one count. The OP was located on the top floor of the schoolhouse, the roof of which had been ripped off by mortar fire. It was cold, but McDonald stayed there all day directing the use of the few precious shells.

All day long Signal Corps maintenance men moved from one stronghold to the next to keep the phone net in operation. Despite mortar fire and MG fire which frequently pinned them to the ground, Pfc. Max D. Troha of Hamtramck, Mich., and Pfc. Stanley R. Presgrave of Arlington, Va., kept the phones working. One mortar burst landed in the Ourthe River only 15 feet from where they were repairing a broken line. They were unhurt by the blast, but several ducks swimming nearby were killed.

Late that afternoon a Jerry mortar sailed through an open window of the mortar OP in the schoolhouse. Lt. McDonald was knocked 15 feet across the room and suffered minor abrasions of the legs and arms. He was returned to the treatment station he had left just a few hours before. Another officer took over the mortar platoon.

An hour later the Germans launched a heavy attack — later identified as a full battalion in strength—against the Americans defending the sawmill and lumber yard. First Sgt. Denver Calhoun had 35 men armed with bazookas, a few machineguns, and small arms. The attackers overran part of the position and started infiltrating into the houses on the outskirts of the village. That split the defending force in two, leaving Copeland with 23 men cut off in the north outpost.

Then the Jerries on the ridge brought their newly arrived artillery into action for the first time. They scored three hits on Hotton's main industrial building, leveled the sawmill, and set fire to some of the lumber piles. Two of the Americans were killed and three others wounded in the blast.

Maj. Fickessen ordered Sgt. Calhoun to withdraw his forces to the railroad tracks and told T-4 Copeland to cut back to the west and try to get around the Jerry spearhead set up around the sawmill. An hour later the Special Services noncom brought his men, who now numbered 23, including two wounded, and all equipment back to Maj. Fickessen's CP. He had swung 300 yards west, then infiltrated through gaps in the Jerry positions without the loss of a single man or weapon.

Setting up their line along the railroad track, the reconsolidated force of cooks, clerks, and mechanics awaited the next enemy attack. It came about 0200 next morning with an estimated force of two Jerry companies driving against the defenders' line. This time the cooks and clerks held fast.

After their second failure in trying to overrun the Hotton positions, the Germans withdrew to houses on the outskirts of the town. Just before dawn five U. S. medium tanks with infantry support rolled into Hotton from division headquarters, and more came in later in the day. The cooks, clerks, and company barber had combat support at last. Although they remained at their positions for the next two days, Hotton's original defenders had finished their job. It included the destruction of four Mark IV tanks and five Mark Vs, plus more than 100 German casualties. They pulled out of Hotton on Christmas Day to rejoin the 3d Armored Division Headquarters which had left them behind in this safe place while it went forward to meet the Germans.

. . .

Early in the afternoon on the second day of the counteroffensive along the Western Front, a convoy of Battery B, 283d Field Artillery Observation Battalion, was moving along three miles south of Malmedy, Belgium, on a road leading to St. Vith. About 300 yards beyond the crossroad of the cut-off to St. Vith, the convoy was ambushed by riflemen, machinegunners, and mortarmen hidden in the surrounding woods. All the American vehicles halted immediately. The men jumped off and took cover in the ditches lining both sides of the road. Several minutes later they were flushed out of their hiding place by Tiger tanks from an armored column which lumbered along the ditches spraying machine-gun fire. Other tanks quickly knocked out some 24 American trucks and other vehicles. Armed only with small-caliber weapons, the Americans had no alternative but to surrender. They were ordered by their captors to line up in a snow-covered field south of the crossroads.

While the Americans were lining up, an enemy halftrack mounting an 88 gun made an effort to swing around and cover them but was unable to do so. In lieu of that, the Germans parked tanks at either end of the field where their machineguns had a full sweep over the prisoners. Just then a German command car drew up. The German officer in the car stood up, took deliberate aim at an American medical officer in the front rank of prisoners, and fired. As the medical officer fell, the German fired again and another front-rank American dropped to the ground. Immediately the two tanks at the end of the field opened up with their machineguns on the defenseless prisoners who were standing with their hands over their heads. No effort had been made to segregate the noncombatant medical corpsmen, all of whom were wearing medic brassards and had red crosses painted on their helmets.

When the massacre started, those who were not wounded dropped to the ground along with those who had been shot. Flat on their stomachs, with their faces pushed into the snow and mud, the Americans were raked by withering machine-gun and small-arms fire from the column of tanks which began to move along the road 25 yards away. Each of the estimated 25 to 50 Tiger tanks and half-tracks took its turn firing on the prostrate group.

Of the approximately 150 American prisoners who were herded up as human targets, only 43 were definitely established as having escaped the German slaughter. More than three-quarters of those who escaped had been wounded. Only 25 men of Battery B's 138 were reported safe.

Pvt. James J. Mattera was the first American

to make a dash for freedom and one of the six members of the surviving field artillery men who escaped without injury. Here is his sworn account of what happened when his outfit was ambushed by the Germans: "About three miles outside of Malmedy on the road to St. Vith our convoy was forced to stop because of machineguns shooting at us and also 88 shells hitting the trucks and blowing them off the road. Everybody dismounted and lay in the ditch along the road for protection. We were forced to surrender because we were not armed heavy enough to stop the tanks.

"The outfit was put into one group and a German officer searched us for wrist watches and took our gloves and cigarettes. After the officer was through we were marched to an open field about 100 feet from the road where the German tanks were moving by. There was about 150 of us, counting officers and medics. We all stood there with our hands up, when a German officer in a command car shot a medical officer and one enlisted man. They fell to the ground. Then the machineguns on the tanks opened up on the group of men and were killing everyone. We all lay on our stomachs, and every tank that came by would open up with machineguns on the group of men lying on the ground. This carried on about 30 minutes and then it stopped all at once.

"Then about three or four Germans came over to the group of men lying on the ground. Some officers and non-commissioned officers were shot in the head with pistols. After they left, the machinegunners opened up. I lay there about one hour sweating it out. My buddies around me were getting hit and crying for help. I figured my best bet would be to make a break and run for my life.

"I was the first one to raise up and I yelled, 'Let's make a break for it!' About 15 fellows raised up, and we were on our way. About 12 of the men ran into a house, and myself and two other soldiers took out over the open field. They fired at us with their machineguns, but by luck we made it into the woods, where we hid until dark. The house into which the 12 men ran was burned down by the Germans. Anyone who tried to escape from the fire was shot by machineguns. After it was dark my buddy and I made our way back to our troops. We landed with an engineering battalion, told them our story and what had happened. They gave us chow and a safe place to sleep."

Pfc. Homer D. Ford, an American MP of the 518th Military Police Battalion, was directing traffic at the crossroads when the shelling started. Along with several American soldiers who had abandoned their trucks, he took shelter behind a nearby house. Then the Germans knocked an ambulance off the road, and on hearing the blast Ford and his companions came back to the barn and tried to hide in the hay. They saw the Germans continue on toward the American armored men, who were marching with their hands up at the point of Nazi bayonets. After searching and disarming their prisoners, the Germans ordered them to line up in the field. Then they surrounded the barn where the MP and others were hiding. Realizing they were spotted, the Americans came out and surrendered. They were herded into the fields with the others after having been disarmed and robbed of their valuables.

Here are sworn excerpts from Ford's testimony as to what happened after the firing started: "They started to spray us with machinegun fire, pistols, and everything. Everybody hit the ground. Then, as the vehicles came along, they let loose with a burst of machinegun fire at us. They said: 'You dirty bastards! You will go across the Siegfried Line!' Then they came along with pistols and rifles and shot some that were breathing and hit others in the head with rifle butts. I was hit in the arm, and of the four men who escaped with me, one had been shot in the cheek, one was hit in the stomach, and another in the legs.

"The men were all laying around moaning and crying. When the Germans came over, they would say, 'Is he breathing?' and would either shoot or hit them with the butt of the gun. The closest they came to me was about ten feet. After they fired at us, I lay stretched out with my hands out and I could feel that blood oozing out. I was laying in the snow and I got wet and started to shiver, and I was afraid they would see me shivering but they didn't. I had my head down and couldn't see but they were walking around the whole bunch and then they went over toward the road junction. I heard them shoot their pistols while next to me; I could hear them pull the trigger back and then the click. Then men were moaning and taking on something terrible. I also heard the butt hit their heads and the squishing noise.

"As I lay there I saw about 25 big tanks and I would hesitate to say how many half-tracks— they went by for two hours. When all the armor and stuff. had cleared the road, we got up and ran, and two Germans sprayed us with tracer bullets, but we kept on running. We ran through the field toward Malmedy, and after running for approximately two and a half miles a jeep picked us up and brought us in."

Testimony of German PWs, captured since the massacre, has substantiated the account of atrocities as related by the Americans who escaped. Here is an extract of testimony given by a German Prisoner, Pvt. Fritz Steinert, a member of the 1st *SS* Panzer division: "On Dec. 17, 1944, at about 3:30 P.M., I saw approximately 50 dead American soldiers lying in a field near an intersection where paved roads radiated in three directions. This point was near Malmedy and between two and three kilometers from Stavelot. The bodies were between 30 and 40 meters from the road and were lying indiscriminately on the ground and in some instances bodies were lying across each other. There were a burning house at the intersection and a barn and shed."

Questioning the German PWs, together with evidence of *SS* uniforms and insignia supplied by the Americans, convinced First Army Officials that members of an *SS* Panzer Division were responsible for the atrocity at Malmedy.

During the interrogation of two of the prisoners, both members of the 1st *SS* Panzer Division but not of the outfit near the burning house, one of them—Pvt. George Conrath—was asked about the appearance of the bodies which caused him to think something improper had happened. "It was such an unusual sight I thought it was murder," he said.

Asked if anyone told him how these American soldiers met their death, Conrath replied, "No, no one told us. We were all *SS* men on the tanks and it was strictly forgotten."

The second prisoner, Cpl. Hans Strasdin, who had not personally seen the bodies but who had been told the story by German comrades, was asked if he knew why the German soldiers killed their American prisoners.

"I have no idea," he replied. "Of course, there are people among us who find great joy in committing such atrocities."

•   •   •

The evacuation of a city is an awesome thing. It gives you the same feeling you get at a wake; you go in, mumble some incoherency to bereaved relatives because you can't think of anything really satisfactory to say, take a brief, self-conscious look at the corpse, and then tiptoe into another room, where you converse with fellow mourners in whispers, even though you know you couldn't possibly be disturbing the person you came to see for the last time.

That's how it is when you are present at what appears to be the last hours of a city before it falls to the enemy. There's no really satisfactory answer when a frightened Belgian woman tearfully asks you if the Americans are going to leave her town to its fate before the advancing vengeful Boche. She doesn't understand when you try to explain in mixed English and French that it is only the rear-echelon troops who are being evacuated, and that the combat men are staying behind to fight, and that this whole thing is really just a consolidation of American lines to

stop the German advance before it gains too much momentum. Rear echelons and consolidated lines and the military wisdom of moving back to take advantage of natural defense terrain mean nothing to her. She only remembers the four years the Nazis spent in her town and what their return will mean to her and her people.

It is hard to look at the clusters of old men and women and children standing silently on every street corner, watching the U. S. Army six-by-sixes, command cars, and jeeps assembling in convoy for evacuation. They remind you of a bereaved family at its father's bier.

Then suddenly there is the sound of planes overhead and bombs being dropped on the convoy road that runs west of the town. On a street corner nearby, a little girl with blonde curls buries her head in her mother's coat and cries. The mother pats the blonde curls tenderly and keeps repeating: "C'est fini. C'est fini." But there is no belief in her voice.

A little farther down the street is a U. S. Army hospital, formerly a Belgian schoolhouse, which was evacuated this morning. The wounded and sick who slept there last night are now in ambulances and trucks, bouncing over that road which has just been bombed.

The whole population of the town seems to be lining the cobbled streets to watch the Americans leave. The men stand silently, but some of the women and young girls cry softly. Only very small children still smile and wave as their elders did a few short months ago when the Americans first came to town.

Out on the convoy road the traffic going west is already jammed. Stretched for miles ahead are the six-by-sixes, half-ton trucks, command cars, ambulances, jeeps, weapons carriers, and heavy-ordnance vehicles linked in the moving chain of the bumper-to-bumper escape caravan.

Our jeep stalls beside a bomb crater on the right side of the road. Hanging on a fence post

_____

◄ **Winter war: frost-bitten feet and death by freezing.**

is a pair of torn and muddy OD pants. Half-buried in the mud below are the remains of a GI shirt, matted with blood and torn as if whoever took it off was in a great hurry. In the muddy crater are two American bodies and an abandoned stretcher. They have been pushed off the road so that the passing vehicles would not run them over. An Army blanket covers each corpse. Beside one body is a helmet with a medic's Red Cross painted on it. There is a hole drilled clean through it.

On the other side of the road, going east, is a long convoy of tanks, TDs and half-tracks of an armored unit moving up to the front. Our jeep passes slowly through a village, wedged between a weapons carrier and an ordnance truck, and the people of the village line both sides of the street, watching the movement of war. The people on our side are silent and grave, and their eyes have a mixed expression of dread and reproach. They look at our column without warmth, because it is going west. But on the other side there are young girls waving and laughing at the Americans in the tanks and half-tracks who are going east to meet the Germans. Older men and women smile behind their fears and give the V-salute to the men in crash helmets. An old lady stands in the doorway of a house by the road, urging a little boy by her side to wave at the Yanks.

At the edge of the village, still going west, are long lines of refugees, carrying suitcases and blankets and tablecloth packs, plodding slowly and painfully along the shoulders of the road. Some of the more fortunate ride bicycles with their packs balanced on the handlebars. Others push carts loaded with lamps and favorite chairs and loaves of bread and sacks of potatoes. A baby too young to walk sits on a sack of potatoes and smiles at everything.

There is a feeling of security along the road when it gets dark, and there is no longer the fear of planes. The convoy travels blacked out, with only cat's eyes and tail lights to mark its progress, and the drivers are very careful to avoid the tanks and half-tracks on the left and the long lines of civilians on the right. Suddenly there is a murmuring from the human line on the right. Everyone turns to the east. There is a low humming sound that grows gradually more ominous, and a long fiery streak flashes through the black sky. It is a German buzz bomb headed toward the Belgian cities to the west. Everyone breathes in half-takes until the flaming arrow has passed over the slow-moving convoy.

Finally the rolling country gives way to scattered black buildings, which can be sensed rather than seen. A city is coming up, far enough away from the lines to be a city of refuge. But it's not that now. Enemy planes are overhead; sirens are moaning, and red and yellow and green anti-aircraft tracers are reaching up through the blackness. They make you think of a giant Christmas tree in an enormous room, blacked out except for the red and yellow and green lights on the tree. The lights suddenly shoot up, spend their brilliance, and then sink back into blackness.

Now you start to think about the people who said so confidently that the European war would be over by Christmas, and when you think about them you begin to laugh. You can laugh now—in spite of the ack-ack Christmas tree before you, the little blonde girl who cries at the sound of bombs, the old men pushing rickety carts on a convoy road running west, the Americans in crash helmets and combat overalls who ride east, and the people of the evacuated town that gives you the same feeling you get at a wake.

· · ·

The battered Belgian village, with its narrow, rubble-heaped streets and worn, cold-looking houses and barns, was a far cry from the spaciousness of the Champs Elysees and the war-forgetting warmth of Paris' swank nightclubs and bars —too damned far for the men of the 82d Airborne Division regiment who held off on their 48-hour passes so they could spend part of their Christmas holidays in Paris.

Marshal Karl von Rundstedt's counteroffen-

sive screwed up that deal, leaving the paratroopers with nothing more than Paris rainchecks redeemable once the Jerry drive had been rolled back. But the guys in the regiment had one consolation. They, in turn, screwed up a few of Von Rundstedt's holiday plans—and they didn't issue him any rainchecks, either.

According to German prisoners taken since the counteroffensive started, Von Rundstedt had promised they would have Aachen and Antwerp for their Christmas stockings and would spend New Year's Eve in Paris. The Jerries were heading for New Year's Eve in Paris by way of Belgium. That's where they met up with the Yanks, who had similar plans for ushering in 1945.

The meeting took place on a hilly road that leads down into this Belgian village. B Company of the 1st Battalion started out at 1500 to look over the town, which was reported to be lightly held by the Germans. That was a slight understatement. When the Americans got within half a mile of the town, they were promptly tied down by Jerry flakwagons that came out to greet them. Lacking artillery and tank-destroyer support and armed only with M1s, light machineguns, flak, grenades, and bazookas, B Company was in no spot to start trading punches. Regimental headquarters was notified of the situation and urgently requested to send something to get the German flakwagons off B Company's tail. Just about that time, somebody hit on the idea of sending in a previously captured Jerry half-track, mounting a 77, as a pinch-hitter till our own TDs and artillery arrived. A hurry call was sent out for five volunteers to man the German vehicle.

The first guy to stick his neck out was Pfc. Russel Snow of Burbank, Calif., a regimental code clerk. Snow, who was a clerk in the Los Angeles Board of Education office before the Army got him, volunteered to drive the half-track although he had never handled one before. Two members of the regiment's 57mm. antitank squad —Pfc. Harold Kelly of Chicago, Ill., and Pfc. Harry Koprowski of Erie, Penna.—offered to work the 77. Pvts. Thomas R. Holliday of Henderson, Ky., and Buland Hoover of Hobbs, N. M., two BAR men, volunteered to cover the driver and the 77 gunners.

After Kelly and Koprowski had been given a brief orientation on how to operate the 77—they had never fired one before—Snow drove the half-track onto the frost-hardened rutted road, and they went off to relieve the pressure on Company B. For three hours the Yanks operated their one-vehicle armored patrol up and down the hilly road that led into the German-occupied village. Seven Jerry flakwagons, mounting 20mm. guns, and several heavy machineguns were deployed around the edge of the village, well hidden by thick underbrush and heavy ground fog that reduced visibility to 100 or 200 feet. Most of the time Kelly, who was at the sights of the 77, was firing practically blind, aiming in the direction the 20mm. and machinegun tracers were coming from. Once, however, the men on the half-track saw a column of German infantrymen coming down the road toward positions taken up by B Company. Moving in for the kill, Kelly raked their tanks with his 77, forcing them to abandon the attack. Another time Hoover, the BAR man, spotted a Jerry machinegun nest through the fog and silenced it permanently.

Just before dusk, a blast of a 20mm. hit the brace of Kelly's gun. He got several pieces of flak in his lower lip and chin. At that point Snow, the clerk, started doubling in brass. He maneuvered his vehicle into position against the tracers coming from the enemy 20mm. or machinegun, then moved back to take Kelly's place on the 77. A moaning German half-track got into Snow's sights on the crossroads just outside of the village and went up in flames, and there were two probables on the machinegun nests, but Snow couldn't be certain because of bad visibility. Finally, with his ammunition almost gone and Kelly in need of medical attention, Snow turned the captured Nazi vehicle around and headed back to the command post to resume his regular duties there as regimental code clerk.

After determining the real strategy of the German occupying force, Lt. Col. Willard E. Harrison of San Diego, Calif., battalion commander, ordered an attack on the town that night. The battalion kicked off at 2000 after a 10-minute artillery barrage, with two TDs for support.

It had started to snow, and a thick veil of white covered the huge fir trees that lined the hill road leading into town. B Company, advancing on the right side of the road, yelled over to C Company on its left: "The last ones in town are chicken. Get the lead outta your tails, you guys!"

C Company made contact first, taking on a column of 100 German infantrymen who were supported by 19 flakwagons, several tanks, and a big gun. The first wave was pinned down by murderous fire from Jerry advance machinegun emplacements. But when the second wave came up, they overran the enemy position and wiped out both guns and crews. S/Sgt. Frank Dietrich of Detroit, Mich., emptied his Tommy gun on a machinegun crew, and, when the last Jerry started to break and run, Dietrich threw the Tommy gun at him. The shock of being hit by the gun slowed up the fleeing German just enough for another C Company man to finish him off with a BAR.

Meanwhile B Company had attacked the flakwagons with bazookas and hand grenades, mixed in with spine-freezing Texas cowboy yells and self-exhortations to "get those bastards!" It was not phony heroics, as one B Company man proved by the way he finished off a Jerry flakwagon gunner who wouldn't surrender. The kraut was injured, but he still leaned over his gun, firing at the advancing Americans. Suddenly one tough, battle-maddened GI made a direct break for the flakwagon, yelling: "You German sonuvabitch!" He jumped up on the vehicle and stabbed the German with a knife until he fell over dead.

Another Company B man, S/Sgt. William Walsh, of Winnetka, Wis., had sneaked up on a flakwagon, ready to throw a grenade inside, when he was hit on the left arm and side by small-arms fire. Unable to pull the pin, Walsh had another GI pull it for him, then turned and hurled the grenade into the flakwagon.

The battalion got into the first building on the outskirts of the town that night, set up a CP there, and dug in. The Germans launched a five-hour counterattack supported by flakwagons and a tank. This failed, but only after the tank had hit the CP three times.

During daylight hours, the Yanks and Jerries fought it out at long range, with nothing particularly startling happening except for the experience of S/Sgt. Edgar Lauritsen, Headquarters Company operations sergeant from Limestone, Me., and Pfc. Theodore Watson, a medic. While a German tank was shelling the CP, two jeeploads of soldiers in American uniforms—a captain and eight enlisted men—pulled up in front, got out, and started walking around the other side of the building toward the German lines. Watson hollered to them that they were going too far, but they ignored his warning. That aroused the medic's suspicion. He demanded to know what outfit they were from.

"The 99th," said the captain, and he continued on his way.

Sgt. Lauritsen, who had just come out of the CP, caught the tone of the conversation, got suspicious, and shouted: "What outfit in the 99th?"

"Headquarters," replied the captain in a slightly gutteral voice as he kept on walking.

The accented answer convinced Lauritsen. He hollered, "Halt!" and when the eight American-uniformed strangers started running Lauritsen opened up with his M1. The captain staggered, shot in the back, but his companions grabbed him and hurried him toward a steep embankment which led down into the woods.

The other Americans in the CP, attracted by the firing, thought Lauritsen had gone flak-happy and was shooting Yanks. They were all set to drill Lauritsen himself until they realized what had happened. By that time the eight fugitives had escaped into the woods, presumably making their way back to German lines.

Regardless of any information the phony Americans may have carried back to the German lines, it didn't do the Nazis who were there much good. That night the 3d Battalion came up the valley and joined with elements of the 1st Battalion to clear the village, destroying one Mark IV tank and seven flakwagons in the process.

The joes in the 82d figure that's some solace for the 48-hour passes they didn't get to Paris—but not enough. Mark IV tanks are poor substitutes for G-stringed blondes at the Folies Bergere, and flakwagons and dead Germans will never take the place of champagne and cognac.

•   •   •

The Ardennes campaign was more than a fight against the strongest German attack we had faced since the early days in Normandy. It was also a fight against almost daily snowstorms in near sub-zero temperatures and face-freezing winds which doubled the difficulty of rolling back the German advance.

We learned a lot about winter warfare in the Ardennes. Some of it was learned the hard way by frost-bitten hands and feet, pneumonia, and even death by freezing. Besides physical difficulties, there was the added trouble of frozen weapons, equipment, and even food. But out of it all came the GIs' usual improvising and home-made remedies.

Line-company men of the 83d Division, who cleared the Bois de Ronce of German opposition in a continuous eight-day push that enabled the armored spearheads to follow through to the vital St. Vith-Houffalize highway, learned a lot of ways to fight winter weather during that operation. Their methods were often makeshift and crude because there was no time to waste on details. But the men of the 83d are sure those hastily improvised methods of keeping themselves moderately warm and dry and their weapons and equipment workable played an impor-

At last, the reinforcements came.

tant part in the ultimate success of the operation.

T/Sgt. Wilbur McQuinn of Helechawa, Ky., a platoon sergeant in the 331st Regiment, used the usual method for frostbite prevention in his platoon by insisting on frequent toe and finger-clenching exercises to keep the blood circulating. But he and his men learned some other tricks, too.

"Some of the men took off their overshoes and warmed their feet by holding them near burning GI heat rations [fuel tablets] in their foxholes," McQuinn said. "Others used waxed K-ration boxes, which burn with very little smoke but a good flame. Both GI heat and K-ration boxes are also fine for drying your socks or gloves. I also used straw inside my overshoes to keep my feet warm while we were marching. Some of our other men used newspapers or wrapped their feet with strips of blankets or old cloth."

McQuinn's company commander, Capt. Robert F. Windsor, had another angle on keeping feet warm. "We found our feet stayed warmer if we didn't wear leggings," Capt. Windsor explained. "When they get wet from snow and then freeze, leggings tighten up on your legs and stop the flow of blood to your feet. That's also true of cloth overshoes which are tight-fitting.

"Another 'must' in this weather is to have

the men remove their overshoes at night when that's possible. Otherwise their cloth arctics sweat inside, and that makes the feet cold. Of course, the best deal is to have a drying tent set up so you can pull men out of the line occasionally and let them get thoroughly dried out and warm."

The drying tent to which Capt. Windsor referred is nothing more than a pyramidal tent set up in a covered location several hundred yards behind the front, with a GI stove inside to provide heat. There an average of seven men at a time can dry their clothes and warm themselves before returning to their foxholes. This procedure takes from 45 minutes to two hours, depending on how wet the men's clothes are. All the front-line outfits in the 83d Division used this method.

Because of their almost continuous advance, it was all but impossible to get sleeping bags and straw up to the front-line troops. In place of straw, the men used branches of trees as matting for their foxholes. Logs and more branches were used as a roof to protect them from tree bursts. GI pioneer tools, which include axes and saws, were issued to each outfit for foxhole-construction work. Raincoats, overcoats, and the usual GI blankets were used for covers. Two or three men slept in each hole, close enough so that they could pool their blankets. Some slept with their helmets on, for an extra measure of warmth.

The chief difficulty men had in carrying their own blankets was that they got wet with snow and then froze, making them hard to roll and heavy to carry. The same was true of GI overcoats, which became water-logged after several days in the snow and slush.

On some of the more frigid nights the men abandoned any hope of sleep and walked around and exercised all night to keep from freezing.

The front-line troops of the 83d were issued a pair of dry socks each day. However, wading through icy streams and plodding through knee-deep snowdrifts often resulted in men soaking two or three pairs of socks within a few hours. In such cases, the men wrung out their socks thoroughly and placed them inside their shirts or under their belts, where the heat generated by their bodies gradually dried them out. Another sock-drying method was to put them under the blankets and sleep on them at night.

Marshlands in some sections of the Bois de Ronce added to the infantrymen's troubles. When digging in for the night, they hit water two feet down. That meant two or three inches would accumulate in their foxholes before they were ready to go. This also forced them to move around gingerly on branches to avoid sinking into the water. One night, a platoon of the 83d had to dive into muddy foxholes without any preliminaries when a German tank came along a forest path spraying MG bullets. By the time the tank had retreated, every man in the platoon had had the front of his field jacket and pants, plus shoes and socks, thoroughly soaked. Enemy pressure that night was so strong that none of the dripping soldiers could be spared to go back to the drying tent. They spent the entire night in wet clothes with the temperature less than 10 above zero.

The standard GI gloves proved unsatisfactory for winter fighting,. 83d men reported. When wet they froze up and prevented the free movement of the fingers. Nor were they very durable, wearing out in a few days under the tough usage they got in the forest fighting. When their gloves wore out, many of the men used spare pairs of socks as substitutes.

Another improvisation was the use of sleeping bags for combat suits. To be sure of having their bags with them at all times, some of the men cut leg holes in them and drew them up tight, like a pair of combat jumpers. During the day they made a warm uniform; at night they served the original purpose as sleeping bags.

Web equipment was a problem. It froze solidly on cold nights and had to be beaten against a tree in the morning in order to make it pliable enough for use.

Frozen weapons were one of the most dangerous effects of the winter warfare in the Ardennes. Automatic weapons were the chief concern, although some trouble was experienced with M1 rifles and carbines. Small arms had to be cleaned twice daily because of the snow, and none of the larger guns could be left unused for any length of time without freezing up.

"The M1s were okay if we kept them clean and dry," said T/Sgt. Albert Runge, a platoon sergeant from Boston, Mass. "You had to be careful not to leave any oil on them or they would freeze up and get pretty stiff. But you could usually work it out quick by pulling the bolt back and forth a few times. Sometimes the carbines got stiff and wouldn't feed right, but you could always work that out, too."

However, during the fighting at Petit Langlier, Pvt. Joseph Hampton found himself in a spot where he had no time to fool around with the above method. Just as his outfit started into action, Hampton found that ice had formed in the chamber of his M1. With no time to waste, Hampton thought and acted fast. He urinated into the chamber, providing sufficient heat to thaw it out. Not five minutes later he killed a German with his now-well-functioning rifle. Hampton's company commander vouches for that story.

"The BARs gave us the most trouble," Runge said. "They froze up easily when not in use. Ice formed in the chamber and stopped the bullet from going all the way in, besides retarding the movement of the bolt. We thawed them out by cupping our hands over the chamber or holding a heat ration near it until it let loose."

Some other outfits reported that the lubricants in their light machineguns and antitank guns froze. Heat tablets were ignited to thaw out the machineguns which couldn't be cocked. But blow torches were needed before the antitank guns were put back into firing condition.

Communications men of the 83d had headaches in the Ardennes fighting. Breath vapors wet the inside of their radio mouthpieces and then froze, cutting off transmission of their speech. Most of the time, the mikes were thawed out with cupped hands or by placing them inside sweaters.

Pfc. Grank Gaus of Pittsburgh, Penna., solved the problem by inserting a piece of cellophane inside the mouthpiece to prevent the moisture from accumulating there.

Other communications difficulties were experienced when radio batteries froze up and went dead. Signal Corps wire-maintenance crews were kept on 24-hour duty by numerous torn-out lines which resulted when tanks and other vehicles slid off the icy roads and ripped out wires.

The 83d medics were also hampered greatly by winter wartime conditions. Not only did snowdrifts make their litter-bearing jobs doubly difficult, but the severe cold caused their morphine syrettes and blood plasma to freeze. The medics remedied the morphine situation by keeping the syrettes under their armpits, thawing them out with body heat. When stoves were not available to melt the frozen plasma they stuck it under the hood of a jeep whose motor was running. Slippery roads and snow-drifted fields often stymied jeeps, half-tracks, and tanks, which were pressed into service to haul supplies and evacuate the wounded. Some units improvised crude toboggans made of strips of tin taken from shell-shattered roofs with two-by-four planks as runners.

The 83d men found only one compensating factor amid all the misery of the Ardennes. That was when they occasionally plodded across snow-covered German minefields without accident because the mines failed to explode. Melted snow seeped down around the firing pins of some of the mines and then froze them up when the temperature fell at night, thus preventing them from detonating. Chemicals in other mines turned to mush and failed to go off.

That was the only good thing the 83d men could find about winter war in the Ardennes.

—SGT. ED CUNNINGHAM

Iran: cargo route to Russia

"SARKISS SHAHIJANIAN! Adranik Markarian! Ahmas Khamnai! Koocheck Hussain Memtaza! Aram Khatchikian! Nickolai Boodaghian! Abbas Rasooli!" the sergeant yelled.

S/Sgt. Forest Neely of Columbia, Ind., wasn't reeling off the cast of characters in a Saroyan story. He was just calling the roll of native Iranian truck drivers who are learning to navigate the important United Nations overland motor route from the Persian Gulf to Russia.

It's quite a road, the Road to Russia. In the winter there is driving snow and treacherous ice. Sudden rains in spring wash out whole sections of roadbed. And in the summer and fall there is dust.

Starting out, before the dust gets too thick, we get a glimpse or two of Eastern atmosphere—an Arab with a hooded hawk on his wrist, some old ruins. But soon dust has engulfed the convoy, clinging to trailer tarps and truck fenders, settling so thick that even after a mile of good black-top roadbed there's still a stifling cloud behind us.

This is the U. S. Motor Transport Service's main supply line to Russia. Quartermaster Corps units, white and Negro, drive the loaded trucks northward and bring back the empty ones. They have been making the trip for many months; some of the drivers were in the very first convoy when the going was toughest. Supplementing these Army units now are native drivers, trained by the MTS at special schools.

Riding with Sgt. Rufus Johnson of Athens, Ga., who belongs to a Negro QM unit, you realize with a sudden crack on the head that desert travel isn't smooth. What looks like a stretch flat enough to rival Daytona Speedway turns out to be full of hidden ruts and bumps. Even Johnson, with the steering wheel for an anchor, scrapes his noggin. "This bouncin' and jumpin' is about to get me down," Rufus says.

After endless dust, heat, and shaking, we get a break for lunch at a Motor Transport Service installation. Trucks are fueled up here and checked by Ordnance mechanics. Drivers take a stretch, wash the dust off their messkits, and down the chow they've been looking forward to since their before-dawn breakfast.

Lunch is good-humored but not leisurely. The boys want to get rolling again toward dinner and bed.

"Gas up 'at old P-40 of mine, man," shouts Pvt. Willy Hoover of Panama City, Fla., to the mechanic. "I'm flyin' low this afternoon."

Willy's in the same convoy as Sgt. Johnson, only a little farther back and getting a little more dust. Sometimes, when a curve permits, we see the third or fourth truck ahead looking as small as a jeep, with a tail of cotton-thick dust waving behind it.

Like most drivers, Willy's forgotten what a day off means. It's up in the morning and roll on your trip. Sleep here one night, another place the next. The driver's home is a musette bag, a couple of blankets, and his messkit. When enough native drivers have been trained, they'll run regular schedules with days on and days off. But war doesn't wait for anyone, and supplies to Russia must go through.

We stay tonight at an MTS station. It's a tent camp; laborers are constructing more permanent quarters. One of the lads who is supervising the work is Pfc. Nockie Sims of New Augusta, Miss., who shares our chow. Nockie's from the district engineer's office, and he's only slightly less transient than the drivers. As soon as his job here is finished, he'll be on his way to another spot where they may need an instrument man to help lay out a camp.

Some time before daylight we're shaken out of our sleep to grab a bite of chow. Willy and Rufus are rolling back to their starting point, driving empties. The loaded trucks, re-checked overnight by Ordnance, roll northward with new drivers.

On this next stretch—the toughest of the entire road—the truck is handled by a native driver, Nadjaf Paidar Towhair, an Isfahan boy who's been trained by Sgt. Neely and Sgt. Paul Sayre of Pomeroy, O., at a Motor Transport Service school. This is his first trick on a regular, and he's as nervous as a bride.

Nadjaf tries carefully to remember everything he learned at drivers' school, and he does all right in spite of occasional difficulties with bumpy roads and shifting gears. He knows only two gears, first and second, but he knows them well.

Patroling the road are members of the Iranian Rural Constabulary, decked out in natty blue uniforms. These military-looking gents have been trained by Col. Norman H. Schwartzkopf, former head of the New Jersey State Police, who had charge of the Lindbergh baby-kidnaping investigation, and their gorgeous dress reminds you of the troopers who used to police the stretch between Newark and Trenton.

At the change-over point the native drivers turn back, and Pfc. Alan Black, a Negro boy

from Jasper, Ala., takes over this truck. He used to drive for the Alabama Highway Express and would sell out right now for a roadside spot where a trucker can get a hamburger and a juke-box version of "In the Mood."

Around a bend we come upon a tribe of nomads. Like their fathers and grandfathers, they are following good pasture with their flocks. Our horn sounds constantly as we crawl through a moving block of sheep, goats, cattle, horses, men, women, and children.

Our overnight stop is a repetition of the last. Blackie, who has been driving for 12 straight days, drops off to sleep in nothing flat, undisturbed by the noise of Ordnance crews working over his truck near the tent. The Ordnance men work while the QM drivers sleep. Their job begins when the first truck rolls in and doesn't end until the last one rolls out. Their work day may be as long as 20 hours in 24.

S/Sgt. Wilfred Heinen of Branch, La., and Sgt. Joe Detrieux of Kenner, La., NCO Ordnance bosses here, direct the crew of men who straighten out all the mischief that Persian roads play on trucks meant to roll over concrete highways. Valve trouble, pushed-in radiators, and loose gas tanks cause most of the hell. Somehow our truck is shipshape when we wake up. Pvt. Alfred Eccles, a Negro boy who used to run an elevator in Atlantic City, N. J., and still gets as many ups and downs as ever in the Persian mountains, is the driver now. He alternates with a white driver, Pvt. Samuel Sabel of New Orleans, La., who came to Iran with the first batch of GIs and worked in the first truck convoy to Russia.

Mountainous scenery and rough roads gradually give way to gentler slopes and good paved black-top. We pass native road workers, filling in holes with queer flat shovels, and wearing head-tight casque-shaped felt hats. Farther along is a labor battalion of British Indian Engineer troops, dressed in shorts and in their shirtsleeves. They are busy improving the road.

Native peddlers dot the road, too. You can

get a handful of hard-boiled eggs for only five rials, or 15 American cents. Some of the salesmen, anxious to get their message across, stand along the roadside waving eggs in one hand and a live chicken in the other. It's the closest thing to a billboard on the whole road.

Another stop overnight, then once more we rise before dawn for the last lap. Driving this time is one of the saddest soldiers in Iran. Pvt. Edward O. Kepping of Hazelton, Penna., who thought he'd gotten this country out of his system in 1931. He was here then as chauffeur for an American contractor and left when his job was finished, planning never to return. The Army brought him back, but it didn't change his feelings.

This last stretch is fairly good road, almost monotonous after some of the earlier tough going, but don't be fooled. Over there are whitened bones, picked clean and bleaching in the sun. That was where a camel caravan froze to death, hemmed in between impassable snowdrifts, only a few months ago.

Just ahead of us a truck goes through a soft shoulder and winds up mired in the mud. Capt. Jeff English dashes up in his jeep. As a good transport man, the captain doesn't like wrecks, but there's a wild and happy gleam in his eye whenever he sees one he can untangle.

Capt. English is principal trouble-shooter for Brig. Gen. Don G. Schingler, a wiry West Pointer who takes the beating of the road, good weather and bad, as the chief of the Motor Transport Service. The general's a staff officer for Maj. Gen. Donald H. Connolly, commanding the Persian Gulf Command, but he's no chairborne soldier.

Another driver runs out of oil. First Lt. Byron Block, an Ordnance officer from Philadelphia, who's on convoy patrol duty today, wangles a quart from a British petrol dump and gets him moving.

Pvt. Kepping takes our truck to a depot, where it is unloaded under the eyes of 2d Lt. Martin Steenbock of Laurel, Neb., and S/Sgt. Andrew Eirman, who hails from Copiague, Long Island, N. Y. They check every unloading job to see that the cargoes are in readiness for the Russians.

They find the Russians good to work with. The worst of the language difficulty is bridged by Pvt. Alex Pinkewich, who speaks pure Chicago American and adequate Russian. "Russian is easy to sling my way," he explains, "but the Russians do it a little harder."

Once the goods have been checked and unloaded from the trucks, the American end of the job is over. The cargo is in Russian hands. But traffic on the road goes on. The empties roll back and the loaded trailers bounce and grunt northward. The drivers crawl out of bed and rub their eyes and climb into their cabs to fight desert heat and dust and mountain hairpin turns. The Ordnance mechanics try to grab some shuteye in the morning before incoming trucks put them back to work again. The Road to Russia never rests.

—SGT. AL HINE

Beginning of the end

SOME SOLDIERS of the 99th were talking it over.

"There's hardly anybody left. You look around now and they're all new faces . . ."

In Europe, at the end of January 1945, there was no waiting—only the painful push ahead, day after day, with more guys getting hit and everyone trying to get it over and everyone wondering if the damn thing would ever end.

The high brass summed up:

"It's true the Germans' Ardennes offensive cost us heavy casualties and heavy loss in equipment. But it also shortened the war's end by at least six months because it chewed away most of the Germans' strategic reserves. If we break through now, they won't have enough troops left to stop us."

People back home said the Germans were scraping the bottom of the barrel. Some people said the German Army had been whittled down to old men and cripples with glass eyes and wooden legs.

The doughs up front knew better.

"I don't care if the guy behind the gun is a syphilitic sonuvabitch who's a hundred years old—he's still got enough fingers to press triggers and shoot bullets . . ."

It was pay-off time. In the East the Russians, driving steadily ahead on a continuous 300-mile front in eastern Germany, were within 63 miles of Berlin. The Russians took town after town; counted dead and German prisoners in the increasing hundreds of thousands. Hungary had surrendered unconditionally.

In the west the Allies were in Germany. 'A great offensive was in the making. The signs were everywhere. People back home were sure this was the Last Offensive.

The doughs kept looking around and seeing new faces. There was hardly anybody left.

Assault across the Roer

I JOINED K COMPANY, 406th Regiment, 102d Division, the night before the shove-off, as an artist, not an infantryman.

We were part of a reserve regiment several miles behind the line and would not be committed until after the Roer had been crossed by forward elements.

I felt everyone of us sweated it out as we went to sleep that night. At 0245 our barrage awoke us, but we stayed in our sacks until 0400. After hot chow we saddled our packs and headed for an assembly area in a wrecked town about five miles away. It was a silent company of men spaced on either side of the road—the traditional soldier picture of silhouettes against the crimson flashes of shells bursting on the enemy lines in the distance.

In the assembly town, we waited in the shattered rooms of a crumbling building. It was not pleasant waiting, because a dead cow stank in an adjoining room. We shoved off at daylight and came to gutted Rurdorf. I remember passing crucifixes and a porcelain pee pot on the rubble-laden road and pussy willows as we came to the river. A pool of blood splotched the side of the road. We crossed the Roer on a pontoon bridge and moved on. The forward elements were still ahead of us a few miles.

We passed a still doughboy with no hands on the side of the road; his misshapen, ooze-filled mittens lay a few feet from him. Knots of prisoners walked by us with their hands behind their heads. One group contained medics. In their knee-length white sacks, emblazoned with red crosses, they resembled crusaders. In another group were a couple of German females, one of them in uniform. Mines like cabbages lay on either side of the road.

They passed a still doughboy with no hands by the road; his misshapen mittens lay beside him.

We entered the town of Tetz and set up the CP in a cellar. Two platoons went forward a few hundred yards to high ground overlooking the town and dug in. We were holding the right flank of the offensive finger. Several enemy shells burst in the town. Some tracers shot across the road between the CP and the dug-in platoons, seemingly below knee-level. Night fell.

The CP picked up reports like a magnet:

In a German church GIs await orders for the jump-off.

"The Jerries are counterattacking up the road with 40 Tiger tanks. . . . The Jerries are attacking with four medium tanks." Stragglers reported in from forward companies. One stark-faced squad leader had lost most of his squad. The wounded were outside, the dead to the left of our platoon holes. It was raining. I went to sleep.

The next day, when I went to our forward platoons, I saw a dough bailing his hole out with his canteen cup . . . saw our planes dive-bomb Jerry in the distance . . . saw our time-fire burst on Jerry, and white phosphorus and magenta smoke bombs. I saw platoon leader Lt. Joe Lane playing football with a cabbage. I saw a dead GI in his hole slumped in his last living position—the hole was too deep and too narrow to allow his body to settle. A partially

Two doughs had their arms around each other . . .

smoked cigarette lay inches from his mouth, and a dollar-sized circle of blood on the earth offered the only evidence of violent death.

Night fell and I stayed in the platoon CP hole. We didn't stay long, because word came through that we would move up to the town of Hottdorf, the forward position of the offensive finger, preparatory to jumping off at 0910.

K Company lined up in the starlit night—the CO, the 1st Platoon, MGs, the 3d Platoon, heavy weapons, headquarters, and the 2d Platoon in the rear—about 10 paces between each man and 50 between the platoons. The sky overhead was pierced by thousands of tracers and AA bursts as Jerry planes flew over. Again it was a silent company.

At Hottdorf we separated into various crumbling buildings to await H-Hour. We had five objectives, the farthest about two and a quarter miles away. All were single houses but two, which were towns of two or three houses. We were the assault company of the 3d Battalion.

H-Hour was approaching. A shell burst outside the window, stinging a couple of men and ringing our ears. We huddled on the floor.

It was time to move now. The 1st Platoon

went out on the street followed by the MGs and the 3d Platoon and the rest of us. We passed through doughs in houses on either side of the street. They wisecracked and cheered us on. We came to the edge of town and onto a broad, rolling field. The 3d and 1st Platoons fanned out in front of us. Headquarters group stayed in the center.

I followed in the footsteps of Pfc. Joe Esz, the platoon runner. He had a light aluminum case upon which I could easily focus the corner of my eye to keep my position and still be free to observe. Also, I felt that if I followed in his footsteps I would not have to look down at the ground for mines. He turned to me and commented on how beautifully the company was moving, properly fanned and well-spaced.

Several hundred yards away I noticed Jerries running out of a gun position waving a white flag. A black puff of smoke a few hundred yards to my right caught my attention, then another closer. I saw some men fall on the right flank. The black puffs crept in. There were whistles and cracks in the air and a barrage of 88s burst around us. I heard the zing of shrapnel as I hugged the earth. We slithered into the enemy 88 position from which I had seen the prisoners run. Somebody threw a grenade into the dugout.

We moved on. Some prisoners and a couple of old women ran out onto the field from a house, Objective One. There was the zoom and crack of 88s again. A rabbit raced wildly away

to the left. We went down. I saw a burst land on the running Jerries. One old woman went down on her knees in death, as though she was picking flowers.

A dud landed three feet in front of T/Sgt. Jim McCauley, the platoon sergeant, spraying him with dirt. Another ricocheted over Pfc. Wes Maulden, the 300 radio operator. I looked to the right flank and saw a man floating in the air amidst the black smoke of an exploding mine. He disappeared just in front of the squad leader, S/Sgt. Elwin Miller. A piece of flesh sloshed by Sgt. Fred Wilson's face. Some men didn't get up.

We went on. A couple of men vomited. A piece of shrapnel cut a dough's throat as neatly as Jack the Ripper might have done it.

The right flank was getting some small-arms fire. I was so tired from running and going down that it seemed as though my sartorius muscles

On the right flank, men fell.

would not function. The 300 radio wouldn't work and we couldn't get fire on those 88s. Pfc. George Linton went back through that barrage to get another one from Hottdorf. Medic Oliver Poythress was working on wounded in that barrage.

Objective Two loomed ahead—a large building enclosing a courtyard. Cowshed, stables, toolshed, hay loft, living quarters opened on the inner court. I saw an 88 explode over the arched entrance.

We filtered into the courtyard and into the surrounding rooms. The executive officer started to reorganize the company. The platoons came in. First Sgt. Dick Wardlow tried to make a casualty list. A plan of defense was decided on for the building. A large work horse broke out from his stable and lumbered lazily around the courtyard. T-4 Melvin Fredell, the FO radio operator, lay in the courtyard relaying artillery orders. An 88 crashed into the roof. The cows in their shed pulled on their ropes. One kicked a sheep walking around in a state of confusion.

A dying GI lay in the tool room; his face was a leathery yellow. A wounded GI lay with him. Another wounded dough lay on his belly in the cowshed, in the stench of dung and decaying beets and another GI quietly said he could take no more. A couple of doughs started frying eggs in the kitchen. I went into the toolshed to the dying dough.

"He's cold, he's dead," said Sgt. Charles Turpen, the MG squad leader. I took off my glove and felt his head, but my hand was so cold he felt warm. A medic told me he was dead.

Lt. Bob Clark organized his company and set up defense. FO Philip Dick climbed the rafters of the hayloft to report our artillery bursts. The wounded dough in the cowshed sobbed for more morphine. Four of us helped to carry him to bed in another room. He was belly down and pleaded for someone to hold him by the groin as we carried him: "I can't stand it. Press them up, it'll give me support." A pool of blood lay under him.

I went to the cowshed to take a nervous leak. A shell hit, shaking the roof; I ducked down and found I was seeking shelter with two calves. I crossed the courtyard to the grainshed, where about 60 doughs were huddled.

Tank fire came in now. I looked up and saw MG tracers rip through the brick walls. A tank shell hit the wall and the roof. A brick landed on the head of the boy next to me. We couldn't

◀ *A partially smoked cigarette lay near his mouth.*

see for the cloud of choking dust. Two doughs had their arms around each other; one was sobbing. More MG tracers ripped through the wall, and another shell. I squeezed between several bags of grain. Doughs completely disappeared in a hay pile.

We got out of there, and our tanks joined us. I followed a tank, stepping in its treads. The next two objectives were taken by platoons on my right, and I don't remember whether any 88s came in for this next quarter mile or not. One dough was too exhausted to make it.

We were moving up to our final objective now—a very large building, also enclosing a courtyard, in a small town. Jerry planes were overhead but for some reason did not strafe. Our tanks spewed the town with fire and led the way. Black bursts from Jerry time-fire exploded over our heads this time. We passed Jerry trenches and a barbed-wire barrier. Lt. Lane raced to a trench. A Jerry pulled a cord, setting off a circle of mines around him, but he was only sprayed with mud. S/Sgt. Eugene Flanagan shot at the Jerry, who jumped up and surrendered with two others.

Jerries streamed out of the large house. Women came out too. An 88 and mortars came in. I watched Pfc. Bob de Valk and Pfc. Ted Sanchez bring out prisoners from the basement, with Pfc. Ernie Gonzalez helping.

We made a CP in the cellar. The wounded were brought down. Stray Jerries were rounded up and brought to the rear. Jittery doughs relaxed for a moment on the beds in the basement. Pfc. Frank Pasek forgot he had a round in his BAR and frayed our nerves by letting one go into the ceiling. A pretty Jerry girl with no shoes on came through the basement. Doughs were settling down now. The CO started to prepare a defense for a counterattack. Platoons went out to dig in. L and M Companies came up to sustain part of our gains.

Most of us were too tired to do much. The battalion CO sent word he was relieving us. All of us sweated out going back over the field, al-

Dud shells landed close, sprayed men with dirt.

though this time we would go back a sheltered way. We were relieved and uneventfully returned to a small town. The doughs went out into the rain on the outskirts and dug in. A few 88s came into the town.

Early the next morning, K Company returned to its former position in the big house with the courtyard as the final objective. Just when I left, Jerry started counterattacking with four tanks and a company of men.

—Sgt. Howard Brodie

The village bridge, Remagen: target for 10 days.

The bridge at Remagen

FOR 27 YEARS the Ludendorf Bridge connecting the picturesque riverside villages of Remagen and Erpel was just a country cousin to Cologne's famous Hohenzollern Bridge and the other Rhine bridges at Bonn, Dusseldorf, and Coblenz; it was known to very few people outside the wine-growing Ahr Valley. But for ten days during World War II this obscure span across the Rhine was probably the most important military property on the whole of the Western Front.

Built in 1918 during the last weeks of the First World War, the bridge at Remagen carried trainloads of wine and mineral water and occasional tourists during peacetime. Most of the visitors to the Ahr stopped briefly to look at the winding waters of the Rhine and then hurried north toward the more industrially important cities of the Rhineland.

The prestige of the Ludendorf Bridge rose slightly with the outbreak of World War II when military traffic started rolling across its double-track railroad toward the defenses at the southern end of the Siegfried Line. But strategically the Ludendorf was still a country cousin.

Even the Allied Air Forces, which made repeated attacks on the other Rhine bridges, all but ignored the Ludendorf. The bridge suffered only one serious blow, an air attack which destroyed its left-bank arch span. That, however, was soon repaired by German engineers.

But the Ludendorf was to have its share of importance.

On Mar. 7, 1945, the U.S. Army's 9th Armored Division rumbled into the Rhine village of Remagen for what it thought would be the climax of its seven-day drive across 40 miles of German territory. The tankmen and armored infantrymen expected to reach the banks of the Rhine and stop there for a rest while the Allied high command completed plans for the crossing of that last barrier to the heart of Germany.

The bridges spanning the Rhine at Cologne, Bonn, and Coblenz had been blown up by the retreating Germans. When the 9th Armored reached Remagen it naturally looked for the blasted remains of the Ludendorf Bridge. Instead, the three-span structure was still standing. The German engineers assigned to destroy it had apparently delayed their work too long.

Realizing the value of their find, the armored infantrymen rushed past the pair of fortress-like towers guarding the bridge's main spans and headed for the east bank of the Rhine. The Germans on the far bank, now equally conscious of the Ludendorf's importance, set off two demolitions. One of the explosions damaged the eastern span, but it failed to stop the armored infantrymen from continuing across the bridge and establishing the first Allied bridgehead on the east bank of the Rhine.

The Ludendorf Bridge, overshadowed for 27 years by its more important sister spans across the Rhine, had won its place in history.

For 10 days the Ludendorf basked in its glory as the world's most important bridge. It was a high-priority military objective now. American troops and tanks rolled across it to enlarge the bridgehead. German air and artillery, realizing its importance, attacked it daily. Maybe such belated attention was too much for the Ludendorf. Anyway, on the afternoon of Mar. 17, the bridge suddenly crumbled and its three spans dropped into the Rhine. But the Ludendorf, while meeting the same fate as the other bridges of the Rhine, had won a place in history that the more important bridges could never attain.

The Ludendorf's 10 days of fame began at 1550 on Mar. 7. 1st Lt. Karl Timmermann of West Point, Neb., was telling his men of Able Company of the 27th Armored Infantry Regiment that he had just received orders to cross the bridge. The Germans were scheduled to blow it at 1600, according to a PW.

The lieutenant had barely finished his announcement when an explosion shook the east span of the structure. Timmermann hollered, "As you were!" Then, seeing the three spans still standing, he repeated the order of attack and shouted, "Let's go!"

The 1st Platoon, led by T/Sgt. Mike Chinchar of Rochelle Park, N. J., started across, followed by the 3d and 2d Platoons, in that order. With them went three armored engineers, a lieutenant, and two sergeants, to cut the demolition wires so the Germans would not set off further charges.

Running and ducking like halfbacks on a broken-field gallop to avoid the machinegun and sniper fire, A Company reached the towers on the far side of the bridge.

"The bullets didn't worry us half as much as the bridge," T-5 Gaccarino Mercandante, a mortarman from Brooklyn, explained later. "We expected the Heinies to blow the bridge right out from under us at any minute, so we didn't waste any time getting to the other side. It didn't matter how many Germans might be there; we just wanted to get off that bridge fast. And if there's anybody who thinks he can't doubletime 400 yards, he's got marbles in his head."

Rushing up the winding stairs of the right tower, T/Sgt. Joseph Delisio of New York City, the 3d Platoon leader, broke in on a Jerry machinegun nest on the second floor, expecting a fight with the two-man crew who had been

spraying the advancing Americans. Instead, he found the two Jerries meekly waiting to be captured. Mike Chinchar, aided by S/Sgt. Anthony L. Samele of the Bronx and Pfc. Artus Massie of Patterson's Creek, W. Va., got the same result in the left tower. The lone German manning the machinegun there surrendered immediately. They sent him back across the bridge with a PW guard and threw his machinegun into the Rhine.

Meanwhile the three armored engineers had cut all the wires on the west and center spans of the bridge which prevented electricity getting through to set off the caps on the 40-pound charges the Jerries had planted under the decking on the bridge's crossbars. Then they made a dash for the far side to cut the main cable which controlled the entire demolition set-up. When they found it, it was too heavy to cut with their small pliers. But Sgt. Eugene Dorland of Manhattan, Kans., solved that problem by riddling the cable with three well-aimed shots from his carbine. Then he went back to hunting other demolitions along with his platoon leader, 1st Lt. Hugh Mott of Nashville, Tenn., and S/Sgt. John Reynolds of Lincolnton, N. C., the other two engineers.

They found one 500-pound TNT charge set up with time fuses near the north railing, about two-thirds of the way across the bridge. It had not exploded, even though the cap went off. Across the board-covered railroad tracks was another charge, which had been set off just before Able Company started across the bridge. That blast knocked out one of the main diagonal supports on the upstream side of the main arch, destroyed a section of the bridge flooring, and left a six-inch sag at the damaged pier point.

"Both piers had 350-pound TNT demolitions in them which hadn't been set off," Lt. Mott said. "The Germans had enough stuff in that bridge to drop it right to the bottom of the Rhine but we were lucky. The one heavy charge that didn't explode had either a faulty cap or something was wrong with the explosive itself.

Besides that, before we started across, one of the cables to the main charge had been cut in two, evidently by a million-to-one direct hit by our artillery."

Under the cover given the Able Company men in the two towers, Sgt. Alexander Drabik of Holland, O., and Pfc. Marvin Jensen of Slayton, Minn., ran down the bridge approach and on to the east bank of the Rhine. They were followed almost immediately by Samele, Delisio, Chinchar, Massie, and S/Sgt. Carmine J. Sabia of Brooklyn, Pfc. Martin Read of Assaria, Kans., and Pvt. Joseph K. Peoples of Warrenton, N. C.

For the first 30 minutes of the crossing, Able Company fought alone on the east bank of the Rhine. The men cleared the nearby village of Erpel and the roads leading to the bridge. At the same time, Mott, Reynolds, and Dorland worked under intense sniper fire from the upstream east bank to cut every demolition wire they could find.

At 1630, with the bridge safe for heavy traffic and a company bridgehead firmly established on the pay-off side of the Rhine, Brig. Gen. William H. Hoge of Lexington, Mo., commander of Combat Command B which swept through Remagen to grab the war's most unexpected prize, gave the orders for reinforcements to cross. Armored infantrymen, engineers, tanks, TDs, and antiaircraft crews started rolling.

The Ludendorf Bridge literally found it hard to stand up under its newly acquired importance. Its demolition-weakened spans strained under the massive weight of heavy tanks and supply trucks which rumbled across it day and night. Two of its overhead supports were severed by enemy artillery fire, and 23 other hits, none serious, were scored on other parts of its framework. Hit-and-run German planes, making their first large-scale appearance on the Western Front since the Ardennes breakthrough, made almost daily attacks on it, none of which were successful. Railway guns were also fired at it,

but they, too, failed to land on their target. Floating mines were directed toward it, necessitating the use of a special squad of GI sharp-shooters on each span to fire at any object floating down the Rhine.

Among its other claims to lasting fame, the bridge was probably the best antiaircraft-supported bridge in the world during its 10 days of glory. As soon as the bridge was captured, ack-ack crews were rushed to the crossing area to ward off enemy air attacks. The self-propelled and heavy-gun units set up on the zone of action are believed to have made up the heaviest AA concentration ever assembled in such a small area.

When the bridge collapsed at 1505 hours, almost 10 days to the hour after its capture, scores of engineers were thrown into the water. Several were pinned beneath the wreckage and drowned. However, prompt rescue work by other engineers, together with ack-ack crewmen and passing soldiers, cut the fatalities to a minimum. In all, the engineer battalion suffered about 100 casualties, most of whom had only slight injuries.

No official explanation of the collapse of the Ludendorf Bridge has yet been issued. However, some engineers believe that it was due to a combination of the damage done by the German demolition on the day it was captured plus the gradual weakening caused by the vibrations and the weight of the traffic it carried.

But all the Monday morning quarterbacking on the cause and effect of our unexpected crossing of the Rhine can't dim the importance of the village bridge at Remagen. During its 10 days of military importance, the Ludendorf Bridge made up for a lifetime of playing second fiddle to other bridges across the Rhine. It may not rate many lines in German history books, but the 9th Armored Division and other units which crossed the Rhine on its weakened spans will never forget the Ludendorf.

—SGT. ED CUNNINGHAM

Last jump on Germany

[*The following story by Cpl. Bob Krell,*YANK *staff correspondent, was written about 12 hours before he was killed in action on Mar. 24, 1945, shortly after he jumped with the 17th Airborne Division to cover the airborne operation across the Rhine. Krell and three other soldiers were firing at a partly demobilized German tank in a woods near Wessel, Germany, when German riflemen opened fire behind them and killed all four. Krell was 21 when he died.*]

• • •

"KEEP STRAIGHT AHEAD and you'll come to the loading platform about a quarter of a mile down the road," said the MP. And he waved our truck on into the darkness with his flashlight.

The loading platform was along a railroad siding about a hundred yards from the main line. It was a long piece of track, and the American box-cars on it seemed to stretch for miles into the black night.

It was crowding 2100 hours. Two hours ago, as darkness fell, huge semi-trailers carrying as many as 75 soldiers with full field equipment pulled out of the garrison area and moved to the waiting train. The latter was on a siding for security reasons. And all of the men had removed the Eagle's Claw insignia of the 17th Airborne from their clothing so that anyone who did see them loading could not identify them.

Our car was about eight feet wide and 24 feet long, with doors on either side. When we left the siding, both doors were open. We closed them, but it was still cold. We threw our blankets on the wooden floor and huddled as tightly as possible in the corners to stay out of the draft that blew in from around the doors. We were ten in our car; none of the others were over-crowded either; none had more than 12 men. This was a priority special, this rattler, and only parachutists could get tickets.

It's hard to sleep on the cold, wooden floor of a box-car. The clickety-clack of the wheels over the tracks isn't as soothing as it is on the Broadway Limited. So you roll and toss.

The clickety-clack is gone now but the overpowering roar of the C-47s being preflighted has replaced it, and sleeping in the marshalling area isn't much better. C-47s from all over England are massing at different airfields in France, and this is one of them. The huge troop carriers come in at all hours of the day and night. Once they land, they are lined up in long rows, and some are less than a hundred yards from where the men are sleeping—or trying to.

Your feet are freezing, or anyway you think so. And the plaintive bitching of the others in the tent tell you that your buddies think they are suffering the same fate. You roll over and try to catch a few more winks, but the cold and the planes make it impossible. So you kick off the covers and get ready for your first day in the marshalling area.

There are three distinct phases in a marshalling-area operation. The first is the movement from the garrison to the airfield. The second involves the briefing of all officers and enlisted personnel and a final inspection of all equipment. The last step takes place when the men fit their parachutes and load the ammo, guns, and other equipment in the parapacks from which they will be released during the attack.

As we go through these phases we couldn't ask for better weather. It is warmer now and a hot sun beats down. Some of the men are shirtless, some have taken off their pants, and some have taken off everything.

Working or loafing, there isn't too much wise-cracking among the men. To many of them this is no new experience. A lot of them went through the same thing on D-Day with the 82d Airborne. All but a few are veterans of the Battle of the Bulge.

Pfc. Walt Leonardo of East Palestine, O., is busy tying the base plate for his mortar into his bundle. He runs out of rope, and after the usual argument Pfc. Paul Hines of Harlem goes off to get some.

While they wait for Hines to come back, someone points to Leonardo and says: "There's a guy with a real TS tale."

Leonardo, a D-Day and Bulge veteran, doesn't say anything. He just grins. He's a sawed-off guy with a bushy mustache. His skin is Latin-dark, and when he smiles he flashes out a set of toothpaste-ad molars.

"I guess I did get a bit of a screwing," he says. "Three days ago they tell me to pack my bags. I'm going to the States for a furlough, they say. Now it seems like I ain't going to the States."

He thinks it over for a minute, and then adds: "But hell, I ain't got too much kick coming. Look at Walley, there. Three years in the Pacific, and he comes back home and joins the parachutists. Then he has to go AWOL for five days so he can get married before coming overseas."

Pfc. Ralph Walley of Little Rock, Ark., had a short comment about his marriage.

"They fined me thirty bucks, but it was worth it," he said.

We enter the briefing tent to see where we are going to drop. The sand table, on which is reproduced the terrain that we are to occupy, gives you a remarkably realistic picture. The terrain is of green sand, the Rhine River and the other water areas are marked with blue sand, the main highway is of red sand, and the secondary roads are in white. Tiny trees and houses dot the terrain. The parachutes and glider landing zones are plainly marked in yellow.

The briefing officers tell us our objective, who will support us, and what we anticipate the enemy will do. He explains the preparatory artillery barrage and the air-going-over that the Germans will get. It makes you feel better, and when you leave you feel that you know where you are going and, above all, which direction you are going to move in when you hit the ground.

Other troops go into the briefing tent and you listen to their comments as they leave. One barrel-chested lad with his jump-jacket thrown open to reveal a hairy chest says, "It looks good to me." A sergeant with him isn't so confident. He says: "The drop zone will probably be lousy with krauts." Another kid says: "You mean just like Normandy, where we were to outnumber them six to one. Oh, yeah?"

When there was nothing else to do, some of the men read; others wrote letters home, and the volley-ball court was always filled. And, of course, there were the movies. There was an out-of-this-world thing called "Rainbow Island" which had Dorothy Lamour and her sarong.

You crawl deeper in your sack, but you can't get away from the noise. Over the roar of engines somebody is shouting a bunch of names . . . Andrews . . . Burger . . . Edwards . . . Fairbanks . . . Jones, Jack Jones . . . and on down the roster. C Company is falling out to fit their 'chutes.

Tomorrow there will be an early breakfast—0400, the order said. Then we will climb into our parachutes as dawn breaks. We will trudge out to the planes and climb in, not saying much of anything about anything. The men will know where they are going and what they are going to do. Some have done it before; for others this is the first time. But they all know this will be the end for the krauts. They'll sweat a bit, as any paratrooper sweats before making a parachute jump. They will get the same old butterflies. But they'll all jump. And when they hit the ground they will get down to cases.

—CPL. BOB KRELL

How the Germans killed

Most GIs were brought up to be suspicious of "atrocity stories." Their suspicions carried over into World War II, and they were, some of them, wary and unbelieving when they heard the first stories of Nazi concentration camps. Until after the invasion of France they weren't very close to the fact of Nazi terror, and the strange names of the camps—Dachau, Lublin, Buchenwald—and the unpronounceable names of the victims made it all a little unreal.

Then American soldiers opened some of these sores of Hitler's Reich. They freed concentration camps and prison camps and found starvation and murder and torture applied as Nazi weapons to American prisoners of war with the same ruthless violence with which they had long been applied to Germany's slave laborers of "lesser races." GIs saw wrecked bodies that once belonged to Americans with names like Jones and Johnston, starved hulks of men with faces like skulls who used to take the New York subway to work in civilian life or plow a field in Missouri or lie on the beach in California.

•   •   •

SITTING IN THE PARLOR of a German home which had been requisitioned as an MP billet, a dozen Yanks who had been released from a German PW cage when the 104th Division overran it told what had happened to them during their captivity.

The dean of the prisoners had spent two years and eight months in a PW camp. He had been captured in August 1942 and had been shot in the ankle and thigh by a German sniper just before he was taken prisoner. Despite his wounds, the Germans made him walk 12 miles to a prison camp without medical attention.

After a week in a French prison, he and 1,500 other Allied prisoners were herded into French 40-and-8 cars and taken to Stalag VIII-B at Lamsdorf in Ober Silesia. The rations for each man on the four days' and four nights' train ride were a loaf of bread, a third of a tin of meat, and a quarter pound of margarine.

"When we got to Lamsdorf," the dean of the prisoners said, "they put us in a compound by ourselves. We couldn't have any contact with the other Allied prisoners. There were 400 men in a hut, and each hut was built to hold only 200. Just to make sure we weren't too comfortable, they tied our hands with binder twine from eight in the morning until eight at night. Later they used handcuffs instead of twine. That went on for a whole year. Sometimes some of the boys managed to slip out of their bonds, but if they were caught they got five days of solitary confinement in a bunker with no food at all."

Despite temperatures that dropped to 10 and 20 below zero, the Germans made no effort to heat the prisoners' barracks. Men had to sleep in their clothes with their overcoats for blankets. Many of them suffered frozen feet and fingers. Later some of these frozen feet and fingers had to be amputated by Allied military doctors in the prison.

"The food at Lamsdorf was terrible," the soldier said. "They gave us a loaf of bread for seven men, and it was usually green with mold. Sometimes we'd get about a quart of watery soup made from the water the Germans boiled their own potatoes in, with a few cabbage leaves thrown in to make it look like soup. I lost about 50 pounds in two years and five months."

Along with 8,000 other Allied prisoners at Lamsdorf, he was evacuated from the Silesian prison camp on Jan. 23, 1945, because the Russian Army had advanced to within five miles. All the men who were able to walk were forced to do so. A few invalid prisoners went by freight.

"They put me on a train, but some of the other boys who had frozen feet and hands never made it. Their guards clubbed them with rifles and left them lying there along the roadside in the snow and zero weather when they dropped out because of bad feet. God knows what happened to them."

"The bastards did the same thing to our guys," another GI said. "They beat them with rifle butts when they couldn't walk any further. And if any of the stronger ones tried to help a guy they saw was getting weak, the guards clubbed them too. Besides that, they egged on German kids in the towns we went through to throw stones at us."

Another GI, an infantryman from the 14th Armored Division, was captured at Bitchie on Jan. 2, during the German breakthrough in Belgium and Luxembourg. Along with 200 other Americans he was loaded on a freight train and sent to eastern Germany. They had neither food nor water on the trip, which took four days and five nights. Their overcoats, blankets, field jackets, and shoes were taken away from them, together with their watches and other personal belongings.

"We licked the ice on the hinges of the box car for water," he said. "There were 60 or 70 of us in each car with no blankets or warm clothes or even straw to sleep on. And just to make sure we didn't get any sleep, German guards stopped outside our car several times a night and fired a couple of rounds in on us. They weren't trying to hit us, because they always fired high, but they kept us awake, so we wouldn't have energy to try to escape."

Until now, it had all seemed a little unreal.

A medic, who was one of the 12 ex-prisoners, got in the conversation then. He was a medic of the 101st Airborne Division, and he had been captured at Bastogne on Dec. 19, 1944.

"They not only wouldn't give us medical supplies," he said, "they even took our own away from us. After they captured us they made us turn over our kits and left us nothing to treat wounded and sick prisoners with.

"They marched us from Bastogne to Coblenz in zero weather and with two and three feet of snow on the ground. I saw guys who dropped out along the road clubbed on their bare tails with the butts of rifles by their guards. At Gerolstein they made 60 of our boys clean out buildings which had just been bombed by our planes and which were still burning. While they were working, the guards kicked them, hit them over the heads with pitchforks, and then turned the fire hose on them, spraying them with water that froze their clothes on them.

"They marched us seven days, then gave us two days' rest and started us off again. Finally they put us in box cars for a five-day ride to Stalag II-A, about 85 miles north of Berlin. From Dec. 19 until Jan. 3, when we reached Stalag II-A, the total food given each of us 600 prisoners was two cups of ersatz coffee, a sixth of a loaf of bread, and two cups of barley soup. That's all. It wasn't much for a two-week trip, most of it on foot."

After six days at Stalag II-A, his group was put on freight trains for a ride back to another camp.

"They would only give us some straw and two blankets for the sick and wounded prisoners," he said. "That was their bed and bedclothes, even though the temperature often got down around zero. Then they forbade us to use bedpans for patients and ordered that all the patients had to go to the toilet themselves. Some of the guys were just too weak to do it."

"The sonsuvbitches," a listening MP sergeant said.

—SGT. ED CUNNINGHAM

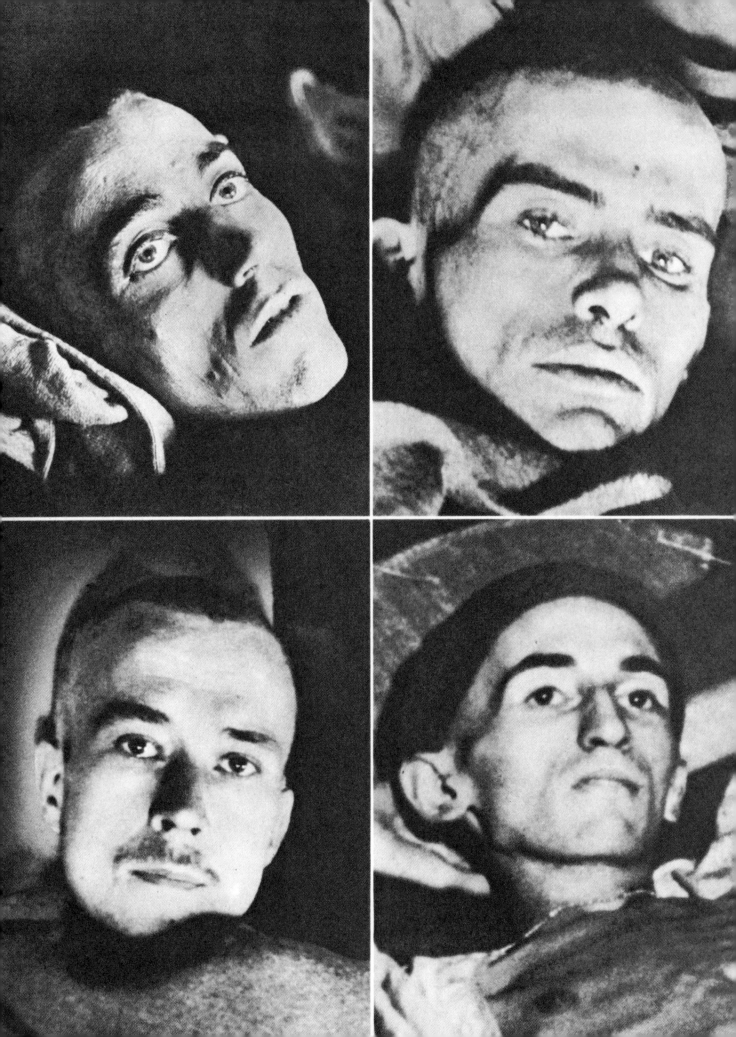

AT BUCHENWALD concentration camp I saw bake ovens. Instead of being used to bake bread they were used to destroy people.

They were most efficient. Each was equipped with a door and a sliding board down which victims could be slipped to eventual destruction.

There were various stories about how the victims were knocked out before they were "baked," and I saw one club which had been used for that purpose. There was also a table where gold fillings were removed from the teeth of skulls.

There were long steel stretchers on which the prisoners, often still alive, were rolled into the stinking heat of the ovens. I don't know how far German efficiency went, but I'm sure the heat from so much good coke and so many tons of sizzling flesh could not have been wasted. Perhaps it was circulated through asbestos pipes to warm the quarters of the SS guards.

The Germans had an inspirational four-line stanza painted on a signboard in the cellar. The stanza explains that man does not want his body to be eaten by worms and insects; he prefers the purifying oblivion of flame.

Before purification the prisoners lived in barracks-like structures about 200 feet long. On either side of the buildings are four layers of shelves about five feet deep and three feet apart. Two-by-fours, spaced five feet apart, cut these building-long shelves into compartments. The final compartment is about five feet wide, five feet deep, two or three feet high.

In each of these compartments, the Germans put six men—or seven, when, as was normal, the camp was crowded.

And, remarkably enough, there is room for six or seven men. After all, a man whose thighs are no bigger around than my forearm doesn't take up much room.

The stench of such a place became something to dread on a hot spring afternoon. Vomit and urine and feces and foul breath and rotting bodies mingled their odors—the smell of 1,500 men in a single room half again or at most twice as long as one of our model barracks back home.

The camp used to be well guarded to keep the townspeople away, but they couldn't have lived in ignorance or innocence of what was going on here. Many of the prisoners worked in the nearby Weimar factories. They collapsed of hunger at their benches, and no one asked why. They died along the road on the long walk back to camp, and no one expressed surprise. There existed a spirit at Buchenwald when the Americans arrived, however, that even the Nazis had been unable to destroy.

Still at Buchenwald after nine years were hundreds of Spanish Loyalist prisoners, who greeted their liberators with a large placard proclaiming: "THE FIGHT AGAINST FASCISM MUST NOT STOP AT THE PYRENEES; DEATH TO FRANCO AND THE FALANGE."

—CPL. HOWARD KATZANDER

A spirit even the Nazis had been unable to destroy: a freed Spaniard and his placard.

Wrecked bodies that belonged to American names.

How a German-American died

THIS IS THE STORY of Herman Bottcher, an American soldier and an antifascist from way back.

In December 1942, when Stateside newspapers were hailing him as "our greatest hero of the New Guinea campaign," Bottcher, not a U. S. citizen then, said, "I have tried to live as a good American and I want to die as one."

Last New Year's Eve he got his wish in a burst of motar fire while his company was holding off 300 Japs during the Ormoc campaign on Leyte Island. By that time, Congress had naturalized him by a special act so he could be commissioned. He already had the DSC with Oak Leaf cluster and the Purple Heart with two clusters. At the time of his death, recommendations were in for a promotion to major and for a Silver Star.

The *Wehrmacht* lost some good material when Bottcher left his native Germany in 1928 at the age of 19. He was a cabinetmaker with ambitions to become something more. After tarrying in Austria for a couple of years, he emigrated to the United States with citizenship in mind. He worked at many jobs and, during the depression, was more than once "on the bum." By 1936, when Franco launched his fascist revolt in Spain, Bottcher had knocked about enough to know which side he was on. He joined the Abraham Lincoln Brigade, recruited in America to help the Spanish people against German, Italian, and Spanish fascists.

In Spain Bottcher learned a lot about soldiering, participating in seven battles in 25 months. He was wounded twice and decorated three times, and he rose to be a major before the Loyalist Government was overwhelmed. Of that experience, Bottcher said later, "I've always hated dictators. That's why I joined the Spanish Loyalists. Gee, that was a tough war. Now we at least have bullets."

Meanwhile the American citizenship Bottcher had earned during his first years in the States was revoked because of his enlistment in the Abraham Lincoln Brigade. He reapplied and started all over. Living with an aunt in California, he worked his way through college by washing dishes and such. Intending to become an architect, he lacked only six credits for a degree when the Japs struck Pearl Harbor.

One month later he had managed to convince the War Department of his loyalty, despite his German birth and accent, and began basic as a private in the Army. Assigned to the 32d Division, a former National Guard outfit, he became a staff sergeant in a year.

The first anniversary of Pearl Harbor found Bottcher fighting with his company in the Papuan campaign. He turned out to be a terrific jungle fighter. He knocked out enemy machine-gun nests single-handed, slaughtered Japs by the half-squad, and rescued wounded comrades with utter disregard for his own safety. When all ranking officers were knocked out, Bottcher took command of his company and drove a wedge to the sea between two Jap groups at Buna Village and Buna Mission. He held this dangerous position for a week until the battle was won.

He was breveted a captain while machinery was set going to restore his citizenship so he could be permanently commissioned. He was not one of those GIs who scorn the responsibilities of command. "If they'd only commission me," he fretted, "I'd get something done."

But joining the brass did not separate Bottcher from his men. As Pvt. Tex Pitcox of Amarillo, Tex., put it, "There ain't a man in the outfit who wouldn't have followed him through hell carrying a bucket of ice water." When his outfit was being shipped and the men had to sleep on deck, Bottcher spurned his cabin to lie there with them. If the men had K rations, Bottcher, too, ate K rations, regardless of what his fellow officers thought of such conduct. What is more, after the Papuan campaign, Bottcher probably could have gotten out of the Army because of his three wounds. His shooting hand was partly crippled.

But after a rest in Australia, Bottcher was back with the 32d at Saidor and Aitape in New Guinea. While in Australia, incidentally, he thought so little of the DSC coming to him that he didn't show up for the ceremony of presentation. They found him later, working out with some enlisted men on a jungle-training course.

At Aitape, Bottcher led a recon troop behind Jap lines for 57 days, penetrating 36 miles into enemy territory. The men learned to trust blindly their tall, raw-boned captain with the thick German accent. On any patrol Bottcher himself was point man. The outfit boasted of their light losses.

One man said, "I never feel safer out in the jungle than when I'm with Capt. Bottcher." And Pvt. Harold Endres of Madison, Wis., declared, "If the Old Man wanted us to enter Manila Bay in a rubber boat, we would go and, furthermore, we'd bet nothing would happen."

In the Leyte campaign, Bottcher was up to his old tricks. For 48 days he led a recon troop, sometimes reinforced by Filipino guerrillas, behind Japanese lines. They destroyed many supply dumps. They ambushed Jap units and killed innumerable enemy soldiers. Their daily reports prepared the way for successful drives at Kanaga, Palompon, and other places. And through it all, until the last terrible shellacking the troop suffered on Dec. 31, Bottcher's outfit suffered only four casualties—one man killed (in an accident) and three wounded.

Bottcher's outfit lived mostly off the land, killing game for meat and getting vegetables and fermented coconut milk from the natives.

On Dec. 30, Capt. Bottcher's unit was instructed by radio to return to Division HQ, since the Leyte campaign was virtually concluded. No Japanese had been seen for several days. At 0235 hours on Dec. 31, the 90 men of Bottcher's outfit were awakened by heavy fire from rifles, machineguns, knee mortars, and 90mm. mortars. It was later learned that 300 Japs, trying to fight their way to the sea in the hope of being evacuated safely by boat from the island, had run across Bottcher and his men.

When Bottcher got it, he was about four feet from T-5 Edwin Essman of Portsmouth, O., who was setting up his radio to advise headquarters. There was an explosion and Bottcher called out, "They blew my leg off!"

Lt. Royal Steele of New York twisted a tourniquet on the captain's thigh. Sgt. Tony Gaidosik of Milwaukee, Wis., a medic, gave the CO a shot of morphine. Another medic raced for blood plasma stored in a shack but found the shack and the medical supplies destroyed by gunfire.

Bottcher stopped S/Sgt. Jim Calbe of Chattanooga, Tenn., and ordered his men to leave him and withdraw. They withdrew, but, of course, they carried the captain with them. They made it to the main infantry lines just before dawn. A radio call had been sent for plasma, but by the time it arrived by Cub, Bottcher was unconscious. The medics kept up a frantic radio conversation with the station hospital, describing Bottcher's condition and receiving doctor's directions for treatment. But Bottcher's pulse weakened. About 0600 hours no sign of life could be detected.

His men said later they couldn't believe their captain could be killed by the Japs. They didn't talk much about it. They just sat around staring wearily at the constant drizzle of Leyte.

Bottcher had no wife or parents. All he had was the aunt in San Francisco and a hell of a lot of friends in the Army.

—CPL. IRA FREEMAN

JINX FLIGHT

"Berkeley gave the order to bail out, then followed his crew into the night."

K. GREENHALGH

Nine Men Played Peek-a-Boo With Death Over Rangoon— And Lived to Tell the Tale

By Sgt. ED CUNNINGHAM
YANK Staff Correspondent

AT A U. S. BOMBER BASE, INDIA—There are nine Yank airmen at this U.S. base who will give you odds they can make any nine-lived cat turn green with envy. They're members of a combat crew who played tag with borrowed time so often on a recent bombing mission that the law of averages is in grave danger of being repealed. .

Here are the names of these nine guys with the charmed lives. Don't put a wooden *anna* on the line against them until you've read their story.

1st Lt. William R. Berkeley, 25, pilot, Cleveland, Ohio.

2nd Lt. Thomas L. Murphy, 22, co-pilot, of Shreveport, La.

1st Lt. Francis N. Thompson, 25, navigator,

M/Sgt. Howard C. Darby, 32, bombardier, Plattsburg, N. Y.

T/Sgt. William O. Frost, 25, engineer, Jaffrey, N. H.

S/Sgt. John E. Craigie, 25, radio operator, West Haven, Conn.

S/Sgt. Bernard L. Bennett, 23, tail gunner, Peru, Ind.

S/Sgt. Adolph R. Scolavino, 22, belly gunner, Providence, R. I.

Sgt. Edward M. Salley, 22, waist gunner, Houston, Tex.

This tale starts at Rangoon, where the boys were headed recently to drop a few explosive calling cards on the Japs. Fifteen minutes from the target area, a fire broke out down in the nose of the plane. A parachute placed too near the electric heater had caught fire, flooding the plane with smoke. Lt. Thompson's fire extinguisher quickly drenched the blaze and averted the first threat of disaster.

Then, right over the target, all four motors cut out. The plane dipped down toward the spitting Jap ack-ack guns, while Berkeley feverishly twisted the controls trying to get the motors back. He succeeded momentarily, only to have them conk off again. For seconds that seemed hours, the B-24 started losing altitude. Then the motors came on again and Berkeley leveled off.

After Darby had dropped his load of thousand-pounders, the B-24 headed for home. Berkeley and his crew stopped sweating then, bolstered up by the fact that they had weathered three threatened disasters. Other than a few frayed nerves, the only damage was the burned parachute. But what the hell, there was an extra chute anyway. A ground crew man had left one back in the cabin by mistake. It was the first time the B-24 had ever carried more than the usual nine chutes.

But the headaches were just beginning. The B-24 was still 100 miles at sea when its electrical system went out. So did the auxiliary. Shortly after, the batteries went, too. The ship had no electrical power at all. That meant no electric governor for the propellers which were fast approaching the red danger line on the RPM gauge. No means of putting out distress signals or radio identification. No landing lights.

Everything was dead except the vacumatic instruments. Only the flight indicator and the gyro compass were working. Murphy's flashlight, trained on the instrument panel, was the only light available for the pilot to watch his course.

Sgt. Edward M. Salley, Waist Gunner · 1st Lt. William R. Berkeley, Pilot · 2nd Lt. Thomas L. Murphy, Co-Pilot · 1st Lt. Francis N. Thompson, Navigator · S/Sgt. Bernard L. Bennett, Tail Gunner · S/Sgt. John E. Craigie, Radio Operator

T/Sgt. William O. Frost, Engineer · S/Sgt. Adolph R. Scolavino, Belly Gunner · M/Sgt. Harold C. Darby, Bombardier

You have to have a charmed life to survive the accidents these men had. Everything that could happen to a bomber crew happened on this one flight.

Frost, the engineer, worked frantically trying to get the power back. But no soap. Only a tight-rope walker standing against a 170-mile-an-hour gale out on the wing tip could get at the source of the trouble. The electrical system was unrepairable in the air.

They were over land by now, but still without landing lights. Circling over a city, they were looking for an airfield when a British Hurricane fighter made a pass at them in the darkness. Unable to radio their identification, they had been spotted as an enemy bomber. Fortunately, the Hurricane pilot must have recognized the B-24 twin-tailed design. He didn't open fire on them.

The No. 3 engine was running away now. The finger on the RPM gauge was up to 3,300, far beyond the danger point and way too far beyond the normal 2,700 revolutions per minute. That No. 3 engine might fall off at any minute.

When it started to splinter, Berkeley gave the order to bail out. He cut off the main switches, to prevent explosions, then followed his crew into the night. His was the spare parachute.

The nine parachutes floated earthward through 7,000 feet of darkness. Seven of them swayed crazily, their riser lines unguided by the seven unconscious men strapped to their rubber seats. Only Darby and Scolavino saw the B-24, with its No. 3 engine falling to pieces, plunge past them. The others had been knocked out by the flailing buckles of their chest straps just seconds after they had pulled their ripcords. They hadn't had time to adjust them properly before jumping. When they hit the cool layer of air about 5,000 feet up, they came to.

Only the wind lapping against the billows of their flying canopies broke the silence of the night. They could control their riser lines now, but that didn't prevent the wind from carrying them apart. It would be every man for himself when they hit the ground.

Darby was better prepared than the rest; he had his .45 with him. Frost had jumped ready for action, too, carrying a tommy gun, 125 rounds of ammunition, a camera and a musette bag.

But he hadn't figured on that strap buckle. When he recovered at 5,000 feet, he had nothing left in his hands but his flight cap. That had been on his head when he bailed out.

Darby, uninjured and armed, took his delayed descent in stride. He pulled a pack of cigarettes out of his pocket, lit up and settled back to enjoy his trip down to earth.

The others weren't so comfortable. Salley, with a gaping lip wound where two teeth had been driven through by the strap buckle, landed in a tree. Fortunately, he managed to shake his chute loose and fall to the ground without injury. Craigie, bleeding profusely from a broken cartilage in his nose, landed in a lake. He had to swim and wade through mud for nine hours before being rescued by an Indian boatman. Frost barely missed a tree, landing by pulling his legs up under him and tugging on the riser lines.

Some of the crew landed in rice paddies, others in swamps. All but Murphy, Darby and Craigie spent the night where they landed, sleeping on the ground with their parachutes as pillows. The co-pilot and bombardier reached Indian villages after walking several hours, and spent the night there. Craigie swam and walked until dawn. Ironically enough, he was the only one who heard the yells of any of his crewmates. He heard Bennett calling soon after they landed but couldn't call back because of his wound.

Some of them had to do a little improvising

before being rescued. Lt. Berkeley lost a shoe coming down. He made a substitute by cutting off a piece of canvas from the back of his parachute and sewing it into slipper-form with a fish hook and fishing line from his jungle kit. Berkeley managed to wet his parched lips during the night by collecting a little dew on a waxed candy paper. Murphy went native and draped himself in a silk shawl while the villagers were drying his uniform.

When the sun came up, all nine of the crew started for a nearby Indian city by different routes. Some of them met along the line. Craigie and Salley ran into each other in a native village and boarded a train together. At the next station, Bennett got on. Scolavino and Lt. Thompson had caught an earlier train, at different stations, but the conductor put them in the same coach.

Frost met Darby along the river and got a boat to take them to the city. Lt. Berkeley was also making his way by boat when he was hailed by Lt. Murphy from a village along the river bank. He picked up his co-pilot and they, too, caught a train that took them to the city.

The entire crew met that night at a hotel in the city. And that's where their luck ran out, according to Salley.

"We stayed at that hotel eight days waiting for travel orders back to our base. But do you think we drew expenses? Like hell! We all had to pay our own hotel bills!"

Battle for Iwo

ANYONE WHO LANDED at Iwo Jima will tell you that naming the stretch of beach just north of Mount Suribachi "Green Beach" was inaccurate, to say the least.

The sand of "Green Beach" got into the eyes of members of the 5th Marine Division who landed there and caked around their eyelashes. It became mixed in their hair like gritty dandruff. It invaded small cans of K-ration ham and eggs as soon as they were opened. It crept over the tops of men's leggings and worked to the bottom of their shoes. The sand was both friend and enemy. It made foxhole-digging easy, but it made fast movement impossible for men and vehicles.

For two days the men who landed on Green Beach were pinned to the ground. Murderous machinegun, sniper, and mortar fire came from a line of pillboxes 300 yards away in the scrubby shrubbery at the foot of the volcano. No one on the beach, whether he was a CP phone operator or a front-line rifleman, was exempt. The sight of a head raised above a foxhole was the signal to dozens of Japs, safely hidden in concrete emplacements, to open up. Men lay on their sides to drink from canteens or to urinate. An errand between foxholes became a life-and-death mission for the man who attempted it.

For two days the Marines stayed pinned to the beaches in what seemed to many of them a humiliating stalemate. Hundreds of green-clad bodies hugged the ground, spread out helplessly in a scattered pattern, furnishing marksmanship practice for the Japs on the mountain with their telescopic gunsights.

The Marines had been hopelessly cut up and disorganized when they hit the beach. Their vehicles bogged down in the sand when they were brought in. Their supplies were ruined. Many of their wounded still lay where they fell, in spite of the heroic efforts of the tireless medical corpsmen. Bad weather and a choppy ocean prevented the landing of many small boats on the second day and held up the supply of new ammunition and equipment and evacuation of the wounded. Though scores of dead marines lay everywhere, few of our troops had seen a single Jap, dead or alive.

Towering over them was Mount Suribachi, a gray unlovely hulk with enemy pillbox chancres in its sides. Marines on Green Beach grew to hate the mountain almost as much as they hated the Japs who were on it. Reaching the summit was almost as much of a challenge as destroying the men who defended it.

The supporting air and naval fire did much. Hour after hour of surface and air bombardment couldn't fail to wipe out many emplacements, imprison many Japs in their caves, and slowly eat away the mountain fortress itself. But when it came to the specific four-foot-square machinegun emplacements and the still smaller snipers' pillboxes there was little the offshore and air bombardment could do except silence them for a few minutes. Everyone knew that in the end the troops would have to dig them out.

The foot troops made their drive on the third day. They were aided by a naval and air bombardment so terrific that the Tokyo radio announced that the mountain itself was erupting. They were aided also by our own artillery and rocket guns, landed with superhuman effort the previous day in spite of a choppy ocean and the enemy's guns.

But the foot troops were aided most by the tanks that advanced with them and lobbed shells into the stone-and-concrete revetments that blocked the way of the foot troops. The Japs were afraid of our tanks—so afraid that they ducked low in their shelters and silenced their guns when they saw them. They dug dozens of tank traps, but that is all they did. They didn't dare challenge our tanks with their guns.

As soon as the tanks had passed on or had been blown up by mines, the Japs came out of their holes and attacked our men from behind with machineguns and mortars. Between the foot of the volcano and Green Beach the enemy had hundreds of pillboxes and emplacements connected by a network of tunnels. When the Japs were driven from one pillbox, they would disappear until the Marines advanced to another, and a moment later they would appear at their old emplacement, lobbing grenades at our men who had just passed.

By early afternoon of D-plus-two the Japs at the foot of Suribachi had been silenced. However, everyone knew there were still Japs around. There were Japs in the tunnels between the caves, and there were Japs in the "spiderwebs" —the one-man sniper pillboxes—who would lift the camouflaged lids of their shelters and take pot shots at Marines trying to reorganize.

There were also many Japs who were dead. There were dead Japs in every conceivable contortion of men who meet death violently. Their arms and legs were wrenched about their bodies, and their fists were clenched and frozen. Those who had been killed by flamethrowers were burned to a black darker than the ashes of Suribachi or scorched to a brilliant yellow. Their clothes had been burned off, and the heat vulcanized their buttocks together with ugly black strips. It was good to see these sights after having been pinned down to Green Beach for two terrible days.

There were dead marines, too. Some platoons had been entirely stripped of their officers and noncoms. Some had lost more than three-fourths of their men since morning.

But the worst of the battle for Suribachi was over. Our men had fought their way in under the guns higher up on the mountain. Many of these guns had been knocked out by our tanks and artillery and our naval and air bombardment. Many others couldn't be depressed far enough to menace our new positions.

There was still much to be done at the foot of the volcano. There were still many emplacements to be cleaned out with flamethrowers and tanks, and there were still snipers sneaking through the subterranean tunnels. The third afternoon a detachment of marines fought around one side of the mountain and another detachment fought around the other. Then they dug in for the night. At 0100 hours the Japs counterattacked. They kept coming until daybreak, but the Marines held them back. And all day the Americans were busy cleaning out the tunnels, caves, and concrete emplacements at the mountain's base.

On the fourth night S/Sgt. Ernest R. Thomas of Tallahassee, Fla., led a platoon whose officer had been killed; it was accompanied by the company's executive officer, 1st Lt. Harold G. Schrier of Richmond, Mo. They dug in for the night at the base of a tortuous path leading to the top of the mountain. It was a bad night. Rain streamed down the mountain in small rivulets that trickled under their clothes and washed sand across their bodies. The cold wind made them shiver.

They huddled in foxholes, keeping their weapons dry with their ponchos.

At 0800 hours the following morning they began the ascent. The volcanic sand on the steep path offered poor footing. Stubby plants broke off in the men's hands or pulled out by their roots. But the only resistance encountered was the occasional *ping!* of a sniper's bullet. As the

men reached the summit they found a few more emplacements that were manned by live Japs. These were cleaned out with flame-throwers, BARs, and satchel charges.

At 1131 hours the Marines were in undisputed control of the top of the volcano. Sgt. Henry O. Hanson of Somerville, Mass., looked around for a pole and found a lead pipe on the ground. At 1137 hours he, together with Lt. Schrier and other 5th Division marines, raised the American flag on Suribachi.

Far below, Green Beach was rapidly taking on the appearance of any other beachhead. The volcanic sand was littered with abandoned equipment, and the shores were lined with boats delivering more supplies and evacuating the wounded.

Iwo Jima was far from being secured. But the Marines were on the summit of Mount Suribachi, the fortress that had made them wallow in sand for two days. Not far from where the flag flew a communications man shouted, "This is easy!" into his field phone.

The Marines intended to stay. Green Beach had been avenged.

—SGT. BILL REED

The Japs were cleaned out with flame-throwers.

With victory near

IT WAS SPRING, and the feel of victory was everywhere. In the Pacific American troops had landed at Okinawa and were pushing ahead. In Europe it was a rat-race. Allied armies had broken through German defenses along the Rhine, looped through the valleys and across the plains.

German resistance was stubborn in some places, easy to convince in others, and nowhere was it the organized resistance of a coordinated army.

German kids came out of the cellars, stood in the rubble, made the V-sign, and asked for chocolate.

It was a rat-race, and the tankers speared forward so fast that the high brass lost count of the prisoners and of the towns taken. A press association correspondent in a jeep driven by a GI raced into a little German town, left the jeep, and went running through the deserted houses trying to find out when the town had fallen and whether it had been defended.

The correspondent couldn't find anyone. He went through the bombed buildings and down the broken streets. Finally he met a GI.

"What is your name," the correspondent asked, "and what is your home town?"

The GI told him.

"Did you help take this town?" the correspondent asked.

The GI said, "Take this town? No, sir."

"Are you in the Third Army?" the correspondent asked.

The GI said no.

"Then what are you doing here?" the correspondent demanded.

"It's this way, sir," said the GI. "I'm the fellow who drove you here in the jeep."

It was the biggest, wildest jig-saw puzzle in history, and part of the pieces were missing. Everyone agreed on only one thing: The Germans were licked. The Allies went barreling eastward, and German refugees came straggling back to the west.

American spearhead outfits moved faster, competing to make a juncture with the Russians.

The American Ninth Army crossed the Elbe and rolled to within 57 miles of Berlin. The Third Army captured Weimar. The Seventh Army took Schweinfurt and Heilbronn. First Army tanks swept 22 miles over the Thuringian Plain. The French stormed Rastatt. The British moved west from a line five miles south of Bremen.

In the East, the Russians crossed the Oder and were within 30 miles of Berlin.

At this hour of high triumph—Apr. 12, 1945 —with victory sure and the Nazis all but beaten, President Franklin D. Roosevelt died at Warm Springs, Ga.

Commander-in-Chief, 1933-1945

Death of Roosevelt

THE FUNERAL MARCH stretched for a thousand miles. The train, with the flag rippling from the engine, had come up from Georgia, past the old battlefields of another war fought 80 years ago. There was a great hush over the land. The people came and stood by the tracks as the long train rolled on, bound for Washington and later a quiet garden high above the Hudson. The President was dead.

The train moved slowly through the night. At Charlotte, N. C., a troop of Boy Scouts started to sing "Onward, Christian Soldiers," and massed thousands took it up in a mighty chorus. Along the way people dropped to their knees in prayer. Bells tolled a requiem.

By countless thousands the people came to say good-bye to Franklin Delano Roosevelt. Men in overalls, men with gnarled hands, women with shawls, kids, wet-eyed and solemn, lined the tracks and bowed their heads.

•   •   •

"There is the hope of the future," said the economist who once had been a Brain Truster. "If Franklin Roosevelt's hopes and dreams are deep enough in the heart of the people, the people will make them come true."

•   •   •

There had been only one other pilgrimage like this in American history. That had taken place 80 years before, almost to a day, when a wartime President had been borne on a long trek to Illinois and a tomb that became a shrine. His name was Abraham Lincoln.

Across the silent countryside soft with spring, past the sprawling green fields of Virginia, Franklin Roosevelt came back to Washington. There in the Capital, shimmering in the hot sun, where he had four times come in triumph after Presidential campaigns, the President rode again. The last campaign had ended for the man who once described himself as an "old campaigner who loves a good fight." Now he rode in a flag-draped coffin on a black caisson drawn by six white horses.

At the Union Station and along the broad streets leading to the White House, where the President had ridden so often to the crowd's acclaim, the silence was broken only by the muffled roll of drums and the muted dirge.

Five hundred thousand persons saw the coffin on the caisson and sensed that men would speak of this hour 100 years from now.

•   •   •

"Once when I was traveling on a campaign train with Franklin Roosevelt," said the senator, "a little boy came running up the tracks as the train started pulling out of the station. And the little boy yelled, 'Hey, Mr. President, thanks for our new WPA toilet and thanks for everything.' Franklin Roosevelt was the people's hero. The people were his hero. A long time ago he whipped infantile paralysis, and after that he wasn't afraid of anything. No wonder they called him the Champ."

•   •   •

Mrs. Eleanor Roosevelt had asked that no one send flowers to the funeral, yet in the stately East Room of the White House, where the closed coffin rested, flowers banked three sides of the room, high against the wall. There were flowers sent by kings and flowers sent by obscure people whom the President never saw. A little boy in Chicago sent a bouquet picked from his back yard. "I was sorry," he wrote, "that I couldn't come to the funeral."

The weather was sultry on this funeral day,

much as it had been on Apr. 14, 1865, the day Abraham Lincoln was shot in Ford's Theater. And in the East Room, where Lincoln had lain in state, the mourners gathered at the bier of Franklin Roosevelt. Great men of the world were there. Foreign Secretary Anthony Eden had flown to Washington from London. He looked grave and worried. Prime Minister Winston Churchill had planned also to attend the funeral of this "cherished friend" but canceled his plans because of the urgency of the war situation.

Cabinet members and diplomats were there. Supreme Court justices, congressmen, and men famous in literature were there. Mrs. Eleanor Roosevelt was drawn and tired, but her step was firm and her head was high. Harry Hopkins, closest of the Presidential advisers, who had flown to Washington from the Mayo Clinic in Rochester, Minn., where he had been ill, grasped the back of the chair in front of him so tightly that his knuckles gleamed white.

Near the Roosevelt family sat President Truman, his wife and daughter, Mrs. Woodrow Wilson, and Crown Princess Martha of Norway. The new President and his family entered the room so quietly that no one had time to rise. He stared straight ahead, his jaw outthrust. In this hour of mourning, he seemed quietly confident, as though at this flag-draped coffin of his fallen leader he was gathering will of spirit for the task ahead.

The coffin was flanked by flags and rested on a catafalque centered near the east wall. From the wall on either side looked down full-length portraits of George and Martha Washington.

At each corner of the coffin was a guard. Two GIs, a corporal and a pfc, and a marine and a sailor all stood rigidly at attention. The stillness was broken only by the gentle whirring of a fan. To one side of the room sat the President's wheel chair, empty.

And in the park across the street from the White House, where the people had gathered to talk in low tones, the old man said: "The greatest thing that Franklin Roosevelt did was teach the people that this land was theirs; that the earth's abundance belongs to the people; that they need only the will to gain the power."

•   •   •

In the East Room, rich with history and heavily fragrant with flowers, the Rt. Rev. Angus Dun, bishop of the Episcopal Diocese of Washington, prayed for "steadfast courage in adversity; for sympathy with the hungers and fears of common men; for trials met without surrender, and weakness endured without defeat; for unyielding faith in the possibility of a more just and more ordered world, delivered from the ancient curse of war."

The bishop, at Mrs. Roosevelt's suggestion, quoted the words with which Franklin Roosevelt on a bleak inaugural day more than 12 years before had restored a desperate nation's faith: "The only thing we have to fear is fear itself."

The bishop closed with familiar words that rang through the long room: "Through Jesus Christ, to whom be glory forever and ever. Amen."

The mourners left the White House. Outside, other mourners still stood, crowds of them. They had stood through a sudden downpour of rain, and now their clothes steamed in the sun.

That night, again through hushed, crowded streets, the President's coffin was carried to the train for its journey to Hyde Park, N. Y. Twelve years before, Franklin Roosevelt had come to the White House at a time of crisis, with millions of unemployed roaming the nation's streets, and he had offered sympathy, hope, and bold experiment. Now he was no longer untried. Twelve years before he had reassured the people with the solemn word that the "money changers have abdicated . . . the people have not failed." Now the people were telling him quietly and reverently that he had not failed.

They watched the hearse roll to the train, and they bowed in honest grief. His place in history secure, the President was leaving the White House forever.

.   .   .

"Some people compare him to Lincoln," said the professor who had once helped draft New Deal legislation, "and it's true that he was attacked and abused like Lincoln. But Franklin Roosevelt patterned himself after Jefferson and Jackson. He proved, as Jefferson did, that a man can be a great gentleman and at the same time a great commoner. And he was tough like Jackson, a hell of a fighter."

.   .   .

Once more the body of Franklin Roosevelt was borne through the night. And again the people in the villages, towns and farms waited in the darkness while the train rolled past.

Riding with the President on this last journey were the men and women who had come to Washington 12 years before, eager to wipe out old laws and write new ones. This night they were tired and troubled. The New Dealers were getting old, and they had lost their leader. Secretary of Commerce Henry Wallace and Secretary of the Interior Harold Ickes had boarded the train together, walking arm in arm. "Roosevelt's musketeers," said a man in the crowd.

The train moved through the night, and the dim lights of the towns etched the faces of the people standing near the tracks. Across one station there was a line of boys and girls—boys holding caps in their left hand and girls with pigtails. They stood with chests thrust out at attention. A band played "Hail to the Chief." Some of the kids were crying.

Northward the train rolled, taking Franklin Roosevelt home. At the edge of a little town an old man was spearing waste paper with a pointed stick. In his right hand he carried a greasy cap. As the train passed, the old man put on his cap, drew himself jerkily up, and saluted. His heels were together, his chest was out. Clearly he had saluted before, maybe in some war long ago.

"I rode with him on all four of his campaigns," said the reporter. "A lot of people praising him the most now are the ones who fought him the hardest. That would amuse the old man. He always knew the pitch on those phonies."

.   .   .

At lonely crossroads and in great cities, the common people had come to say their own good-bye to this crippled man who had taken a crippled nation and helped it walk once more.

The next morning was Sunday, Apr. 15, 1945. At 10:15 A.M. Franklin Delano Roosevelt, four times chosen by the people as President of the United States, was committed to the earth of his beloved Hyde Park birthplace.

Against a 15-foot hemlock hedge surrounding the old garden which the President long ago had designated as his burial place, files of soldiers, sailors, and marines stood rigidly at attention, their eyes fixed on the flag-draped coffin. A battalion of gray-and-white-clad West Points cadets were massed at one end of the garden. The cadets' crepe-hung drums rolled mournfully across the chill morning air.

The Rev. Dr. George W. Anthony, rector of St. James Church of Hyde Park, quoted from "Requiescat" by John B. Dykes:

"Now the laborer's task is o'er;
   Now the battle day is past;
Now upon the farther shore
   Lands the voyager at last.
Father, in thy gracious keeping,
   Leave we now thy servant sleeping."

Three cadets fired deliberately spaced volleys across the President's grave. A bugler stepped forward and softly blew "Taps." A sergeant of the honor guard selected to carry the coffin lifted the American flag from the top, folded it carefully, and handed it to Mrs. Roosevelt. Mrs. Roosevelt, ashen-gray but dry-eyed, accepted it proudly.

.   .   .

"Last time I talked with him," said the neighbor, "the President told me he didn't know how

history would record him as a President, but he said he knew for sure that he was one of the best doggoned tree-growers ever to come up the pike."

•   •   •

Within a half-hour after the burial all the mourners had left. Franklin Roosevelt was alone in the garden where he had played as a boy and where he had teased a childhood playmate named Eleanor. The only sound was the foot-beat of sentries walking their posts.

—SGT. DEBS MYERS

BEFORE THE NEWS CAME over the radio from San Francisco, the GIs in the Eighth Army casual camp in the Philippines were talking mostly about the new adjusted service rating cards that two men, fresh from the States, had brought along with their service records and Form 20s. Then an infantryman back from morning chow said that the President had died from a heart attack.

When they got the story straight and realized that it wasn't just another rumor, everybody in the camp was stunned and bewildered.

Pvt. Howard McWatters of Nevada City, Calif., just released from the hospital and waiting to go back to the Americal Division, shook his head slowly. "Roosevelt made a lot of mistakes," he said. "But I think he did the best he could, and when he made mistakes he usually admitted it. Nobody could compare with him as President."

In Rome the Allied Command closed its places of amusement, and the Italian officials shut down the civilian movies, the schools, the banks, and the opera. "I came out of my tent this morning," said Pfc. Fred Carlson of New York City and the 1st Replacement Depot, "and I saw the flag at half mast. I asked who was dead. Then they told me. I hope it won't work out like when we lost Wilson after the last war."

A Navy lifeguard spread the news among the GIs and sailors on Waikiki Beach in Honolulu.

Most of them walked into the exclusive Outrigger Club, which is ordinarily reserved for members only, and sat silently by the radio in their swim suits, listening to the reports of what had happened in Warm Springs.

Sgt. Bob Bouwsma was reading the final item of the five-o'clock newscast in the Armed Forces Radio Service station in Panama when Cpl. Reuben Diaz, the station's Spanish announcer, handed him the flash. GIs hearing it at supper in the mess halls didn't believe it at first. Then the station's phone started to ring. Sgt. Jim Weathers would pick it up and say, "Yes, it's true." "Yes, it's true," he said to each call, "Yes, it's true."

In London, the British civilians lost their traditional restraint. They stopped American soldiers on the street to tell them how sorry they were, how much the President had done for Britain and for the world. They talked about his trade of the over-age destroyers for their Western Hemisphere bases, about lend-lease, about the times they had cheered him in the newsreels.

Cpl. Louis Schier of Chicago, Ill., an armored-division artilleryman just back in England from the German front, said it was like the loss of the major who had command of his task force. "I was just about a hundred yards away when they killed him with a machine pistol," said Schier. "We had a tough time after that pulling ourselves together. It's the same way with all of us now that FDR is dead."

In Sydney, Australia, Sgt. Lloyd P. Stallings of San Antonio, Tex., said, "I came down here to have a good time, but now I don't feel so cheerful."

Outside the Grand Hotel in Paris, Pfc. Lester Rebuck, a medic from the 104th Division, said: "It was just like somebody socked me in the stomach when I wasn't looking. I just couldn't get it through my head he was really dead. For my money, that guy was one of the greatest guys that ever lived. You can put him next to Lincoln or Washington or anybody."

He was a small, gray, weary little guy, and the men called him Ernie.

Death of Ernie Pyle

ERNIE PYLE covered Okinawa on D-Day with the Marines. Many of them did not recognize him at first and stared curiously at the small, oldish-looking man with the stubby white whiskers and frayed woolen cap. When they did recognize him they said, "Hi, Ernie. What do you think of the war here in the Pacific?" And Pyle smiled and said a little wearily, "Oh, it's the same old stuff all over again. I am awful tired of it."

The men watched him climb from the boat, his thin body bent under the weight of his field pack and draped in fatigue clothes that seemed too big for him, and they said, "That guy is getting too old for this kind of stuff. He ought to go home."

Ie Shima, where Pyle died, is a small, obscure island off the western coast of Okinawa. The operation was on such a small scale that many correspondents didn't bother to go along. Pyle had been in the ship's bay sick for a week with one of his famous colds. The weather was perfect, with balmy air and bright sunshine. Pyle was ashore on D-plus-One. He stretched out on the sunny slope with Milton Chase, WLW radio correspondent, soaking up the sun and gazing at the picturesque landscape and gently rolling fields dotted with sagebrush-like bushes and clumps of low pine trees. The country, he said, was the way Italy must be in summertime. That was only a guess, he added, because he was in Italy in the middle of winter. Most of all, it reminded him of Albuquerque.

"Lots of people don't like the country around Albuquerque," he said, "but it suits me fine. As soon as I finish this damned assignment I'm going back there and settle down for a long time."

A young officer came up to report that the Japs were blowing themselves up with grenades. "That's a sight worth seeing," he said.

Chase asked Pyle what his reaction to the Jap dead was. Pyle said dead men were all alike to him, and it made him feel sick to look at one.

A wounded soldier with a bloody bandage on his arm came up the slope and asked Pyle for his autograph. "Don't usually collect these things," he told Pyle sheepishly, "but I wanted yours. Thanks a lot."

The operation was going so well that most of the correspondents left that night. There had been hardly any casualties, and only a very few of these were killed. Pyle was in the midst of preparing a story on a tank-destroyer team, so he stayed on. He was wearing green fatigues and a cap with a Marine emblem. He was with a few troops when he died, standing near Lt. Col. Joseph B. Coolidge of Helena, Mont. The Jap machinegun that got him took the group by surprise.

Pyle had proceeded to the front in a jeep with Col. Coolidge. As they reached a cross-roads, still some distance from the front lines, the Jap machinegun, hidden in a patch of woods, suddenly opened up on them. The gun was a sleeper. Our troops had been moving up and down the road all morning and most of the day before. This was the first time it had revealed itself.

Pyle and the others jumped from the jeep and took cover in a ditch beside the road. The machinegun fired another long burst, and Pyle was dead. The rest withdrew. Several groups attempted to recover his body, once with the support of tanks, but each time they were driven back.

At 1500, Chaplain N. B. Saucier of Coffee-ville, Miss., received permission to attempt to recover the body with litter-bearers. T-5 Paul Shapiro of Passaic, N. J., Sgt. Minter Moore of Elkins, W. Va., Cpl. Robert Toaz of Hunting-ton, N. Y., and Sgt. Arthur Austin of Tekaman, Neb., volunteered to go with him. The cross-roads lay in open country that offered no cover. The men crawled up the ditch, dragging the litter behind them. Army Signal Corps photographer Cpl. Alexander Roberts of New York City preceded them and was the first man to reach the body.

Pyle lay on his back in a normal resting position. His unmarked face had the look of a man sleeping peacefully. He had died instantly from a bullet that penetrated the left side of his helmet and entered the left temple. His hands folded across his chest still clutched his battered cap, said to be the same one he carried through his previous campaigns. The litter-bearers placed the body on the stretcher and worked their way slowly back along the ditch under sniper fire. The battle for Ie Shima still remained to be won.

The island probably will be remembered only as the place where America's most famous war correspondent met the death he had been expecting for so long.

—EVAN WYLIE CSp (PR), USCGR

Mussolini: end of the rope

ON APR. 27, 1945, a German convoy of 13 trucks, two passenger cars, and a tank was driving north from Como to the Swiss border. As the convoy rolled into the village of Dongo, Peter Bellini and a group of 11 Partisans jumped up from behind a roadblock with their guns leveled.

Bellini told the convoy commander, an SS lieutenant, that he had orders to search all vehicles to make sure Italian Fascists were not escaping with the Germans. The lieutenant objected to the search, and for four hours they argued until Bellini, bluffing his way, warned that he could summon enough Partisans to wipe out the convoy.

The lieutenant submitted to search. In the back of a truck Benito Mussolini was found, hiding under a blanket. He was wearing a Jerry helmet, sun glasses, and, over his Fascist uniform, a coat belonging to a Luftwaffe sergeant. One of the Germans in the truck told the Partisans that Mussolini was "our drunk comrade," and the Duce burped.

But the trick failed, and Mussolini was taken from the truck. Seventeen other Fascist leaders were found in the same caravan, including Mussolini's 25-year-old mistress, Clara Patacci.

Fearing a possible rescue attempt by the Germans, the Partisans took Mussolini to a secluded mountain cottage. The others were held in the city hall at Dongo. At 4:10 the next afternoon Mussolini and his mistress were shot to death

◄ Benito Mussolini: Once he said, "It is better to die like a lion than live like a lamb . . ."

after a brief trial; the others were executed an hour later.

That night the bodies were taken to Milan in a moving van and dumped in the Piazza Loreto, where they were mutilated and strung up by a mob of angry Italians. The Duce was later buried in a pauper's grave.

The night before he died, Mussolini talked freely with his two Partisan guards, and in this interview with the guards a YANK correspondent tells how Mussolini spent his last hours of life.

•   •   •

IN A COTTAGE in the small mountain hamlet of Giulino di Mezzerge, Benito Mussolini paced the floor nervously. He looked old and drawn in his gray Fascist uniform. He was 62.

Outside the rain fell in the darkness. The room was cold and damp. Mussolini paused in front of the table where Peter Bellini, the Partisan commander, sat smoking a cigarette. He placed his left hand on his stomach, in the old familiar Duce pose, and leaned forward.

"You played a big hand," he told Bellini sarcastically. "The order was to defend me."

Bellini smiled and winked at his lieutenant, George Buffeli, who stood guard at the door. "This makes the second time you have been captured," Bellini said.

"My dear fellow," Mussolini said, "from dust to altar, altar to dust."

"What do you think will become of you?" asked Bellini.

"I know my destiny," Mussolini answered. "I shall be taken to San Donino prison in Como and then to San Vittore prison in Milan." (Mussolini served time in both prisons 30 years ago as a political prisoner.) "I shall be given a trial, and I will tell the world I have been betrayed nine times—the last time by Hitler."

"But why do you arrest me?" Mussolini asked. "What can you accuse me of? The people wanted the war. In 1943, everybody asked me why Italy was so late in declaring war. I didn't declare war. The King signed the declaration of war."

"Why didn't you put the names of all the people in Italy in one bag, and draw out one, and ask that man if Italy should have gone to war?" Buffeli suggested. "Any Italian would have said 'No.'"

Mussolini laughed. "You are a very clever young man."

"Why did you tell the people Germany would win the war?"

"My dear fellow," Mussolini said, "you must know that Hitler's Gestapo was so strong around me I could be alone only in bed."

"Do you realize now," Buffeli continued, "that you were allied with a madman?"

"Hitler was a foolish man," Mussolini answered. "He should have known that it was impossible for one man to become master of the world. Every human force has a limit. A tree cannot grow to the sky."

"Are you convinced now that it is impossible for the Italian people ever to live with the Germans?"

"Yes," Mussolini said. "The Germans, unfortunately, are too cruel."

Mussolini walked to the table in the center of the room and sat down. He shivered slightly. The room had become colder. Bellini offered him the Luftwaffe overcoat which he wore at the time of his capture.

"*Basta Tedeschi*," Mussolini growled and pushed the coat away.

Bellini then asked Mussolini if he wanted something to eat.

"It is not important that I eat," Mussolini said. "But I would like to have a few vegetables and hot coffee."

Bellini smiled. "You forget we do not have coffee any more."

The dicator's last full meal consisted of vegtables, one egg, spaghetti, butter, and warm tea. After dinner he talked again. He recalled his last meeting with Hitler.

"Hitler asked me what I intended to do. I told him I wanted to be a politician, not a militarist. Hitler became angry. 'You must fight as I do,' he said. 'This is the war of the party.' Then he said, 'Remember, Benito, I have lead for my enemies and gas for traitors!'"

"Why did you say in your last speech that Germany would win the war with new secret weapons?" asked Buffeli.

"Germany has no new secret weapons," Mussolini confessed. "Only the V-1 and V-2."

"You mean it was just a bluff?"

"Yes, just a bluff."

"Do you think Italy will ever go to war again?"

"For 50 years, surely not. But after that we cannot be sure," Mussolini said. "The Anglo-Americans will help to bring rebirth to Europe; they will make a barrier against Communism."

Buffeli then asked Mussolini to explain two statements made at the time of Roosevelt's death —Hitler's remark that the world's biggest criminal had died and the Japanese radio comment that a great statesman had died.

"Which was correct?" Buffeli asked.

"Hitler was wrong," Mussolini said. "The world lost a great statesman when Roosevelt died."

"Do you consider Stalin a great man?"

"Yes," answered Mussolini. "Stalin is a very great man. Only a great man could take such a big country with so many different people and accomplish so much."

Commander Bellini turned the conversation to the Duce's family. He asked Mussolini if he knew where his wife Rachele and the two youngest children were, Mussolini said he thought they were probably somewhere between Milan and Como.

"Why didn't you send them to Switzerland?"

Mussolini shrugged his shoulders.

Bellini looked at his watch. It was 11 o'clock. He put on his cap and started to leave; Mussolini stopped him at the door.

"Will you do me a great favor?" Mussolini asked haltingly. "Take my respects to the Madame. Tell her I am well."

"Who is the 'Madame'?" asked Bellini.

Mussolini was silent for a moment. "She is Signorina Petacci," he said reluctantly.

When Bellini had gone, Mussolini asked if he could lie down and rest. "My feet are cold," he said, looking down at his muddy boots. "I would like to warm them."

As Mussolini walked toward the bedroom, Buffeli became suspicious of a black object in the Duce's trouser pocket. He felt to see if it was a gun, but Mussolini smiled and pulled out a black leather glass-case.

In another few minutes Mussolini dropped off to sleep.

In the city hall at Dongo, Clara Petacci sat back, her thin legs crossed, filing a fingernail she had broken during the excitement of the capture. She had asked the Partisans for a manicurist, but they laughed at her. She was wearing a blue woolen suit under her beaver coat; a green scarf was tied in a turban around her brown hair. On her breast was a delicate gold locket. In the lower right corner it bore the inscription: *"Clara—io sono te, tu sei me* (Clara —I am you, you are me)." It was signed "Ben" and was dated Apr. 4, 1939 (when Mussolini met Clara) and Apr. 4, 1941 (when he gave her the locket.

Clara stood up smiling when Commander Bellini approached her. "Mussolini asked me to bring his respects," Bellini told her. "He is feeling well."

"But why should Mussolini greet me?" Clara asked innocently. "I do not know Mussolini."

"Don't play with me," Bellini said impatiently. "I know who you are."

"You will not kill me," she pleaded. "I have done nothing."

Bellini didn't answer.

"All right. Since you know who I am," she said, "please do me one favor. Let me be with him during his last moments of life."

The commander turned to a guard and told him to take Clara to a nearby cottage while he went to get Mussolini.

The Duce was sleeping when Bellini went to his room. Bellini shook him.

"Get up. I'm taking you to Petacci."

Mussolini sat up, rubbing his eyes.

"I was waiting for this," he said.

Clara was at the cottage when Mussolini arrived. They looked at each other as though they were strangers. Then Mussolini said, "Why, Madame, do you choose to share this terrible moment with me?"

"I want it so," Clara answered, and walked into the bedroom. Mussolini followed her and closed the door behind them.

—SGT. DAN POLIER

Fall of Berlin

BERLIN IS WET AND SAD and the smoke of its fires boils up to join clouds that hang low over the city, allowing a shrouding rain to drift down first on this block, then on that. And the sun fights through an occasional thin spot in the clouds, but its light is intercepted by the haze and the smoke. The effect is of the interior of a cathedral at dusk. It is weird, this view of the corpse of a city at midday.

This is two days after Berlin fell. From a deserted street comes the rattle of an automatic weapon and the staccato echo with a metallic ring, and then there is quiet. Down the block somewhere men face each other in the ultimate moment of decision by gunfire, and the effort of attack or defense consumes them wholly. There is no physical sign of the men who fight.

Berlin, the capital city of Nazi Germany, has come to a violent end. Berlin looks dead, and not only dead but desecrated. Its people, fearful and bewildered, wander without purpose in its streets, and the streets are befouled by the remains of a city devastated.

Along one mound of debris a family group—men and women—have formed a line and are passing bricks, one at a time, from hand to hand, to some one who places them in his own way, perhaps to brace a sagging foundation or perhaps only to stow them for future use at some place unseen from the street.

Physically there is a great deal more to be said of the wreckage of Berlin than might have been said of the wreckage of Aachen or Essen or Cologne. In Berlin buildings still stand as they did in Essen. Streets have been blocked by falling walls as they were in Cologne, and the damp smell of decomposition is the same. And in Berlin, as in the early days during and after the taking of Aachen, there seem to be fewer citizens of the city than there should be.

But in Berlin there is a feeling that here has ended not only a city but a nation, that here a titanic force has come to catastrophe.

Russians swarmed along the Tiergarten—walking, riding bicycles, driving shrapnel-studded automobiles, riding the backs of tanks which roared their powerful insolence past the shell of the Adlon Hotel.

In the Tiergarten, a park bisected by an avenue called Charlotteburger Chaussee, a German fighter crashed, and its bulk is a masterpiece of humiliation — the humiliation of a defending plane flung back upon the ground it was sworn to defend.

Berlin is a series of impressions . . . the strange twisted mouth of a horse that died by shrapnel, the brilliant grin of a Russian girl directing traffic as she flips a salute with the pert grace of a wren flipping its tail, the parked cars in front of the Reichstag, and the obviously important Russians who stand on the steps as conquerors.

There is the unceasing sense of powerful movement as the Russians explore this city which they have just taken, driving around with a boundless enthusiasm. There are Russians eating beside a chow wagon, and a soldier washing down his food with vodka. In Unter Den Linden are the bodies of civilians, the dust of their famous street like grease paint on their faces. And by Brandenburg Gate, in a small building that has spilled its guts inward on the floor, is an old woman, alone. She lies on the debris, trying to support herself on an elbow. She has stockings but no shoes on her feet. The woman slowly moves her head from side to side, dying.

—SGT. MACK MORRISS

Hitler: end of the Reich

GIs saw *the same story everywhere: broken cities, women standing dazed in the ruins, long lines of German prisoners heading for the cages. The end of the Fourth Reich, which Hitler said would last a thousand years, was approaching.*

At Berchtesgaden in the great banquet hall where the leaders of the National Socialist Party once met to chart plans of conquest, a grand piano stood in the center of the ruins.

With one finger a GI picked out "Deep in the

"Heil Hitler—the bastard!"

"Heil Hitler, the bastard!" was the GI's toast.

"Heil *batard!*" toasted the Frenchmen.

It was hard to tell which caused more damage to this palatial hideout in the Bavarian Alps— the 350 Lancasters which bombed it on April 25, or the 2,000 SS men who looted and burned it a few days before the Americans arrived. The net result was the same: The place was a weird jumble of twisted and burned buildings.

The roads and woods were littered with empty wine bottles. "It looks to me," said a sergeant, "like they were expecting to defend the place with wine bottles."

At the Eagle's Nest, a stone cottage high above Berchtesgaden, GIs poked among the books and furniture—now marked with the prints of GI combat boots—and talked about what happened to Hitler.

Most of the servants were sure that Hitler and his mistress, Eva Braun, had either killed themselves in Berlin or had been killed by Russian artillery fire and buried where their bodies could never be found.

"The Fuehrer was a good master," said Elly Danat, a housemaid. "My four children shall know about him. Tell me, are the Jews coming back? Will they kill my children?"

A rifleman named Arnold Patterson said he hoped Hitler was still alive and that the Russians would catch him.

"I once read," he said, "about a bunch of natives who caught a fellow on an island and tied him, behind-down, on a bamboo sprout. When they came back later, the bamboo was growing out of this fellow's ears."

At the bottom of the mountain, below Hitler's estate, Pfc. William Crawford and T-5 George Liekhues, 3d Division medics, looked up the winding road. "When I was at Salerno," said Crawford, "I never figured I'd wind up the war in Hitler's home."

"Can't think of a better place to wind up a war at," said Liekhues.

"I can," said Crawford. "My home town."

—SGT. HARRY SIONS

Heart of Texas." The doughs with him cheered.

In the spacious hallway, a 3d Division rifleman and two French soldiers sat around a mahogany table, taking turns swigging from a bottle of Moselle.

Fall of Germany

THE TWO WEEKS *that ended with the Germans signing an official surrender at 2:41 A.M. on Monday, May 7, 1945, were crammed with more important happenings than any other equal period thus far in the war. From the fall of Cologne and the massing of Russian assault forces on the east bank of the Oder, the fact of final German defeat had been obvious. The climax came in these last two big weeks, and when it came news flash tumbled upon news flash, rumor upon rumor, surrender upon surrender, so quickly that the average GI could hardly grasp one Allied triumph before he was caught up by the impact of the next. . . .*

·   ·   ·

The two weeks before Germany's surrender began with the Russian battle for possession of Berlin in full swing. Below Berlin, near Torgau on the Elbe, tankmen of the U.S. First Army were beginning to pick up snatches of Russian combat directions on their mobile radios. Marshal Ivan Konev's forces were moving to meet them. All along the Western Front an Allied nutcracker was breaking up the vaunted "hard core" of German defense. U.S. Lt. Gen. William H. Simpson's Ninth Army was pushing east from Magdeburg; Gen. George S. Patton's tankmen were cowboying toward the Czech border; the First Canadian Army was at Emden; the first French Army was past Stuttgart; Lt. Gen. Alexander Patch's U.S. Seventh Army was south of the Danube near Lauringer, and other units of Gen. Jacob L. Devers' Sixth Army Group threatened Bavaria; British Field Marshal Sir Bernard L. Montgomery's Twenty-first Army Group was bringing complete freedom to the Netherlands and Denmark. From their side the

Russians continued the same inexorable squeeze that had forced the Germans back from their high tide of eastern aggression before Leningrad and Stalingrad. Marshal Gregory Zhukov's First White Russians were in Berlin. Marshal Konev was almost to the Elbe River. Gen. Tolbukhin's Third Ukrainian Army cut into the Nazi redoubt. Gen. Rodion Malinovsky had pushed through Vienna and was following the Danube deeper into Austria. In Italy the long, dull stalemate of Lt. Gen. Mark W. Clark's polyglot armies had been broken. The U.S. 10th Mountain Infantry Division had spearheaded a breakthrough, and the war in Italy had a moving front again—a moving front of Fifth Army veterans, including American Negro troops and Japanese-Americans and Brazilian Allies and Free Italian troops, and British and Indian GIs of the famous Eighth, which had swept across Africa in 1943—all of them aided by the sabotage and behind-the-lines action of Italian partisans in the north and by the sharp, constant pressure against the German eastern flank from Marshal Tito's Yugoslavs. Hitler's Germany was going down in flames.

·   ·   ·

Moving forward with the U.S. Ninth Army into the confusion of a dying Reich, YANK *staff correspondent Sgt. Allan B. Ecker observed the symptoms of collapse:*

A ferryboat, a big barge propelled by the hand-over-hand cable system, was loaded to the gills with about 60 displaced persons, German nationals, and American GIs crossing west over the Elbe from a strictly unofficial American 35th Division bridgehead on the other side of the river. A patrol of K Company of the 137th

Infantry under Lt. Howard Pierson of Huntington, Ore., and S/Sgt. Denzil Lindbom of Peoria, Ill., had made a crossing to the eastern bank for a brief reconnoitering, but they'd run into a peculiar situation.

Everybody and his uncle in the little town of Ferchland insisted on going back with them. So the boys set up a ferryboat. One of the passengers on the way back was a German woman with four kids, the youngest five months old, all of them wailing to beat the band. Asked where she was coming from and where she was heading, she replied in words which seemed to sum up the whole plight of the German nation crushed between two fronts: "We left Brandenburg two days ago because the Russian bombs and shells leveled our home there. Where are we going? To a big city where we have relatives.

"Perhaps you've been there? It's called Aachen."

Among the prize catches of the 102d Division was an attractive and much-married female Gestapo agent whose current and fourth husband is an *SS* major general. Interrogated at her hideaway house in the woods by German-born Edward Hoffer of New York City, the frau was much embarrassed by one question. She couldn't remember the first name of her first husband with whom she had lived for seven years until 1929.

As Russian and American forces converged on the Western Front, a rumor started back among the 8th Armored Division men around Braunschweig that a junction had already been effected. "Just take a look at those two guys if you don't believe it," GIs advised cynics.

"Those two guys" were honest-to-God Red Army first lieutenants, one of them an ex-member of the Crimea General Staff. They were, to be sure, a trifle out of uniform: GI ODs and field jackets, German leather boots and Lugers, Russian shoulder insignia and GI helmets with big red stars and the words "Soviet Union" painted on them.

Picked out of a horde of Russian slave labor-

ers and war prisoners wandering along the highways and byways of Germany, the two officers had been given razors, baths, and equipment by the 8th Armored's 88th Cavalry Recon Squadron. Thus transformed, they were ready—with the aid of Russian-speaking Pfc. Frank Ilchuk of New York City—to organize some of the thousands of their countrymen into orderly communities in each village. Many starving Russians, newly liberated, had taken to pillaging and cluttering up important roadways. The use of Red Army officers to control them and the requisitioning of rations from local German burgomeisters was put into effect to take the load off American combat units until military-government authorities arrived in sufficient numbers to take over.

IN THE NEWS, as the first of the two last weeks wore on, you heard less about Adolf Hitler and more about Heinrich Himmler, his Gestapo chief. There were increasing rumors of Hitler's disappearance or his death or his madness and with them increasing rumors of a Himmler bid for peace. The peace rumors reached a climax in a false Armistice announcement in the U.S. on Apr. 28.

The story behind the false armistice—Himmler's attempt to surrender to the U.S. and Great Britain and leave Russia holding the bag—was true. But the chief fact behind the Himmler trial balloon was fear, German fear before an assault the Germans now knew they could not withstand.

Gen. George S. Patton's Third Army was an arrow aimed at Hitler's Berchtesgaden mountain hideaway. U.S. troops took Italy's chief naval base at La Spezia. Genoa fell. The aged ex-chief of Vichy France, Marshal Petain, came through Switzerland to give himself up for trial in liberated France. The Germans in Italy were shoved back into the Alps, and their lines of possible retreat were all but cut off. Great Britain and the U.S. refused to be parties to any peace overtures which did not include their Russian ally. At Torgau, advance groups of the First Army's 69th Division made contact with the 58th Guards Division of Konev's First Ukrainian Army.

• • •

Sgt. Ed Cunningham, YANK staff correspondent, was with the First Army to report the meeting:

A 28-man, six-jeep patrol of the 69th Division Yanks under the command of 1st Lt. Albert Kotzebue of Houston, Tex., and his platoon sergeant, T/Sgt. Frederick Johnston of Bradford, Penna., and a Russian cavalry patrol made the first link-up between the Eastern and Western Fronts. The meeting took place on a hill outside the village of Zautwitz just before 1330 hours on Apr. 25.

The jeeps roared up the hill smack into the middle of a group of hard-riding Cossacks who were patroling the area in search of stray pockets of German resistance. Both units recognized each other so there was none of the confusion that attended some later Russki-Yank meetings.

The Cossacks detailed a Russian civilian to guide Lt. Kotzebue and his men to where the CG of the Russian division was waiting to greet them on the other side of the hill. Then they galloped off in search of more Germans.

The American patrol crossed the Elbe in jeeps ferried on a platform raft and fell headlong into a lively Russian celebration.

A Russian major who spoke a few words of English set the tone of the celebration with a toast. "Today," he said, "we have the most happy day of our lives. The years 1941 and 1942 were a most difficult time. Germany was at Stalingrad. It was the most difficult time of our lives. At that time we do not think of our lives; we think of our country.

"Just now, our great friends and we have met one another, and it is the end of our enemy. Long live your great leader. Long live our great leader. Long live our great countries."

Maj. Fred Craig of Friendship, Tenn., and 2d Lt. Thomas R. Howard of Mississippi were in command of the second patrol to meet the Russians. They made contact at 3:45 P.M. Apr. 25 at Clanzchwitz with a column of Russian cavalry.

The Russians galloped across an open field to meet them, throwing their helmets in the air. Maj. Craig was ferried across the river and taken back to the Russian corps headquarters to meet the lieutenant general commanding. The general asked him if he were the highest American officer available to greet him, and Maj. Craig explained that his was only a patrol, not the official greeting party.

The major and his men had two meals with the Russians, one at 1900 and one at 0930 the next morning. Once again there were toasts and mutual greetings. The Russians had several cameramen on hand to record the meeting and seemed sorry we didn't have any of our own. The general told the major he was sending a message direct to Stalin to inform him of the meeting. The Russians and Yanks fired each other's weapons and criticized them. Red Army men found our M1 too heavy for their taste but liked our carbine and .30-caliber machineguns.

During the night the radio operators at the major's CP on the west bank of the Elbe relieved each other so they could cross and enjoy the Russian party. A Cossack column stopped by the CP and put on a two-hour serenade of Russian songs with harp, mouth organ, and accordion accompaniment.

In the morning a Russian barber shaved the Yanks in bed.

The third U.S. patrol to contact the Russians had a more confusing time of it. It was led by 2nd Lt. William D. Robertson, 1st Battalion, 273d Regiment, 69th Division, who had studied Japanese as an ASTP man, a factor which was as useful as an extra toenail in establishing friendly relations.

Robertson and his three-man patrol reached the town of Torgau on the banks of the Elbe after a 27-mile jeep ride through the no-man's-land then separating our forces. He spotted Red Army men on the opposite bank and shouted to them: "Amerikanski! Come over. Friends! *Tovarisch!*" But the Russians weren't having any, since a German patrol had tried to get next to them by pretending to be Americans the day before.

Robertson and his three-man GI patrol weren't daunted and proceeded to manufacture an American flag from cloth and red, white, and blue paint procured at a Torgau store. They waved their flag at the Russians from the tower of a castle. The Russians fired two colored flares, the agreed link-up signal. But Robertson had no flares to fire back.

The Russians were now thoroughly convinced that something phony was afoot. They opened up with an antitank gun and small-arms fire on the castle and scored two direct hits.

An American naval lieutenant, a newly freed PW, came up about that time. He spoke Russian and so did a Russian liberated slave worker who was nearby. Between the two of them, they managed to shout the news across the Elbe that the patrol was really Americans and wanted to meet the Russians.

Then and then only did the Russians relent and allow Robertson and his men to cross to their bank. Once across, the meeting followed the pattern already set. There were vodka and backslapping; there were toasts and mutual congratulations.

The climactic meeting, of course, was when Maj. Gen. Emil E. Reinhardt of Decatur, Ga., CG of the 69th, made his official visit to Lt. Gen. Rosakov, CG of the 58th Guards Division. The major general and three staff officers crossed the Elbe and returned in a slim German racing boat, so delicately balanced that all officers had to sit at attention in order not to tip themselves over into the drink. The shell had been designed for sport, not transportation, but it was the only craft available at the section of the Elbe where Gen. Reinhardt crossed and where the Germans had blown the only two bridges.

Sgt. Andrew Marriack, of Hudson, N. Y., served as an interpreter for a Russian captain who told some of the Americans gathered by the river how his men had taken Torgau. Marriack had learned his Russian as an ASTP student at City College in New York.

"They took this town two days ago," he translated. "It wasn't much of a fight, but the captain got sore because the Germans ambushed one of his patrols. He says a gang of krauts held up a white flag and, when his patrol came over to take them prisoner, they threw down the flag and opened fire, killing two of his men. He says the Germans don't fight like human beings; they're treacherous and they destroy towns and civilian populations without any cause. He says the Russians will stay in Germany until the Germans are capable of respecting the rights of other people. He doesn't . . ."

The roar of an exploding grenade, which landed in the river several yards away from the party, interrupted. Some of the Americans who had just arrived hit the ground. Marriack, who didn't seem disturbed, said, "That's nothing to worry about. Just one of the Russian soldiers showing one of our guys how their grenades work. They always fire their weapons when you ask about them; they figure a demonstration is the best answer they can give."

Outside of the actual meetings, the unoccupied area which separated the Russian forces on the Elbe from the American forces on the Mulde River was the most interesting and the screwiest part of the link-up picture. Hundreds of German soldiers streamed along the roads leading to the American lines, unguarded and all but forgotten in the excitement of the Russki-Yank junction. They had been disarmed by advance American patrols and ordered to make their own way to our PW cages because we didn't have enough GIs around at the time to escort them. Most of them seemed to be happy to be out of the fighting.

Unlike the reception we got in the dash from the Rhine to the Mulde, where the civilians accepted our entry in sullen silence, the people between the Mulde and the Elbe welcomed us like returning heroes. They stood on the curbs of no-man's-land towns, waving and laughing.

None of their waves and smiles were returned.

FEAR WAS BECOMING an all-pervading thing in Germany. No matter which way the Germans turned they found the Allies moving in on them. On Apr. 29, the 12th Armored Division, the 20th Armored Division, and the 42d Infantry Division of Gen. Patch's Seventh Army took Munich, birthplace and shrine of the Nazi party. The Fifth Army took Milan and the British Eighth took Venice, and from the north of Italy, from the village of Dongo on Lake Como, came word of the death of Mussolini.

Pierre Laval, the "honest trader" who had sold France out to Hitler, fled from Germany to Spain and was interned. The Seventh Army took Dachau, the most infamous of all Nazi concentration camps and one of the oldest. The Ninth Army made its contact with the Russians just north of the First near Wittenberg.

•   •   •

YANK correspondent Sgt. Ecker was still with the Ninth and observed sidelights of the second junction of Allied armies:

It doesn't take a second look to know the Russians are planning to stick around for a while in Germany. In our area, American flags are few and far between, mostly on military-government offices, but over on the Russian side almost every window of the occupied town buildings flies a red flag instead of the white surrender flags we leave up. There's another more conclusive proof of the permanence of Russia's intentions: German signposts, left up in our area, have been torn down by the Russians and new ones in their language substituted.

Among the many other things that the Russians can do better than the Germans is the fine art of sloganeering. The Germans in many

cities have painted a vast number of inspirational mottoes on the walls of the houses and public buildings, but none can quite measure up in concise impact to this Soviet slogan lettered in white on red banners flying in the street here: "Death to the Fascist aggressors!" For the benefit of the American allies, a special two-language flag was displayed in Wittenberg, scene of a meeting between the Russian and American corps generals. This is the way it read in English: "Long live the great leaders, President Trumen, Marchall Stalin and Premer Churchill." Lots of wiseacres bet Stalin's name came first in the Russian version of the same slogan, but they were wrong.

THE ALLIED FLOOD rolled on. It was a great period for capturing Nazi field marshals like Wilhelm Ritter von Leeb and Wilhelm List, both of whom had been kingpins in the Nazi drives that overthrew Poland and France and both of whom had had less luck in the invasion of Russia. Adm. Nicholas Horthy, Nazi-controlled dictator of Hungary, was captured. All three were picked up by the Seventh Army. Lt. Gen. Kurt Dittmar, leading German military commentator, surrendered to the Ninth. And then came the biggest story of all. The German radio announced that Hitler had died in action in Berlin. The Russians, who had by this time freed Berlin of all but street fighting, agreed that Hitler was dead, not as a fighting soldier but as a suicide. They said that Goebbels, his warped little propaganda minister, had also died by his own hand. Tired of too many German tricks, most Allied authorities reserved comment; they would believe Hitler dead when they saw his body. But a dead Hitler made for cheerful talk.

•   •   •

In Paris, Sgt. DeWitt Gilpin, YANK field correspondent, took a sample of public opinion on the subject of Hitler's death:

Lt. William J. Cullerton of Chicago, a fighter

pilot who was left for dead a few weeks ago after a German *SS* man fired a .35 slug through his stomach, sat in a Paris hotel and talked about the late Adolf Hitler.

"I hope the sonuvabitch was as scared of dying as I was when that *SS* officer let me have it through the stomach," he said. "I thought I'd had it.

"Now they say Hitler is dead. Maybe he is. If he is, I don't believe he died heroically. Somehow I can't figure Hitler dying in action. And I don't think Hitler's death changes anything about Germany. It might be just part of a deal to soften us up so they can stick another knife in the soft spot."

Two Eighth Air Force aerial gunners, who like Cullerton were sweating out a ride back to the States from the same hotel, said that they hadn't believed the news of Hitler's death when they first heard it shortly after the 104th Division liberated them from the Alten Grabow PW Camp.

S/Sgt. Henry J. Smith of Scranton, Penna., said: "I came down near Stutlitz about nine months ago and I just had time to get out of my 'chute before German civilians started beating me up. One old man of about 60 broke a .22 rifle over me. But when we left Germany all the people were forcing smiles for us. And that old guy would smile too, now. Mussolini is dead, Hitler is dead—but what's the difference? There are lots more."

S/Sgt. William Cupp of Tipton, Ia., who came down in Belgium and beat his way to within 200 yards of the American lines—then near Paris—before the Germans got him, said: "They want to make Hitler a martyr for the German kids. Most of them are pretty much for him as it is."

At the 48th General Hospital, Sgt. Allan Pettit of Verndale, Minn., and the 78th Division, was well enough to be going out on pass. He had been hit twice before on the Roer River, but this time it was only concussion, and now he had a chance to see Paris.

"Why waste words on Hitler?" he asked. "And how do you know for sure? Anyway he picked a damned good Nazi to take his place. That crazy Doenitz fought us in the last war."

Over in another ward filled with combat men just in from the front, it was the entertainment hour and as a special favor to Cpl. Peter Stupihin—a Red Army man suffering from prison-camp malnutrition—a singer rendered "Kalinka." The GIs thought that was fine, and those who felt strong enough called for tunes like "Stardust" and "I'll Be Seeing You."

A red-headed Southerner from the 4th Division was feeling good because the doctor had finished dressing the shrapnel wound in his chest, and he had something to say about Hitler and his Germany between songs.

"I wish I was the guy who killed him," he said. "I'd have killed him a little slower. Awful slow."

In the Tout Paris Bar some men from the 101st Airborne and the 29th Divisions worked at having a good time with pilots from the Troop Carrier Command. There were Wacs in the party too, but the attention they were getting came mostly from pilots. Some infantrymen were arguing about what their outfits did and where.

A pianist was pounding out what he considered American swing, and it wasn't the place for a name-and-address interview. An Infantry captain who'd had a few drinks didn't waste much time on Hitler.

"Yeah, I guess he's dead," he said, "but so are a lot of *good* guys. And you just remember that."

Then the infantrymen went back to arguing about what had happened at Bastogne.

IN A VERY DIFFERENT SETTING, *in the PW section of a Third Army post in Bavaria,* YANK *correspondent Cpl. Howard Katzander got a very different slant on what might lie behind Hitler's death from a source a little closer to Berchtesgaden:*

The colonel was out of uniform—regrettably so for an officer of his rank in the Third Army area—but he carried it off well. He was average in height, slim, and blond-haired. He carried a crooked cane and was dressed in green cotton trousers and a pepper-and-salt sport jacket zippered up the front. He wore grey suede gloves, and as he talked he sat crosslegged, occasionally slapping at one trim brown oxford, composed and nonchalant as if he were back on his father's East Prussian estates in the heart of Germany's Junkerland.

The story he was telling was the story of why the war did not end last July. It was the story of the attempt to assassinate Hitler and he knew all about it. Because this was Lt. Col. Wilhelm Kuebart, a member of the Wehrmacht General Staff, and one of the original plotters.

Kuebart was a Junker gentleman of the Prussian militarist class with a long military tradition behind him. His wife was the daughter of a Junker general. His uncles were Reichswehr officers and before them his grandfather and great-grandfathers as far back as his memory went. Only his father had departed from the tradition to embrace a profession as an architect.

In the fall of 1932 Wilhelm Kuebart entered the Reichswehr as an officer-candidate. He was commissioned as a second lieutenant in the fall of 1934.

From then on his rise was rapid and in the best Junker tradition. He participated in the Polish campaign in the late summer of 1939 as a first lieutenant and in the summer of 1940 he became a captain and was transferred to the staff of the 18th Panzer Division. In the early spring of 1941 his talents and family background received due recognition and he was sent to the Kriegsakademi—the General Staff School—after which he joined Von Leeb's staff in the Central Army Group on the Russian front.

It was there that Kuebart was inoculated with the anti-Hitler virus in its most violent form. Almost the entire staff of this army group was anti-Hitler.

This was not unusual. The Junker officer class was probably the most exclusive club in the world. Its members regarded the military as the only career fit for a gentleman and the Wehrmacht as its own private sphere.

Kuebart had taken a pretty dim view of the Nazi regime from the begining, the way he told it, and had never joined the National Socialist Democratic Workers Party. Kuebart and his fellow officers felt that their ranks had degenerated under Hitler, and they were particularly resentful of Himmler's attempt to spy on the officers and impose SS control over them.

Hitler's spectacular failures as general and Supreme Commander of the Armies led to open revolt. The disaster at Stalingrad was the last straw.

From that time on the most popular subject of conversation among officers of the old school was the question of how to get rid of Hitler and Himmler. Kuebart had been sponsored for a place on the General Staff by Col. Hansen, Chief of the Wehrmacht Intelligence Service, and Hansen was the brains behind the plot against Hitler's life. The burgomeister of Leipzig, Boerdler, was to take political control. Hansen went to Zeitzler, Chief of the General Staff, and persuaded him that immediate action was necessary.

The date for the assassination was set for July 13. The weekly conference between Hitler and his generals was to be held as usual on that day. But, at the last minute, there were two hitches. Himmler was going to be present and Hitler decided to hold the conference in a flimsy wooden barracks.

The bomb that had been prepared to wipe out Hitler and Himmler was designed for use in Hitler's underground headquarters where heavy concrete walls and the earth itself would confine the force of the blast to the small room.

When the bomb was exploded in the frame building above ground—it had been brought to the conference in a briefcase—its force was dissipated. Hitler was injured, but not seriously.

The attempt to assassinate him had failed.

It could not be proven definitely that Kuebart had plotted against the Supreme Commander, but it was felt that he had betrayed his trust as an officer of the Wehrmacht. Accordingly, a crushing blow was dealt him. He was expelled from the Wehrmacht as *undwirdikeit,* unworthy of the honor of wearing the uniform. He was forbidden to reenter the Army even as a buck private. He was kept under constant Gestapo surveillance, apparently in the hope that his movements would betray others who had taken part in the plot.

Kuebart said that 120 high German officers were hanged as a result of the plot, and 700 others were waiting execution.

When American troops overran the area where Kuebart had been living with his wife and two children since his expulsion from the Army, he calmly walked into the CP of B Battery, 551st Antiaircraft Artillery Battalion, and told his story. He expected to speak his piece and go home to his wife and kiddies. He had papers to show that he had been expelled from the German Army. He assured his interrogators that his group had been prepared to sue for peace immediately if their plot had succeeded.

But he did not go home to the wife and kiddies. Somehow or other, the Third Army did not feel that his expulsion from the Army relieved him of responsibility for the part he had played up to that time. He is now in a PW cage and knows no more than anyone else of what actually happened to Hitler this time.

ADM. DOENITZ was named as Hitler's successor—the new Fuehrer. It was asserted that Hitler himself had nominated the Grand Admiral of the German Fleet to carry on his job. It was possible: Doenitz was a devout Nazi; he was also the man who had helped perfect wolf-pack submarine warfare. Goering, once head of the Luftwaffe, was no longer a factor in anything except guessing games—he was crazy; he was a suicide; he had escaped abroad. Von Ribbentrop was out as German Foreign Minister, and cagey Count Lutz Schwerin von Krosigk was in. Berlin fell on May 2. Field Marshal Arnim von Rundstedt had already been added to the list of captured field marshals by the Seventh Army. Also on May 2 it was announced that German forces in Italy and southern Austria had surrendered at Caserta. Free Czechs started their own revolt and battled Germans in Prague. The Fifth and Seventh Armies met at Vipiteno, Italy. On May 4 all the German forces in Holland, Denmark, and northwest Germany surrendered.

By now the Allied advance had gathered unstoppable force. On May 5 the First and Nineteenth Armies, comprising German Army Group G, surrendered to Gen. Jacob L. Devers' U.S. Sixth Army Group in Western Austria and Bavaria; the German First and Nineteenth surrendered to the U.S. Seventh and French First; the German Twenty-Fourth Army surrendered to the French First. The Germans were preparing to give up Norway.

•   •   •

On Sunday, May 6, at Reims, France, Col. Gen. Gustav Jodl signed a formal surrender for all German armed forces. YANK's *Sgt. Gilpin was at Reims when GIs there got the news:*

The 201st MP Company, whose members handled the guard details when the Germans came to Reims to surrender, is a celebrity-wise outfit. Gen. Eisenhower knows many of the men by their first names, and some of them have dined at Churchill's home. They have been the gun-carrying soldiers on hand during a succession of visits to high headquarters by Nazi bigwigs like Franz von Papen, who was described by one of them as looking like "an old goat in golf knickers."

The MPs said Gen. Jodl looked and acted more like the popular idea of a German militarist than any of the other German officers with him at the surrender meeting. He walked and talked with the arrogance that the Junkers have developed through a long series of wars. He didn't seem to drink as much as some of the others, and before and after each conference the MP outside his bedroom window could see him examining his face in his mirror. After the last conference session Jodl came back to his room, threw open the windows, and looked down at Pfc. Jack H. Arnold of Lancaster, Penna. After peering at Arnold, he inhaled deeply and then twisted and pulled at his face before the mirror.

Adm. Hans von Friedeburg, of all the Germans, seems to have impressed the MPs most as what they called a "character." In the words of Pfc. Joseph Fink, who used to build Burroughs adding machines in Detroit, "The Admiral had enough medals hanging on his chest to decorate a Christmas tree."

The house in which the Germans stayed during the conference looked like a shack on the outside and a palace on the inside. There were paintings on the walls and a grandfather clock, inlaid tile in the bathrooms, and comfortable double beds in the bedrooms. There was a bit of a fuss over the first meal because someone had forgotten to get the red wine. Pfc. Frederick A. Stones of Pittsburgh, Penna., commented privately, "If I was running this show I'd throw them a can of C-rations."

Stones say that his proposed diet had a practical as well as a vindictive side in that it might have helped shorten the negotiations.

Once Pfc. Joyce Bennet, Wac manageress of the German billets, asked two of the GI orderlies to straighten up the beds of the German officers. The GIs complied but bitched. "We're usually assigned to British Air Marshal Tedder," one of them said, "and he straightens up his own bed and so could these guys."

Speaking of the Germans, a little blackhaired Wac from Tarentum, Penna., said, "I felt terribly uneasy serving them coffee. Some officer made a crack about my waiting on Germans while my husband was still shooting them. He didn't stop to think that I'd have preferred to have been spilling the hot coffee down their necks."

Jodl's firm Junker penstroke made it official. ▶

THE NEWS *of the surrender was to have been held up for a simultaneous announcement by President Truman, Premier Stalin, and Prime Minister Churchill, but, in spite of censorship precautions, it leaked out and set off celebrations in all Allied capitals.* YANK *reporters in overseas posts from Paris to Saipan heard the good news as it spread from soldier to soldier, in combat, in camp, and on the streets of pass towns:*

The announcement came as an anticlimax to men of the Ninth Army, just as it did to most of the rest of the world. They had been relieved for the last time on the Western Front some days before the signing at Reims and their relief was to them the real end of the war in Europe. Pfc. S. L. Gates, who has a brother in the Marines in the Pacific, figured he'd be heading there soon. Most of the talk was like that—either of home or of possible Pacific duty.

In Paris, where the news had begun as a phony rumor and then turned true, it was an anticlimax, too. A photographer staged a shot with some French babes kissing some over-happy doughs in front of the Rainbow Corner. "I keep telling everybody that it's over," said an MP at the door of the Red Cross Club, "but nobody believes me."

Finally, when Paris believed the news, it was just a big-city celebration—crowds and singing and cheers and lots of cognac and girls. People stopped work, and airplanes of all the Allied forces buzzed the Champs Elysees. Pvt. Ernest Kuhn of Chicago listened to the news come over the radio at the 108th General Hospital. He had just been liberated after five months in a Nazi PW camp, and he still had some shrapnel in his throat. "I listened to Churchill talk," he said, "and I kept saying to myself, 'I'm still alive. The war is over here and I'm still alive.' I thought of all the guys in the 28th Division Band with me who were dead now. We used to be a pretty good band."

In London there were crowds too, and singing and kissing and cheering. Everybody you spoke to said the news was swell, but they all added a postscript about the Japs. The end of the war in Europe seemed to bring the Pacific war closer than ever to GIs here. Cpl. Robert M. Rhodes of Kittanning, Penna., who works in a base ordnance depot in the U.K., said, "I just can't believe it's over on this side. That is, I can't realize it yet. I figure this VE-Day is just one step nearer New York and the Statue of Liberty. I figure it'll take 10 to 12 more months to get rid of the Japs. I'm just going to write home to my wife, 'So far, so good. I'll be seeing you.' "

Nobody got very excited on Saipan when the news came over the B-29 squadrons' loudspeakers in the morning. It was like the Hawaiian reaction, only stronger. M/Sgt. Wilbur M. Belshaw, a flight engineer from Vesta, Minn., said what was uppermost in GIs' minds: "The Japs thought they could lick the world. Well, now they've got their chance."

On Okinawa, GIs and Marines continued to kill Japs and to be killed by them. It was raining when the VE announcement was broadcast over loudspeakers, and the artillery and the noise of planes made it hard to understand. Besides, almost everybody was too busy to pay much attention to it.

Ordeal on Okinawa

THE G-2 CAPTAIN was leery about calling it a typical night on Okinawa. On the other hand, it could not be considered particularly unusual.

However G-2 wanted to classify it, the night of May 15 had been another night in the battle for Okinawa. And to infantrymen of the Army and Marine divisions inching south toward Naha, Shuri, and Yonabaru each day and each night was pretty much like another. The pattern was well established—planes and artillery pounded the positions; foot soldiers fought their way up each hill, held it against counterattacks, and fought their way down the reverse slopes. There were a lot of hills and a lot of Japs. Progress was slow and costly.

When night came the men who had fought all day stopped trying to advance and dug in, not so much to sleep as to hide. For it was then that the enemy, who did his daylight fighting from caves, tombs, and concealed pillboxes, came out to counterattack and infiltrate, to probe and harass. When dawn came he was gone again, leaving only the dead behind. And the tired men counted bodies and wondered how many they had really been fighting.

On the left flank the 96th Division moved slowly down the east coast toward Yonabru. The 382d Infantry was trying to take Dick Hill. At 0700 on the 15th they moved forward. The Japs on the rear slopes blanketed them with mortars. Machineguns hidden in caves pinned them down. Snipers hung on their flanks. Men fought forward, but casualties were heavy.

By late afternoon there were only three non-coms and one officer left in L Company. The second and third platoons were combined to make one unit.

At dusk they were halfway up the forward slope of Dick Hill. Word was passed to dig in for the night. This turned out to be not so easy as it sounded. Underneath a thin surface of churned earth and patches of torn grass lay a substantial stratum of shale; pack shovels made little impression on it. Long after dark some of the company were still digging. Others had doubled up, two or three in a one-man foxhole.

Sgt. Bill House of Portland, Ore., had a command hole in the center of the slope. It was hardly big enough for one, but he was sharing it with S/Sgt. Ludas and Pfc. Nordgren. The hole was cramped and uncomfortable, but they had to give up trying to enlarge it. Every movement of an arm, leg, or shoulder caused another cave-in in the wall of loose dirt they had erected around them to make up for the foxhole's shallow depth.

It began to rain, a steady, cold drizzle that brought with it a thick, clinging ground mist. The men ate a supper of C-ration meat-and-vegetable stew and set a night guard—one man on watch while the other two tried to sleep. House had the first watch. He settled himself in the limited space, one leg folded under him, his M1 across his knees.

In his mind he reviewed his position. His men were spread out across the slope. Further over to the left was K Company. That made that flank pretty sure. On the right, however, things were not so good. After the line crossed the slope, it dropped back, leaving the company's flank exposed.

The nightly artillery duel was under way. Jap heavy stuff rushed across the valley. House could hear it landing far behind the lines. American artillery became interested in the slope of Dick Hill. Shells whistled overhead and began bursting in Jap positions. The enemy replied with mortars. The first few rounds dropped haphazardly until some Jap was satisfied he had the range he wanted. Then they began to work the slope over methodically. Bursts moved up and down and across the hill. Each one was a little nearer to the center.

House wanted to get down further in the hole, but he was afraid to stop watching. The barrage might be a cover for an attempt at in-filtration. He slid down as far as he dared, peering out into the murk through the slit formed between the rim of his helmet and the ground. Raindrops splattered mud in his face. Nordgren and Ludas stirred beneath the poncho. "Mortars coming," House whispered. Both men muttered acknowledgment. They had not been asleep after all. Another round landed—about 40 feet away. The next would be either right on top of them or safely beyond. There was nothing to do but wait.

House lay motionless, gritting his teeth. He

The rain on Okinawa was a steady, cold drizzle . . .

knew the hole was not deep enough. Suddenly there was the quick whispering noise of shells coming. The men in the hole were fused together in a taut huddle of shrinking flesh. There were two blasts, very close, almost simultaneous. Dirt, mud, and pieces of shale flew into the hole. They waited for the next round. It landed further down the slope. Then, abruptly, the mortars stopped.

The men stirred cautiously. Whispers went from hole to hole: "You guys over there okay?" "Yeah, we're all right. But that last sonuvabitch landed damn close."

Suddenly gunfire started in down on the right. It was followed by muffled blasts and bursting grenades. What the hell was happening now? The firing subsided; time dragged.

A message finally came up the hill: "Jap patrol trying to come around the right flank. Stand by for an attack." House passed the word along. Men prodded others into wakefulness. Mortars started in again. On the slope House and his men gripped their weapons and waited.

Down at the right where the gunfire had come from, Platoon Sgt. Richard Stickley of Detroit, Mich., T-5 Gurch and Pfcs. Kirby and Shriner had ended the day in a foxhole on a knobby projection of ground close to the Jap lines. Somebody in the rear decided they should remain there as night outpost. Snipers had them pinned down, making any movement outside the hole impossible. Rations were tossed up to them. They ate them cold and settled down for the night. Jap artillery was falling short just in front of the hole. The four men ducked constantly as rocks and dirt, thrown up by explosions, rained down on them. Around 0230, Shriner nudged Stickley.

"There's something moving down there."

"Where?"

"Down there—coming uphill toward us. I've been watching him for about five minutes to make sure. Here he comes."

A shadowy figure rose up and charged them. Shriner's carbine cracked five times. The figure screamed and rolled back downhill. The men lay and listened.

Shriner said: "I think there was more than one of them."

A noisy scuffle broke out further down the slope. Another Jap had jumped into a hole occupied by two men. Shriner's firing had alerted them, and they were ready. One grabbed the Jap, the other battered him with the back of a shovel. Finally he stopped struggling. The men put two shots in the body and pushed it out of the hole. Nobody went back to sleep. When you get a couple like that it usually means there are more close by.

In the center of the island the 77th Division, closing in on the fortress of Shuri, had reached the forward slope of Chocolate Drop Hill. K Company, 307th Infantry, dug in for the night around its base. The rain that was bothering House was worrying them, too.

The Japs on the rear slope were altogether too active. Sgt. Thomas and Pfcs. McCurdy and Major huddled together under their poncho listening to the machinegun firing sporadically off on the right. The Japs, they decided, must be trying to sneak through over there. They strained their eyes, trying to pierce the mist. Suddenly Major yelled, "Japs!" and started shooting. The enemy was right on top of them. The slope flamed into activity. Dark shapes raced among foxholes hurling grenades. One blew himself up just before he reached Thomas' position. Then, just as suddenly as it had begun, the firing ceased. There were no more targets. Had they killed them all, the men wondered, or just driven them off?

The right-flank riflemen of the 22d Regiment, 6th Marine Division, had reached the banks of the Asato River and were looking into the rubble-strewn streets of Naha. The 3d Battalion had established a CP in the shelter of the ridge about 500 yards behind the front lines. The row of tombs set in the side of the ridge had been unsealed and then obligingly abandoned by the retreating enemy. Marines lost

Observation post at Itoman: Acting on information it supplied, U. S. artillery pounded the Japs' positions.

no time in moving in. Besides offering an escape from the rain, the tombs were perfect protection against all manner of shells; some of them could withstand even a direct hit. The men spread their blankets, stretched out, and talked in low tones about K Company.

At 0230 that morning K Company had begun moving up the slope of Sugar Loaf Hill. At 0300 they had sent back the message: "We are on top and intend to stay here." The enemy was determined they wouldn't. Knee mortars fell like hail. Grenades flew back and forth. Snipers crept around the base of the hill and ambushed the amtracks trying to evacuate the wounded. Daylight brought no relief.

Six times the enemy banzaied a way to the crest. Six times K Company threw them back. Not until almost noon did fighting subside long enough for another Marine unit to relieve them. Seventy men had gone up the slope that morning; less than 30 came down. "Those guys had a lot of guts," someone said.

Gradually conversations in the tombs died away. Except for the man on guard outside the CP, they slept. An hour or two passed. In one of the tombs Cpl. Paul Stewart of Waukesha, Wis., awoke with a start. A struggle was going on outside. He sat up, reaching for his carbine. Somebody tossed something inside the tomb. Instinctively Stewart rolled over against the wall. There was a deafening explosion as a grenade went off, killing the man next to him. Stewart was unhurt. He scrambled out of the tomb. Pfc. Spencer Klatt of Alton, Ill., had the grenade thrower by the throat and was slowly strangling him. The Jap gasped and kicked and bit Klatt's arm. But Klatt wasn't letting go. Stewart used his carbine.

The Jap soldier stopped struggling and died.

He had not been alone. The whole CP area was swarming with Japs. Two tombs away a Lt. Brown of Denver, Colo., found himself face to face with a charging Nip. Brown killed him with his .45. Another jumped down from the top of the tomb with his hands full of grenades. Brown got him before he could pull a pin.

In the midst of the confusion Pfc. Donald Houghtaling of Poughkeepsie, N. Y., was trying to help the wounded. Plasma and a doctor were needed. The medic station was on the other side of the open field. Lt. Buenos Young of Ellington, Conn., risked the crawl to the message center and got the medics on the phone. "We have some wounded over here who need help. There are Nips all over the place. I don't know whether you can get through." Word came back over the phone: "We will try it."

The doctor, Lt. John Tuthill, and Infantry Lt. Davis Curtis started across the open field. They did not dare crouch for fear the men in foxholes would mistake them for the enemy. "We are marines," they called. "Let us through."

They had gone about halfway when two figures rose up out of the darkness. Curtis had his .45 ready; he fired three shots at close range. The two officers ran about 10 yards and stopped to see if they were being followed, but the Japs had disappeared. Curtis was very happy about it—he had only one round left in the .45. Tuthill cursed; when the Nips appeared he'd been so startled he'd dropped most of the plasma.

They tried another dash, and this time they made it to the wounded. Just as he had feared, Tuthill found he needed more plasma. Another call went over to the medics. Corpsman George Perrault of Evanston, Ill., and a chief pharmacist's mate volunteered to bring over another load. In the middle of the field the Japs jumped them. The medics threw the case of plasma in their faces and took off. A grenade exploded behind them. The chief, hit by fragments, dropped. Perrault made it.

A game of blindman's buff was going on around the CP. Groups of marines moved cautiously about, stalking down Japs in the dark. When they sighted something there was a quick challenge. If there was no answer whatever, the "something" was well sprayed with lead. Gradually they got things under control. But firing had started in down on the beach. Whether enemy survivors had retreated down there or a larger force was on its way up, the marines did not know. They dug in around the tombs and waited to find out.

Late that afternoon five amtanks of Able Company, 1st Armored Amphibian Battalion, had crawled into the sea on the west coast a few miles behind the lines, churned across the estuary, and taken up positions on the beach just north of the mouth of the Asato River. Mounting a 75mm. pack howitzer and a .50-caliber machinegun in an open turret, they were there to discourage any attempt at a night counterlanding by bargeloads of Japs sneaking up from Naha. The beach was protected by a six-foot seawall. The platoon commander, Lt. R. Leroy Robertson of Memphis, Tex., deployed his tanks tight up against it in column formation. Two men remained on watch in each turret.

The tide, rising slowly, crept in across the reef. It reached the seawall and rose around the amtanks, lapping softly against their steel hulls. In tank No. 15, Pfc. Junior Howell of Muncie, Ind., munched an handful of salted peanuts. They were damp and sticky but helped him to stay awake. In No. 11, Cpl. Alex Worden of Roslyn, N. Y., yawned and watched a figure approach, walking casually down the seawall. "Some damn marine," he thought.

"Hey, you!" he called. "You want to get your butt shot off?" Instead of replying, the figure turned and sauntered off in the opposite direction. Howell had heard Worden challenge. He looked down the wall. Suddenly he realized there were not one but several figures. "Shoot those sonsuvbitches!" he shouted through a mouthful of peanuts. "They're Nips!"

In a foxhole nearby, tank commander Floyd

Harvey of Colfax, Wash., stuck his head up to look around and pulled it right back in again. Howell's tracers were zipping overhead. Three dark forms rushed by the hole, bullets flying around them. Harvey made a dash for the turret. He jumped in, grabbed the machinegun, and opened up on two more coming downhill toward the seawall. Other Japs were running around out on the reef. Tracers flew out to meet them. A dripping figure rose from a pothole, brandishing a grenade. Somebody dropped him. Lt. Robertson was shouting, "Don't let them get close! They may have satchel charges!"

On the radio he called the amtank liaison officer back at the regimental CP: "You better give us some flares quick if you expect us to be around in the morning."

Offshore a destroyer's gun crew went into action. Flares began bursting up and down the reef. Japs trapped in their glare made beautiful targets. On the interphone, Cpl. Daniel Sullivan of Los Angeles, Calif., pleaded, "Shoot 'em high, they may have nice sabers." The 3d Battalion CP, which had been having its own troubles, called down on the radio: "We can hear you firing, do you need any help?" Cpl. Harvey had an answer ready: "Yeah, send us down a bulldozer to help cover up these Nips." The CP was unimpressed. "Brother, you're not telling us anything new. We got 'em all over up here too."

Dawn came slowly. There was no sunrise, only gradual, almost imperceptible transition from darkness to misty daylight. Rain fell fitfully. Flares continued to burn weakly overhead. Along the front on Okinawa shivering men stood up, stretched, and looked cautiously around. On the slope of Dick Hill, the cooks brought breakfast to Sgt. House and his men: cold spaghetti and meat balls and water. Off to the right, Stickley's group cursed. Someone had passed off a batch of Australian rations on them. They tried to eat the hash, but it had a funny taste. They mixed the tea with cold water and drank it. Then they went down the hill to look

at the Japs killed during the night. They noted they were in good shape—healthy, clean, wearing almost new uniforms.

"If they're all like this," one GI observed gloomily, "the bastards aren't even close to being licked."

On the west coast the 3d Battalion CP was evacuating its wounded. When dawn came they had found the chief pharmacist's mate still alive in the field he had tried to cross with the plasma. Unable to move, he had played dead all night.

Down on the beach the amtank men counted bodies in the shallows, scattered along the base of the seawall. Pvt. Sullivan had guessed right; some of them did have good sabers. Damp wood sputtered and smoked. The marines were going to have bacon and coffee for breakfast.

In the air there was suddenly a high, thick noise. It changed to a piercing whistle, ended in a tremendous crash a short distance down the beach. Before the men could make up their minds whether the shell was a freak, more began to land around them. There was no doubt about it. Some Jap over in Naha had spotted them and was zeroing in.

Lt. Robertson decided that this was too much. "Get your engines started," he shouted, "we're pulling out!"

The marines, with their mess kits full of sizzling bacon, hurdled the seawall and piled aboard. Engines roaring, five amtanks crunched painfully out across the reef in single file. If they could make deep water they would be fairly safe. Shells burst just behind the last one, throwing up geysers of mud and water. The crew ducked and thought about what perfect targets they must be making—"like the line of beginners' targets in a shooting gallery."

Then the last tank bumped down in deep water. The Japs gave up.

Platoon Sgt. John Spelce of Clearwater, Fla., looked back over his shoulder and shook his head. "What a helluva night that was," he said. "I thought it would never end."

—Evan Wylie CSp (PR), USCGR

Kamikaze: Jap suicide

THE SKIPPER of the destroyer stood on the bridge, his head thrown back, peering through glass at the ack-ack fire high on the horizon. "They're at it again," he said. He lowered the glasses and pulled his baseball cap down over his eyes. "They're licked, but they keep coming back for more. Now it's suicide planes with suicide pilots—the Kamikaze Corps. Means 'divine wind,' they tell me. Kids with a little flight training hopped up with the idea of joining their ancestors in the most honorable way possible."

He smiled, and the lines of fatigue and strain made deep furrows in his weatherbeaten face. "It's a weird business, something only a Jap would dream up. Almost every day they claim they've sunk another hundred of our ships. Actually we shoot most of them down before they get to us. Some get through, of course. They're bound to. A few hit. If they only knew how few, maybe they'd quit."

The destroyer was the USS *Newcombe*. She had taken the worst the kamikaze boys could offer. Seven Jap suiciders had hurled their planes at her, determined to destroy the ship and themselves in one big moment of beautiful everlasting glory. Three had been shot down. Four had connected. The *Newcombe* was still afloat, and most of her crew were still alive. Some of them were sitting crosslegged on the deck below playing cards. They didn't look as if they were very much awed by the attention of the Japanese Navy's special-attack corps.

The weather that day had been good. The *Newcombe*, patrolling off Okinawa, slid easily through the slight swell, her crew at battle stations. Air defense had passed word that an attack by Jap suicide planes was expected, but the afternoon wore on and there were no visitors. The crew, restless from their long stay at the guns, watched the sun drop down toward the horizon. It would soon be time for evening chow.

"Bogies coming in ahead!"

In the turrets the men stretched out on the deck beside the guns leaped to their stations. On the 20s the gunners who had been dozing in their harnesses snapped erect. The electric motors whined. The gun muzzles arched around, sweeping the target area. The destroyer shivered as the throbbing engines picked up speed. The seas began to curl away from her bow. In a moment the *Newcombe* was knifing through the water at better than 25 knots.

"Bogies in sight, bearing three zero zero!"

What had been mere specks in the sky grew suddenly larger. They were Japs, all right—a whole swarm of them. One detached himself from the group and headed for the *Newcombe*. The can's heavy guns challenged him. Dirty brown bursts appeared in the sky. One Jap bore through them, jigging from side to side as he tried to line up the ship in his sights. He was a suicider, deliberately trying to crash the ship. The *Newcombe* shook as her 40s and 20s joined in. Their bullets hammered into the Jap. He faltered, lost control, and splashed into the sea 400 yards away.

Another plane tried it. The *Newcombe's* guns blazed savagely. The second plane disappeared in a wall of ack-ack. For a moment the gunners thought they had him, too. Then he burst into view, much closer. A yellow flame flickered along his left wing. He was starting to burn out, but still he came on.

Cmdr. Ira McMillian of Coronado, Calif., stood on the wing of his bridge, eyes fastened on

Kamikaze plane afire: If only they had known how few got through, maybe the Japs would have quit.

the approaching plane. At the last minute he shouted an order. In the wheel house the quartermaster spun the wheel. The speeding destroyer heeled over in a sharp, rivet-straining turn. It was too late for the Jap to change his course. There was a splash and a great ball of yellow flame as he plunged into the sea at the spot where the *Newcombe* had been a moment before.

The bogies buzzed warily about out of range, seeking an opening. One thought he saw it. Zooming up, he made a quick diving turn, leveled out and came in low, the belly of his fuselage a few feet above the waves. The *New-*

combe's five-inch batteries pointed. A burst threw the Jap down against the water. He staggered, recovered, and kept coming. Cmdr. McMillian barked his order for a change in course. But this time the onrushing plane swerved freakishly in the same direction. For an instant the pilot could be seen hunched forward in the cockpit, his begoggled face an impassive mask. Then the plane ripped through a gun mount and shattered itself against the after stack. There was a blinding flash. The *Newcombe* shuddered and rolled heavily to starboard.

On the signal bridge Richard Hiltburn SM3c of Tacoma, Wash., was flung high into the air by the explosion. Before he landed unhurt on the deck he caught a glimpse of bits of plane, guns, and men flying in all directions. Wounded men struggled to gain their feet. Others lay motionless, already beyond help. Escaping steam roared from broken pipes.

But the *Newcombe* had been hit before. The rest of the crew remained on station. Up in the wheel house the quartermaster wrote carefully in the ship's log: "Plane hit our stack, causing damage not known at present." A mile behind the *Newcombe* another ship saw the flash of the exploding plane. Altering her course, she started for the scene at full speed.

She wasn't the only one who saw the plane hit the *Newcombe*. One of the bogies noted it too. He banked around and came for a closer look. He probably wasn't expecting much opposition, but a surprise was waiting for him. The *Newcombe's* guns still packed a punch. The startled Jap veered as the five-inch batteries opened up. He wasn't quick enough. The burst hit him. He caught fire. One of his wings dropped off, and he spun into the water.

From his post on the bridge wing Jesse Fitzgerald SM1c noticed the ship's photographer lying helpless on the platform halfway up the undamaged forward stack. Running aft, he climbed the ladder to the platform. As Fitzgerald bent over the photographer, the *Newcombe's* guns started again. Whirling around, he saw not

one but two planes attacking, one from the port bow, the other from the port quarter. As they closed in, the guns in their wings started winking. The bullets ricocheted from the bridge and whined around Fitzgerald.

Aboard the *Newcombe* the gunfire rose to a crescendo. Again Cmdr. McMillian tried to dodge at the last minute, but the ship had lost too much speed. The planes were upon her. One buried itself in the base of Fitzgerald's stack; the other dove into the hole made by the first suicider. There was a tremendous explosion. A giant fist seemed to descend upon the *Newcombe* and drive her down into the water. Men and gun tubes alike disappeared skyward. The heavy steel hatches which had been tightly dogged down were blown off their hinges, twisted like sheet metal. Engulfed in flame and billowing black smoke, the *Newcombe* lost headway and slowly came to a dead stop in the water, all her power and communications knocked out.

Up forward the dazed men picked themselves up and stumbled out to see what had happened to their ship. The bridge and forward portion of the *Newcombe* were relatively undamaged, but the flame and smoke amidships hid the stern from view altogether. Was the stern still there? There was no way of knowing. "Stern is gone!" someone cried, and many men believed him.

Signalman Fitzgerald had ducked at the last minute. Miraculously he and the wounded photographer had been untouched by the explosion. Looking down, Fitzgerald found the base of the stack surrounded by burning gasoline and wreckage from one of the planes. Above him the coils of wiring in the broken rigging whipped about, crackling and spitting, showering the decks below in a cascade of blue sparks. Fitzgerald took his man down the ladder and found a path through the burning gasoline to the forward part of the ship. He applied a tourniquet to the photographer's bleeding leg and then rushed back to the bridge to help put out the fires in the signal flag bags.

Men on the other destroyer had seen the

second and third planes hit the *Newcombe,* had seen her go dead in the water half-hidden in the clouds of smoke. As the distance between the two ships narrowed they could make out figures stumbling about in the dense smoke that covered the *Newcombe's* stern. Other figures lay along her starboard deck, too badly hurt to move. Into the smoke went the other destroyer.

At almost collision speed she swept up alongside the *Newcombe.* There was a grinding crash as the two ships came together. The men jumped across and made the ships fast. Fire hoses were snaked across the rails. Powerful streams of water leaped from their nozzles and drove the flames back from the prostrate men. Rescue parties rushed in and dragged them to safety.

The suicide boys were not through. Another plane was roaring in, headed straight for the *Newcombe's* bridge. Looking up, Joseph Piolata WT2c of Youngstown, O., saw the other destroyer firing right across the *Newcombe's* deck. The gunners did their best, but the *Newcombe's* superstructure hid the plane from their sights. On both ships the men watched helplessly. This was the kill. The *Newcombe* could never survive another hit.

But the battered, burning can still had fight in her. Incredulously the men of the *Newcombe,* crouched on her stern, struggling in the water, lying wounded on the deck, heard their ship's forward batteries firing. There was no power, but the gunners were firing anyway—by hand.

The gunnery officer stood at his station shouting the range data to the men in the forward five-inch turrets. In the No. 2 turret Arthur McGuire GM1c of St. Louis, Mo., rammed shells with broken, bleeding fingers. His hand had been caught by a hot shell while he fired at the third plane, but he was still on the job. The Jap had the *Newcombe's* bridge in his sights. It looked as if he couldn't miss. But the burst from McGuire's gun caught him and blew him sideways. The hurtling plane missed the bridge by a scant eight feet, skidded across the *Newcombe's* deck and plowed into the other destroyer.

With a gaping hole in the afterdeck and the portside a tangled web of broken lines and wildly sprouting fire hoses, the second destroyer drifted slowly away.

Without water to fight the fire still raging amidships, the *Newcombe* was doomed. But the destroyer's crew contained some obstinate people. Donald Keeler MM2c of Danbury, Conn., was one of them. Keeler had been at his station in the after steering compartment. He was knocked down by the explosions but got up and put the ship in manual control. When it became evident that all the power was gone he joined the crowd on the stern just in time to hear that the after ammo-handling rooms were burning and the magazines were expected to go any minute.

Keeler elected to fight the fire. His only hope lay in a "handy-billy," a small, portable pump powered by a gasoline engine. The engine was started like an outboard motor—by winding a rope around the flywheel and giving it a quick tug. Like all outboard engines, sometimes it started and then again sometimes it didn't.

Groping around in the blistering heat, Keeler found the handy-billy. Carefully he wound the rope around the flywheel, held his breath and yanked. The engine kicked over and kept going. Now Keeler had water. He and Donald Newcomer WT1c of Portland, Ore., took the hose in the No. 4 handling room and went to work on the fire. Malcom Giles MM3c of San Jose, Calif., and Lt. David Owens of Waukesha, Wis., joined them. The four men got the fire under control. Then they dragged the pump forward.

The No. 3 handling room was a roaring furnace. Steel dripped like solder from overhead. In the galley next door the heat had already transformed the copper kettles into pools of molten metal. Flames shot from the ammo hoists like the blast of a huge blow torch. It looked hopeless, but Newcomer shoved the hose in the doorway. No sooner had he done so than a wave came over the side and doused the pump. The chattering handy-billy spluttered and died. Keeler rushed back to the pump. Again he wound the rope around the flywheel, gritted his teeth and yanked. "I think I even prayed that second time," he said. "But the damn thing popped right off, something it wouldn't do again in a million years."

The men went back into the handling room. They kept the hose in there, taking turns. The magazines didn't blow up.

Up forward sailors were trying to fight the fire with hand extinguishers. A withering blast of heat drove them back. Their life jackets were smoking; their clothing was afire. The Newcombe's doctor, Lt. John McNeil of Boston, Mass., and Edward Redding QM3c found one of the crew battling the flames with hair ablaze, half blind from the blood dripping from the shrapnel wounds in his face and forehead. With difficulty they dragged him off to the emergency dressing station in the wardroom. Many of the pharmacist's mates were out of action. Men with only first-aid training helped McNeil mix blood plasma for the burn cases.

Early Sayre CPhM of Roseville, O., was trapped on the stern unable to get his casualties forward. He was working on a fracture when someone tugged on his sleeve. "Blue Eyes has been hit bad. Looks like he's bleeding to death."

Blue Eyes was the youngest member of the crew. He had come aboard claiming 18 years, but the men had taken one look at him and decided he must have lied to get in. Now he lay on the deck, blood spurting from a vein in his neck. Sayre had no instruments. He knelt down beside Blue Eyes and stopped the flow of blood with his fingers. He stayed there while the second plane came in and hit the other destroyer 20 feet away. He stayed there for almost an hour longer until they could come and take Blue Eyes away and operate on him and save his life. But Early Sayre had saved it already.

The rest of the Japs had been driven off. It was beginning to get dark when a ray of hope came to the exhausted men of the Newcombe. Keeler's volunteer fire department seemed to be holding the fires. Perhaps now they could save their ship. But the wave that had stopped the handy-billy was followed by another and another.

The Newcombe was sinking. The weight of the water that the hoses had poured into her after compartments was dragging her down. The rising water moved steadily forward. It reached the after bulkhead of the forward engine room. If it broke through, the Newcombe was done for. And the bulkhead already was leaking.

Back on the stern Lt. Charles Gedge of Detroit, Mich., and torpedomen Richard Mehan of Verona, N. J., Richard Spencer of Roddick, Penna., and Joseph Zablotny of Boswell, Penna., had neutralized the depth charges and dumped them overside. After them went the wreckage, anything that would lighten the stern.

In the forward engine room the damage-control party shored up the bulging bulkhead. Water oozed from it, but it held. With less than one foot of freeboard between sea and her decks, the Newcombe stopped sinking.

Now the blinkers flashed in the darkness. Other destroyers were coming alongside. Over their rails came men with fire hoses and pump lines, doctors and pharmacist's mates with plasma and bandages. Tugs were on the way. The fight was over.

The Newcombe's men had answered the question: Just how much punishment can a destroyer take? The answer was: just as much as any gang of Japs can dish out, provided her crew never stops trying to save her.

—EVAN WYLIE CSp (PR), USCGR

The new Big Three: Potsdam, Germany, July 1945.

Potsdam plans the end

IN TOUGH, SIMPLE LANGUAGE, *the men at Potsdam told the world of the Allies' plans for the vanquished Reich and for victory over Japan.*

First, the new Big Three—President Harry S. Truman, Prime Minister Clement Attlee, and Generalissimo Josef Stalin—settled on pre-peace-conference terms for conquered Germany and its puppets.

Then the President of the United States and the Prime Minister of Great Britain joined with Generalissimo Chiang Kai-shek in issuing a last warning to Japan: Surrender or perish.

In the Potsdam declaration of July 26, 1945, the leaders of three great Allies told Japanese

soldiers to lay down their arms and reject forever the supremacy of the military caste.

"We do not intend that the Japanese shall be enslaved as a race or destroyed as a nation," the declaration stated, "but stern justice shall be meted out to all war criminals, including those who have visited cruelties upon our prisoners."

Talking with the hard assurance of men who are looking down the enemy's throat, the leaders of the United States, Great Britain, and China concluded: "We call upon the Government of Japan to proclaim now unconditional surrender. . . . The alternative for Japan is prompt and utter destruction."

Fred Canfil, U. S. Marshal from Missouri and a member of the Presidential party at the Big Three meeting, was running around checking on the kitchens of the 2d Armored Division here. "The Boss doesn't like the kind of bread the soldiers have been getting," he said.

Canfil was a fellow officer of the President's in the 35th Division in the last war. "No man in the Boss's old outfit would ever have had to eat bread like the stuff they're getting," he said.

The Boss is a familiar figure to the GIs of the 713th MP Battalion, who draw most of the guard duty for the conference.

Pvt. Floyd Jenkins of Caruthersville, Mo., one of the MPs who gets a guard's-eye view of some of the Truman-Churchill-Stalin banquets at the Little White House, hasn't gotten around to passing the time of the day with the President yet, but that, he figures, is inevitable and not in the nature of anything establishing a precedent.

"The Trumans make our country fair in my home town every year," said Jenkins, "and I suppose he will this year unless he gets tied up. When he comes around to talk to me I'm going to tell him that here is one cotton-picking GI that would like to be back to pick a crop this fall."

That is how GIs in general size up the conference. With the hard logic of men who are personally involved in the outcome of the conference, they reason that the more unity there is among the conferees, the quicker will come the decisions that will eventually get them home.

Beefing among soldiers is, of course, a universal privilege that transcends armies, and the GIs around the conference refuse to let the fact that history is being made around them still their natural instincts. As they see it, too many people around the conference are trying to look to their postwar future by doing unsolicited favors. On the night of July 18, for example, some of the local brass went to work and surprised the President by getting Mrs. Truman on the phone in Independence, Mo.

"Everything is strictly Big Deal around here," said a guard, expressing the attitude of a tired man who has been doing four on and eight off, "including apple-polishing."

Fortunately for the cause of the non-VIPs (Very Important Persons in the GI jargon here), at least one from their ranks was accorded privileges above his station because of an accident of birth. When Sgt. Harry Truman, the President's nephew from the 44th Division, got a chance to fly in and see his uncle, he alighted from a plane at night without orders and transportation. Suspicious guards finally let him contact M/Sgt. Albert Garfinkel of the 713th, who then bucked young Truman through channels until he got him in the conference area. Once there, things changed suddenly for the 44th Division sergeant, and, as he explained to fellow soldiers, he was overwhelmed by officers who wanted to carry his luggage.

"That was the first time that ever happened to me," said Sgt. Truman. "Boy, that was fun!"

The President supplied the final touch to this version of a sergeant's dream by taking a PX wrist watch away from a VIP with the explanation that "you can get another one, and Harry can't."

Because of his free and easy manner of associating with soldiers, most of the GIs seem to regard Truman simply as one of them who fulfilled the old American formula of growing up to be President. Conversely, they feel no such familiarity with Marshal Stalin of the Soviet Union, who is easily the greatest drawing card for soldiers' interest that this galaxy of VIPs presents. And this was so before the rumor grew that Joe had Japan's surrender in his hip pocket.

Cpl. John Tuohy of Long Island, N. Y., who used to be a booker for Paramount Pictures, now stands guard in front of the celebrity-packed Little White House.

He described Stalin as "smaller than I expected him to be, but an immaculate man who wears beautiful uniforms."

"But," added Tuohy, "he's the kind of man

that would attract attention in overalls. And that mustache of his is a whiz."

On one occasion, however, Mr. Winston Churchill made an entry from the Little White House that completely stole the show from Stalin. It was near dusk on the night of July 19 after a banquet that had included, according to those who tried to keep count, at least 25 toasts. Stalin left first, emerging from the door surrounded by his usual escort of fruit-salad-bedecked generals. With all the lusty flourishes for which the Russians are noted, Stalin was paraded down to his long, black Packard, which straightaway roared down the street. After him the then Prime Minister of Great Britain came out—minus any VIPs. He took a breath of fresh air, chewed at that cigar and strode off resolutely down Kaiserlautern Strasse while a couple of chaps who looked like British "SS" men—as the soldiers called FBI and Secret Service men—tagged belatedly after him. GIs and Wacs ogled him, then snapped to and saluted. His Majesty's Minister returned them all, and everyone noted that the line he walked down Kaiserlautern was as straight as a drill major's.

Most of the soldiers around the conference seemed more alert to the possibility of Churchill's passing out of the Big Three picture than were the correspondents writing about the same thing. At any rate, few of the Yanks expressed surprise when they learned the results of the British balloting, and they explained this by quoting their British buddies who were sharing details with them at Potsdam.

"Not one English soldier that I talked to thought that Mr. Churchill would be re-elected," said S/Sgt. Max Adams of Angola, Ind., who is in charge of the Presidential bodyguard detail.

From time to time soldiers make contacts with other notables beside the Big Three. Sgt. E. F. Radigan of Albany, N. Y., spotted the Russians' Deputy Commissar for Foreign Affairs, Vishinsky, recalled his prosecution at the Moscow trials, and assumed there was a rough time coming up for war criminals.

Pvt. Dale Horner was told by a general who had just left the VIP mess hall that "I had a wonderful dinner," and replied: "Sir, you should have ate what we did."

Disproving those "reliable sources" from which emanated journalistic dope stories of American-Russian disagreements, guards like Cpl. Wallace Calvin of South Bend, Ind., and Cpl. Floyd Stewart of Springfield, O., work with their Russian guards outside the conferences in the Cecelienhof Building with no friction. The Russian guards range in rank from majors to first lieutenants. They rate it a great honor to guard people like Stalin, Truman, and Churchill; hence no privates. As officers, the Russian guards rate a vodka ration which they sometimes share with the Yanks—off duty hours.

Wallace and Floyd get along well with the pert Russian girl interpreters at the conference building, but they think that this fraternizing is the only thing that sometimes makes the Russion guards take a dim view of them. Another thing that the Russians find hard to understand is the American soldiers' habit of making up funny stories that poke ribald fun at all the national leaders. Most-told joke here concerns watches (five minutes in Berlin convinces any one that the Russian soldier will buy any watch for 10 times its value). The story has Stalin saying to Churchill on the occasion of their first meeting: "How much for your watch?"

The social life around the conference has not, incidentally, been restricted to the conference area, and on one occasion the Femina, Berlin's frowsy nightclub, was filled with cops from the American, British and Russian "SS" details.

American combat officers who are lucky enough to draw liaison assignments to the meeting come in for such unexpected pleasures as squiring American girl secretaries into Berlin for a look at the night life, and one first lieutenant from the 2d Armored—dated up with one of Jimmy Byrnes' secretaries—said: "I just hope an MP stops me with her in a jeep."

—SGT. DEWITT GILPIN

YANK

THE ARMY WEEKLY

VJ ISSUE

SEPT. 7, 1945
VOL. 4, NO. 12 • 5 CENTS

The answer to the biggest question on any GI's mind is still iffy. YANK assembles here the best dope at the time of going to press on what the WD plans.

By Sgt. H. N. OLIPHANT
YANK Staff Writer

WASHINGTON—The plan the War Department has announced for demobilizing some 5,000,000 men within a year may or may not be your idea of a good deal. But the big question to GIs who remember and were POd by the rotation deal is: Good or bad, will it work?

The WD answers that $64 job this way: The demobilization plan will work okay *if*:

1) We get the breaks on the occupation detail. (Widespread internal disorders in Japan or the threat of a renewal of hostilities would demand the retention of an army considerably larger than that now planned for.)

2) Congressional action doesn't snafu the basic principles of the demobilization pattern as it now stands. (Congress could, for example, abruptly abolish the draft; such action, the WD says, would shut off the monthly supply of thousands of inductees slated to be replacements.)

3) The transportation set-up functions with a minimum of hitches.

All this may sound as if the WD is getting ready to send out TS slips instead of discharge papers. Luckily, that's not quite the case. The WD says it is merely playing it safe by taking into account any snags that may occur in the future. Actually, the sentiment around the Pentagon is that the demobilization machinery ought easily to be able to spring 5,000,000 men out of the Army within 12 months.

The high brass doesn't appear to feel that either Separation Centers or shipping will prove to be bottlenecks. As far as Separation Centers are concerned, the WD points out that the post-VE-Day Readjustment and Redeployment plan gave them a four-month "trial run" and a chance to iron out a lot of wrinkles that emerged.

In addition, the Separation Centers have been expanded and plans are in the works for them to take over certain reception center facilities should the need arise.

A colonel who helped in the evolution of the separation procedure told YANK that further expansion of Separation Centers probably won't be necessary. At the peak, he added, Separation Centers should be able to handle at least 500,000 dischargees a month.

The other possible bottleneck, shipping, should also be a cinch to break. During May, June and July, despite the fact that the overwhelming emphasis was on winning the Far East war, 800,000 men were returned from Europe to the U. S. The Pacific run is twice as long as the Atlantic run. But distance won't matter so much because thousands of tons of shipping formerly used for the redeployment of troops and supplies from Europe to the Far East will now be available for demobilization uses.

The demobilization plan, like the old Readjustment plan put into effect last May, is based on the old point system, and the same point values go for the same four factors: Service credit, overseas credit, combat credit and parenthood credit. But there are at least two important differences between the two plans:

1) R-Day (Redeployment Day), May 12, 1945, the date at which all computations of point scores stopped under the old set-up, will be discarded just as soon as our occupation needs in the Far East are ascertained, and a new date will be substituted, allowing troops credit for service after May 12, 1945.

2) A lower critical score will be established for both EM and Wacs and "further reductions in this score will be made periodically to insure that discharges proceed at the highest rate permitted by transportation." As of the day of Japan's surrender, no definite score had been announced, but most authorities at that time were pretty generally agreed that it would be in the neighborhood of 75 for EM.

Under the demobilization plan, you will compute your score in exactly the same way as you did under the Readjustment plan. When a new critical score is announced, the only difference will be that instead of using May 12, 1945, as your deadline for points, you will include all points you have earned up to the new deadline date.

The demobilization plan does not provide credit for dependents other than three children under 18, and no point credit is given for age. The age limit for the Army, however, has been lowered from 40 to 38, and this limit, according to a Pentagon colonel, will be progressively lowered as demobilization takes full effect.

That worn-out bit of double-talk—the "military necessity" gag—should just about disappear under the demobilization plan. For all practical purposes, the WD insists, the words "essential" and "non-surplus" will be tossed out.

Actually, only men with four types of jobs can be stuck; they really fall in specialized categories: *1)* orthopedic attendants; *2)* acoustic technicians; *3)* electroencephalographic specialists; *4)* transmitter attendants, fixed station.

All this doesn't mean that you can't be retained temporarily even if you don't belong in one of the foregoing groups, but under a regulation being considered by the WD, you can't be held longer than six months after VJ-Day.

THE first job is to get the armies of occupation set. "That job," a Pentagon colonel explained, "takes priority over everything in this plan, just like beating Japan took priority over everything in the Readjustment plan. We've got to make damned sure, in a hurry, that the Japs don't hole up and get a chance to start an underground movement that could cause us plenty of grief later on.

"Therefore, our No. 1 task is to get enough men on the spot as soon as possible and in the right places to insure a real peace. After that has been accomplished and the system of supply for the occupation troops is clicking, the demobilization process can go forward in full swing."

How many men will be needed for occupation duty? The answer to that one depends on several things. First of all, we have no way of knowing as yet what problems we'll encounter in Japan. There is a terrific density of population to consider, and that fact added to the screwy twist in the Japanese mind will in all probability force us to keep plenty of manpower around to police the area constantly and thoroughly. At the same time, our occupation army in Europe—possibly 400,000 men—will continue on the job until Congress decides there's no further use for it.

In addition, we'll have to keep, according to the WD's estimate, around half a million men on duty in the U. S., Alaska, Panama and Hawaii. These will be used to man permanent garrisons and to see that transportation and supply for the occupation armies don't bog down. Finally, all or most of the islands we have captured in the Pacific will have to be garrisoned for an unspecified time. All these needs, the WD figures, will ultimately require a peacetime Army of at least 2½ million men. Presumably, the 2½ million would consist of guys with extremely low point scores, regulars and new inductees.

Many more men than that will be needed at first, principally because of our uncertainty over what the internal situation in Japan will develop into, but most of the big brass here believe that the normal discharge procedure, spreading demobilization over a 12-month period, will insure there being enough troops around to take care of any incidents that may occur in the early phases of the occupation.

Granting priorities to the occupation armies doesn't necessarily mean, however, that the process of getting eligibles out of the Army will be impeded much, if at all. The mechanism for demobilization, says the WD, is tuned so that it can go simultaneously with the machinery that builds and maintains our armies of occupation.

First to be released under the demobilization plan are the 550,000 men who had 85 or more points under the Readjustment plan. According to the colonel, these men are being discharged just as fast as they can be moved to separation centers, or in the case of high-pointers overseas, loaded in ships and planes and returned to the States. While he was reluctant to make any definite prediction as to the exact time it would take to spring *all* high-pointers, the colonel did say, "It is perfectly possible that most of them will be back in civvies within 60 days after VJ-Day."

Of the half-million high-pointers under the original Readjustment plan, those who were in the States when Japan surrendered were necessarily slated to get out first; indeed, the War Department announced that it would try to get all these out by August 31. Accordingly, some guys in the U. S. with a bare 85 points got out sooner than some men overseas with 100 plus.

That may appear unjust, but WD spokesmen justify it on the score of expediency. They describe the demobilization process as a giant funnel. The eligible men already in the States (or en route) would clog the funnel if they were kept sweating it out until overseas troops with higher scores reached the States.

There has been a lot of latrine talk lately about a so-called Army plan to regulate the flow of dischargees back into civilian life, not on the basis of high-point scores but on the basis of whether a guy has a job waiting for him when he gets out. There is no such regulation in the War Department's plan for demobilization and none is being considered, although Congress could conceivably make such a regulation if it decided that it would be in the best interests of the national economy. But not the WD. The WD says its sole job is to get 5½ million men out of the Army just as soon as possible.

Another latrine rumor has it that men eligible for point discharges will be given furloughs in the States before their release so that they can look around for jobs on the Army's time. That's a phony, too. When your number is called you can do only one of two things. You can walk up and get your discharge papers, or you can choose to stay in the Army.

The choice to remain in the Army may sound a little wacky to most of us, but some GIs are thinking seriously about it. High-pointers who elect to remain in the Army have three choices:

1) They can enlist in the regular Army.

2) If they are overseas they can volunteer to remain for the duration-plus-six-months with the occupation army in the theater to which they are presently assigned.

3) Whether they are overseas or in the U. S. they can volunteer for duty in the U. S. for the duration-plus-six.

If you decide to enlist in the regular Army, you'll be required to take a three-year hitch. You'll be able to keep the rank you had at time of discharge, but how much freedom you'll have in choosing your arm of service hasn't been decided. The WD is working on plans for an intensive stay-in-the-Army campaign which is expected to include inducements in the way of educational opportunities, easy promotions, retirement privileges, and so on.

The other two deals—volunteering for continued duty for the duration-plus-six—involve several *ifs*. First, if you are overseas you can elect to stay in the theater in which you are presently stationed provided your CO decides there's a legitimate need for your services and if he wants you around. If he accepts you, you're stuck only for the duration-plus-six. You won't be required to join the regulars.

You can volunteer for duty in the U. S., too, without joining the regulars. If there's room for you, you'll probably be accepted. On this deal you also sign for the duration-plus-six.

In case you're still baffled over the "duration-plus-six" business, here are the facts: You were inducted under the law for the duration and six months "after the date of the termination of hostilities." This termination-of-hostilities date has nothing to do with the cease-fire order. It will be a date, defined by law, as "the date proclaimed by the President . . . or the date specified in a concurrent resolution of Congress, whichever is earlier."

THE Marine Corps is using exactly the same plan as the Army used for its Readjustment plan. As of August 14, the day the Japs said they'd quit, it took 85 points to get out of the Marines. The Navy and Coast Guard have a different plan. The Navy gives half a point for each year of age, figured to the nearest birthday; half a point for each full month of active duty since September 1, 1939, and 10 points for a dependent. (It doesn't matter whether you have more than one dependent; you get just 10 points for your total of dependents.) The critical score for Navy EM is 44 points; for enlisted Waves, 29; for male officers, 49; for Wave officers, 35. The Navy, too, will lower its critical scores as "military commitments permit." From 1½ to 2½ million men and women will be released under the Navy's plan within a year to 18 months.

"How soon OUT?"

VICTORY

THREE years, eight months and seven days after Pearl Harbor total victory came to the United States of America and all the Allies. On the 14th of August, 1945, the last Axis enemy went down to that total defeat which the democracies, some of whom had faced up to Rome-Berlin-Tokyo aggression long before the 7th of December, 1941, had solemnly pledged themselves to bring about.

In this nation, and throughout the Allied world, the contrast between those two days was the contrast between shock, dread and near-defeat and relief, thanksgiving and unqualified triumph. There was another difference, too.

To the citizens of the United States—and indeed of all the countries that later became the United Nations—Pearl Harbor had been a blow-without-warning. In its unexpectedness it had brought a mental shock almost as severe as the physical shock of the bombs that fell on Hickam Field and on the ships in harbor. VJ-Day came to a nation waiting for and well schooled in victory.

America's armed forces had had a major share in Allied triumphs all over the globe. The weapons forged in its factories and carried on its ships and planes to every part of the world had proved its industrial supremacy. VJ-Day had come sooner than most Americans had dared hope, but for months none had doubted that it would arrive.

When it did come, after a five-day wait while the Samurai fumed and quibbled over the details of defeat, there was such an outpouring of emotion as Americans had never known. Wherever Americans were gathered together—whether in Louisville, Ky., Berlin or Manila—the pattern of celebration was much the same. There were roars of rejoicing, high hopes for reunions, and prayers. The prayers were offered in gratitude and in remembrance of those who had died for a day they could not mark.

In America the celebration outdid anything within the memory of living men. It made VE-Day seem silent; it far overshadowed Armistice Day, 1918. On the Continent of Europe and on continents and islands where end-of-war had never found U. S. troops before, it was a day without precedent. A chapter, perhaps a whole book, of history had ended, and a word that had figured much in American thoughts for three years, eight months and seven days—a word often spoken, but always in terms of the past or of an unsure future—could be spoken now in terms of the living present. The word was peace.

DALLAS Peace came to Dallas like a mixture of Hallowe'en and Christmas. The day itself had been quiet, because, as everywhere else, there had been too many false alarms and people had grown cautious. But a White House announcement at 6 P.M. changed all that.

It took just 30 minutes for the celebration to get under way here. From all parts of the city thousands flocked into the downtown area. Bus and streetcar schedules were hopelessly disorganized. The howlingest mob in Dallas's recent history made short work of the anti-noise ordinance, conceived by the city fathers to speed war production.

Sirens came on 30 minutes late, but made up for their tardiness by their volume. Paper cascaded out of downtown office windows, while street sweepers looked on helplessly, then laughed and joined in the fun.

Centering at Commerce and Akard Streets, the celebration fanned out to take in the entire downtown area, with parades of yelling and chanting pedestrians weaving through lines of cars with horns blaring full blast. Elsewhere shirt-tail parades and group singing swelled the volume of sound.

Pillows in the rooms of the Adolphus and Baker Hotels were ripped apart, and their feathery contents floated through the air. Socks came next, with other odds-and-ends following, while Abe Berger, publicity man for the Adolphus, looked worriedly up at the windows and wondered how long they'd stay put.

The long-awaited announcement left many pedestrians silent, however. For one woman the news had come too late. On her shoulder, between the arms of a silver V, was a picture of her son in uniform. He had been killed in action several months ago.

Mrs. Mary Williams, a pretty redhead, said she had been waiting to eat, but her appetite had vanished. "I stepped outside just as the news came," she said. "Then a chill came over me and I had a feeling that was more like sadness than joy." She couldn't help crying, she was so thankful. Her husband, Boyd Williams, is somewhere in the Pacific with the Navy.

A solid mass packed Akard between Commerce and Elm, with cars lined up from signal light to signal light. An Army private walked up to an MP standing at Akard and Commerce. The soldier had made the rounds of the liquor stores just before a telephone conference of owners had resulted in their closing for the night in the midst of a tremendous run. Toting one bottle under an arm and drinking steadily from another, the soldier stared the MP in the face. "Mercy on you, MP," he murmured, "mercy on you," and walked off.

At the USO on Main Street a crowd of servicemen hung over a radio waiting for the President's announcement. When the news came they remained quiet, listening attentively to every word. Then they cut loose with a yell, most of them pouring out into the street to join other celebrators bent on organizing a demonstration.

Some stayed behind. There was Pfc. William E. Boynicki, 39, who sat down at once to write to his wife in Miami, Fla. "All I want to do is go home and tie myself to my wife's apron strings and never leave home again," he murmured. "I've been in this man's army five years. That's enough."

Pfc. Guy Rogers of Dallas, just back from two years and two days overseas, was ready to sit down for a discussion of chemical warfare, a field in which he had worked. The atomic bomb, he figured, had really done the job. Then he paused, struck by an idea. "Now if they would just say that all of us fellows were going to be discharged," he said, "we would really blow our tops."

NEW YORK CITY

At 7:30 A.M. on Friday, August 10, 1945, the thermometer in New York City read 66 degrees, the sun was shining, the humidity wasn't bad, and all in all it was one of the town's better summer mornings. The atomic bomb and Russia were in the war now, and the 7:30 news broadcasts were much concerned with the accomplishments of these new allies.

A moment later it came. Japan, according to the Tokyo radio, wanted out. Word of the momentous broadcast spread quickly, but in New York there was no immediate sense of jubilation. Instead, a mood of trance-like suspense prevailed. Nothing was official, nothing was definite, no one could do anything but hope.

Thin lines of earnest people gathered almost at once in Times Square to await developments as they were flashed on the electric news sign running around the Times Tower Building. They didn't know it then, of course, but they were the advance guard of a host of New Yorkers who would be keeping vigil there for five days and nights to come.

"Whadya say, sarge?" said one GI to another in the ranks of an expectant throng listening to a sidewalk radio in the entrance to a newsreel theater on East 42d Street. "Kinda quiet, ain't it, for a big deal like this? People seem to be walking around in a dream. Yep, that's what the whole thing seems like—a dream."

Among the first in the city to act on the news were the proprietors of establishments in the Times Square area who feared for the safety of their plate-glass windows. By 8 A.M. Toffenetti's Restaurant, on the southeast corner of Broadway and 43d Street, had a crew of carpenters busy putting up barricades as a precaution against crowds, and the Astor Hotel and other vulnerable spots were quick to follow suit.

And so the long morning wore on. Civilians stopped GIs in the streets, offering to buy them drinks, but by and large the GIs didn't seem inclined to accept. Everything was still too uncertain to get party-minded. Down in Wall Street, where ticker tape can be counted on to fly at the first sign of exuberance in the big town, there wasn't so much as a shred of paper in the gutters. A recruiting station for Waves, situated in front of the Sub-Treasury Building at the corner of Wall and Nassau, remained open for business, but there were no customers.

Thousands shouted together when news of Jap surrender came to Times Square in New York.

Word went out that President Harry S. Truman was calling a Cabinet meeting at 2 P.M. Somehow or other this was distorted in Manhattan's garment center into a rumor that he had accepted the Jap peace offer, and a celebration, as cockeyed as it was short-lived, began. Seventh and Eighth Avenues from 34th to 40th Streets and the side streets in the area became a crazy quilt of bits and patches of brightly colored cloth thrown from the windows of buildings by excited dressmakers. Vendors popped up from nowhere to peddle VJ-Day buttons at two bits per button. The Department of Sanitation rushed sprinkler trucks around to wet down the mess, but not in time. In the midst of all the excitement, some of the pieces of cloth on Eighth Avenue caught fire from a cigarette butt, and traffic had to be stopped because of the danger to gasoline tanks. "In the garment center, we've always prematured our celebrations," said one disgusted elevator operator.

During the afternoon, 5,000 policemen were stationed in the midtown area to handle anticipated crowds, but at 3:30 P.M. came an announcement that the White House would have no further news until morning and the cops were called in. And so the restless, indecisive day petered out. In the theater district that night there were no more than the usual summer crowds and local radio stations hammered home this message at frequent intervals: "If you have a war job, keep plugging. The war is not yet over."

Nor was the war over during the long weekend that followed. Saturday it was hot—sunny again, and hot. Just after dawn the *Queen Elizabeth* came in with 14,800 GIs from the ETO, a

A sailor and a Wac tore up the sidewalk o[n] Broadway with a swinging, strutting victory jiv[e]

lot of whom figured that now they wouldn't hav[e] to take another free ocean ride on Uncle Sam, a[s] they'd been expecting to. By afternoon the street[s] were all but deserted and from one end of th[e] city to the other girls sprawled on tenemen[t] roofs in skimpy bathing suits, picking up sun[-] tans for their legs in place of the silk stocking[s] they couldn't buy. The Japs, the radio said, ha[d] been told that Hirohito could stay but that we'[d] be the boss, and everyone realized it would no[w] be some time before we'd have an answer to thi[s]. That evening the West 54th Street police statio[n] reported fewer people in Times Square tha[n] there usually are on a summer Saturday nigh[t]. There was nothing to do but wait.

The skies were clear again Sunday, as indee[d] they were throughout the five days of waitin[g] that seemed like a century, and the thermomete[r] was in the low 80s, making it a fine day to go t[o] the beaches. Thousands turned up at Cone[y] Island and Orchard Beach, toting portable radio[s] along with them so that they could keep u[p] with developments, of which there were non[e]. Learned commentators went on the air to expla[in] at was holding up Japan's surrender, although ..y obviously had no more idea than their ..eners of what the deal was. A mass of thanks-..ing for the peace that had not yet come was ..d at St. Patrick's Cathedral on Fifth Avenue. ..yor F. H. LaGuardia broadcast this plea: "Do ..celebrate unless there is good reason to cele-..te."

..hen, as it apparently must at the end of any ..r, came the phony report of surrender. At ..4 P.M. the United Press sent out this flash: ..SHINGTON—JAPAN ACCEPTS SURRENDER TERMS ..THE ALLIES. Two minutes later came the ..ntermanding order: EDITORS—HOLD UP THAT ..SH. But by then it was too late. Radio stations ..l already broadcast the false news and ..usands upon thousands of people had dashed ..m their living rooms out into the streets.

..he U. P. later explained that it hadn't sent ..the report and it put up a $5,000 reward for ..ormation leading to the identification and con-..tion of the culprit who in some manner had ..naged to slip the hot but screwy dope out ..r its wires. By that time, however, crowds ..re whooping it up in Times Square, a bit syn-..tically, to be sure, since all they had to do ..s to look up at the electric news sign and read ..t the war was definitely not over. Most of ..he hullabaloo was kicked up by kids of bobby-..k age just raising the roof for the hell of it. ..midnight it was way past their bedtimes and, ..erly pooped out, they straggled home.

..Monday was a stinker. The weather was hot ..d humid and a sweating city was fretfully ..eating the surrender out. Whereas at first ..eryone had more or less taken it for granted ..t Japan would accept our terms, now as the ..urs passed people began to fear that it wasn't ..er yet by any means. The day dragged on, a ..y on which most New Yorkers had thought ..ey would be celebrating and on which they ..tead had to return reluctantly to their routine ..ores. Then, that evening at 6:25, came a radio ..ort that a broadcasting station in Brazzaville, ..rica, had picked up an announcement from

nitely in the bag. Frenzied babes rushed through the crowds kissing servicemen, and wolves, in uniform and out, prowled about mousing any and every likely-looking number while the cops looked on, grinning indulgently. At 3:17 in the afternoon a sailor and his honey were to be seen lying flat on the pavement necking furiously as the throngs shuffled about them. Traffic was barred from the Times Square area all day so that the mob, which ultimately numbered 2,000,-000, could run loose.

All the way from Staten Island to Van Cortlandt Park, from the Hudson River to the remotest outposts of Queens, the streets were littered with tons of paper torn up and scattered about by New York City's seven and a half million elated citizens. In Chinatown, where the residents have relatives in the land the Japs first tried to overrun, they put on the sacred dragon dance ordinarily staged only on the Chinese New Year. Up in Harlem there was jive and jitterbugging in the streets. Flatbush Avenue and Fulton Streets, two of Brooklyn's main drags, were jammed.

Frantic and madcap as the shindy was by day, however, it was nothing compared to what it became at night after President Truman made his 7 o'clock announcement that the war was over. This, at last, was the official end, and at once the whole city, already a seething turmoil, seemed to explode. To the blasts of automobile horns and the shrilling of whistles the *Queen Elizabeth*, docked in the Hudson, added the deep, throaty boom of her horn. Some of the bars around Times Square closed down, unable to cope with the crush, but it was a cinch to get a drink since scores of people were wandering around carrying quart bottles of the stuff and all were in a generous mood.

On, on, on it went into the night and the next night as the biggest city in the world went its way toward picking up the biggest hangover in its history. It was a hangover few would ever regret.

—Sgt. SANDERSON VANDERBILT

a 40-year-old, rather liquefied, bald-headed gentleman who chose that moment to try to slide, no hands, down the Willard's banister. He made it halfway.

The number of bottles which were passed freely among strangers would have startled anyone who has ever paid $50 for a quart of the stuff in such far-off places as New Georgia. One officer, standing in the middle of Pennsylvania Avenue outside the White House, waved a fifth of rye at arm's length, repeatedly inviting passers-by to "have a drink on the European Theater of Operations."

A T/Sgt. rounded off his night's excitement by shinnying up a light pole in front of the White House and leading the crowd in song, beating time with a small American flag. He concentrated on corny numbers like "Keep the Home Fires Burning" and "Home on the Range," and between songs he led yells of "We Want Harry!" But the President did not repeat his early-evening appearance. There were many officials in Washington that night who were too busy with the new problems of peace to celebrate the end of the war.

Not everyone on the streets was demonstrative, either. "I can't get that jubilant," said a T-5 thoughtfully. "You'd be surprised how many didn't get drunk tonight. I didn't."

And a middle-aged white-haired man with a Scottish burr remarked sadly, "You know, soldier, it's a nice celebration, but I lost two sons—two sons. It might be a joke to some, but . . ."

And the middle-aged man shook his head and walked slowly away.

—Sgt. BARRETT McGURN

CAMP KILMER, N. J.
Dusk had just about settled over the rolling Jersey countryside when the factory whistles of nearby New Brunswick began screaming that the second World War was over.

In War Department Theater No. 1 a captain in a clean, crisp tropical-worsted uniform adorned with an American Defense ribbon was standing on the stage. He was delivering the standard "welcoming lecture" to some GIs who had just got off a ship from Europe and were to be redeployed to the Pacific.

"Now in conclusion, men," he said, "I wish to warn you that any demonstration that results in damage to camp property will result in the postponement of your home furloughs. May your brief stay at Camp Kilmer be pleasant."

Someone hurried onto the stage from the wings and whispered to him: "Captain, President Truman has just announced that the war is over! Tell 'em that before they leave."

"No," replied the captain. "As far as Camp Kilmer is concerned there is to be no announcement of peace until the Colonel hears it from the War Department through channels and announces it officially."

"But President Truman announced it over the radio—it *is* official."

"Sorry, I'm only following orders."

Over in the barracks area a BAR man was outside in the yard burning the fuzz off his brandnew combat boots in the flame of a can of shoe polish. He heard the factory whistles, looked up and then bent his head to his task again.

Inside barracks T-241 some of the newly-arrived GIs were reading or snoring in their sacks. Others were sitting in little groups, shooting the bull. Still others packed the shower room, luxuriating in the steam.

A little buck sergeant came into the barracks, went over to one group sitting among the double-tiered bunks and said, "The war's over. Just heard about it." They grunted and continued shooting the bull.

A permanent party soldier came in with a handful of overseas caps. "Who wants to buy a hat with blue Infantry braid on it?" he asked. "Only two-fifty. Ya can't buy a cap with braid on it in camp and you can't get outta camp and you gotta take off yer wools tomorrow, so ya better get one."

"Two-fifty!" muttered a big corn-haired guy. "What a racket! Probably cost ya no more'n a buck. You commandos got all the angles, ain't ya! About half an hour ago one of yer pals come in and got rid of two bottles of gin for 15 smackers. Probably cost him about five bucks. Just because we can't get outta camp . . ."

Several of the men bought caps, and the per-

..kyo that Japan would have an important an-..uncement to make at 8 o'clock the following ..rning. That made it look as though the situa-..on would remain on ice for the rest of the ..ght and a large slice of New York City's swel-..ng populace nursed itself to bed early with ..oling drinks.

..That was the last sleep for a lot of people for ..ot of hours. Tokyo jumped the gun and at 1:49 ..esday morning broadcast a statement that ..pan would accept the Allied surrender terms. ..roughout the city late stay-uppers hopped ..the phone to rouse their friends and tell them ..e good news. Some made immediately for ..nes Square, setting off a celebration that was ..last well over 48 hours. It was still going ..ong at dawn and carried on right through the ..y and the next day as more and more yelling, ..ughing, horn-tooting thousands poured into the ..ea.

..By Tuesday noon there was still nothing official, ..t from the way the crowds carried on you would ..ver have suspected that peace wasn't yet defi-

In the White House President Truman, surrounded by members of his cabinet, reads the Jap surrender message. Seated by him are Admiral Leahy, Secretary of State Byrnes and ex-Secretary of State Hull.

WASHINGTON
This capital city, over which the Japs boasted they would raise their flag within a year after the attack on Pearl Harbor, relaxed its worn nerves and celebrated the winning of the war with a screaming, drinking, paper-tearing, free-kissing demonstration which combined all the features of New Year's Eve and Mardi Gras.

Fraternization among officers and enlisted men was the order of the night in this usually dignified stronghold of brass, where seemingly every second person in uniform is adorned with bars, leaves, eagles or stars. Every girl was fair game, and rank was no obstacle. A buck sergeant and a corporal chased two WAC captains into the doorway of a shop on F Street and kissed their superiors soundly, despite giggled orders to the contrary.

Two Navy officers who warmly invited a victory kiss from a redheaded Wave ensign in the hallway of the Willard Hotel did not make out as well, but their confusion was covered by

This was part of a hilarious two-night celebration in San Francisco. A crowd, a large part of them being sailors, took over some cable cars, stopping traffic.

In Louisville, Ky., soldiers and sailors reacted pretty much as they did in other parts of the country. They hoisted their girls into the air and yelled.

manent party soldier flashed a sardonic grin at the corn-haired guy.

"By the way," he said, as he headed for the door, "the war's over. Guess you guys won't have to go to the Pacific after all."

"Like hell we won't!" someone shouted from the other end of the room. "We'll get shipped an' you commandos will stay here an' get out."

"Army of occupation in Japan," mused a little Italian from the Bronx. "Geez, why didn't we go over the hill in Austria so's we could of stayed there, fraternizing every night with them gorgeous Heinie babes."

"Oh, Japan ain't so bad," someone chimed in from an upper bunk. "This here book by Roy Chapman Andrews, the explorer, says they got some classy dames in Japan. He says they're one whorehouse there has a huge sign in front of it which says, 'Short time, one yen. All night, including breakfast, three yen.'"

"How much is a yen?"

"You'll find out soon enough, Jack."

"Baloney," said the corn-haired guy. "They ain't gonna ship us to Japan. We at least been overseas 10 months. They'll grab some of these 18-year-olds with peach fuzz on their face."

"That's what you think. Ain't you been in the Army long enough to know it ain't never done a logical thing?"

"Brother," piped a soldier with a Storm Trooper's skull-and-crossbones ring on his finger, "you can say that again!"

"Well, look," said the little Italian from the Bronx, "The war's over. Let's go over to the GI beer hall and toss a few."

Four others went with him. There was a line of more than 200 men in front of the door of the "Gay Nineties," the Area 1 beer hall. They dropped into line. Three-quarters of an hour later they were sitting on the grass outside, drinking beer out of paper cups.

"Nice cool evening, ain't it?" said the corn-haired guy.

"Yeah, quiet, too."

"Shall we sweat out the line for another four cups?"

"Naw, let's hit the sack. We'll be ridin' a train fer purty near two days startin' tomorrow night."

The four ETO veterans got up off the grass and ambled leisurely through the cool, dark night toward barracks T-241. From the direction of New Brunswick came the blaring of horns and the banging of dishpans.

"Well, the war's over."

"Yup."

—Sgt. DAVE RICHARDSON

PASADENA

"A hospital is one hell of a place to be in when a war ends."

That was the majority opinion of the men ranging from private to two-star general who found themselves, on the day of Japan's surrender, patients in the Army hospital which was formerly the swank Vista del Arroyo Hotel. There was bedlam in the hospital, according to Lt. Helen Span, ANC, of Savannah, Ga., when the radio at 4 P. M. brought the official word from the White House.

"They went wild," Lt. Span said of her patients. "They slid down banisters, they chinned themselves on the hospital's chandeliers. The remark most of them made was, 'No Pacific trip now!'"

WAC Sgt. Rayetta Johnson, a former San Diego policewoman, was on MP duty at the hospital's door when the news broke. She held the door open for Maj. Gen. Thompson Lawrence, for the past two years commanding general of the Replacement Training Center, Camp Roberts, Calif., and Mrs. Lawrence. The general, carrying a barracks bag and a suitcase, was entering the hospital as a patient. Leaving off the "sir," Sgt. Johnson said to the general, "It's all over."

The general dropped his bags and grabbed Sgt. Johnson; he and his wife told her that they had two sons in the Pacific.

The hospital rang with shouts, and convalescing patients scurried through the corridors, their maroon robes trailing after them. "All I want," a nurse commented, "is a discharge and some nylons."

"Wotta place to be," moaned a staff sergeant who had been a prisoner in Germany for several months after his B-17 exploded in a raid on Munich. He had come home all in one piece, got his furlough and then banged himself up riding a motorcycle.

Passes were hard to get at the hospital, surrender or no surrender, but the WAC lieutenant who was officer of the day slyly said that as soon as the news came in she had resigned herself to a large number of AWOLs and to much smuggling-in of liquor by visitors. Typical of the passless patients was Pvt. Ted Chuinski of Chicago, back from 14 months in Europe. He sat dejectedly on the front steps, calling out to passing GIs to lend him some clothes. "I couldn't get far in this goddam bathrobe," he said glumly.

—Sgt. LARRY McMANUS

BOSTON

Boston's peace celebration exploded suddenly after the official news of Japanese surrender poured out of countless radios. All morning and afternoon, while many other cities were already wildly celebrating, the Hub, with true New England caution, waited soberly for confirmation.

But this staid attitude was swept away in a surging tide of mass enthusiasm a few minutes after the news came. In a celebration that topped Boston's two-day madness following the collapse of Germany in 1918, over three-quarters of a million people crammed narrow, twisting downtown streets and the famous Common in the wildest riot of noise in the city's long history. It was like 50 New Year's Eves rolled into one.

The most general impulse seemed to be to shout, sing and hug passers-by. For men in uniform the celebration seemed to be more of a kissing fest than anything else. They were seized by girls and women of all ages, and their faces soon burst out in what the movie ads would have called "flaming Technicolor," because of the varied hues of lipstick prints.

Doors of hundreds of churches were opened, and many thousands entered them briefly, if only to pause in silence for a few moments in gratitude

in the midst of an evening in which many ordinarily powerful Boston inhibitions were swept aside.

Though nearly 200 persons required treatment for minor hurts, as they were squeezed and pushed around in the throngs, there were no serious accidents.

The next day, happily, was a holiday, so Boston's celebrators enjoyed a late morning's sleep. They needed it.

SAN FRANCISCO

Peace brought something akin to a state of chaos to the Pacific's largest port of embarkation. The good news was almost too much for San Francisco. Hundreds were injured and a number killed in a celebration that lasted two nights and that at no time had any element of the peaceful about it.

Some of the highlights: Firecrackers, hoarded in Chinatown for eight years, rattled like machine guns. . . . Servicemen and civilians played tug-of-war with fire hose. . . . Market Street, the wide, bar-lined thoroughfare that has long been the center of interest for visiting GIs and sailors, was littered with the wreckage of smashed War Bond booths and broken bottles. . . . A plump redhead danced naked on the base of the city's Native Sons monument after servicemen had torn her clothes off. A sailor lent the woman a coat, and the pair disappeared.

Marine Pfc. James Prim, 34, had as much to celebrate as anybody in San Francisco. He had come safely through bitter South Pacific campaigns. In the early hours of August 15, when the mass hilarity was at its height, Prim fell down a flight of stairs. He died of a fractured skull.

There were thousands of San Franciscans who marked the day soberly and with prayer, but the end of the second World War seems likely to be remembered here as a celebration that got way out of bounds.

NEW ORLEANS

After celebrating the end of the war prematurely three times, New Orleans let loose with everything it had when the official word finally came through from the White House.

A snowstorm of paper had pelted down from office buildings all during the afternoon as optimistic citizens hoped for an immediate announcement of the war's end. The feel of victory in the air kept office workers downtown past their normal working hours, and the announcement caught mobs of shoppers and workers on Canal Street.

So wary of unconfirmed rumors were the people of New Orleans that it took a newsboy three minutes to sell the first copy of the extra proclaiming the real peace. But once they were convinced, no Mardi Gras was ever as gay or as wild as the celebration that followed. Although all bars closed immediately for 24 hours on orders from the police, civilians and servicemen alike were not slow to bring out bottles.

Mobs jammed the "widest street in the world" from sidewalk to sidewalk. Traffic moved with the greatest difficulty in spite of the efforts of the 150 extra policemen called out to handle the crowds. Sailors swarmed up to street cars as they stopped, kissing willing girls through the open windows. A loaded watermelon truck stalled in traffic on the big street, and sailors took over, handing out the melons to passing celebrants.

As every type of paper, except toilet tissue, which was notably absent, fell to the streets in ankle-deep piles, the Commissioner of Public Works announced that three extra street crews would be put to work cleaning up the mess.

In direct contrast to the shouting in the streets was the quiet of a Jesuit church in the business district crowded with parents, wives, and sweethearts of servicemen, offering prayers of thanksgiving for the end of hostilities and the safety of their loved ones. Men and women clutching newspapers with the banner-line PEACE mingled in front of the church, wiping their eyes unashamedly.

With all the bars closed, the French quarter was deserted as both civilians and servicemen hurried to Canal Street to join the festivities. A scattering of foreign soldiers and sailors were seen among the joyful crowd. A young French aviator, seeking refuge in a recruiting booth, spread a newspaper on the floor in an effort to translate the headlines. A passer-by, seeing his problem, shouted "*La guerre est finie!*" and the aviator jumped to his feet with a shout and disappeared into the mob.

Shipyards, aircraft plants and other war industries ceased operations shortly after the news was announced.

The *Times-Picayune*'s weather forecast read: "Peaceful showers and clouds will be enjoyed by New Orleanians. . . ."

HONOLULU

In Honolulu, where the war began for the U.S., the first news of its ending reached a sleepy-eyed Chinese-American radio technician shortly after 1200 hours when he had just finished making his regular weekly check on KGU's station transmitter and was ready to leave for home.

When technician Harry Chu received the U. P. flash that the Japs had offered to accept the Allied peace terms, he put the transmitter back on the air, telephoned the assistant station manager and marked time until an announcer could arrive by playing records interspersed with the following announcement: "Stand by for important news about the Potsdam ultimatum."

The assistant station manager and two announcers arrived at the studio at about 0245 hours. Ten minutes later the first real broadcast of the news went on the air, and reaction from the late-listening radio audience was immediate.

One of the most spontaneous celebrations was

Victory didn't stop the draft. The day after Jap surrender these men were inducted in Cleveland.

at Hickam Field, where hangars, planes and barracks were strafed by the Japs December 7. Crewmen, technicians and passenger-terminal personnel, working on a 24-hour shift to keep bombers and supplies flowing to the battle lines, heard the first news flash and quickly spread the word. GIs in jeeps and command cars and trucks raced up and down the roads with their horns held down. A soldier woke up six members of the AAF band and their noise soon woke up others. When the first parade started down Fox Avenue there were 40 assorted musicians playing "Hail, Hail, The Gang's All Here."

Flight nurses, Wacs and GIs all streamed from their barracks and joined the howling procession. Forty vehicles, lined up three abreast in back of the paraders, loaded with shouting men, women and children, must have looked pretty puny compared with a Times Square celebration, but nothing ever surpassed them in enthusiasm.

Waikiki Beach, where the Army has its rest camp, Fort DeRussy, and the Navy has the Royal Hawaiian Hotel, at first took the news quietly simply because nearly everyone was asleep. But soldiers and sailors who heard the flash went from door to door pounding and shouting, and within 15 minutes all lights were on and groups had gathered to talk over the historic news.

In the replacement training command depot where men are assigned to combat units in the forward areas, jubilation was high. Even though men realized that Jap capitulation would not necessarily cancel their trip west, they knew now it would be for occupation duty and not for actual combat.

By 0600 hours thousands of civilian workers, many of them of Japanese descent, began to arrive at the base. They talked excitedly as they went about their jobs, but now it was beginning to look like just another routine day, as busy as ever with nothing slowed down.

Downtown Honolulu didn't seem to be changed much by the news either. Soldiers and sailors filed along Hotel Street doing the same old things they'd always done on pass days—staring at traffic, shopping in curio stores, having their pictures taken with hula girls. But there was a broad grin on the face of Pfc. Nobuichi Masatsugo, a Japanese-American soldier, as he read the headlines.

"I always knew we had them licked, but I never thought the end would come this soon," he said. He wore a Purple Heart won in Italy, where he had fought with the 34th Division.

"I guess my 76 points will be good after all," commented T-4 Cyril D. Robinson of Klamath Falls, Ore., another soldier on pass in town.

Pvt. Mitchell Rosen, a New York City marine who saw action at Iwo Jima, was taking the news soberly.

"You can credit the Marines, the atomic bomb and the Russians for bringing the Japs to their knees," he said, and he emphasized the word "Marines." —**Cpl. TOM O'BRIEN**

PARIS

The GIs had managed to keep their VJ spirit bottled up through most of the phony rumors, but when the real thing was announced the cork popped with a vengeance. A spontaneous parade, including jeeps and trucks and Wacs and GIs and officers and nurses and enlisted men, snaked from the Red Cross Club at Rainbow Corner down to the *Place de l'Opera* and back.

Jeeps crawled along in the victory celebration so loaded down with cheering GIs that the shape of the vehicles could hardly be discerned. Some GIs showed up with flags to add both color and an official note to the procession. By the time the demonstration hit its full stride trucks and cars were moving five abreast with pedestrian celebrants marching before and behind and between.

The most unusual note of the day was the spontaneous contribution campaign for the Red Cross which started up out of nothing at all except good humor when a GI at the Rainbow Corner pinned a couple of franc notes to a tree, announcing: "This is for the Red Cross."

His idea caught on and soon other GIs were unloading their spare currency. The sport was enlivened considerably by kissing French girls at the tree, whether as a bonus for contributions or just for the hell of it. At any rate, a late afternoon check showed some $14,000 raised for the ARC by what had begun purely as a half-gag gesture of good will.

The whole show was a soldier—especially an American soldier—performance. French civilians were happy and pleased, and they showed it,

SAD SACK
PEACE AT LAST
JAPAN SURRENDERS
SGT GEORGE BAKER

but they still went about their work as much as usual as was possible. They had been drained of celebration first when their city had been freed and later when the European war had ended.

ATLANTIC OCEAN

GIs aboard troopships at sea, heading back for the States from Europe, heard about the Japanese surrender over the ship's p. a. system barely three minutes after the Washington news flash was received in the radio room, and read details in "extras" of mimeographed and typed ship's newspapers as quickly as the folks back home.

On the *Cape Flattery*, carrying 600 returning officers and low-point EM who'd thought they were headed for the Pacific after a Stateside furlough, each premature announcement was greeted with cheers and then with groans when it turned out to be a false alarm. The *Flattery's* news sheet, the *Bilge*, appeared with a daily news roundup.

One false flash came through at 2 A.M., long after "lights out," so almost nobody heard the news until morning. A pfc was rudely informed by a sergeant who rolled him out of bed at 5:30: "Wake up. The war's over and you're on KP."

But—unlike the boy who cried wolf—the first mate never lost the confidence of his p. a. listeners, and when President Truman made it official, everybody cut loose.

A minute later the chaplain took command of the loudspeaker, leading troops and crew in a prayer for their fallen comrades.

—Sgt. ALLAN B. ECKER

MANILA

The headline, in type so big that the words ran together across the top of the page, said: "NIPS QUIT." The Japanese prisoners of war crowded around the superior private who held the paper. They stood in the sun-baked courtyard of the new

open. About 30 Japs, most of them newly arrived at the prison, lay or sat on blankets spread on the concrete floor. On one side of the room were the day's crop of newcomers. Most of them were just skin and bones, and the GI shorts they wore hung loosely on their flanks as they lay with their thin arms clasped behind their heads, their dead eyes staring at nothing.

On the other side of the room were healthier specimens waiting to be assigned to work companies. It was easy to tell how long they had been prisoners by the amount of meat on their bones.

When the visitors were seated around the superior private's cot (he has a cot because he's a trusty and in charge of this part of the processing center), the interpreter asked him how he felt about the news of Japan's capitulation.

The soldier rubbed his eyes with the palm of his hand and figured out just what he wanted to say.

"I'm not sorry," he told the interpreter. "I'm in a happy mood." He smiled cheerfully to show how happy the mood was. There was a murmur in the room as the word passed from pallet to pallet, and some of those who had been lying down sat up and watched.

He was asked if he wanted to go home now. This was a ticklish one. He wanted to go home, and he didn't want to go home. His relatives and his friends at the aluminum plant where he worked in Tokyo might point at him, he said, and he didn't want to be pointed at. The Japs who had edged into the group all looked at the floor. Nobody said anything for a moment. The superior private looked up and smiled again— his happy mood smile. He was happy that the

After he told the interpreter about his surrender, he spoke rapidly for a moment and the interpreter laughed.

"He wants to go to America," the interpreter said.

"Houseboy!" yelled the sergeant in clear English, the first he had spoken.

—Sgt. ROBERT MacMILLAN

ROME

The people of Rome—Italian civilians and U. S. GIs—took the news of the Japanese surrender in their strides. There weren't any parades, bells didn't ring and there were few drunken soldiers. People went about their business as usual, including the girls on the *Via del Tritone*.

In front of the *Ristorante San Carlo*, a GI restaurant on the *Corso Umberto*, there was the usual line of hungry soldiers waiting to eat. Aside from the fact that most of them were grinning as if they'd just heard a joke, they showed little reaction to the news. A big, beefy corporal wearing a Bronze Star ribbon and a blue combat Infantryman's badge, with the Red Bull patch of the 34th Division on his shoulder, said, "I don't know. Can't believe it. Only two bombs and they give up. Don't sound like all that stuff we hear about the Japs fighting to the end. Seems to me there's a catch somewhere. Hey, what the hell's holding up this line?"

Outside the PX Italian kids were begging for cigarettes with "Joe, war *finito*. You give me one cigarette?"

On the night when the papers hit the streets of Manila with headlines of Jap surrender, thousands of Filipinos celebrated.

In London, on Piccadilly Circus, bunch of GIs and a New Zealand sailor (left) hoist an English bobby onto their shoulders when they heard the Japs had offered to qu

Bilibid Prison south of Manila, where some 8,000 former soldiers of the emperor are confined.

An elderly Japanese civilian interpreter lifted his eyebrows, adjusted his spectacles and translated.

"*Nippon*," he said. "*Nippon kofuku*."

The superior private glanced sidelong at the older man and laughed at him. The civilian thumped the paper with his forefinger and repeated the translation.

The superior private frowned and stared at the page that said that the war was ending and that his country was offering to surrender. The Japs behind him chattered and stuck their heads over his shoulder to see for themselves. The superior private left the paper with them and walked into the long concrete building where he lived.

I followed with the interpreter.

The room, which was part of the processing center for incoming prisoners, was about the size of a Stateside Army barracks. The windows were barred, but the door was unlocked and

war had ended and that the world could know peace again, he said.

The others, watching him, all smiled, too. They put on their happy-mood smiles, and there was the sound of polite hissing.

A muscle-jawed Jap sergeant joined the group. He'd been a prisoner for about a month and was in pretty fair condition. He, too, had been aware of what was going on.

"I'm much relieved," he told the interpreter. "All my friends [he indicated the Japs along the wall], all my friends have such a mood of mind." The Japs along the wall stared impassively. The sergeant gave his name and said he had no objection to having it published in an American magazine. He was a medical sergeant about 40 years old, and he had an abscess on one leg. He had given up after four months hiding in the hills.

A Nisei staff sergeant from the 442d Regimental Combat Team came out carrying a paper bag full of rations. He grinned and said, "Wonderful news. Almost too good to be true. I'm anxious to get home. I hope people there'll realize the war's over. But it's sure fine news—best ever."

In front of the Red Cross a gray-haired tech said, "The best news I've ever heard on the radio. It's a funny thing. I came out of an Engineer outfit that's headed for the Pacific. They pulled me out because I got 95 points. I wonder if the boys have left Italy yet. They'll sure have the laugh if they beat me home."

At a sidewalk cafe on the *Via Nazionale* stood a bald-headed GI who was getting a buzz on. Laughing and sweating, he showed two Italians pictures of his wife and kids.

". . . and this garage here, you can just see part of it sticking out from the side of the house. I got the sweetest little Buick, what a car. You *capito* Buick?"

Inside the Florida Club, a GI hot spot, things

ked about the same—a band giving out with
he strictly Roman version hot jazz, about 30
ples dancing and several soldiers singing at
ir tables. A private who said he was attached
the 34th Station Hospital was drinking with
over-bright thin blonde. The private said, "I
't know why, but the thing sort of sneaks up
you. I started out to raise hell tonight but
ehow I can't get started. It seems hard to
ieve. No more worrying about points, stripes
anything. Bud, when ı get home now, it's to
y. Maybe when I get home I'll celebrate, really
ch some hell."

War finito," the blonde said. "Buono. Ameri-
s leave Rome, no?"

t was hard to tell from her voice whether
thought the GIs leaving Italy would be a
d or a bad deal.

he private put his arm around her and said,
ssir, baby, from now on it's home sweet home.
ay 'Home Sweet Home,' " he shouted at the
estra leader.

GI at the next table said, "That ain't dancing
sic."

he nine o'clock show at the Barberini Thea-
was out and the crowd of GIs and Tommies
eamed into the streets fresh from seeing Lana
rner in "Slightly Dangerous." An English ser-
nt said, "Wonderful news. I went to the
ema because I didn't know what to do with
self. Five years of it for me, you know.
arly four overseas. I was slated for Burma so
glad the show's over."

couple of soldiers were walking down the
del Tritone singing hillbilly songs. Three
zilian soldiers were sitting in a parked jeep
tching the girls as they passed under the
et light, laughing and making cracks in
rtuguese. On the corner an Italian was selling
ermelon slices to a small crowd of civilians
o stood around his cart eating and spitting the

**Out in Guam, advance headquarters of the Navy,
these servicemen gathered around to cheer the news.**

"When you guys get papers from home now you
better start reading the want ads columns." The
crack brought a wave of laughter.

The Negro GI smiled. "That's a fact. Start
thinking about jobs, but after the Army it'll be
a pleasure."

An Air Force master sergeant and a Wac corporal were standing in front of the Rome Area
Command building, opposite the famous balcony
in Piazza Venezia where Mussolini used to ha-
rangue crowds. The six-striper said, "It's great
news all right, although I guess we've been
expecting it. Japan can't stand against the world.
I'm in an occupation bomb group down at Fog-
gia. You think they'll still keep us here now?
I've got 18 months overseas. They ought to send
some of these new guys for occupation work."

"They certainly ought to send over men
who've never been out of the States," said the
Wac. "I think they could even get a volunteer
force. I wonder if we or the Chinese will occupy
Japan."

"My God, don't even talk about that," said the
sergeant, laughing. "Can you imagine Japan
with a Chinese occupation force? Damn!"

It was a little after midnight and St. Peter's
looked very solemn and impressive against the
stars. The church was shut. GIs kept coming up
and then standing and looking at the church as
if they didn't know what to do. One soldier said
"I thought it would be open tonight."

An elderly Italian said that in Italy all churches
close at dark.

"I know, but tonight . . ." the soldier said.

At the entrance to the Swiss Guard barracks
a heavy-set guard in the ancient uniform of this
small army was standing at the gate. His face
was expressionless—his army life not dependent
on the war's ending or beginning.

On the day when the greatest and most terrible war in world history came to an end, on
the day when fascism was finally broken in the
world, Rome—where fascism was born—was quiet
and orderly. Rome has seen its share of this war.
Maybe there should have been a lot of noise and
great rejoicing. Here, where people know war,
there wasn't shouting, ticker tape showers or
hysterical parades, but the people were happy.
In Rome most people were merely smiling
quietly.   —Cpl. LEN ZINBERG

ALASKA GIs from Fort Richardson tried
to take over the nearby town of
Anchorage when the final surrender news came
through, but the town's six blocks of bars and
liquor stores folded under the impact. Anchorage's seemingly inexhaustible supply of liquor
just wasn't enough to meet the demand.

The celebration got under way early Tuesday
afternoon and continued till 8 P.M. when the bars
closed. Civilian neckties keynoted the rejoicing
here. GIs bought up all the available ties in
Anchorage stores and when the tie supply was
exhausted they exchanged OD ties with civilians.
MPs removed OD ties from soldiers; the MPs
wore civilian ties themselves.

The difficulty for the MPs was telling soldiers
from civilians. Officers and EM exchanged insignia and stripes and one sergeant made full
colonel during the evening.

Local girls did a strip tease for a couple of
hundred GIs. They stripped in a hotel window
and tossed their garments to soldiers gathered

ese GIs crowded on top of a jeep and drove
rough the streets of Paris celebrating victory

ds out. You could hear them saying, "Guerra
ta . . . bomba atomica . . . molti morti . . ."
ile a loud-mouthed buck sergeant from II
rps was happily stuffing himself with melon
d explaining how the atomic bomb worked.
n the Borghese Gardens a Fifth Army T-5
s sitting with a slim, pretty Italian girl. "I
ared something like this would come. It's been
long war and nobody's sorry it's over. Of
urse, I married here—this is my wife. Now I
nder how soon I'll go home and if she'll be
le to go to the States at the same time. If she
s stuck here, I'm going to ask for a discharge
re and sweat out Italy till we can both go to
 States. But no more sweating out Japan!"

ear the Galleria Club a Negro sergeant from
 92d Division, wearing a silver star ribbon
der his combat Infantryman's badge, said, "I'm
d we didn't have to invade Japan. That
uld've been a bitch. Got a brother in the Navy
 the Pacific and I bet he's shouting now."

nside the club somebody yelled over the music.

below. Telegrams to and from the States quadru-
pled over the previous day.

The reaction was summed up by Sgt. Bob Kirk
of Chicago: "How long is the duration?"
                                    —Sgt. AL WEISMAN

LONDON Two Canadian soldiers walked
into a restaurant talking quiet-
ly about the Japanese surrender offer. A GI sitting in one of the American-style booths caught
their words and let out a whoop. "We're going
to tear this place apart!" he announced.

Then he lapsed into silence. Other Americans
in the restaurant reacted pretty much the same
way. As one soldier remarked, "We're still in
Europe, bud."

There was a little more excitement as the evening wore on and there were crowds in Piccadilly Circus and Leicester and Trafalgar Squares.
Quite a few people got rid of their waste paper
by throwing it out of windows, a sign that the
need for saving such things for the war effort
was just about over.

Five hundred GIs who arrived that evening on
furlough from the continent weren't exactly on
fire about the news, either. Duffel bags and toilet
kits on their shoulders, they queued up to register
for rooms at the Red Cross Club as quietly as
they have been queuing up for everything else
during their army careers. A lot of the furlough-
ing troops said they didn't believe the war was
over and even if it was they'd still have to sweat
out transportation home for a long time yet.

Quite a few GIs were more interested in talking about the atomic bomb than about Japan.
They were afraid of the new weapon and its
potential force for evil. Cpl. Paul Martin of
Vauxhall, N. J., an anti-tank gunner with the
9th Division in France, Belgium and Germany
and now with the army of occupation in Germany, was a little dazed.

"The news that Japan gave up seems impossible to me," he said. "Especially since the Russians have only been in the thing for one day.
This atom bomb is sure a lotta hell; it had a lot
to do with the surrender. I have to go back to
Germany, but I'm glad for the guys who're
sweating it out in the Pacific now. I'll get home
eventually and it might be a little quicker than
I thought this time last year. How long will we
have to stay in Germany? Depends on how long
we take to get those buergermeisters working
right."

"Yeah, I know the atom bomb helped a lot,
but it wasn't the only factor in the surrender.
Right now I want to go home; I've got 134 points,
and I've got a son two years old I never saw and
a girl that I only saw once. Who doesn't want to
go home, brother?"

Sgt. Bernard Katz of Pittsburgh, Pa., now with
the 36th Bombardment Squadron, Eighth Air
Force, has been in the Army for five years and
had special reactions.

"I'm one guy who ought to be glad, because I
saw my first action on Dec. 7, 1941. I was at
Wheeler Field on Oahu, the first island the Japs
attacked.

"We thought it was an earthquake until we
found out that it was war, and war was worse.
I jumped under a theater for shelter and found
myself lying beside a two-star general. He didn't
say anything about saluting, and neither did I.

"Now it's all over. For good, I hope. I think a
combination of the Russians and the atom bomb
did the trick in about equal proportions. I think
the atom bomb is the best weapon to prevent
future wars, and I also think it should be given
to the whole world so it can be developed to its
fullest extent. Even the Japs and Germans should
be given it when they're domesticated enough."
                                    —Sgt. FRANCIS BURKE

BERLIN The city that had seen its own
brand of fascism and international
banditry tumble only a few months before had
little energy left for reaction to the fall of
Japan. The American Forces network broadcast
the first authentic VJ news at 0210, and most of
Berlin's polyglot occupation population, as well
as most native Berliners, were asleep.

The U.S. Army newspaper Allgemeine Zeitung was the only Berlin paper which carried
the news the next day. But the four days of false
alarms made even the real thing seem unexciting.

Russian GIs interviewed had the same responses as their American counterparts. Said one
of them, typically, "Now maybe I can get home
to see my wife and children."

Generalissimo Stalin was the only one left of the original Big Three as the Potsdam conference ended.

but equally historic. To San Francisco came delegates from 46 nations bent on creating a world security organization that was to enforce justice among nations and redeem the sacrifices of the war. The conference itself had been heralded weeks in advance, but the question of whether or not it would result in agreement was uppermost in millions of minds. Success would not necessarily guarantee the peace of the world for all time, but failure would almost certainly be the first step toward a third World War—and for a time it seemed touch and go. Would Russia's position on Poland upset the apple cart? Would the admission of Argentina open the way to a renewed lease of life for Fascism? Would the small states rebel at a concentration of power in the hands of the Big Three? Could a sound peace rest on a basis of power? All these doubts, and the rumors that accompanied them, contributed to the jitters of a nation.

While the earnest delegates successfully struggled through political mists thicker than the fogs that rolled in from San Francisco Bay, word came from Milan that the first of the dictators—Benito Mussolini, "modern Caesar," founder of Fascism, and chest-thumper extraordinary—had been shot, along with his mistress, Clara Petacci.

THE LAST 125 DAYS

ALL OVER THE WORLD THINGS SEEMED TO HAPPEN ALL AT ONCE IN THE FINAL FOUR MONTHS OF WAR

Men and women everywhere took the death of President Roosevelt, on April 12, as a deep personal loss.

dragged through the gutter and strung up by the heels from the girder of a gas station. Public figures had been assassinated before, but here was a melodrama of revenge more startling than the blood-and-thunder of the most far-fetched spy thriller.

THAT was April 28—and for the last time Mussolini was showing the way to his colleague in tyranny. Within three days came the startling announcement from Hamburg that Adolf Hitler, too, had ceased to dishonor the planet with his presence, that he had "died at his post" in the ruins of Berlin. It took a while for the news to sink in that the man who had plunged the world into the greatest misery it had known in centuries, who had made fanatic cruelty the law of a nation, who had conquered nearly the entire Continent of Europe and spread his poison to all parts of the world—was at last dead and done for. But here, too, melodrama crept in and made a big news story doubly intriguing; nobody could be quite sure that Hitler really *was* dead, and the groundwork was laid for the mystery of the century.

Hitler's reported end was the natural prelude to an even bigger story—the collapse of Germany, the Nazi state that was to endure for a thousand years and make slaves of all the lesser people of the earth. That story broke — unofficially—on May 7, when morning radio programs in the East (Californians were still asleep) were interrupted for a flash report that the Allies had officially announced the unconditional surrender of Germany (which, in fact, they didn't get around to doing until the next day). Even though victory could have been seen approaching at a gallop for weeks before it arrived, the news was a breathtaker. Celebrations were jubilant, but on all sides they were tempered by words of warning: there was still Japan to conquer, and that might be a long, costly and bloody business. Six months to a year, said the optimists. A year and a half to two years, countered the cautious. Gradually the excitement died down.

June was, for these feverish times, comparatively calm. There was, of course, the rounding up of the once-proud leaders of the "master race," the stepping up of the war in the Pacific, including the great victory at Okinawa, and the successful windup of the San Francisco conference. But the next really big story, No. 6 on our list, did not break until July 15. On that day the British were able to announce, in the

By Pfc. ROBERT BENDINER
YANK Staff Writer

NEVER before — to take off on Winston Churchill's famous phrase—has so much history affecting so many people been made in so short a time. In the 125 days starting with April 12 of this year no fewer than 10 world-rocking headlines were splashed across the newspapers of the country, any one of them explosive enough to furnish the average human being with his excitement quota for a year. Raining down in breathless succession, these news bombshells found their target in a public nervous system which should logically be so frayed by this time that it will be fit to take nothing stronger than accounts of tiddly-winks tournaments for at least a year to come.

It is hard to believe that the first of these four-alarm stories broke on a stunned world only four months ago. On the 12th of April at 3:35 P.M. in the "Little White House" at Warm Springs, Ga., President Franklin Delano Roosevelt died. Papers from one end of the country to the other broke out with the 260- and 300-point woodblock heads reserved for moments of history. Commercials vanished from the air waves, which for 24 hours echoed almost exclusively to solemn tributes and words of mourning. Men and women everywhere took the death of the President as a deep personal loss but beneath this profound emotion ran another—and equally taxing sensation—a strong current of excitement over possible political changes, the feverish speculation that naturally accompanied the first presidential shift in more than 12 years.

Less than two weeks after this emotional outpouring came a story less personal, less dramatic, unruffled way that characterizes their country; that they had just experienced the biggest electoral upset in their history.

By a two-to-one count they had voted Winston Churchill, one of the greatest war leaders of British history, out of office in order to install a government that had pledged itself to nationalize whole sections of the country's economy and push toward the goal of socialism. Not since that remote period before Hitler had embarked on his first aggression, even before Mussolini had pitted his legions against the Ethiopians, had Britain had a national election. The result was a revelation.

WHATEVER its long-range significance, the election's immediate consequence was the second substitution in the cast of the Big Three. At Potsdam, on the outskirts of Berlin, the seventh of our heady headlines was in the making. What Roosevelt, Churchill and Stalin had started long ago was carried to completion by Marshal Stalin, President Truman and Britain's new Prime Minister, Clement Attlee. On August 2, after sessions of the strictest secrecy, the fate of Germany and much of Europe was announced —the decision to make Germany a third-rate industrial power, incapable of waging war, stripped of East Prussia and of large areas along the Oder, and denied a central government for an indefinite future. Equally sensational was the ultimatum issued from Potsdam to the Japanese Terms were laid down, and for the first time the enemy had a concrete picture of what it could expect in the event of unconditional surrender. Failure to accept, it was pointed out by the American, British and Chinese governments, would mean the utter destruction of Japan.

That was only a starter for the month of August, which was to bring the wave of history to a towering crest. Before August was half over three of the biggest news stories of the war—and one of the biggest in the history of the world— had broken on a public almost immune to eight-column streamer heads and "flash" interruptions of the morning soap opera.

On August 7, a date that will probably be memorized by schoolboys for generations, the world of the future was ushered in. The power of the atom, the basic energy of the universe, had at last been harnessed to the uses of man. Its first employment was to blow 60 percent of the Japanese city of Hiroshima completely out of existence. The tiny atom promised a speedy end of the war. And, more important in the long run, it marked out alternative roads for men of the 20th century to follow: the suicide of our civilization through atomic warfare, or the salvation of that civilization through peaceful application of this monumental scientific advance.

People were still rubbing their eyes and trying to stretch their minds enough to take in the overwhelming significance of the atomic bomb when Story No. 9 crashed through. Three months from the date of the German surrender the Soviet Union entered the war in the Pacific. Long poised on the borders of Manchuria, the Red Army of the East plunged across the line from east and west, and Americans rejoiced that the Japs' crack Kwantung Army could be left to the Russians while our own forces concentrated on the enemy's jittery home islands.

IT seemed impossible for the war to go on for more than a matter of months, but the public was hardly prepared for the swiftness of the Japanese collapse. Early on the morning of August 10 the enemy threw in the sponge. By way of Domei, the Japanese news agency, came word that the Tokyo government was prepared to accept the Potsdam terms provided the "sovereignty" of the Emperor was left intact. Four days of uncertainty followed, days of feverish consultation in high places and tentative jubilation in places both high and low. One thing was certain: the end of the second World War was imminent. The day longed for by an entire world through six tortured years was about to dawn.

In four short months this planet had come a long way. Three figures who had dominated the news of a decade were gone—Roosevelt, Mussolini and Hitler—and a fourth, Winston Churchill, had passed from leadership of an empire to leadership of His Majesty's Loyal Opposition. Nazi Germany had been ground into the dust and its ruthless leaders either driven to suicide or brought to the prisoner's dock. The foundations for a durable world security organization

Whether or not Hitler died in Berlin made a big story but a bigger one was the German surrender on May 7.

had been laid, and the outlines drawn for a reconstructed Europe. A Labor government had swept into power in England, with possible repercussions in all the liberated countries of the Continent. And the most widespread and devastating war in history was brought to an end with the capitulation of those Japanese jingos who had threatened to fight if necessary for a hundred years. Finally, towering above even these massive events, a revolution had taken place in science, which promised in time either to make the mighty atom work for man or to destroy man and his world in another war.

After a streak like that it would not be surprising if a revulsion against "big news" should set in. It may well be that people long to pick up a paper in which nothing more cosmic is reported than the city's reception of a visiting channel-swimmer, and nothing more violent than a tie-up on the Magnolia Avenue trolley line.

On the other hand, "big news" is a potent drug. On the day between Russia's entry into the Pacific war and the Japs' bid for peace more than one American was heard to complain that things were slow, "nothing new." For such jaded addicts nothing will do now but an extra with the eight-column streamer: MOON COLLIDES WITH EARTH AS MARTIANS CHEER—unless it is that equally exciting head: ALL GIs DISCHARGED AS ARMY SCRAPS RED TAPE. But let's not be fantastic.

Word came from Milan on April 28 that Mussolini and his mistress had been shot and strung up in the square.

THE MIGHTY ATOM

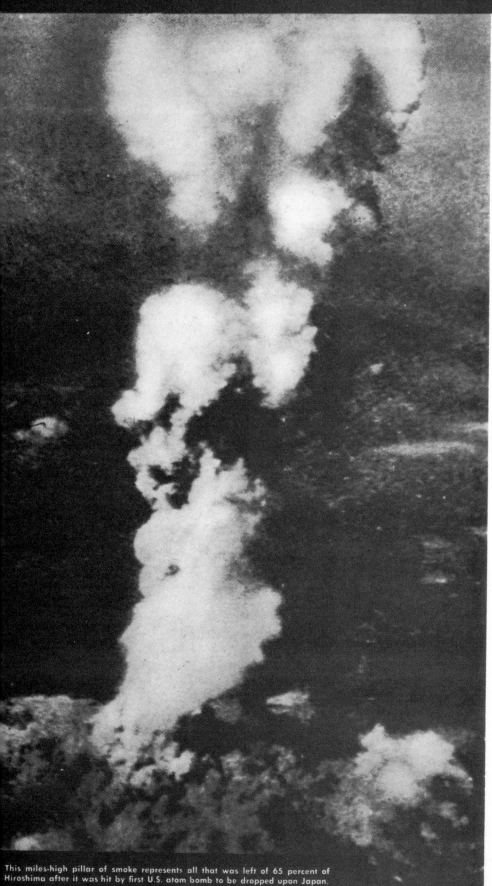

This miles-high pillar of smoke represents all that was left of 65 percent of Hiroshima after it was hit by first U.S. atom bomb to be dropped upon Japan.

From it science forged the war's most fearful weapon, gave Japan the final blow and opened a new era of vast energy that can, man willing, be harnessed for peace. These six pages tell the story.

By Cpl. JONATHAN KILBOURN
YANK Staff Writer

THINK of the smallest thing you can conceive of, then divide it by two billion. That will give you an approximate idea of the size of the atom, which provides the energy for the most destructive weapon in the world, the atomic bomb.

The bombs that devastated Hiroshima and Nagasaki contained billions of atoms.

An atom consists of almost inconceivably tiny particles of electricity, negatively charged, positively charged and "neutral."

Any given amount of any "thing" consists of atoms—billions of them, like the small particles of sand on an ocean beach. Everything you see around you, everything you see or touch is made of atoms. You are, too.

Each atom is like our solar system in the smallest miniature. In the center is the sun, the nucleus. Around it revolve the planets, called electrons. But they whirl billions of times faster than our world.

Science has broken down into component parts the sun of the atom world. This nucleus is composed of a conglomeration of individual particles of two kinds, protons and neutrons. Protons are positively charged, neutrons are neutral.

The atom solar system would burst apart if there were not a force to bind it together. This force is supplied by the attraction between the one or more protons in the nucleus and the atom's electron planets, which are negatively charged.

HOLDING our little atom system together takes terrific energy. This energy, released, means not only the end of the atom world but, within its sphere, unimaginable pandemonium, like a minute Judgment Day. Temperatures of millions of degrees are developed. Pressures produced are far and away the most violent reactions known. Until this reaction was first discovered, human beings couldn't even conceive of such power.

The reaction depends on no chemical element for combustion; it is entirely self-sustaining. The crashing destruction continues until the entire atomic solar system breaks apart.

What happens to the exploded particles and how can this miniature cataclysm be created? Because the explosion is over so quickly—it takes place in only 1/1,000,000th of a second—the details of the reaction are hard to trace.

And bringing about this cataclysm is doubly difficult because atoms are not packed tightly together. Trying to smash just any old atom in a molecule or piece of matter would be, as Albert Einstein puts it, like trying to shoot ducks on a dark night in a section where ducks are rare. There would be millions of misses for every hit.

The component parts of the atom world are few and far between, too. Like our solar system, the atom is mostly space. The atom sun occupies only one millionth of a billionth of the atomic solar system's reaches.

If all the electronic planets and empty space were taken from the myriad of atomic solar systems that compose a 150-pound man, and only the nuclei remained, there would be left a lump no larger than a ball of buckshot.

Taking the electrons and space from this 150-

pound man's miniature solar systems would not, however, leave a neat little lump without producing an explosion beyond imagining. For atomic disintegration is not the kind of explosion we are familiar with. Ordinary explosions and fires are started by the separation from one another, and the rearrangement, of molecules. The molecules themselves remain whole, but the energy that held them together is released in heat and light and explosive force.

We daily see atomic explosions, but from afar, so far that we are not familiar with their characteristics. The sun's heat and light and the many rays it sends forth are produced by such explosions—explosions that go much farther than the mere separation of molecular groups. Atoms separate from one another, and the disintegration goes farther still. The atoms themselves break down.

An incredibly greater amount of heat and light results. Other forces are released, some so powerful that they have only been guessed at.

The disintegration of one atom in the laboratory causes havoc in the atom's solar system but none in the room itself. This is because a chain of atom worlds—great numbers of them—would have to go off to equal the detonation of a firecracker. Yet a combination of atoms little larger than a pea could cause terrible destruction because of the billions upon billions of atoms it contains.

To create such a combination, and favorable circumstances for bombarding that combination, are the primary problems of the atom-smasher and the makers of the atom bomb. Haphazard bombardment of the atom is like shooting peas at an electric fan. The speed of the electrons in their orbits makes the atom practically impenetrable. Moreover, the electrons successfully resist most positively charged particles.

A neutron, however, has no electrical charge. But neither can it move unaided. Because it has no charge, scientists who wish to break into the well-defended atom world cannot whirl the neutron by itself in their giant atom-disrupting cyclotrons or in the atom bombs.

To give the neutron motive power, scientists sometimes use the heavy hydrogen atom, which contains a nucleus in which a proton and a neutron are combined. The heavy hydrogen atom is whirled in the magnetic field of the cyclotron. When the heavy hydrogen atom hits the target—the uranium atom to be smashed—the hydrogen nucleus breaks apart. Into the uranium atom goes the neutron.

The atom target of the neutron can be uranium 235, one of the uranium atoms and the atom with the most powerful electric guards of all. U-235 has 92 positively charged particles in its nucleus which repel any protron stranger that tries to crash its world. Ninety-two electron planets revolve around it, and these satellites repel all negative strangers.

The reason why scientists use unsociable uranium instead of some more companionable material is that U-235 (the number is its atomic weight), one of the atoms in uranium, becomes unstable when its weight is increased by one unit by shooting a neutron into it. The same is true of plutonium, the artificial chemical element created by science to provide a super-atomic energy source, which has an atomic weight of 239, heaviest in existence.

Whenever the balance of its system is broken by a neutron, either U-235 or plutonium smashes into two nearly equal parts.

The heavier the atom, the greater the binding energy necessary to hold it together. When the uranium atom is split in two parts and two lighter atoms are formed, these two together require less energy to hold together than the atom from which they were formed. What's left goes out in the form of excess energy—it explodes. And what's left is 200,000,000 electron volts.

That sounds like a lot, but it's just a flicker of a match in the atomic universe. Within its sphere the effect is utterly destructive. But unless the atomic system's disintegration spreads to other similar systems, it is not observable by the naked eye of man.

When the rapidly traveling neutrons hit a 235er, nothing happens in the ordinary nature of things. At high speeds the 235s are immune. Just slow the neutron down a bit, however, and the atom splits. When neutrons float through the air they penetrate the 235s with the greatest of ease.

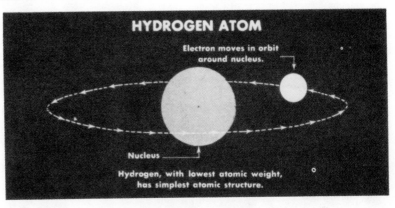

HYDROGEN ATOM

Electron moves in orbit around nucleus.

Nucleus

Hydrogen, with lowest atomic weight, has simplest atomic structure.

URANIUM ATOM

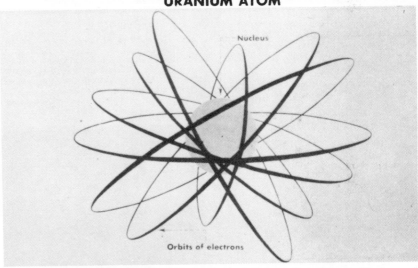

Nucleus

Orbits of electrons

Uranium atom is most complex and rarest of atoms. Its nucleus consists of 92 protons and 143 neutrons, around which whirl 93 electrons in seven orbits.

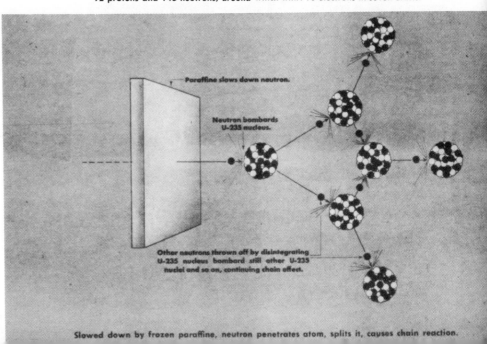

Paraffine slows down neutron.

Neutron bombards U-235 nucleus.

Other neutrons thrown off by disintegrating U-235 nucleus bombard still other U-235 nuclei and so on, continuing chain effect.

Slowed down by frozen paraffine, neutron penetrates atom, splits it, causes chain reaction.

To cause a successful chain reaction, scientists must arrange things so that the free neutrons are slowed from their dizzying pace.

The neutrons can be caused to collide with frozen paraffine. Hydrogen atoms in the paraffine, about the same weight as the neutrons but active agents, practically stop the neutrons in their tracks—much as one billiard ball can be stopped dead by hitting another.

The neutrons are now shot at the 235s, and the chain reaction ensues. Out of the blast that tears the uranium atom in two come also gamma rays —powerful radiations that sometimes tear electrons off atoms and otherwise shatter them, creating further flying fragments and debris.

The chain reaction is on, carried forward by the swarms of neutrons released from each atom that is split. Rebounding back and forth, the neutrons are sufficiently slowed so that the process is continued, and vast energy is released.

It is this energy that created chaos in Japan. It is this same energy which poses the possibility of a new era, the era of atomic power, in which the vast energies of the atom, harnessed as the atom bomb shows they can be, may give mankind power greater than it has ever had.

This 20-ton cyclotron at Notre Dame is one of many in scientists smashed atoms prior to invention of the

THE ATOMIC BOMB

"Sixteen hours ago an American airplane dropped one bomb on Hiroshima. . . . That bomb had more power than 20,000 tons of TNT. It is an atomic bomb . . . a harnessing of the basic power of the universe."

THAT simple statement, made by President Truman at 10:30 A.M., August 6, electrified the world. It came as the climax of one of the most dramatic stories in the history of man's long search for the secrets of matter.

The story behind the atomic bomb is a detective story with no Sherlock Holmes for a hero. The number of scientists who took part in the search was without parallel. And when the first of the bombs hit Hiroshima it was a victory for the whole force. No star-performing "special investigator" could claim credit for the breath-taking, earth-shattering climax.

Brilliant deductions had been made, clue after clue tracked down to climactic discoveries. But although the individual findings of many men share the credit for the final, almost incredible success, that success was made possible primarily by the kind of leg work and laboratory work in which a metropolitan police force would take part—leg work and lab work entailing years of drudgery as well as drama, ill-omened activity as well as inspiration, false scents as well as cosmic clues.

The dramatic story opens with Dr. Lise Meitner, a woman scientist and director of the Kaiser Wilhelm Institute in Berlin. In 1938 Dr. Meitner is bombarding uranium atoms with neutrons and then submitting the uranium to chemical analysis.

To her amazement, she and her associates, Drs. Otto Hahn and F. Strassmann, find the element barium in the smashed remains of the uranium. They remember they had put in barium as a chemical "carrier" to precipitate a powerful new radioactive substance present in the debris, but when they try to separate the substance from the barium, it cannot be done.

There is one possible answer, and only one. The mysterious substance is itself barium—a radioactive barium that had been there before the other barium was put in.

But where did the radioactive barium come from? It was a scientific mystery of the first order. It was like finding champagne flowing from your faucet. It just couldn't be.

And then Hitler's racist theories came into the story. Dr. Meitner was a Jewess. Hitler had over-ruled his own Nuernberg anti-Semitic laws in order to try to compel her to stay in Germany, but Dr. Meitner, outraged by the "new order," escaped over the Dutch border and fled to

Sweden, stopping in Denmark on the way.

With Dr. Meitner in Copenhagen, her former colleagues refused to face the facts of their revolutionary discovery. They reported in a German scientific publication that they could not bring themselves to believe that the radioactive barium came from the uranium.

Lise Meitner was more imaginative. Since the barium was not there to begin with, she reasoned,

it must have come from the uranium. That meant it was the result of the uranium atom being split into two nearly equal parts.

She lost no time in getting in touch with her nephew, Dr. Otto Robert Frisch, who worked in the Copenhagen laboratory of the famous Danish physicist, Dr. Niels Bohr. Testing together for the radioactive barium, they saw for the first time the possibility of a geyser of atomic energy.

In the first weeks of 1939 Dr. Frisch succeeded at his task. He split the uranium atom.

Dr. Frisch cabled the news to Dr. Bohr, who was in the U. S. With Dr. John Dunning, Dr. Bohr and Prof. Enrico Fermi, both Nobel prize winners in physics, repeated the experiment at

Little was left of Hiroshima when a reconnaissance plane flew over the devastated city to take this photo day after the first atom bombing. Many buildings and whole city blocks were vaporized.

Columbia University and announced the news to an astounded scientific world.

Prof. Fermi then revealed that five years before he had been firing atomic bullets and had been prevented from making the discovery of uranium fission—the splitting of the uranium atom in two—only by a mischance in his technique.

Prof. Fermi, incidentally, is pretty happy today about his failure. When he came so close to making that fateful discovery he was in Mussolini's Italy. Had he succeeded before his exile the Axis might have had atomic bombs with which to begin its war.

• The Axis was thwarted again and again by its own tyranny. Among the scientists who helped produce the atom bomb were two Jewish physicists who were forced by the Nazis to emigrate to England and a Danish professor who was smuggled out of German-occupied Copenhagen with atomic secrets which he carried with him to London and Washington. The Nazis raided his laboratory but found nothing.

Another near-miss for the Nazis came when the collapse of France was imminent. Premier Edouard Daladier had sent a secret French mission out of Norway past German spies with heavy water for French physicists, among them Frederick Joliot-Curie, son-in-law of the great Mme. Curie. Heavy water is invaluable in certain methods of atomic fission and is difficult to produce. The water arrived in France just before the capitulation and was carried to England on one of the last ships to leave Bordeaux.

Germany nevertheless continued work on the atom, and Allied leaders were worried. Reports had the Germans working feverishly to forge a weapon from the atom's power. In Britain, alarmed scientists speeded their efforts to solve the secret of atomic fission.

In the U.S., American-born nuclear physicists were so unaccustomed to the idea of using their science for military purposes that they hardly realized what needed to be done. The early efforts to restrict publication on atomic subjects and to obtain Government support for further research were stimulated largely by a small group of foreign physicists living in the U.S. Up to 1940 information on research which was to

lead to America's greatest secret weapon was open to any one.

One of the European physicists-in-exile in the U.S., the great Albert Einstein, had written in 1905 a simple equation which was to be the background for all the research in atomic energy. The equation was part of his relativity theory and indicated that light, which is a form of energy, has mass just as much as a particle of what we usually think of as matter, and that any particle of matter therefore is energy.

The astonishing thing about his equation was that it showed that if only a tiny bit of matter should be destroyed, the result would be enormous energy.

Backed by Einstein and his theory, a little band of scientists—native Americans and exiles from Axis-dominated lands—went to President Roosevelt to interest him in the possibilities of atomic power. The President, convinced that much might come from atom research, appointed a committee to look into the problem. Up to the end of 1941 the total expenditures on atomic research were small, although the amount of work done on the problem by scientists all over the country was great.

Shortly before Pearl Harbor the President wrote Prime Minister Churchill suggesting that any efforts toward the development of an atomic bomb should be coordinated or even jointly conducted by the U.S. and Great Britain.

That December the U.S. National Academy of Sciences issued a report supporting the efforts already made in the atomic field and expressing optimism about the future. Information received from the British was even more optimistic, and the President, the Prime Minister and their advisors decided that the time had come really to push the program. The atom bomb began to take shape.

It was decided to build production plants on a vast scale in the U.S., since Great Britain was already up to her neck in war production and was in range of German bombers and open to sea attack. Britain would therefore furnish her scientists to the U.S. and Canada would furnish indispensable raw materials.

There were many questions for the scientists to decide. First, they had to select a material to give the bomb explosive force. They had several forms of uranium to select from—the uranium "isotopes." There were three of them—uranium 234, 235 and 238, plus plutonium, the artificial element that can be created from uranium. Of these, the scientists knew that only 235 and plutonium could be used.

In a ton of uranium ore there are only 14 pounds of 235, and these are intricately mixed with the other isotopes. It would have taken more than 191 years to obtain a single gram of 235 and more than 75,000 years to obtain a single pound, under methods then in use.

Worst of all—uranium was one of the rarest elements in the world. It was found in pitchblende, which exists only in Canada and Africa in any quantities.

The project and its problems were put under the direction of a group of top-ranking U.S. and foreign scientists working in the newly-formed Office of Scientific Research and Development; its director, Dr. Vannevar Bush, noted electrical engineer, was detailed to report directly to the President. Later, the military value of the experiments became obvious to everybody, and the major part of the work was transferred to the War Department. Practically the same scientific staff continued working, with Maj. Gen. Leslie R. Groves, former Deputy Chief of Construction in the War Department and a veteran Engineer Corps man, in charge.

From here on, work on the atomic bomb became "top secret." In wartime Washington, where practically every project was hush-hush, the atomic work became the best-protected secret of the war.

Information on atom research was so compartmentalized that each person connected with it knew only what he or she had to know to carry out a particular job. A special intelligence organization was set up independent of G-2 to control the security side of the project. Even the FBI was barred from the various installations throughout the country, except where its operatives had special permission to enter.

Congress had to content itself with no more than an assurance from the Army that the $1,-950,000,000 appropriated for atom research was "absolutely essential to national security." Mere

mention of atomic work on the floor of Congress might have been a tip-off to the Nazis and Japs.

Once the whole House Appropriations Committee became skeptical of the work, since progress was not so rapid as had been expected. One of the Congressmen called the project "too fantastic" and threatened to tell the House what he knew and demand more information. That threat brought Chief of Staff George Marshall before the committee in a hurried secret session; the committee heeded his plea to keep silent.

The Nazis and the Japs actually did have agents in the U.S. with specific instructions to get information on the bomb, if any, and on uranium. The Nazi spies were directed to make contact with key personnel at any atomic work plants and to determine the type of protective devices used. The FBI learned through a foreign power what the spies were up to and stopped them.

To make doubly sure that there would be no leak of information, about 20,000 news outlets—newspapers, radio broadcasters, magazines and book publishers—were asked by the Office of Censorship not to publish or broadcast anything about "new or secret military weapons or experiments." On the whole, they kept mum. But the Army really got in a tizzy when Superman gave a "preview" of the bomb.

One episode showed little Professor Duste challenging Superman to take a 3,000,000-volt charge from a cyclotron. Superman withstood the current, and the professor was so embarrassed by his failure to kill the big guy that he said, "The machine must be out of order."

What followed is still a military secret. At the request of the Office of Censorship, the artists who create the strip promptly discontinued reference to atomic power.

Strictest secrecy was maintained throughout the whole project, which was set up as a new district of the Corps of Engineers and officially designated the "Manhattan District." More than 179,000 workers were recruited throughout the country for work in the various laboratories and plants in which the atomic investigations were carried on. Prospective employees could be told only that the work for which they were being selected was "most secret." Many of the men who were finally chosen were unaware of the purpose of their jobs even after they had been employed for some months.

Although there was still some question as to which of the several theoretically possible methods of producing explosive atomic material was best, the Army decided to go ahead with the construction of large-scale plants—the biggest Army construction program of all time—because of the tremendous pressure of time. Two plants were started at the Clinton Engineer Works near Knoxville, Tenn., and a third at the Hanford Engineer Works, near Pasco, Wash. Here, too, secrecy was essential: Contracts were placed with no publicity. Parts were ordered in many cases without the manufacturers knowing what they were to be used for.

The Clinton site was selected for its large size —59,000 acres—and isolated location, and for safety against possible unknown hazards. The Hanford site, too, was isolated, on a 430,000-acre Government reservation.

At the Clinton reservation a Government-owned-and-operated city named Oak Ridge was built. The settlement contains houses and dormitories, churches, theaters and schools. Today it has a population of 78,000—fifth largest in Tennessee. At Hanford another city was constructed. Called Richmond, it has a population of 17,000.

Near Santa Fe, N. Mex., a special laboratory, most secret of all the secret plants, was built to deal with the hundreds of technical problems involved in putting together an effective bomb. In this largest and most complete physical laboratory in the world, Dr. J. Robert Oppenheimer, brains behind the bomb itself, headed a staff of technicians who worked day and night forging the weapon that gave the final blow to Japan.

All over the country thousands of large and small manufacturing plants and laboratories, universities and schools carried on research and worked to develop special equipment, materials and processes for the project. And all of them worked under a blanket of secrecy.

It was due to these hundreds of organizations and thousands of workers that a study which would ordinarily have taken 20 years was completed in just three.

The Atomic Age was ushered in on July 16,

Maj. Gen. Groves, O-i-C of the Atomic B[...] (seated), with his assistant, Brig. Gen. Thor[...]

1945. A tense band of military men and scientists gathered in a remote section of the Alamogordo Air Base on the New Mexico desert 120 miles southeast of Albuquerque to witness the results of their years of effort—the first fateful test of the atomic bomb. It was 5:30 in the morning. A darkening sky, rain, lightning and peals of thunder heightened the drama.

Tension was tremendous. Failure was always possible, and too great success might have meant not only an uncontrollable, unusable weapon but the death of those who watched. The bomb might blast them and their entire efforts into eternity.

The nearest observation post was 10,000 yards south of the steel tower from which the bomb was to be detonated. Here in a timber-and-earth shelter the controls for the test were placed. At a point 17,000 yards from the tower which would give the best observation, the key figures in the cosmic project took their posts.

The time signals—"minus 20 minutes," "minus 15 minutes"—increased the tension. The watchers held their breaths.

Two minutes before the scheduled firing time most of them lay face down, with their feet pointing towards the tower. The moment came. There was a blinding flash brighter than the brightest daylight. A mountain range three miles away stood out in bold relief. And then there was a tremendous, sustained roar. A heavy wave of pressure bore down upon the observers. Two men who were standing outside the control center were knocked flat.

A huge, many-colored cloud surged majestically upward for more than 40,000 feet. The steel tower was completely vaporized.

The test was over. The bomb was a success.

What is this bomb like? What is its size? How is it constructed? Those are still top military secrets. Popular science writers say it is likely that the bomb contains plutonium, in great concentration, as well as some means to split it and make it release its energy in an explosion.

The detonating mechanism of the bomb must contain a slow-down device for the neutrons which are hurled at the uranium or plutonium atoms to produce an explosion. Only a neutron, which is an uncharged particle found in the atom's nucleus, has much chance of getting through an atom's electrical ring of defenses.

Before the war scientists had succeeded, in their cumbersome cyclotrons, in bombarding uranium with neutrons and getting the neutrons through. It has been estimated that these neutrons had about one chance in 140 of hitting the nucleus. When that happened, the uranium atom split in two, and the result was no longer uranium but barium and krypton, a rare gas. That was transmutation, and together with it came the emission of energy, the mass of krypton and barium being less than that of the original uranium atom.

But major mechanical and laboratory advances have been made. It seems evident that scientists are now able for the first time to separate uranium in quantity and that a means has been devised to release neutrons to bombard plutonium and thus detonate the bomb at a desired period after the bomb leaves the aircraft. The War Department has released information showing that the weapon is fired before it hits the ground to increase its power to shatter buildings and to disseminate its radioactive products as a cloud. The mechanism that effects such a marvel must obviously be far simpler than a cyclotron, which weighs tons.

How quickly research on the bomb itself has proceeded is shown by the disclosure that the second atomic bomb dropped on Japan at Nagasaki, August 9, was a more powerful and a simpler one, which "made the bomb dropped on Hiroshima obsolete."

But the mechanical details of the bomb did not concern most Americans. When the news came that the greatest weapon in the world had been unleashed upon Japan, the nation's main reaction was one of awe. There was little rejoicing.

President Truman voiced the sentiments of the country when he said: "The atomic bomb is too dangerous to be loose in a lawless world. . . . We must constitute ourselves trustees of this new force—to prevent its misuse, and to turn it into channels of service to mankind. It is an awful responsibility that has come to us."

When the awe at the destructiveness of the new weapon began to wear off, the feeling that we were entering a new era—the Age of Atomic Energy—remained. The New York *Times'* three-word headline—the like of which had probably never appeared in a newspaper before—summed it up: "New Age Ushered."

Never before had one discovery so caught the imagination of people everywhere. Never before had it been obvious so soon that a scientific discovery would change the world.

All over the U. S. people started using words they barely understood: "Atom," "electron," "proton," "neutron," "uranium." The nation's press did its best to simplify the scientific principles of atomic energy for its readers. The War Department felt that the subject was too highly complicated for its officers to explain and called in a civilian, the New York *Times'* science expert, William L. Laurence, to handle the press releases on the bomb and its background.

There was much disagreement as to when and to what extent atomic energy could be put to peaceful uses. The power, coal and oil industries protested vehemently that it would be years after the lifetime of any one now living before atom energy would take over.

One scientist close to the development of the atomic bomb compares it with the prehistoric discovery of fire and cautions that there was a lapse of centuries and centuries between the discovery of fire and the development of the steam engine. The atomic discovery does not seem as important as the discovery of electricity, this scientist says, although it may actually prove to be that important in time.

Others were more optimistic. In London, Sir John Anderson, who as Chancellor of the Exchequer in the Churchill Government supervised the British side of the atomic bomb research, said the discovery definitely is greater than that of electricity.

Prof. H. D. Smyth, chairman of the physics department at Princeton University and consultant on the atomic bomb, has written a detailed account of the history of the project and of its scientific background with War Department authorization. Smyth says: "There is good probability that nuclear power for special purposes could be developed within 10 years and that plentiful supplies of radioactive materials can have a profound effect on the treatment of certain diseases in a similar period."

The Rev. Alphonse Schwitalla, S. J., dean of the St. Louis University Medical School, sees in atomic energy a possible key to the mystery of life.

But to make sure that when the secrets of atomic energy become available for peacetime application they will be employed wisely in the interests of security and peace, the U. S., Britain and Canada have taken action to control patents in the field and to obtain control over the uranium ore which so far appears indispensable to the process. In each country, all scientific and industrial figures involved in the work have been required to assign their entire rights to any inventions to their respective governments, subject to financial settlement later.

To consider the long-term direction and control of U. S. atomic research, Secretary of War Stimson has appointed a committee to make recommendations. An advisory group of the scientists and industrialists most closely connected with the development of the bomb is already planning national and international control.

They hope, as the world hopes, that the new Age of Atomic Energy will be an age of peace as well. For if it is an age of war, that war might mean the annihilation of the human race.

—Cpl. JONATHAN KILBOURN

One of the giant production plants of the Clinton Engineering works at Oak Ridge, Tennessee

ATOMIC BOMB AWAY

By ROBERT SCHWARTZ Y2c
YANK Staff Correspondent

G UAM. THE MARIANAS—It was 0245 when the colonel eased forward on the throttle. The B-29 with *Enola Gay* printed in big block letters on her nose vibrated and began to roll forward. She reached 100 mph in a hurry, then picked up additional speed more slowly. She used up half the runway, and she was still bearing down hard on her spinning tires.

The tail gunner, S/Sgt. George Caron, up near the waist for the take-off, began to sweat it out. Capt. Robert A. Lewis, who usually piloted the *Enola Gay*, would have had her off the ground by this time. But Cap Lewis was only co-pilot on this trip and Caron didn't know the colonel, Col. Paul W. (Old Bull) Tibbets Jr., who had the controls now.

The *Enola Gay* neared the end of the runway and was almost on the gravel when she lifted gently into the dark sky. Caron realized suddenly that the colonel had been fighting to hold the ship on the ground the whole length of the runway just to be absolutely safe. And Caron remembered the bomb.

The men knew about the bomb—that it was something special—but they didn't know it was the atomic bomb. It was important, they knew, too, for in addition to Col. Tibbets' taking over for the trip, there was a Capt. William S. Parsons of the Navy aboard. He was a bomb expert of some kind and had come along as an observer.

Sgt. Joe Steiborik, radar operator, a dark husky Texan who was almost uncannily adept at operating his precision instruments, called the pilot on the intercom and told him he would find a large cloud north of the next island. "Better stay away from it, Colonel," he said. "It's pretty turbulent."

Fifteen minutes later the colonel came to the rear to use the tube. Before the trip was over he was to make a dozen or more such trips. "Coffee," was all he would say. "Drink so damn much of it."

Pfc. Richard H. Nelson, a boyish redhead who looks like every kid in every breakfast cereal advertisement ever printed, settled down to read "Watch Out for Willie Carter," a boxing story. Nelson was teased pretty constantly about his reading, just as he was teased about almost everything. The youngest man on the crew ("I've been 20 for over two months"), he had been nicknamed "Junior" by the four other men of the plane crew. Before the flight was over Junior finished the Willie Carter novel.

The flight engineer, S/Sgt. Wyatt E. Duzenbury of Lansing, Mich., a quiet 32-year-old thin-faced fellow with big ears, sat at his control panel reading innumerable gauges. A pure, undiluted flight engineer, Deuce's only concern during the flight was to wonder how the big explosion would affect his gauges. "He's dial happy," say the others.

Up front sat Col. Tibbets, a young (33) man with an accumulation of war flying experience. He was the pilot of the first B-17 to fly over the English Channel on a bombing mission; he flew Gen. Mark Clark to Gibraltar, he flew Gen. Eisenhower to Gibraltar, and then he flew Gen. Doolittle to Gibraltar; he flew Gen. Clark and Canada's Gen. McNaughton to Algiers, landing on a field he knew would be bombed, and which was actually under attack, before he stopped taxi-ing; he led the first mission to bomb North Africa; returned to the U.S., he flew the first B-29 on test missions; he was made CO of the atomic bomb outfit forming at Wendover, Utah; and now, sitting at the controls of the *Enola Gay*, he was on his way to drop the first atomic bomb in history.

The co-pilot was Cap Lewis, the plane's usual pilot. He had flown four missions against Japan in the *Enola Gay* with this crew. The crewmen all call him Cap, and he is an easy man to know and an easy one to like.

The navigator was Capt. Red (Dutch) Van Kirk, a young Pennsylvanian with a crew haircut that gives him a collegiate look. Van Kirk is a good friend of Maj. Tom W. Ferebee, the bombardier, and they had flown together in

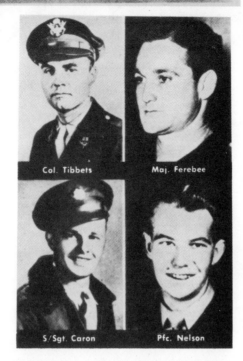

Col. Tibbets   Maj. Ferebee

S/Sgt. Caron   Pfc. Nelson

North Africa and England, usually as navigator and bombardier for Col. Tibbets. They were in on most of the colonel's firsts, and he brought them into his atomic unit as soon as he got it.

The flight was well along now, and Caron, the tail gunner, remembering Cap Lewis' prodigious appetite, crawled forward through the tunnel to get to the food before the co-pilot ate it all. Caron found six apples among the food up forward and threw these the length of the tunnel to Shumard, hoping that they would roll out of the tunnel and fall on a sleeping lieutenant who was flying this mission as special observer. He was Lt. M. U. Jeppson, an electronics officer. Caron wanted to wake him and get him to sit erect, thus taking less space in the waist, but none of the apples went the length of the tunnel, and the lieutenant kept on sprawling.

The flight to the target was routine, and only the thought of what they were going to see kept them active. They read, ate and talked a little and said nothing more historic than "Move over, you bastard, and give me some room," which must have been said on every plane ride since Orville said it to Wilbur at Kitty Hawk.

Occasionally they consulted the various charms and talismans, of which the *Enola Gay* had an inordinate number. These included, in addition to Caron's baseball hat and Shumard's pictures, the following items: Three pairs of silk panties from Omaha, stowed in one corner with a booklet on VD. One picture of Wendover Mary, a group companion during training in Utah. Wendover Mary had on a pair of high heeled shoes. One good conduct ribbon, fastened on the radio set and owned by Junior. Six prophylactic kits, divided equally between Van Kirk and Ferebee and presented by the ground crew in case of forced landing in territory "where the natives are friendly." One ski cap purchased in Salt Lake City and worn by Steiborik. One picture of the lobby of the Hotel Utah at Salt Lake, where Ferebee formed many associations, all of limited length but definite purpose. One lipstick kissprint on the nose, signed "Dottie" and bearing a dateline, "Omaha, onetime," placed there by a civilian girl who worked at an Omaha air base; it had been shellacked over promptly for permanence—source of the crew's common prayer, "Omaha, one more time."

These things were all very important to the *Enola Gay* community and were a binding force. A series of good drunks together in the States had helped weld them into a unit, and they were all very close friends.

They were getting near the target now, and Caron went back to the tail, taking his K-20

along. The plane began to climb, and they pressurized the cabin. The bombardier and the navigator, veterans of 54 and 63 missions, weren't worried about their imminent work, though it dawned on the navigator, Van Kirk, that "I'd be the biggest ass in the Air Force if I missed the target." They passed over several secondary targets and found them visible, then continued into Hiroshima. They saw it, lined it up, opened the bomb-bay doors, made the bomb run, and let the bomb fall. The plane banked sharply to the right and every one craned to look out.

Back at the right waist window, Sgt. Bob Shumard, the assistant flight engineer, turned his polaroids to full intensity and prepared to take advantage of the fact that he had the best seat for the show. When the bomb went off it looked blue through his polaroids, but he noted that the interior of the plane lighted up as though flash bulbs had been set off inside the cabin. He adjusted his polaroids to mild intensity and looked down at Hiroshima. A large white cloud was spreading rapidly over the whole area, obscuring everything and rising very rapidly. Shumard shouted into the intercom: "There it goes, and it's coming right back at us."

Looking way down again, he noted that outside the smoke circle and racing ahead of it were three large concentric circles. These appeared to Shumard to be heat rings, since they looked like the transparent wavy vapors seen coming off hot objects. He craned to see what happened to them, but the lieutenant who had been asleep was now awake and was climbing all over Shumard's neck. He lost the rings during this interval and could not find them again.

The engineer noted that his instruments were still functioning normally, and then he looked out his little hatch. He said nothing.

When Steiborik got no instrument reaction to the blast, he looked too.

"Jesus Christ," said Lt. Jeppson, "if people knew what we were doing we could have sold tickets for $100,000."

Van Kirk said nothing, though newspaper reports later called him "a battle-hardened veteran who exclaimed 'My God!'" when he saw the blast. The crew still kid him about this.

Ferebee, the bombardier, felt only one reaction: he was damn glad to be rid of the bomb. Then he set to work filling out the strike report form which was to be radioed in.

Back in the tail Caron noted the turbulence and called to the pilot: "Colonel, it's coming towards us fast." He got no reply, but the plane changed its course and outdistanced the cloud.

They looked after it as long as they could see it, a great ringed cumulus-type shaft rising higher and higher through the clouds. Then they flew on and it was gone. The tail gunner called to the pilot: "Colonel, that was worth the 25c ride on the cyclone at Coney Island."

The colonel called back and said. "I'll collect the two bits when we land."

"You'll have to wait till pay day," said the tail gunner.

Maj. Ferebee filled out the strike report and gave it to Capt. Parsons who had been in charge of the bomb. Parsons took it to Junior.

"This report," said the captain, "is going directly to the President."

The Navy captain wondered aloud: "How can you destroy so much and sacrifice so little? We didn't even damage a plane."

Some of the men wondered how many it would take to make Japan surrender; everyone wondered if the one bomb would end the war. Finally they dozed off a little, talked a little and ate a little and engaged in brief flurries of speculation. But the *Enola Gay*, the plane that had been named by the crew for the colonel's mother as a gesture for the flight, flew on and on. "She sang," they say now, with the deep pride that airmen feel for a ground crew that can make a plane sing.

Deuce worried about fuel, but Cap kidded him out of it. Time dragged. Everyone got hungry. But then they saw the field, and they were alert again.

"I looked at the Old Bull," says Cap Lewis, "and his eyes were bloodshot and he looked awful tired. He looked like the past 10 months, at Wendover, and Washington, and New Mexico, and overseas, had come up and hit him all at once.

"I says to him, 'Bull, after such a beautiful job, you better make a beautiful landing.'

"And he did."

Separation

By Cpl. MARTIN S. DAY

FORT MEADE, MD.—Even if you have fewer points than I have, you'll probably be seated across the desk from me one of these days while I try to hand you some separation counseling at the Fort Meade Separation Center here in Maryland. We separation counselors figure that for us it's still a long war.

I know how I'll feel when my chance for discharge comes. "Let's cut the chatter, bud," I'll probably say. "Just give me the white paper and let me take off." Equally impatient right now,

One fellow with 74 points squeezed through to 86, because he had an illegitimate child.

many men try to dash past us without taking full advantage of the separation counselor's advice and assistance. But since they've been away so long from the States and from civilian life, maybe they ought to listen to us.

Almost every man getting out on points has plenty of Spam bars for overseas time and has sweated out more than enough time for a hashmark. No one could deny that the great majority of dischargees on points deserve their release. Many times I've written about a dischargee, "Served as rifleman in North Africa, Sicily, Italy, France and Germany," or "Drove light tank in France, Belgium, Holland, Germany, Austria and Czechoslovakia."

Most of these men came into the Army in 1940 or 1941, and most of them have seen far more than their share of combat. They've earned *WD AGO 53-55* (honorable discharge) the hard way.

Every Army system, however, produces its oddities. I talked to a radio operator-mechanic-gunner on a Liberator who was overseas nine months and collected 60 combat points, while many infantrymen overseas three years got only half that number. A buck sergeant drove a refueling truck on Italian airfields and never even saw an air raid but he collected scads and scads of combat points because his entire squadron received those little bronze stars. On occasion rear-echelon units in AGF and ASF have also picked

up some combat points the easy way. But it does seem a bit screwy for a man who never left England to get the Ardennes star and five more points simply because some planes of his squadron got in the scrap.

One fellow I interviewed had 74 time and combat points and squeezed through to 86 because of an illegitimate child. He had recognized and supported the child for several years, but some of the boys around here were sarcastic. "You do what the medics and the chaplain tell you," they complained, "and you only gyp yourself out of points."

A very few have sweated out the points pleasantly. Recently I had a topkick who was forced to endure the rigors of downtown Honolulu from 1940 until this summer in order to get his release. A fortunate T-4 spent more than three years in Hamilton, Bermuda, before returning to the States in 1944. Early this year he was snipped to India, but the point system tagged him and sent him back for discharge after only three weeks residence in India.

A Regular Army man beat a peacetime desertion rap and is getting a perfectly white discharge that lists more than 900 days bad time. Men with as many as 12 courts-martial are copping the lovely white paper. One youngster is getting a blue discharge because of four AWOLs and a total of 121 days bad time. I've stopped trying to figure this thing out.

If anybody has put this war on a paying basis, I think it's the guy whose feet completely collapsed in basic and sent him back to his wife and three kids after only one month and 12 days in service. In addition to his regular pay he hit Finance for $240 in dependency benefits, $100 in mustering-out pay and 5 cents a mile for the trip back to upstate New York. What are the odds that the joe would have been on flying pay if he'd stuck it out another week or so?

Point system separatees up till now have been about evenly distributed among Regular Army,

His feet collapsed in basic and he went home after one month and twelve days service.

This kid boosted his age to get in the AAF. In two years he got 90 points and is out.

National Guard and Selective Service. Most of them have ranged from 22 to 35 years of age. There's a good percentage of youngsters who lied about their age to get into the Army a few years back. We recently had a kid who boosted his age to join the AAF; in a trifle over two years he amassed more than 90 points and is now back in corduroy pants and polo shirts. He's just a few months past his 19th birthday.

A while back I used to try feebly to kid Regular Army dischargees by saying, "Why don't you RA men stay in and let us civilians out?" I've cut out that sickly gag, largely because most of my RA first-three-graders plan to re-enlist.

One grizzled first sergeant with five hash-marks put it up to me: "They won't let me take my family to Germany. I've got a baby boy I've never seen, and I want to get reacquainted with the missus. Taking a discharge means for me a trip home and $100 a month for a three-month furlough. But after that's over I'll be in for another hitch."

Talking about family reunions, I had one man going to meet his father for about the first time. He was the son of an English girl and an American soldier of the first World War. Born in 1921, he was taken to England by his mother in 1923 when she left her husband in a huff.

After more than one and a half years in the RAF, this man, who was an American citizen because he was born in the States, transferred to the AAF. Coming back to his native land was coming back to an unknown country and to a virtually unknown father. He had been in the States just four days when I talked with him in the interview booth. Very enthusiastic about his brave new world, he remarked in an Oxford accent, "D'you know, old chap, I was always quarreling with those English about how much better the States were."

The GI is more than usually talkative when he gets to us counselors, because he suddenly realizes that for him the Army is on the verge of becoming just a memory, so you ought to come around to this office if you want to hear about Dachau, Bilibid Prison, Anzio or Salamaua.

Older men appear more inclined to want to return to their pre-war jobs than younger men, but 80 to 90 percent of the dischargees I talk with seem to want new and different and, of course, better jobs. The guy who wrote, "How're

separation center counselor
ts a bird's-eye view of all
e problems a discharged GI is
ely to run into. Here one of
em tells what he's learned.

you gonna keep 'em down on the farm after they've seen Paree?" wasn't just kidding.

From what they tell me, only a very small proportion of farmers plan to return to the farm for good. One pfc blurted out, "I never got much more than 15 miles from home. The Army's taken me through 15 countries from Brazil to Iceland and from Trinidad to Czechoslovakia. After where I've been and what I've seen, I couldn't settle down on any farm."

The number of dischargees expecting luscious jobs paying a la Hollywood is far smaller than I, at any rate, expected. Most men want steady, lifetime work, and they're willing to study and sweat and take average wages to clinch that permanent job. This generation seems to think pretty much in terms of security.

One ex-farmer said: "The Army's taken me to 15 countries. I couldn't settle down on a farm."

Army counselors can offer extensive referrals and perhaps give you the right steer. Some veterans claim the old run-around is given them by the multitudinous agencies, departments and what-have-you-to-perplex-the-veteran. Tempers and time may be saved, and something vital to you may be gained, if you talk over your job problem with your separation-center interviewer. The T/O lists him as a vocational counselor (262); that means that he should be able to give you advice on job placement.

Surprisingly few of the men I've talked with expect to use the GI Bill of Rights for a full-time education, but many want to take refresher courses at night or other part-time education in the hope of upping their future earning capacity. Many separatees don't realize that all the unemployment or educational benefits they claim will be deducted from any future bonus that may be given to veterans. This really shouldn't be regarded as a disadvantage, however. You have nothing more than a raffle ticket on a future bonus. Do you want the education or the bonus? The education is certain; the bonus at this moment is as unpredictable as a supply sergeant.

Also, it hasn't been universally understood that almost everyone, regardless of age, is entitled to a full year of refresher training. To be eligible

for more than a year's education you must be able to prove that you were under 25 at the time of induction or that your education was interrupted by military service. Your discharge papers are about all you need to produce to be eligible for the one-year refresher course at any school or college of your choice.

Maybe you think I'm fooling you, but I recently had in my booth a staff sergeant who was president of an Alaskan gold mining company. Now 48, he plans a year of advanced metallurgical study before he follows spring up into the Yukon in 1946.

Full publicity has pretty well scotched the hashish dream that everybody could slap the discharge down on the Government counter and say, "Now lend me $2,000, chum." You'll get a loan only from a private lending agency (usually a bank) and only if the lender is willing to risk his own cash on you and your enterprise. Banks are pretty wary these days because most values are now highly inflated. Many loan agencies are backing only gilt-edged, beautifully solvent veterans because they don't want a black eye in the community for foreclosing on an ex-GI.

There are plenty of veterans who are planning to get ahead without borrowing. Take the case of a brawny, Slavic T-5 from Pittsburgh who owns a plot of ground near his postwar place of work.

"First, I'll build a garage with a second floor," he told me. "My wife and I can live in the garage while I build the house in my spare time. I have a little money and I don't want to owe any man a cent." This plan wouldn't work for everybody, and the steel puddler's family won't roll in luxury for a while but, brother, I'm willing to bet the blue chips on that fellow.

The knottiest problem for most men seems to be what to do about their National Service Life Insurance. I've talked with men who have been subject to separation orientation everywhere from Munich or Manila to my desk without getting a clear picture of life insurance conversion. The best advice here is to hold as much of the stuff as you can and thresh out the details with your counselor and with the Veterans' Administration representative nearest your home.

A very poor substitute for Mr. Anthony, I've sometimes found myself dropped into the middle of family squabbles. Not long ago I talked with a poor guy who had been pestering personnel officers all over the ETO. He divorced his wife in 1941 and thought he had done with her, but although she remarried, she didn't forget her first husband. Not this girl. Last summer she produced the license issued for her first marriage and claimed an F allotment from his pay. The GI complained to Regiment, but all he got in the way of satisfaction was, "Oh, yeah? Let's see your divorce papers."

Sent airmail-registered from the States, those papers crawled after the guy across four countries, through two hospitals and around a handful of reinforcement and casual depots. Meanwhile

He's throwing over a girl in Iceland, a wife and baby in England, for a West Virginia girl.

under protest, he kept paying allotments to another man's wife. I did my legal bit in starting action for him to regain what she had mulcted from him, but I don't know how far he'll push the suit and that's strictly none of my business. "After all," he mused, "she's the mother of my child, isn't she?"

That was a simple case. Sometime ask me to tell you about the medical aidman who has a fiancee in Iceland and a wife and baby in England but wants to throw the three of them over for a gal in West Virginia.

Whatever your problem, we counselors will try to help somehow within the limits of our job. My desk is getting bowlegged from its piles of books and files of addresses and referrals. I'll give you all the time you want, and I've spent as much as 110 minutes with one man.

Usually, the interview here at Fort Meade averages 40 to 50 minutes, and each counselor can handle approximately 10 to 12 men daily. But unless somebody pulls counselors out of a hat, we'll have to speed things up a bit now, because our numbers aren't increasing and the hellbent-for-civvies boys are really pouring in.

One thing more about your interview with the separation counselor. He'll fill out the Separation Qualification Record which constitutes the Army's job recommendation just as the discharge is the character recommendation. The form has been used extensively by the United States Employment Service and other agencies, and it might be useful to you when you present it to prospective employers.

The interviewer will give you all the breaks in writing up descriptions of your jobs in the Army and in your prewar civilian life. However, just because you've sharpened up a lot while you've been in ODs and suntans, you shouldn't try to sell the counselor a bill of goods unless it's on the level.

I haven't had a downright phony yet, but some of the boys who said they were store clerks when they came into the Army want the Separation Qualification Record to call them department store managers when they go out. Even if you fool the interviewer (and he's talked to hundreds of men and shouldn't be a complete sucker) you probably won't be able to fool a future employer when you're called upon to produce on the job. But I've talked to plenty of GIs and I'm convinced that since they've endured the enemy, foreign parts and the Army, they can be counted on to meet anything the American future may happen to toss at them.

Now I'll admit that I've skimmed over lots of subjects that might be of interest to men on the point of getting out. If you have any questions or just want to kick the subjects around a bit more, just drop in to see me for some separation counseling.

And when I finish shooting the breeze with you and wish you the best of luck in civilian life, please don't break my heart with, "Thanks, same to you. Hope you're out soon."

One staff sergeant, 48 years old, was president of an Alaskan gold mining company.

Miss Liberty
YANK
Pin-up Girl

VJ-DAY

THE announcement everybody had been waiting for—through day after day of rumor and counter rumor—was a long time coming, and relief was as audible as celebration when final word came through. It was what we had been fighting for, the reason we had been in uniform for a year or two or five. Now the war was over

It is a little hard to analyze the immediate meaning of anything you've been thinking about for so long so intensely. The first feeling is bound to be a bit of a let-down. After you say "It's over" for the first few times and get used to the idea, after you celebrate, after the shouting dies down, there is bound to be a certain hollowness.

The war is over and you suddenly realize that you have been living with war for a good slice of your life. You certainly aren't going to miss the war, but it's hard for a moment for most of us to think of how things will be—are—without it. It's like an itch that you've not used to scratching and all of a sudden along comes a drug that cures it; you still feel a slight inclination to go on scratching and you have to remind yourself that there is nothing to scratch. You have to make an effort to apply yourself to all the things you dreamed of doing if you ever got time off enough from scratching to do them.

The end of the war means for most of us that we will be getting out of the Army—not tomorrow, certainly, and probably not next week or next month, but more or less soon. There is no doubt that this is the biggest immediate meaning of peace to the average man or woman in the service.

One reaction is impatience. All of us are going to be very damn impatient about the speed with which we will be discharged. No matter what system of discharges is put into action there will be kicks, and no matter how good the system is there will be confusion. Recognizing this may make it easier to bear some of the inevitable snafus that will raise their heads in the months to come. We will save a lot of steam if we resist the temptation to belly-ache about some of the minor injustices that are in the cards for us, and gripe only when our beefs are legitimate enough and large enough to warrant some attention and action.

Getting out of the Army also means a return to a way of life—a civilian way of life—that has become strange to some of us. It isn't easy to keep from overglamorizing civilian life when you're in uniform and so some of us are going to be disappointed when we get the chance to put on that blue serge or blue denim. Nothing could be so wonderful as the ideal you dream of when you are stuck on some Pacific island or abandoned in some obscure supply command or when you have been engaged in a succession of D-days, each one worse than the one before. It will save a lot of disappointment and bitterness if we can remember that civilian life is not perfect, that there are snafus there, too, and that the mere changing of a uniform for a department store ready-made is not going to solve problems automatically.

Some of the more excitable of civilian editorialists have been doing a heap of worrying about our reabsorption into normal civilian life. YANK thinks a lot of this worry is groundless and it also thinks that one of the biggest jobs we will have as veterans is to prove how groundless it is.

We are not coming back to the States as a bunch of problem children. We have certain rights as veterans and we have certain responsibilities as citizens. We cannot accept the rights without taking the responsibilities, too.

The responsibilities include more than pulling a blind down on our war past and living as useful citizens. We *have* been in a war and most of us know what war means in terms of death and hardship and hunger and dislocation. One responsibility should be to keep an eye always open for forces that might throw us into another war. We don't want one.

There are eventually going to be over ten million of us. We will have a hell of a lot of potential power. We are going to have to keep continually alert as to how we use that power. There are going to be people who will try to use us for their own ends. There are going to be other people who are going to try to confuse us so thoroughly that our power will be dispersed and useless. Let's not be suckers.

Let's remember that, among other things, this war taught us how costly war can be. And let's, as civilians, pay enough attention not only to our own government but to the affairs of the rest of the world so that another war may be averted.

It may seem silly to worry about far-away places when we will all be so glad to be home again. It may seem silly, but a lot of us spent a lot of time in far-away places and a lot of us died in them to end this war. Unless we pay attention to what goes on in the world today, we may be scattered all over its face, fighting again, tomorrow.

These are the things to remember now that we have the time to think about them. But the most immediate reaction is still the strongest one. The war is over.

YANK
THE ARMY WEEKLY

YANK is published weekly by the enlisted men of the U. S. Army and is for sale only to those in the armed services. Stories, features, pictures and other material from YANK may be reproduced if they are not restricted by law or military regulations, provided proper cerdit is given, release dates are observed and specific prior permission has been granted for each item to be reproduced. Entire contents Vol. 4, No. 12, copyrighted, 1945, by Col. Franklin S. Forsberg and reviewed by U. S. military censors.

MAIN EDITORIAL OFFICE
205 EAST 42d STREET, NEW YORK 17, N. Y.

EDITORIAL STAFF

Managing Editor, Sgt. Joe McCarthy, FA; Art Director, Sgt. Art Weithas, DEML; Assistant Managing Editor, Sgt. August Loeb, AAF; Assistant Art Director, Sgt. Ralph Stein, Med.; Pictures, Sgt. Leo Hofeller, Armd.; Features, Sgt. Burtt Evans, Inf.; Sports, Sgt. Bill Estoff, Engr.; Overseas Editor, Sgt. Al Hine, Engr.; U. S. Editor, Sgt. Hilary H. Lyons, CA; Navy Editor, Donald Nugent Sp(X)3c; Associate Editors, Sgt. John Hay, Inf.; Cpl. Jonathan Kilbourn, Sig. Corps; Sgt. Merle Miller, AAF; Sgt. Max Novack, TC.
WASHINGTON, Sgt. Barrett McGurn, Med.; Sgt. H. N. Oliphant, Engr.; Cpl. John Haverstick, CA.
PHILIPPINES, Sgt. Chuck Rathe, DEML; Sgt. George Baker, Sig. Corps; Sgt. Frank Beck, AAF; Sgt. Douglas Borgstedt, DEML; Sgt. Roger Cowan, CA; Sgt. Jack Crowe, Med.; Sgt. Marvin Fasig, Engr.; Sgt. Marion Hargrove, FA; Sgt. Dale Kramer, MP; Sgt. Robert MacMillan, FA; Sgt. John McLeod, Med.; Sgt. Licnel Wathall, Engr.; Sgt. Roger Wrenn, Sig. Corps; Sgt. Bill Young, Inf.; Cpl. Hyman Goldberg, Inf.; Cpl. Tom Kane, Sig. Corps; Cpl. James Keeney, Sig. Corps; Cpl. Joe Stefanelli, Engr.; Pfc. Ralph Izard.
CENTRAL PACIFIC, Cpl. Tom O'Brien, DEML; Sgt. Larry McManus, CA; Sgt. Bill Reed, Inf.; Cpl. George Burns, Sig. Corps; Cpl. Ted Burrows, DEML.
MARIANAS, Sgt. James Goble, Armd.; Sgt. Dil Ferris, AAF; Sgt. Jack Ruge, DEML; Sgt. Paul Showers, AAF; Cpl. Justin Gray, Rangers; Robert Schwartz Y2c, USNR.; Mason Pawlak CPhoM, USNR; Vernon H. Roberts PhoM3c, USNR; Evan Wylie CSp(PR), USCGR.
FRANCE, Sgt. Georg Meyers, -AAF; Sgt. Howard Brodie, Sig. Corps; Sgt. Ed Cunningham, Inf.; Sgt. Allan Ecker, AAF; Sgt. William Frazer, AAF; Sgt. Ralph Martin, Med.; Cpl. Pat Coffey, AAF; Cpl. Howard Katzander, CA; Cpl. Debs Myers, FA; Pfc. David Whitcomb, AAF; Pvt. David Berger, Engr.
BRITAIN, Sgt. Durbin L. Horner, CA; Sgt. Earl Anderson, AAF; Sgt. Edmund Antrobus, Inf.; Sgt. Frank Brandt, Med.; Sgt. Francis Burke, AAF; Sgt. Jack Coggins, CA; Sgt. Rudolph Sanford, AAF; Cpl. Tom Flannery, AAF.
ITALY, Sgt. Harry Sions, AAF; Sgt. George Barrett, AAF; Sgt. Donald Breimhurst, AAF; Sgt. Nelson Gruppo, Engr.; Sgt. Dan Polier, AAF; Cpl. Ira Freeman, Cav.; Cpl. Dave Shaw, Inf.; Pfc. Werner Wolff, Sig. Corps.
INDIA-BURMA and CHINA, Sgt. Paul Johnston, AAF; Sgt. Jud Cook, DEML; Sgt. George J. Corbellini, Sig. Corps; Sgt. Walter Peters, QM.
ALASKA, Sgt. Tom Shehan. FA.
PANAMA, Sgt. Richard Douglass. Med.
PUERTO-RICO, Sgt. Donald Cooke. FA.
AFRICA-MIDDLE EAST-PERSIAN GULF, Sgt. Richard Paul, DEML; Cpl. Ray McGovern, Inf.
ICELAND, Sgt. Gordon Farrel, AAF.
NEWFOUNDLAND, Sgt. Frank Bode, Sig. Corps.

Commanding Officer, Col. Franklin S. Forsberg.
Executive Officer, Lt. Col. Jack W. Weeks.
Business Manager, Maj. Gerald J. Rock.
OVERSEAS BUREAU OFFICERS, France, Lt. Col. Charles L. Holt, Capt. H. Stanley Thompson, assistant; Britain, Maj. Harry R. Roberts; Philippines, Lt. Col. Harold B. Hawley; Central South Pacific, Capt. Merle P. Milham; Marianas, Maj. Justus J. Craemer; Italy, Capt. Howard Carswell, Lt. Jack Silverstein, assistant; Burma-India. Capt. Harold A. Burroughs; Alaska, Capt. Grady E. Clay, Jr.; Panama, Lt. Charles H. E. Stubblefield; Africa-Middle East-Persian Gulf, Capt. Frank Gladstone; Puerto Rico, Capt. Francis E. Sammons, Jr.

This Week's Cover

IT may be necessary to tell some of you who haven't seen one in a long time that this is a suit, American style, of man's civilian clothes. The picture was made by YANK's Sgt. Ben Schnall, a veteran cameraman who would much rather wear the suit than photograph it.

PHOTO CREDITS. Cover—Sgt. Ben Schnall. 3—Sgt. Dil Ferris. 5—PA. 6—Upper, INP; center. PA. 7 & 8—PA. 9—Acme. 10—Left, INP; right, PA. 11—Acme. 12—Upper, PA; lower, Sgt. John Frano. 13—Sgt. Eugene Kammerman. 14—Acme. 16—Upper, Acme; lower, INP. 18—Manhattan Engineer District. 19—Left, INP; right, PA. 22—Sgt. Reg Kenny.

Fall of Japan

THREE YEARS, *eight months, and seven days after Pearl Harbor, total victory came to the United States of America and all the Allies. On the 14th of August 1945 the last Axis enemy went down to that total defeat which the democracies, some of whom had faced up to Rome-Berlin-Tokyo aggression long before the 7th of December 1941, had solemnly pledged themselves to bring about.*

In the United States and throughout the Allied world the contrast between those two days was the contrast between shock, dread, and near-defeat, and relief, thanksgiving, and unqualified triumph. There was another difference, too.

To the citizens of the United States—and indeed of all the countries that later became the United Nations—Pearl Harbor had been a blow-without-warning. In its unexpectedness it had brought a mental shock almost as severe as the physical shock of the bombs that fell on Hickam Field and on the ships in harbor. V J-Day came to a nation waiting for and well-schooled in victory.

America's armed forces had had a major share in Allied triumphs all over the globe. The weapons forged in its factories and carried on its ships and planes to every part of the world had proved its industrial supremacy. V J Day had come sooner than most Americans had dared hope, but for months none had doubted that it would arrive.

When it did come, after a five-day wait while the samurai *fumed and quibbled over the details of defeat, there was such an outpouring of emotion as Americans had never known.*

Wherever Americans were gathered together—whether in Louisville, Ky., Berlin, or Manila—the pattern of celebration was much the same. There were roars of rejoicing, high hopes for reunions, and prayers. The prayers were offered in gratitude and in remembrance of those who had died for a day they could not mark.

In America the celebration outdid anything within the memory of living men. It made VE-Day seem silent; it far overshadowed Armistice Day 1918. On the Continent of Europe and on continents and islands where the end-of-war had never found U. S. troops before, it was a day without precedent. A chapter, perhaps a whole book, of history had ended, and a word that had figured much in American thoughts for three years, eight months, and seven days—a word often spoken, but always in terms of the past or of an unsure future—could be spoken now in terms of the living present. The word was peace.

—SGT. HILARY H. LYONS

FOR A WHILE it looked as though the proceedings would go off with almost unreasonable smoothness. Cameramen assigned to the formal surrender ceremonies aboard the battleship *Missouri* in Tokyo Bay arrived on time, and, although every inch of the turrets and housings and life rafts above the veranda deck where the signing was to take place was crowded, no one fell off and broke a collarbone.

The ceremonies themselves even started and were carried on according to schedule. It took a Canadian colonel to bring things back to normal by signing the surrender document on the wrong line.

No one had the heart to blame the colonel, though. A mere colonel was bound to get nervous around so much higher brass.

The other minor flaw in the ceremonial circus was that it was something of an anticlimax. Great historic events probably are always somewhat that way, and this one, to those of us who had taken off three weeks before with the 11th Airborne Division from the Philippines, was even more so. We had started out thinking in terms of a sensational dash to the Emperor's palace in Tokyo, only to sweat it out on Okinawa and later off Yokohama.

When it did come, the signing aboard the *Missouri* was a show which lacked nothing in its staging. A cluster of microphones and a long table covered with a green cloth had been placed in the center of the deck. On the table lay the big, ledger-size white documents of surrender bound in brown folders.

The assembly of brass and braid was a thing to see—a lake of gold and silver sparkling with rainbows of decorations and ribbons. British and Australian Army officers had scarlet stripes on their garrison caps and on their collars. The French were more conservative, except for the acres of vivid decorations on their breasts. The stocky leader of the Russian delegation wore gold shoulder-boards and red-striped trousers. The Dutch had gold-looped shoulder emblems. The British admirals wore snow-white summer uniforms with shorts and knee-length white stockings. The olive-drab of the Chinese was plain except for ribbons. The least decked-out of all were the Americans. Their hats, except for Adm. Halsey's go-to-hell cap, were gold-braided, but their uniforms were plain sun-tan. Navy regulations do not permit wearing ribbons or decorations on a shirt.

Lack of time prevented piping anyone over the side, and when Gen. MacArthur, Supreme Commander for the Allied powers, came aboard he strode quickly across the veranda deck and disappeared inside the ship. Like the other American officers, he wore plain sun-tans. A few minutes later, a gig flying the American flag and operated by white-clad American sailors putted around the bow of the ship. In the gig, wearing formal diplomatic morning attire consisting of black cutaway coat, striped pants, and stovepipe hat, sat Foreign Minister Namoru Shigemitsu, leader of the Japanese delegation.

Coming up the gangway, Shigemitsu climbed very slowly because of a stiff left leg, and he limped onto the veranda deck with the aid of a heavy light-colored cane. Behind him came 10 other Japs. One wore a white suit; two more wore formal morning attire; the rest were dressed in the pieced-out uniforms of the Jap Army and Navy. They gathered into three rows on the forward side of the green-covered table. The representatives of the Allied powers formed on the other side.

When they were arranged, Gen. MacArthur entered, stepped to the microphone, and began to speak.

His words rolled sonorously: "We are gathered here, representatives of the major warring powers, to conclude a solemn agreement whereby peace may be restored." He emphasized the necessity that both victors and vanquished rise to a greater dignity in order that the world might emerge forever from blood and carnage. He declared that his firm intention as Supreme Commander was to "discharge my responsibility with justice and tolerance while taking all necessary dispositions to insure that the terms of surrender are fully, promptly, and faithfully complied with."

The Japanese stood at attention during the short address, their faces grave but otherwise showing little emotion. When the representatives of the Emperor were invited to sign, Foreign Minister Shigemitsu hobbled forward, laid aside his silk hat and cane, and lowered himself slowly into a chair. The wind whipped his thin, dark hair as he reached into his pocket for a pen, tested it, then affixed three large Japanese characters to the first of the documents.

He had to rise and bend over the table for the others.

The audience was conscious of the historic importance of the pen strokes, but watched for something else, too. Gen. MacArthur had promised to present Gen. Wainwright, who had surrendered the American forces at Corregidor and until a few days before had been a prisoner of war, with the first pen to sign the surrender. Shigemitsu finished and closed his pen and replaced it in his pocket. There could be no objection. He had needed a brush-pen for the Japanese letters.

When the big surrender folders were turned around on the table, Gen. MacArthur came forward to affix his signature as Supreme Commander. He asked Gen. Wainwright and Gen. Percival, who had surrendered the British forces at Singapore, to accompany him. Gen. MacArthur signed the first document and handed the pen to Gen. Wainwright. He used five pens in all, ending up with the one from his own pocket.

Sailors have been as avid souvenir collectors in this war as anyone else, but when Adm. Nimitz sat down to sign for the U. S. he used only two pens. After that the representatives of China, the United Kingdom, Russia, Australia, Canada, France, the Netherlands, and New Zealand put down their signatures.

As the big leather document folders were gathered, a GI member of a sound unit recorded a few historic remarks of his own:

"Brother," he said, "I hope those are my discharge papers."

—SGT. DALE KRAMER

THE RECEPTION was uneventful at Atsugi Airfield in Japan. C-54s carrying elements of the 11th Airborne Division were coming in low over the coast of Japan in history's gentlest invasion. The narrow beaches, probably the very stretches of sand we would have stormed, were gray and empty. Crowding the beaches were hills and fields, very green and rolling gracefully out from the base of a range of eroded

carpets. Here and there were clumps of trees —willows, evergreens, maples, and cherries. Hedges laced the rice paddies. Houses with thatched roofs were built close to the dirt roads. Most of the people walking along the roads carried heavy bundles or pulled carts. They didn't bother to look at the planes.

Atsugi Airfield looked somewhat like the Indiana Country Fair. Two long dirt runways were in the center of some feebly camouflaged hangars and ramshackle barracks. Wrecked Jap planes, glinting silver where their green paint jobs had worn off, lay like broken toys at one end of the field, having careened over on their wingtips and noses.

Waiting to meet the ships were members of the 63d Airdrome Squad and the 31st Air Freight Transport, who had arrived on D-minus-Two to ready the field.

These advance elements had expected to be massacred. Instead, they had been greeted by docile Jap officials, plus a few enthusiastic Russians who had apparently stayed in nearby Tokyo after their government's entry into the war.

Hundreds of square old Jap trucks stood at one end of the runway, lined up at close intervals, and hundreds of cars were in a big open field at the other end. It looked like the parking lot outside a college football stadium around 1938.

The baggage was piling up in front of the hangars, and troops heavy with packs were climbing into trucks. Jap interpreters, dressed in uniforms or suits or parts of each, stood around in nervous little groups. They had on yellow armbands to denote their calling. Like the Jap truck drivers and work parties, they tried to be impassive. One skinny interpreter wore a faded uniform of black crepe from which dangled bits of dirty gold braid. He looked like a cross between a scarecrow and a kid at a costume party.

On the far side of the field, around the administration buildings, stood armed Jap soldiers. They saluted every American who happened to come within 100 yards of them. Black-uniformed cops, carrying small sabers in silver scabbards, guarded the roads, looking sinister and self-important. A squad of Jap soldiers lay on thin straw mats in a car barn off one corner of the field. Their shirts were off, but they wore leggings. The squad's lieutenant lay on his back, his feet up against his buttocks, making nervous, wavy movements with his knees.

The barracks and administration buildings were weatherbeaten and somber. They had a bleak look that indicated they had been left to sag in rain and sun. Here and there a hangar roof had been burned off—or maybe never had been put on.

The D-minus-Two men were housed in a big barracks. The Jap Government had supplied them with the services of some waiters from Tokyo's Imperial Hotel. The atmosphere was practically lousy with the quiet selflessness that characterizes the breed of good waiters all over the world. "Hail the conquering hero!" said one GI as he snapped his fingers for more ice water.

American soldiers stood around and cracked about the broken-down automobiles. "I understand Henry Ford is coming over to get the cars out of the ditches by Christmas," a corporal remarked dryly. The MPs didn't like to let the ancient vehicles cross the field because of their tendency to fall apart in the middle of the runways.

In a deserted "shadow factory" dug into the side of the hill next to the field someone found a tissue-paper blueprint; it was a design for a homemade air-raid shelter. Standing on the roads that crisscross the barracks area beside the field, you could feel the ground tremble as trucks rumbled past. Underneath was a huge network of electric-lighted tunnels where the Japs had set up a complete machine shop.

As MacArthur's entourage pulled out from the field a car loaded with Jap officials broke down. An officer squatted on the fender and peered under the hood, his *samurai* sword dangling grotesquely between his knees. Other Japs stood by helplessly while a truckload of GIs wheeled past.

"Why don't you trade that sword in on a screwdriver?" called one GI.

—SGT. KNOX BURGER

AT 0800 ON AUG. 15 it was announced over the radio that the Japanese surrender had been accepted in Washington. At 1000 a force of Japs made a banzai charge on the command post of Co. A, 128th Infantry, on Luzon. Our casualties were one killed, one wounded.

Aug. 15 was the 654th day of combat for the 32d (Red Arrow) Division and wasn't much different from any other day. The 32d had been celebrating premature announcements of peace for four days, and when Aug. 15 came the only loud or emotional voices to be heard were the voices of the men of two platoons arguing over the ownership of a small pile of lumber.

As one rifleman of the division said, "Them Japs out in the hills don't know the war's over."

The Japanese whom the 32d was fighting were believed to be out of contact with their higher headquarters and with Domei, and the division dropped leaflets telling of the war's end, sending over Cub planes with amplifiers to broadcast the news, and sent Jap prisoners back into the hills to spread the word. One of the prisoners stayed in the hills.

"You know that Jap we turned loose a week ago and he said he'd bring back his captain?" the chief clerk asked the major. "Well, the sonuvabitch ain't come back yet."

"If he don't come back tomorrow," said the major, "you might as well mark him AWOL."

From all indications, the Japs were taking the leaflets, the loudspeakers, and the returned prisoners for so much propaganda, and it was pretty much taken for granted that the fighting might go on for weeks.

Such celebration as there had been in the 32d was over. It had come and gone the Friday night before, when the movie was cut off in the middle of a newsreel showing the fall of Baguio and a voice said over the loudspeaker, "We have just received word from Division G-2 that Japan is willing to accept the surrender terms . . ."

The announcer's voice was lost in a roar of whooping and hollering that lasted for a minute and a half, during which time one man fainted from emotion. The announcer broke in to finish his sentence: ". . . provided it can keep the Emperor." This had no effect on the general enthusiasm. Then another voice came in, this one tense and excited. "All guards for the beer dump will report to their posts immediately!" The projectionist's voice was next. "All right," it said, "all right. Do you want to see the movie —or what?" Most of the men wanted to see the movie, so the fall of Baguio continued. The main feature was a Fred Allen picture titled *In the Bag.*

After the show the men went back to their tents, talked late into the night, listened to the orderly-room radios, or dipped into the beer that had been issued that morning. One man had been hoarding his beer and had a reserve supply of four cases when the announcement came. He put on one hell of a toot.

The first sergeant of a rifle company looked off down the road. "August the fifteenth," he said, "nineteen hundred and forty-five." He spoke the date slowly and a little wonderingly. "It's mighty goddam quiet around here to be the day the war ended."

"The base sections are the place to see the excitement," said the T-5 inside the orderly tent. "I hear there were big doings down to Corps the other night. They were shooting holes through the roof—and it was raining to beat all hell."

The first sergeant gave a tolerant laugh. "It was probably the first time some of those boys ever got to shoot off a gun."

The afternoon sun was hot and the air was still and drowsy like an August afternoon in the Deep South. There was an occasional snatch of distant conversation from a bunch of GIs working on a road detail and now and then an excited shout from a nearby court where some junior officers were knocking themselves out in a game of handball. A small group of men leaned against the wall on the shady side of a battalion headquarters.

"Two weeks ago," said a man stretched out on the ground, "you could have got any kind of odds betting that the war would be over in August. Be damned if I thought it would be over any time this year. I thought we'd be digging Japs out of their houses six months after we invaded the homeland."

A scattered force of riflemen on the ridge moved back to let the artillery register on the Japs. The Japs did some quick shifting, and the riflemen were cut off on three sides and part of the fourth. Some supplies were moved up to the riflemen, but the men's position wasn't particularly enviable. When word was sent up that the war was all over the reply came back down: "Yeah, it's all over. It's all over this bloody hill."

On Balete Pass, the jeep hit a good-sized stone and bounced toward the embankment. "He's got a forty-foot road and one little eight-inch rock," said one of the corporals in the back seat. "That's what I call real shooting."

"It's the guys who get killed after the war's over," said the other corporal. "They're the real sad cases."

"Goddammit," said the pfc at the wheel, "any time you want to do the driving yourself you can take over."

Two PRO men showed up at the antitank outfit to photograph eight veterans of the Buna campaign who were leaving that night for the States. The eight Buna men climbed into the back of a truck, and the photographer scratched his chin thoughtfully. "It'd make a better picture," he said to the first sergeant, "if we had a few men standing here saying good-bye to them." "Right there?" said the first sergeant. He went to the head of the company street and blew a terrific blast on his whistle. "All right!" he shouted down the line. "Everybody outside!"

At sundown a cold, penetrating rain came up, and a hard wind drove it in through the doors and under the sides of the tents. The order to cease firing still hadn't come down from Corps, and a battalion commander, presumed to be bucking for a silver leaf, sent two rifle companies out into the rain on a night problem. The two companies had been out on the road for possibly two hours when Division heard about it and sent down word that basic training could be dispensed with for the time being.

The crowd at the supper table was discussing the immediate postwar world. "The way I understand it," said the man at the near end of the table, "athletics and recreation are going to be the thing until they decide to send us home. And if you want to study French or learn how to build birdhouses for money, that'll get you out of calisthenics. Build the body and build the mind; that's the ticket. Let 'em go ahead and see what good it'll do. When I get home I'm cutting body and mind both adrift to go to hell."

The man at the far end of the table broke in. "The way they ort to do it," he said, "they ort to serve breakfast in bed every morning for all the troops. I ain't had breakfast in bed since we left Australia."

The man in the middle looked out the mess-hall door at the relentless rain that separated the mess hall from the kitchen. "Let's odd-man," he said, "to see who goes for coffee."

An elderly private from division headquarters got in late from a 40-mile drive over the mountains in an open jeep. It had rained all the way, and he was soaked to the skin. The first man he met gave him the message that he was supposed to go on guard duty in 45 minutes.

At 0700 on Aug. 16, Co. A of the 128th was attacked again by a force of 60 or 70 Japs. Our casualties were one killed, five wounded.

It was the 655th day of combat for the 32d Division.

—SGT. MARION HARGROVE

THE HEADLINE, in type so big that the words ran together across the top of the page, said: "NIPS QUIT." The Japanese prisoners of war crowded around the Jap private who held the paper. They stood in the sun-baked courtyard of the new Bilibid Prison south of Manila, where some 8,000 former soldiers of the Emperor are confined.

An elderly Japanese civilian interpreter lifted his eyebrows, adjusted his spectacles, and translated.

"*Nippon,*" he said. "*Nippon Kofuku.*"

The private glanced sidelong at the older man and laughed at him. The civilian thumbed the paper with his forefinger and repeated the translation.

The private frowned and stared at the page that said that the war was ending and that his country was offering to surrender. The Japs behind him chattered and stuck their heads over his shoulder to see for themselves. The private left the paper with them and walked into the long concrete building where he lived.

I followed with the interpreter.

The room, which was part of the processing center for incoming prisoners, was about the size of a Stateside army barracks. The windows were barred, but the door was unlocked and open. About 30 Japs, most of them newly arrived at the prison, lay or sat on blankets spread on the concrete floor. On one side of the room were the day's crop of newcomers. Most of them were just skin and bones, and the GI shorts they wore hung loosely on their flanks as they lay with their thin arms clasped behind their heads, their dead eyes staring at nothing.

On the other side of the room were healthier specimens waiting to be assigned to work companies. It was easy to tell how long they had been prisoners by the amount of meat on their bones.

When the visitors were seated around the private's cot (he had a cot because he was a trusty and in charge of this part of the processing center), the interpreter asked him how he felt about the news of Japan's capitulation.

The soldier rubbed his eyes with the palm of his hand and figured out just what he wanted to say.

"I'm not sorry," he told the interpreter. "I'm in a happy mood." He smiled cheerfully to show how happy the mood was. There was a murmur in the room as the word passed from pallet to pallet, and some of those who had been lying down sat up and watched.

He was asked if he wanted to go home now. This was a ticklish one. He wanted to go home, and he didn't want to go home. His relatives and his friends at the aluminum plant where he worked in Tokyo might point at him, he said, and he didn't want to be pointed at. The Japs who had edged into the group all looked at the floor. Nobody said anything for a moment. The private looked up and smiled again—his happy-mood smile. He was happy that the war had ended and that the world could know peace again, he said.

The others, watching him, all smiled too. They put on their happy-mood smiles, and there was the sound of polite hissing.

A muscle-jawed Jap sergeant joined the group. He'd been a prisoner for about a month and was in pretty fair condition. He, too, had been aware of what was going on.

"I'm much relieved," he told the interpreter. "All my friends [he indicated the Japs along the wall], all my friends have such a mood of mind." The Japs along the wall stared impassively. The sergeant gave his name and said he had no objection to having it published in an American magazine. He was a medical sergeant about 40 years old, and he had an abscess on one leg. He had given up after four months of hiding in the hills.

After he told the interpreter about his surrender he spoke rapidly for a moment, and the interpreter laughed.

"He wants to go to America," the interpreter said.

"Houseboy!" yelled the sergeant in clear English, the first English that he had spoken.

—SGT. ROBERT MacMILLAN

THE PEOPLE OF ROME—Italian civilians and U. S. GIs—took the news of the Japanese surrender in their stride. There weren't any parades, bells didn't ring, and there were few drunken soldiers. People went about their business as usual, including the girls on the Via del Tritone.

In front of the Ristorante San Carlo, a GI restaurant on the Corso Umberto, there was the usual line of hungry soldiers waiting to eat. Aside from the fact that most of them were grinning as if they'd just heard a joke, they showed little reaction to the news. A big, beefy corporal wearing a Bronze Star ribbon and a blue Combat Infantryman's Badge, with the Red Bull patch of the 34th Division on his shoulder, said, "I don't know. Can't believe it. Only two bombs, and they give up. Don't sound like all that stuff we heard about the Japs fighting to the end. Seems to me there's a catch somewhere. Hey, what the hell's holding up this line?"

Outside the PX Italian kids were begging for cigarettes with "Joe, war finito. You give me one cigarette?"

A Nisei staff sergeant from the 442d Regimental Combat Team came out, carrying a paper bag full of rations. He grinned and said, "Wonderful news. Almost too good to be true. I'm anxious to get home. I hope people there'll realize the war's over. But it's sure fine news—best ever."

In front of the Red Cross a gray-haired tech said, "The best news I've ever heard on the radio. It's a funny thing. I came out of an Engineer outfit that's headed for the Pacific. They pulled me out because I got 95 points. I wonder if the boys have left Italy yet. They'll sure have the laugh if they beat me home."

At a sidewalk cafe on the Via Nazionale stood a bald-headed GI who was getting a buzz on. Laughing and sweating, he showed two Italians the well wallet-worn pictures of his wife and kids.

". . . and this garage here, you can just see part of it sticking out from the side of the house. I got the sweetest little Buick, what a car! You *capito* Buick?"

Inside the Florida Club, a GI hot spot, things looked about the same—a band giving out with some strictly Roman-version hot jazz, about 30 couples dancing, and several soldiers singing at their tables. A private who said he was attached to the 34th Station Hospital was drinking with an over-bright thin blonde. The private said, "I don't know why, but the thing sort of sneaks up on you. I started out to raise hell tonight, but somehow I can't get started. It seems hard to believe. No more worrying about points, stripes, or anything. Bud, when I get home now, it's to stay. Maybe when I get home I'll celebrate, really pitch some hell."

"War *finito*," the blonde said. "*Buono*, Americans leave Rome, no?"

It was hard to tell from her voice whether she thought the GIs' leaving Italy would be a good or a bad deal.

The private put his arms around her and said, "Yessir, baby, from now on it's home, sweet home."

"Play 'Home, Sweet Home'," he shouted at the orchestra leader.

A GI at the next table said, "That ain't dancing music."

Near the Calleria Club a Negro sergeant from the 92d Division, wearing a Silver Star ribbon under his Combat Infantryman's Badge, said, "I'm glad we didn't have to invade Japan. That would've been a bitch. Got a brother in the Navy in the Pacific, and I bet he's shouting now."

Inside the club somebody yelled over the music: "When you guys get papers from home now you better start reading the want-ad columns!" The crack brought a wave of laughter.

The Negro GI smiled. "That's a fact. Start thinking about jobs, but after the Army it'll be a pleasure."

It was a little after midnight, and St. Peter's looked very solemn and impressive against the stars. The church was shut. GIs kept coming up and then standing and looking at the church as if they didn't know what to do. One soldier said, "I thought it would be open tonight."

An elderly Italian said that in Italy all churches close at dark.

"I know, but tonight . . ." the soldier said.

At the entrance to the Swiss Guard barracks a heavy-set guard in the ancient uniform of this small army was standing at the gate. His face was expressionless—his army life not dependent on the war's ending or beginning.

On the day when the greatest and most terrible war in world history came to an end, on the day when fascism was finally broken in the world, Rome—where fascism was born—was quiet and orderly. Rome has seen its share of this war. Maybe there should have been a lot of noise and great rejoicing. Here, where people know war, there wasn't shouting, ticker-tape showers, or hysterical parades, but the people were happy. In Rome most people were merely smiling quietly.

—SGT. LEN ZINBERG

———————————

BERLIN, the city that had seen its own brand of fascism and international banditry tumble only a few months before, had little energy left for reaction to the fall of Japan. The Armed Forces' network broadcast the first authentic VJ news at 0210, and most of Berlin's polyglot occupation population, as well as most native Berliners, were asleep.

The U. S. Army newspaper *Allgemeine Zeitung* was the only Berlin paper which carried the news the next day. But the four days of false alarms made even the real thing seem unexciting.

Russian GIs interviewed had the same responses as their American counterparts. Said one of them, typically: "Now maybe I can get home to see my wife and children."

—SGT. GEORG N. MEYERS

Separation

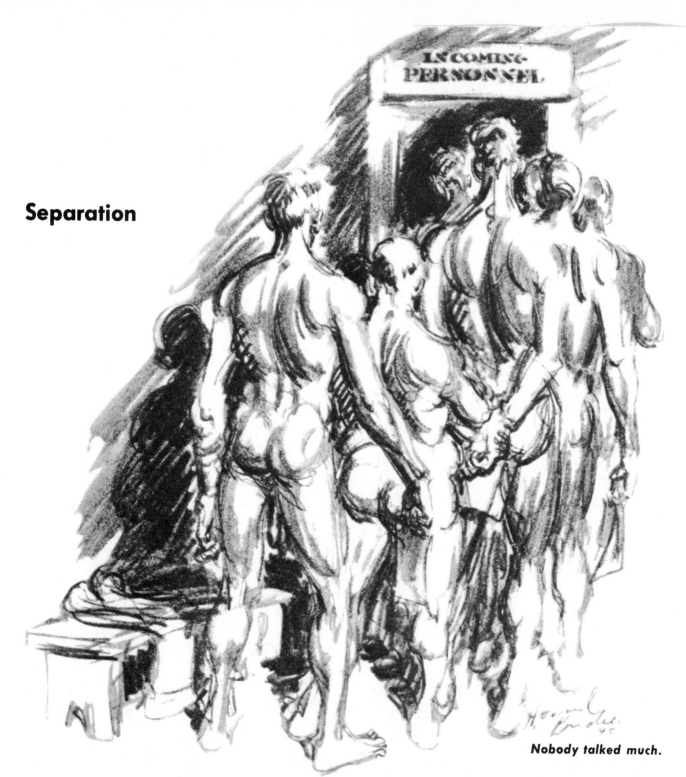

Nobody talked much.

EARLY IN 1942 when I reported to Fort George G. Meade, Md., for induction, fell into my first awkward formation, stripped, was shouted at, jabbed, and endlessly questioned, I rather forlornly hoped something would happen to keep me out of the Army of the U. S.

When, more than three and a half years later, I reported to Ft. Dix, N. J., for separation and went through what is essentially the same process, I was sure something would happen to keep me in. A friend had been unceremoniously yanked off to an Army hospital for a month when the doctors at Dix decided he had high blood pressure; another had had to stay an extra week to have several cavities filled; a third had been returned to his outfit because, it was discovered, five of the points his company commander had approved were illegal.

But nothing of the sort happened to the 14 men from my outfit who stopped at a bar in Grand Central Station for two quick drinks before buying tickets for Dix.

On our arrival at Dix, we were hurried into a cluttered barracks marked "Incoming Personnel" where a captain, apparently anxious to prove that we were still EM and not civilians, treated us with a studied rudeness, ordered a sergeant to take our records, pointed disdainfully at a bench on which we were to sit and, in a speech of welcome to ourselves and a hundred other prospective dischargees who soon gathered, several times screamed at us to "pipe down, dammit, or I'll keep you here all day!"

Then a corporal who wore a Third Division patch handed each of us a white tag on which, he explained, we were to print our last names, initials, and serial numbers before tying the tags to our left breast pockets.

After that, the corporal called out our last names; we shouted our first names and middle initials and stepped up to a counter, where we were given our clothing records and then shown down a long corridor, also lined with counters.

Since my clothing had already been turned in at my previous station, I simply showed a bored private the clean shirt, undershirt, shorts, and two pairs of socks in my civilian overnight bag.

"Me," said the private rather testily, "I'm a lucky bastard. I got 20 goddam points. Twenty."

At the end of the corridor, we were met by a pfc who gave us blue cards on which we again printed our names, ranks, and serial numbers; then we were herded into a bus and driven to what looked like the company area of any Army post anywhere.

Here we were assigned to a barracks and, once inside, lined up for the usual sheets, pillow cases, and GI blankets. As I was making my bunk, slow and easy and being careful to make hospital corners, a weary-looking Fifth Army sergeant said, somewhat sadly, "I'd almost forgotten how,

you know, and pretty soon I won't even have to remember."

A sergeant and a corporal were pacing up and down the barracks nervously, chain-smoking but being careful to put each butt in the GI cans conveniently and familiarly placed in front of strategic bunks.

"Anything might happen," said the sergeant. "I had malaria once; they might keep me in for that. Anything might happen."

"A day or so won't matter," the corporal added. "Not after all this time. I mean, even a week or so isn't so much after four years."

They each lighted another cigarette and continued pacing. A few minutes later a permanent-party corporal, who wore a Combat Infantryman's Badge but was obviously on the defensive, came in to tell us there would be a formation at 1645.

"That's 4:45, civilian time," he said.

"How long's it take, corporal?" someone asked him.

"Forty-eight hours," he answered, "after you get on a roster. But it might be a week before you get on one. Might be longer." He said the last somewhat gleefully, as if he hoped it would take longer.

When the corporal left, I dropped off to sleep for what seemed a few minutes, but when I awakened it was time for the formation. We lined up outside the barracks, almost a hundred of us, and listened to a brassy young first lieutenant with a mustache, steel-rimmed glasses, and almost no chin.

He talked in what he obviously hoped was GI jargon, repeating a number of stale jokes and advising us as if we were rather backward children that "pitching woo" (as he called it) in the nearby guest house was frowned on. Then, rather quickly, he told us that the Army was as anxious to get rid of us as we were to get out and that we should be on a roster in the morning.

When he dismissed us, an elderly technical sergeant wearing a patch of the Ninth Division gave him a mock salute.

"Thanks a lot, sonny boy," he muttered.

By then, it was time for chow, and we fell into a fast-moving line in front of the mess hall.

"I hear the KPs are krauts," said the Ninth Division sergeant. "Dirty krauts." They were krauts, looking surprisingly healthy and well-fed.

"Dirty bastards," the sergeant said, but that was all.

The food was good enough, substantial and unimaginative but plentiful, and after chow we looked at the bulletin boards outside our barracks on which the rosters were posted. We knew our names could not possibly be there until morning, but we looked anyway. It made us feel better.

Then we walked to the PX, bought our cigarette ration, and waited at a table in the beer garden until it opened. The beer was warm and not very good, but we drank a lot of it.

"Relaxes you," someone said. "That's the only thing about beer. It relaxes you."

We all agreed that it did, and we spent the evening talking about what we planned to do when we got out and about officers we'd like to meet again, a few because we suspected that they would really be good guys when they weren't officers any more and a good many more with whom we wanted to settle a score.

When the beer garden closed we were all a little high, but relaxed, really relaxed. I went to sleep as soon as I hit the sack.

After chow the next morning, we hurried to the bulletin boards, and, sure enough, there were most of our names. Those whose names were missing walked slowly back to the barracks.

"I can't prove I'm not still in Casablanca," said one of them. "I'll probably still be here for the next goddam war."

At 10:15 we lined up outside the barracks and in a careless, desultory formation walked to a post theater. It was the old routine again, like basic training.

Everyone filed into the theater quietly and sat down, nobody talking much.

First, there was the chaplain, a huge, hearty man who boomed at us that we were about to be discharged from the Army and he supposed we were all pretty unhappy about that. It was a bum gag, but everyone laughed appreciatively. Then he explained about our discharge pay, pointing out that it would be paid in monthly instalments, one when we got out, another a month later and, for the great majority of us (those who had been overseas), a third payment a month after that.

He bellowed that we probably wouldn't have too much trouble getting adjusted to civilian life—but that we must be patient with other, more settled civilians. Also that dischargees had a lot of trouble with what he called "pitfalls" in and around Trenton, N. J. He warned us to hang on to our money.

"I hung on to a hell of a lot more money than he's ever seen long before I got in the Army," said a somewhat dispirited man in the row ahead of me.

When the chaplain had finished, a young lieutenant rather diffidently explained that in the afternoon we would meet our counselor, who would tell us about our insurance and the GI Bill of Rights and answer any questions. Then we were handed a card on which to check the questions we wished to ask our counselors.

A few men made checks on theirs, but many of us didn't.

"If they don't know the answer, they may keep you here until they find out," said a corporal. The majority seemed to agree with him.

My own counselor was a large, red-faced Irish private who obviously enjoyed beer and drank a good deal of it and explained to me that he had been a newspaper man once himself—and, when he got out of the Army, hoped to be again.

"I guess it's kind of a crowded field, though," he said, rather hopelessly. I agreed that it was.

"You want to know anything?" he asked. I said I didn't.

"Hardly anybody does any more," he said.

Then he carefully filled out my Form 100, listing my jobs in the Army and civilian life.

"It might come in handy some time," he said. "I doubt it, but it might."

Then, quite brusquely, he asked: "You don't want to join the Enlisted Reserve, do you?"

"No," I replied.

"You know," said the private, "I once had a man who did. He was a pretty smart fellow, too. He thought there was going to be one hell of a depression in this country, and he wanted to keep on eating."

After the counseling, we were through for the day and returned to our barracks. On the way, we passed a formation of men carrying their baggage and with the bright golden discharge emblem on their shirts. They grinned at us.

"Hiya, soldiers," one of them said, then repeated, "soldiers," making it sound like a dirty word.

"A lot of things could still happen," said the sergeant with whom I was walking. "The medics hold up a lot of guys."

"I've got varicose veins," said someone else. "I wonder if that'll make any difference." No one answered. We were thinking of our own minor ailments, wondering if they would matter.

We all drank more beer that evening, but it wasn't as much fun as the night before. Civilian life was too close, and there was still the chance that maybe, somehow, for some obscure Army reason, we wouldn't get out at all.

When we marched to the dispensary next morning nobody talked much, and once inside we took off our clothes and waited. The examination was much like the one that got us into the Army. The doctors looked at us with the same bored expressions.

While we waited for the blood tests, one man paled visibly.

"I've only been back from Paris ten days," he said. "Tell the truth, I'm a little worried."

"You got a bad cavity there," the dentist said to me.

"I know."

"We'd just as soon fix it, free," he continued.

"No," I answer, very politely. "No, thank you very much." The dentist merely shrugged.

After lunch, we turned in our bed-clothes and sat down on our empty bunks to wait. The man who could not prove he had left Casablanca was trying to read a book.

"I'll probably have to go back there and then come back home again," he said. "And I'm supposed to meet my girl in New York tonight."

"I heard about a guy that was pulled out at the Finance Office," said the technical sergeant. "It's never too late."

We threw our luggage in a tent that was marked off into compartments, then waited in front of a building marked "Signature Section."

A man had fainted a few minutes before, and the medics had carried him away in a litter.

"They'll probably never let that poor bastard out," said the technical sergeant. He lighted a cigarette, and I was surprised to see that his hand was shaking.

When we got inside the Signature Section, we lined up against a wall and waited until two permanent-party men called off our names. As they reached each name they placed a folder on a counter, and each man walked over to his own folder.

And then we signed our discharges. I blotted mine in two places. I was still blotting when someone mentioned the Enlisted Reserve again.

At the door we fingerprinted our discharge papers. The corporal in charge of that section was having an argument with a dischargee.

"I just asked you to do it the Army way," said the corporal.

The dischargee said an unprintable word, then added, "USO Commando."

The corporal did not answer, but when the dischargee had gone out the door he said, "I guess it doesn't matter, but I was with the 34th."

Then we walked back and picked up our luggage, waiting outside while a few of the men ran to another tent to salvage some equipment.

In a few minutes our guide, a newly inducted private who was an apologetic 18, took us to a squat, unbeautiful building inside of which were rows of men at sewing machines. Each of us had discharge patches sewn over the right pocket of either one or two shirts.

As we put on our shirts again, I felt confident for the first time. But not for long.

"A guy in the barracks got yanked in the Finance Office," repeated the tech sergeant. "Last minute. Been here eight days."

We dropped our luggage in the compartmentalized tent again and walked to the Finance Office. The building was crowded, and our guide told us it would be 45 minutes, at least, before we got in, so we wandered to the PX.

We all ordered cokes, but none of us drank a full bottle.

A corporal, who had loudly sworn off smoking but then borrowed a cigarette, lighted it and said:

"You guys finish your cokes. I'm going back."

We all drank a huge gulp of coke, then set down the bottles and hurried back to the Finance Office. We had been gone exactly five minutes, and we still had almost an hour to wait.

Finally we got inside the building and sat on the same kind of hard benches as in "Incoming Personnel." After about 15 minutes more they began calling our names, and we stepped up to the cashier's cage, where we were each given $50 in cash, the rest of our pay (minus allotments) in a check, plus the first instalment of our mustering-out pay. Also the small gold discharge button.

As we stepped out into the sunshine again the tech sergeant smiled for the first time.

"Not a damn thing can happen now," he said. "Not a damn thing. I'm a damn civilian." His eyes were watering, not much, just enough to be noticeable.

When the last man came out of the Finance Office, we lined up quietly and started for the chapel. We knew what was going to happen there; we'd been told at least a dozen times by men who'd already been through it, but we were a little frightened anyway.

An organ was playing when we marched in,

wearing our ties and silent, and we sat down in neat rows, while the organist ran through "The Old Grey Mare," "Glory, Glory, Hallelujah," and some hymns I didn't recognize.

A chaplain said something, I don't remember what, and then a very old and very small lieutenant colonel stood up, smiling through what were obviously not his own teeth.

I looked out the window and saw a handful of new arrivals walking with their barracks bags toward a company area, and I didn't want to pay any attention to what the old colonel was saying. It was corn, pure corn, about the Army appreciating what we had done and about how most of us hadn't gotten the breaks we deserved, but it was a big army and we knew how those things were, and finally about the war we'd won and what a great thing we'd accomplished for our great country.

It was obvious that it was a speech the old man had made many times, but I didn't care. I thought it was a fine speech.

Then an enlisted man began calling off the names, and men began stepping up to the colonel, saluting him, getting his store-teeth smile and a handshake and their discharge papers.

After I had my discharge papers and was waiting outside, the tech sergeant came up, grinned at me, and said, "I think I could kiss you, but I think I won't." Instead, he just patted me on the back, like a football coach congratulating a player after a winning game.

We walked to where we had left our luggage.

"I was planning to knock the block off that bastard captain we saw when we got here . . ." said the sergeant. Then he paused. ". . . but I don't know why the hell I should bother," he concluded.

As we drove out the gate a few minutes later, a bus load of men who were obviously potential dischargees was just coming in.

"Hiya, soldiers," I said, and waved. "Soldiers," I repeated.

—Ex-Sgt. Merle Miller

WITH FREE CHINA'S FLAG UPON HIS BACK, HE DIED IN A GREAT SKY BATTLE By Sgt. MARION HARGROVE

SOMEWHERE IN CHINA—There was a great battle in the sky and the people stopped their work to look at it. And then the battle moved away until there was nothing left of it but one plane of the *Mei-Kua fi chi* (the American flyers), with its large white star with the red border around it, and two planes of the Japanese devils, the *Yi Bin Kwe-Tse*. There was much shooting and then the first and then the second of the Japanese planes fell to the earth with much smoke and great noise.

And after this had happened the people saw that the little plane of the *Mei-Kua* was also greatly harmed. There was much noise such as one hears from trucks on the great road when they are using gasoline of pine roots and there are too many yellowfish riding on the top of the load. And finally the *Mei-Kua* came down to the earth, not smoothly but with a heavy crash, so that the great body of the plane was crumpled and the wide wings were twisted and bent.

And the people found in the wreckage of the plane the *fi chi* who had driven it in the air and beaten the *Yi Bin Kwe-Tse*. He was tall and large, as are all the *Mei-Kua*, and on the shoulders of his jacket were two narrow strips of white embroidery and on his back was sewn the flag of China, with the white sun of *Kuo Min Tang* in the corner, and the chop of the Gissimo himself was stamped below the writing that said this was one of the men who had come from across the wide waters to help drive the *Yi Bin Kwe-Tse* from the soil of China.

The people took him up gently and carried him to a house and attended to his wounds, although they knew he could not live for long. For his arm and his leg were broken and there were many wounds made by the bullets of the *Yi Bin Kwe-Tse* and his stomach was torn so that the guts of the man could be seen within it. But they did what they could to make him comfortable, although the *Mei-Kua fi chi* knew as well as they that he could not live for long.

And while they did the little that they could for him, he laughed with them and made jests in a poor and awkward Chinese that they could not understand, for it was not the Chinese spoken in that village. But they could understand his labored laugh and they could see the greatness and the goodness and the strength and the dignity of the dying man.

And when he was dead, this man with the flag of Free China upon his back, they wrapped his body in white, for white is the color of the honored dead, and they laid it in the finest coffin in the village and they placed the coffin upon a barge in the river to take it to the people who would return it to the great general of the *Mei-Kua fi chi, Ch'e Ne T'e*, and the others of the *Mei-Kua.*

And in a box beside the coffin they put the clothing they had removed from him when he was in pain, and with the clothing they put the things that had been in his pockets. They put the little leather case with his money, and the pieces of heavy paper with his picture and the other pictures of the woman and the two children, the *Mei-Kua* cigarettes and the little silver box of self-arriving fire, the two small metal plates on a little chain, the knife that folded within itself and the small brown *Mei-Kua* coin with the picture of a bearded man upon it.

And when this had been done four of the young men of the village took poles and poled the barge up the river to return the *Mei-Kua fi chi* to his own people.

And the news ran quickly all along the river that the dead hero was returning to his people. And all of the villagers along the river and all of the people who lived in the sampans tied along the banks of the river waited to see the barge go slowly by. And wherever it passed, the people lit long strings of firecrackers and honored the *Mei-Kua fi chi* who had fought for China and laughed and jested and died as a hero should.

SGT. KEVIN McCARTHY

The Personal History of an Infantryman in the South Pacific

By Sgt. MERLE MILLER

SOMEWHERE IN THE SOUTH PACIFIC—In an obscure corner of his foot locker Sgt. Kevin A. McCarthy keeps a small tin box containing the souvenirs he has collected since April 1942 when he first arrived in the South Pacific.

He has Australian shillings, New Caledonian francs, a sou from the Hebrides and a few Japanese invasion coins he picked up during some 50 days under fire on Guadalcanal.

"They'll make a nice necklace for Lorraine," he explains. Lorraine is Miss Lorraine Meilke, who is head waitress in a cafe in his home town, Jamestown, N. Dak.

In addition, Mac—as he is known to privates and lieutenant colonels in the 164th Infantry Regiment—has a Jap soldier's pay book, some Nipponese machine-gun shells and citations, and his superior officers have recommended him for a Distinguished Service Cross.

But Mac, a blue-eyed, 21-year-old section leader of two machine-gun squads of Company H in the 164th, would gladly swap his citations for a chance to return to his home at 302 Third Avenue, S. E., in Jamestown. There was a time, during the peak of the Battle of Guadalcanal, when he hoped he would be home in a few weeks. In his less optimistic moments he repeats the slogan that is chanted everywhere in this area, "Golden Gate in '48."

Except for one 15-day furlough in June 1941, he has not been home since he was inducted into Federal service with the North Dakota National Guard on Feb. 10, 1941. Since he sailed from the mainland early last year bound for an unknown Pacific destination, his 19-year-old brother William has been drafted and is now a member of a Tank Destroyer outfit at Camp Hood, Tex. Another brother, Robert, 17, has enrolled in the Navy V program for college and pre-flight training at the Valley State Teachers College.

John, 15; Donald, 13; Tommy, 11, and two sisters, Margaret, who is 8, and Mary, 6, are still at home with Mac's father and mother, Mr. and Mrs. William S. McCarthy.

A cousin on his mother's side, Pvt. Don Tracy of Jamestown, is a Japanese prisoner of war; he was a medic on Bataan. Two other cousins, Pvt. Francis Tracy of Hettinger, N. Dak., a field artilleryman, and Pvt. James Tracy of Jamestown, member of a searchlight outfit, have been under fire in North Africa.

Mac gets a letter from Lorraine at least once, sometimes twice a week, and his mother writes every Sunday. Occasionally he hears from Father Gerrity, who is still at St. James', and from some of the nuns who were his teachers at St. John's Academy. He was graduated in June 1939, one of a class of 36.

Like most Americans in the Army, Mac had not planned to be a soldier. At St. John's he took a business course, typing and shorthand. For several summers he worked on Dakota wheat farms. One summer he was a laborer in Yellowstone Park, and another he worked with his father, a section boss for the Northern Pacific Railroad.

Ever since he can remember, Mac has gone rabbit hunting in the winter. He was a Boy Scout, a member of the Catholic Youth Organization, and played football and basketball in high school.

After his graduation he took a job as a short-order cook working nights in a small cafe. That was only temporary. Two evenings a week, from 7:30 to 9 P.M., he drilled in the local armory. He had enlisted in Company H of the 164th in the summer of 1938 mainly "because almost all the fellows I knew were joining the National Guard."

When Company H and the rest of the North Dakota National Guard were inducted into Federal service, he was a private first class, the No. 2 gunner on a Browning heavy .30 machine gun. He was working in a garage then, towing used cars from Milwaukee to Jamestown.

Nobody thought much about it when he and 64 other Jamestown boys left for Camp Claiborne, La. They were going away for a year; that was all.

"It'll do you good," said his father, who had been a private in a Quartermaster outfit on the high seas when the 1918 Armistice came.

Mac thought Claiborne was tough. The 164th was temporarily attached to the 34th Division, which later took part in the first landing in North Africa and fought the famous battle of Hill 609 in Tunisia. Like the others, the men of Company H drilled with wooden rifles and broomsticks. They went on a few night maneuvers, sleeping in shelter halves and bitching, and in August and September took part in the Louisiana maneuvers.

Someone occasionally chalked OHIO signs on the barracks. That meant "Over the Hill in October," and there was a lot of beefing when Congress passed the bill extending service to 18 months.

Late in November a corporal from New York City was making bets that the United States would be at war with Japan by Dec. 12. Everybody laughed at him—until he collected $500 the morning of Dec. 8. That morning the 164th was alerted and on Dec. 12 started for the West Coast.

They were in San Francisco a few days, attached to the San Francisco Bay Defense and sleeping in the stalls of a livestock pavilion. On Christmas Day they were on their way to Oregon, and Chaplain Thomas J. Tracy of Bismarck, N. Dak., said mass in the snow beside the train.

In a few more weeks they were on their way to California again, this time to prepare for shipment overseas. Latrine rumor said their destination was Australia, and Mac bought a map of the Pacific to see how far he'd be from North Dakota. They sailed on Mar. 18.

In Australia he had two dates with a girl whose name he can't remember, but "she was lots of fun, and she thought all Americans, including me, were wonderful. We had a swell time."

A few days later the 164th sailed from Australia for a place Mac had never heard about. It was New Caledonia.

There he walked seven miles to see 2-year-old movies and learned a few words of French, like saying *"bon jour"* or *"tres jolie"* to the girls. He learned to drink hot chocolate instead of coffee and fought mosquitoes that made the memories of Camp Claiborne seem like kindergarten stuff.

The training program was tougher, too. Ten days in the field was not unusual, and Mac and his crew took turns carrying their Browning automatic and its tripod. The gun with water weighed 40 pounds, the tripod 54, and the ammunition 21 pounds per box. There were times both in New Cal and later when he and the crew swore the whole shebang weighed a ton. In the crew were Pfcs. Alvin Knapp of Groton, S. Dak., second in command; James Johnson of Jamestown, No. 1 gunner; Carl Bowlin of Duluth, Minn., No. 2 gunner; and Emory Mercer of Kankakee, Ill., and David Smercansky of Glen Robbins, Ohio, ammunition carriers.

About the time they'd decided they'd be in New Cal for the duration, secret orders came through. Sergeants from headquarters said it was Guadalcanal. On the evening of Oct. 12, 1942, they saw the dim, shadowy outline of the Solomon Islands. It was Mac's twenty-first birthday.

The first scouts left the ship in Higgins landing boats at a spot near Lunga Point on the north central shore of the 'Canal. At 5 A.M. Mac's party landed, and an hour later they were bombed for the first time by two-motored Mitsubishi bombers.

"Sure we were scared," Mac will tell you. "Show me a man who says he isn't scared when he's under fire, and I'll show you a liar."

It took several hours to unload the transports, and Mac piled ammunition on the beach. There were two other raids during the day, and at dusk Jap artillery near Point Cruz fired on them intermittently. That night everyone dug foxholes, deep but not as deep as they were to dig later. About midnight a Jap naval force began firing toward the shore. Fourteen-inchers and star shells zoomed over their heads, but there were no hits.

"It was the noise that got you," Mac recalls. "You thought it would never stop. You thought every shell had your number on it. That night was the worst for most of us, I guess. Probably because it was the first."

The shelling stopped at daylight, and there was another bombing attack at 5 A.M. That made the fourth. There were 30 during the first 10 days.

The 164th moved into the perimeter of defense about a quarter of a mile north of Henderson Field, relieving the Marines. "They were so glad to see us, some of them lay right down on the ground and cried," Mac says.

On Oct. 26, the second day of what has since become known as the Battle of Henderson Field, Mac performed what Col. Bryant E. Moore, then commanding the 164th, said was "commendable service in keeping with the traditions and past performances of our regiment."

What he did seemed ordinary enough to Mac. "Anybody would have acted the same way."

He and his crew were manning the last gun on the Second Battalion flank, about half a mile northeast of Henderson on the perimeter of defense. Japs were moving up with infantry supported by machine-gun and mortar fire. The orders were to hold.

About 50 yards to the left was the Lunga River; to the right was a thick jungle in which a detachment of Japs was firing light machine guns. About 200 yards straight ahead the Japs had established a CP, and in front of the CP and directly in the Jap line of fire was a Marine outpost. There had been heavy fire for about 15 hours, and the Japs were advancing.

That was when Mac got his idea. It was easy to see the marines couldn't last long under the heavy

Nip barrage, so he shouted to Pvt. Thomas Campbell of Minneapolis, Minn., who was driving up a Bren-gun carrier filled with ammunition.

"We can save those marines. Want to help?"

"Okay," said Campbell. Cpl. Floyd Springer of Jamestown, who was in charge of a nearby gun squad, also agreed. So did Knapp. The four of them mounted a light machine gun on the rear of the carrier. There was already one on the front, and they were ready.

Cpl. Bob Havelick and Pfc. Leroy Chilson, both of Jamestown, opened the barbed-wire gate in front of the gun position, and with Campbell driving and Mac, Knapp and Springer keeping up a heavy barrage of fire, they moved to the spot where they thought the marines were.

Although it was only mid-afternoon it was dark as night, and they missed the marines. Then they drove back to their gun, and Mac shouted to the marines. One of them stood up, and Mac shot an azimuth with his compass. They started a second time and brought back seven marines in the carrier. On the third trip they brought back two who were wounded and three others, and on the fourth they rescued the last eight. In all, 20 were saved.

The Battle for Henderson Field lasted until dawn on Oct. 27, when the Jap offensive was repulsed and Mac and his crew, who had been three days and three nights without sleep, were relieved.

They rested for two days and on the morning of Nov. 2 began moving with the rest of the Second Battalion toward Koli Point, where a reported Jap force of 3,000 had been landed. They marched almost 170 miles in nine days, fighting every inch of the way after the second day, taking turns carrying their gun, tripod and ammunition and sleeping on the ground. They had one hot meal in nine days.

They would shout at the Japs "Surrender, you bastards!" and the Japs would holler back "Hell with you" or something less printable. When they charged, the Japs would shout in English, "Blood for the Emperor."

On the evening of Nov. 12, Mac and his squad watched the biggest naval battle of the Solomons, only 20 miles off shore, between the islands of Savo and Tulagi. "It was a pretty big thing, I guess; I mean it was exciting and all, but it just reminded me of the fireworks at the Stutsman County Fair back home," Mac says.

The next day the Japs were driven from Koli Point, and Mac had two days of rest. Then the regiment was sent to Point Cruz to relieve another outfit. Of that engagement, he says: "We didn't get into much of the heavy fighting. We dug in for 28 days; we didn't have one hot meal in all that time, and there were so many air raids I forgot to count them. It was mostly a holding action."

When they were relieved, the battle was nearly over. Company H moved behind the lines and was placed on guard duty. On Dec. 22 Mac came down with malaria, and he spent Christmas in the hospital. After five days he was back on guard duty, but on Jan. 28 the medics ordered his evacuation to this quiet South Pacific island. He had been made a sergeant on Jan. 13.

Mac is no story-book soldier. He does not pretend he enjoys war. He's been in the South Pacific for almost a year and a half now, and he wants to hear American spoken again. First, however, he recognizes that a war must be won.

He is proud of the Infantry, prouder than he was when he became a soldier in February 1941. "They said airplanes would win the war," he says. "Well, they help, sure. They're necessary. But over the 'Canal and in North Africa and every place else they find out that in the clinches it's not the planes or the tanks, it's the Infantry that wins wars."

Sometimes he worries about what will happen after the war, worries about a job and whether he wants to spend the rest of his life in Jamestown or whether he'll stay in the Army. He worries mainly about the fact that in the Infantry he hasn't learned a trade, and he thinks the Army ought to give all infantrymen a chance to learn one after the war.

Meantime, he's anxious only to finish the hard fighting that he knows lies ahead. "It's like going to the dentist; you don't like it, but it has to be done."

Down on the 'Canal he got acquainted with Capt. (now Maj.) Joe Foss of Sioux Falls, S. Dak.

What did they talk about?

"We talked about home, of course," says Mac, "and wondered how the crops had been and if things would be changed when we get back. What else is there to talk about?"

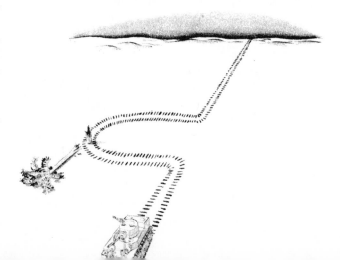

JILTED GIs IN INDIA ORGANIZE FIRST BRUSH-OFF CLUB

BY SGT. ED CUNNINGHAM

AT A U. S. BOMBER BASE, INDIA—For the first time in military history, the mournful hearts have organized. The Brush-Off Club is the result, in this land of sahibs and saris; as usual, it is strictly GI.

Composed of the guys whose gals back home have decided "a few years is too long to wait," the club has only one purpose—to band together for mutual sympathy. They meet weekly to exchange condolences and cry in their beer while telling each other the mournful story of how "she wouldn't wait."

The club has a "chief crier," a "chief sweater" and a "chief consoler." Initiation fee is one broken heart or a reasonable facsimile thereof.

Applicants must be able to answer appropriately the following questions:

1. Has she written lately?

2. Do her letters say she misses you, and is willing to wait no matter how long?

3. Does she reminisce about the "grand times we had together, and the fun we'll have when you come back"?

4. Does she mention casually the fellows she is dating now?

Membership in the club is divided between "active members" and "just sweating members"—the latter being guys who can't believe that no news is good news.

Members are required to give each other the needle; i.e., full sympathy for all active members, encourage "hopeful waiting" in the just sweating members. By-laws state: "As we are all in the 'same transport,' we must provide willing shoulders to cry upon, and join fervently in all wailing and weeping."

One of the newest members of the club was unanimously voted to charter membership because of the particular circumstances of his case. He recently got a six page letter from his fiancée back in Texas. In the last paragraph she casually mentioned, "I was married last week but my husband won't mind you writing to me occasionally. He's a sailor and very broadminded."

This GI, so magnanimously scorned, is now regarded as fine presidential timber.

Present officers of the club, all of whom are active torch-carriers, are: Cpl. Henry W. Asher, Jr., New Orleans, La., president; Pvt. Francis M. McCreery, Marshall, Mo., vice president; Cpl. John McConnell, Garden Grove, Calif., chief crier; S/Sgt. George M. Lehman, Bozeman, Mont., assistant chief crier; Sgt. John Crow, San Jose, Calif., chief sweater; and Lt. Richard L. Weiss, Milwaukee, Wis., chief consoler.

CPL. DOYLE IS TO AFRICA COME!

BY CPL. JOHN J. DOYLE

North Africa

Oh, sound the trumpet and beat the drum!
Cpl. Doyle is to Africa come!
To Africa come in enormous force
To alter the global battle's course.
Already the dastard foemen fly;
We'll all be home the Fourth of July.

Oh, clash the cymbals, sound the tabor!
For Cpl. Doyle, his gun and saber,
His tanks and artillery (self-propelled),
With which the enemy shall be quelled.
Already in dread the Nazi blenches;
By Christmas we'll be out of the trenches.

Oh, smite the zither, rattle the goard!
Cpl. Doyle's in *Afrique du Nord!*
Now for a speedy end to the war;
Summon a hearse for the Afrika Korps,
For here comes the guy the enemy fears—
The paragon of the Engineers.
So smite the zither, rattle the goard!
Cpl. Doyle's in *Afrique du Nord!*

Brenda Joyce

Jean Parker

Alma Carroll

Betty Grable

Virginia Patton

Doris Merrick

Leslie Brooks

Esther Williams

SUNDAY AT SANANANDA

By T-5 DON E. ROHRIG

New Guinea

This is the Huggins perimeter.

As you are standing, Gona's ahead of you,
The green desert of Papua and Dutch New Guinea
Beyond it; beyond the Halmahera Sea, the islands of Molucca
And the far-off places of the Moros and the temple wor-
shipers.

To your left are the Owen Stanleys—
The spinal column of the Papuan tortoise;
And behind you the mightiest of the oceans,
Though from here it is only a breath and a sigh.

To your right, a scant mile up this devious, bucolic trail,
Around many a bend, through the haunted, primordial
tangle,
Past dugout and slit trench, by ford across tropical rivers,
Through mud to your thighs, and the murmuring clouds of
mosquitoes,
Through *kunai* and sun . . . oh, when you get there
You'll know . . . you'll not mistake it, this hell hole:
The bloody black sands, the brown tainted sea water—
This Point Sanananda . . .

Don't mind the skeletons. We haven't had time to remove
them;
And while we sit here with hands limply folded,
We haven't the heart.

No, it isn't the heat or the dampness;
And it certainly isn't sickness, at least not physical sickness—
Though they may come later, the retching, the spewing.
They had it, these grandsons of Heaven,
These stench-making ex-patriots lately of Honshu:
From the slums of Kyoto, from gay Nagasaki,
These pallid-complexioned mother's sons from the rice pad-
dies,
From fermenting Formosa and the smokes of Fujisan . . .
They had the sickness, and not wholly the fevers,
Though the swamp miasmata weren't the least of it.

And so here's what is left of them . . . hell, I don't wonder
Your face grows a bit green . . . it's not a sweet atmosphere
Here with the cadavers.

But after you've slept with them—
There's Charlie the brainless one; and Henry the Horror.
He was clever at sniping, but my cobber resented him,
And even the tree-boys are shy at machine guns!

That beautiful specimen under the quarter-ton
Will have to grow features or else his ancestors
Might fail to remember him among the chrysanthemums
In the honorable Heaven of Japanese heroes . . .
But these are the harmless ones. If you wait until nightfall
You won't be misled by the quiet out yonder;
They're clever, resourceful, and they're not the half of it . . .

The jungle draws in on you, the sound of the wild things
Keeps your heart in your gullet, and I'd not advise you
To sleep with both eyes closed, for fear you might yield
to it—
To sleep—for above all, give the go-by to nightmares.
You see, there's the nightmares, and the start-up in cold
sweat,
The scream that you can't suppress though the darkness is
listening;
And the terror remembered, of the sudden reversal
When these foul, bloody messes that lie here so motionless
Became boys from Brooklyn or Terre Haute or Omaha,
And you recognize all of them and hear the low crying
Just before the death rattle, since none of them wants to die.

And the shadowy shapes glide around in the midst of them,
And the glinting of bayonets and the steaming red rivers
Of warm blood gushing soundlessly . . .

You're pale . . . you're pulling out . . . back to the cities?
Glamorous cities up and down the land.

Well, don't let me detain you
With ranting and preaching. That's just our habit here.
Your blood turns to wormwood.

Though here it is Sunday
We forget the days. Just tell your newspaper
That the boys are still pushing, the Japs still pocketed.

You'd better tone down a bit—don't tell them too much of
it—
Of the corpses and skeletons, the stink and the filthiness
On Point Sanananda.

CAMERAMAN IN CASSINO

BY SGT. GEORGE AARONS

WITH THE FIFTH ARMY IN ITALY—They gave me a Tommy bowler and a leather jerkin and made me take off my combat suit. Otherwise, they said, the British snipers might shoot at my American helmet because it looked like the German one. The captain briefed us, explaining that our load would be rations and barbed wire. He gave us the password and checked to see if everyone knew the rendez-vous at the edge of town.

There were 11 in our party: eight of the men carrying rations; the captain, another man and myself carrying wire. The moon had come up by this time, bringing the slopes of Montecassino out of the darkness.

The captain, the wireman and I started off in a jeep, sitting all three in the front; the back was loaded with the five reels of barbed wire. The windshield was down, so I got the full benefit of the cold night air. It seemed as if we were the only mechanized travel. Soon we began to pass long, slow lines of mules, heavily laden and led by soldiers. The mule lines turned and wound with the road into the valley.

The soldiers leading them were evidently of several nationalities, because whenever our jeep turned a corner and came up unexpectedly on the rear of a column, we heard voices cry out warnings in French and English and sometimes in Italian.

When the mule trains became scarcer, we caught up with jeeps pulling loaded trailers. Occasionally we passed companies of Infantry replacements moving up.

The driver was familiar with the road and he began to speed up, never lingering long on the high points or crossroads because, he said, "they have those spots zeroed in." Although the flats in front of the town were occasionally shelled, nothing fell near us.

I noticed that smoke shells were being put down in front of the town, blocking out the lower slopes but leaving the monastery clearly visible above.

We passed a few dead mules by the side of the road and then a Bren-gun carrier lying in a ditch. There was a heavy smell in the air, a mixture of dead mules and the bright yellow flowers patching the flats in the valley.

Then we came to the flats flooded by the Germans. We made the turn at Hell's Fire Corner, clearly marked by strips of mine tape strung on two shot-up six-by-sixes and two wrecked ambulances.

The driver stepped on the gas, and we raced across the Rapido, bounced past a couple of knocked-out tanks and came to an intersection. The inevitable MP stood there, directing traffic. We turned left at a barracks, and it was then that we began to see the first effects of the terrific shelling and bombardment the town had received. Only a few pillars remained standing above the debris of the barracks on the outskirts. Here and there were dead Shermans, which had thrown their treads as a snake sheds its skin.

Pulling up in front of our meeting place, we quickly unloaded the wire. Before we could acknowledge the hurried "Bye, Yank, see you tomorrow night," the driver raced away, leaving the captain and me alone with our reels of barbed wire.

I'd expected the worst during the ride but nothing had happened, and now I remarked to the captain: "It's pretty quiet tonight." He turned and said quietly that there was an understanding among the men never to mention things like that on these trips. He told me he made a trip like this one every night.

While we waited for the truck to arrive, he demonstrated how to carry a coil of barbed wire. You stand inside the coil and then grab hold of the looped pieces of insulated wire on each side.

Soon there was a terrific clanking down the road, and I was sure every German in Cassino could hear the truck coming. The noise was made by chains carried over the truck's bumper.

The men scrambled out and the captain checked to see that each man had his proper load. The rations were carried in pairs of sandbags tied together at the mouth and then slung over the men's shoulders. Each man also carried a small bag in each hand.

While the captain was attending to the final details, the Germans started. There's a funny thing about mortars: when they're going to miss you they can be heard, but the closer they get the quieter they sound.

There would be a swish-swish, a burst of flame and then a loud explosion. I felt very uneasy. The shells were exploding in the very path we were traveling, and I whispered to the New Zealander behind me: "It's getting kind of noisy." He whispered back: "Jerry's having his bit of hate."

When we moved off, the captain placed me behind him and explained that we must keep five yards between us. He picked up his coil and started off, hugging the bank alongside the road. Picking up my coil, I noticed that it was off balance but decided there was no time to do anything about it now and took up the trail right behind the captain. I heard the man behind me do the same.

Everything was still all around us. Suddenly a burst of machine-gun fire shattered the silence, synchronized with a single tracer that lazily arched its way across us toward our lines. This was followed by a couple of mortars, and then all was quiet again.

It was a beautiful night, filled with all the signs of an awakening spring. A lonely night bird was sounding off over in Purple Heart Valley, and the sting had gone out of the breeze coming down off the mountain.

When we got to the edge of the town, the captain set his coil down near an overturned Sherman and stopped. I was puffing hard and was grateful for this chance to rest. In the distance we could hear the sound of long-range shelling. Occasionally the tanks bedded down in the flats would fire a mission, and then all would be quiet again.

The captain asked me how I was doing and then said that we didn't have much farther to go, but that it would be rougher now; we were coming to the rubble. "I hope Spandau Alley is quiet tonight," a Kiwi whispered in my ear, explaining that it was a spot along our route that the Kraut sprayed every so often in the hope of catching just such a party as ours. "We've been pretty lucky so far," he said. "He's just missed every time."

As we started off again, I hoped silently that he would continue to miss. In a few minutes we were in the rubble, and when someone stepped on a tin can my heart seemed to stop. As it resumed its normal beat, I could see that we were walking on what had once been a street; we were trying to hug the stumps of walls of houses. It was so quiet that I could hear a cat crying.

There was actually no shape to the road as we climbed over heaps of rubble covering the first floor of what had once been a house, down the other side into a bomb crater and then around a tank that lay on its side. I had no idea at times whether we were going up or down a slope and just followed the man in front of me.

Suddenly the near quiet was broken by a very sharp swish, then by the crash of a mortar. The captain shouted: "Take cover, blokes." Everybody dropped what he was carrying, stretched out flat and tried to crawl to some hole or to get behind a heavy wall that was still standing.

I could hear the captain moving about to make sure that everyone was safe. I found myself sprawled out behind a two-foot-thick wall, in the company of a Kiwi who wasn't wearing a helmet. Shivering and sweating at the same time, I whispered to him: "Isn't this a helluva place?" He whispered back: "I wish I was in the desert again." So did I.

There was another crash and a burst of flames, and the ground shook under us. The falling plaster dust tickled my nose, and I tried to get closer to the ground and curl my long legs in under me. Pieces of rubble pelted us, and a pebble hit me in the back of the neck, making me wish I was wearing my deep American helmet.

After a few seconds I raised my head. There was a lot of dust, and the smell of the shell was still hanging in the air. But I could see the captain going from man to man to check whether they were all okay. He had plenty of guts.

I heard a lot of swishing in the air over our heads. Some of it was our stuff, and I remembered someone saying that we give the Kraut about seven for every one he sends over. Any other time I would have been comforted by the thought, but at the moment it wasn't very reassuring because a lot of his stuff was coming at us. We all stayed where we were, but finally no more came, and then our guns stopped firing, too. All was quiet again, but we didn't move until the captain said: "Let's get cracking, blokes."

I went back to where I had dropped the wire. "Quite close, eh, Slim?" the captain said. "Too bloody close," I mumbled.

The dust had cleared away but it was quite dark now; some clouds had blown in front of the moon. Stumbling over huge blocks of masonry, girders and bomb craters large enough to hide a six-by-six, we made our way along.

Every so often we'd pass some Infantry replacements going in, others on their way out. I could understand now why I'd had to change uniforms. Someone seeing my different rig might have thought I was a German who'd infiltrated.

Coming out of a crater behind a tank, I saw the captain step out of his coil. "We're here," he said as I came up to him. All I could see was a ruin similar to those we had passed.

The Kiwis filed in with the rations while we left the barbed wire outside. Squeezing into the entrance, I heard a voice in the dark say: "Give me your hand, Yank." I stuck my hand out, groping, and the owner of the voice grabbed it. I followed him in the dark, turned right and went down some steps into a room. It was dimly lit by a shielded candle in a box.

Coming out of the dark, I found even this light seemed bright. There were many coats and blankets lying on the floor, some American and some British. I plopped down and wiped some of the sweat off my face.

There was a double-decker bunk in one corner of the room. The Germans had built it, but none of our men was sleeping in it because it was too hard. This was company headquarters, and the bunk was serving as a set of shelves.

From here men went to various other houses to deliver the loads. I was introduced to the major in charge and to the rest of the men in the house.

A walkie-talkie was going in the corner of the house and the radioman was trying to contact a forward platoon in another house. The telephone lines were out, and headquarters was using the radio to maintain contact with this platoon.

When the men of the carrying party got back, they threw themselves down and started to light up. The major cautioned them against smoking in the outer room. One fellow lit his cigarette with a match and then passed the cigarette around so the others could light up.

The soldiers occupying the house gathered around the carrying party to get all the latest news and rumors from camp. Loud talking interfered with the radioman's reception and he shouted: "Shut up, back there!"

The captain asked if there was anything else the men wanted, but there was no answer. He picked up their letters and waited for a barrage of shelling to stop before he left. He shook hands and said that he would see me tomorrow. Then he gathered his men together and left. On the return trip they carried back salvage—broken rifles, clothing and even the dead.

The major went out to make the rounds of his forward platoons. After every barrage, the man on the phones checked to see if the wires were still in. If the platoons could not be contacted, headquarters would try to reach them by radio until a man could be sent to repair the break.

When the major came back, he said I could take any place on the floor and handed me two blankets. I picked out an empty spot and spread them out. There was a layer of debris dust insulating the blankets from the bare floor.

The radioman left word with the sentry to call him every hour, the major snuffed out the candle and I crawled in between the blankets with all my clothes and shoes on. All through the night many shells hit near the building; occasionally one would hit the house, but this house had withstood many previous hits. Often I could hear short bursts of machine-gun fire. They say you can tell a German Spandau from our guns because it fires more rounds per minute, but to me they all sound the same.

Early next morning we were awakened by the sound of machine-gun fire coming from every direction. The major leaped up and called out: "Take position, men." It was just beginning to get light, and someone said it was 5 o'clock.

The major called his forward platoons by radio to find out what had caused all the noise. He was told that the Germans had attacked earlier in the night with a strong patrol but had been detected. Flares were sent up, and our artillery had shelled them. The patrol had hunted around most of the night and at first light had attacked again. They had been beaten off and three prisoners taken. The major told me the Germans were just testing our strength.

I didn't feel like going back to bed and decided to look around the place. As I came up the stairs out of the cellar, I saw two Kiwis on guard at the window of a room right across the way. There were two guards at the lookout window at the opposite end of the room and two guards at the only entrance to the house. They all had tommy guns.

The walls of the house were at least a foot and a half thick, and there were two floors of fallen rubble over our heads. The only thing that could knock us out was a direct bomb hit. I could understand now how Stalingrad had held out. We and the enemy were so close that neither side could effectively use heavy artillery or bombs for fear of hitting its own men.

I peered out the lookout window but couldn't see much because of the early morning haze. The guard was reduced to one man at the lookout and one at the entrance, while the others set about preparing breakfast. The room used for a kitchen was also a combined dining room and latrine, and the odor left you in no doubt as to the latter function.

After breakfast two of the men stepped cautiously out of the house and crept to a nearby well to get water. Just as the men reached the well a barrage of mortars let go, and some of the shells hit the house, shaking up the rubble. The men at the well got back safely, though I never thought they would. It was my first lesson in the unwisdom of walking outside in daylight.

Though I spent most of the morning looking out the window with binoculars, I couldn't pick out a living thing. There must have been at least 60 houses occupied by our troops, besides those held by the Germans—more than a thousand men concealed before me. Yet I never saw a soul or heard a human sound. Nothing ever happens in Cassino in the daytime.

The day passed quickly. The men who were not on guard sat around talking sex and politics, except for the night guards who were sleeping. The telephone man was checking up to find out which wires he'd have to repair that night. He said that no repairs are ever made by day and that never a day goes by that wires aren't torn up by shell fire.

From my post at the lookout window I could see smoke shells landing on the flats. Each side uses smoke shells to hinder observation. As I looked out, Cassino reminded me of a ghost town wearing down with the years.

Above the house on a ridge sits the castle—or what's left of it—which we now occupy; and on the ridge right behind is Hangman's Hill, so called because a piece of framework that looks like a gallows stands there. The Germans, who hold Hangman's Hill, look down our backs as we use the outdoor latrine.

Later that afternoon the major asked if I'd like to go visiting. We started off for our next-door neighbor's. Although the distance between the houses was only about 25 yards, it looked like an obstacle course. As the major led the way, I sidestepped our barbed wire, jumped over a block of masonry and leaped in and out of a crater, never daring to look back. We rounded a chunk of wall, wiggled through an entrance that was nothing more than a shell hole in the wall, then slid down a pile of rubble to the main floor, where we ran smack into a Kiwi with a tommy gun. The Kiwi seemed to have heard all about the Yank with a camera, so I figured the communications system was still functioning.

We were barely inside when we heard the crash of mortar shells dropping on our recent route, as if to say: "You're not putting anything over on us."

This house was about the same as the other except that it had more armament. There were Bren guns, and the Kiwis were setting up an antitank gun, carried up during the night. I took a few pictures and then decided to go back. We made the same quick scramble between houses, and a few minutes after we got inside, the Germans loosed a burst of machine-gun fire that hit the outside of the house. "It's not good to run around like we did," the major said; "it angers the Kraut and he wakes up the men who are trying to sleep."

There was little doing the rest of the day, and life in a Cassino fortress seemed pretty dull. The boys had a pin-up of Marguerite Chapman, salvaged from a beat-up British magazine. They also

"Going ashore early tonight, eh, Wilcoxen?"—Sgt. Frank Brandt.

had a bottle of Scotch, donated by some correspondents. They'd had the bottle for a week but there was still some Scotch left. "We're saving it for a tough spot," they said. These boys have been fighting the war for three years now, so I reckon it's going to be a pretty tough spot.

While we were eating supper the Kraut threw over some stuff. "Here comes his iron rations," one soldier said to me, looking up from his stew. "He puts over a stonk every day at this time."

By this time mortar fire sounded as commonplace to me as an auto horn on a street back home. I felt perfectly safe in this temporary home.

Time wore on after supper and there was nothing to do except wait for the ration party. I sat at the entrance and made conversation with the guard. "The ration party is our only link with the outside world," he said. "They bring us our letters every day and anything we want. They had a tough job getting some rat poison we asked for."

Since the bombing of Cassino, the rats have increased in number and boldness. They feed on the dead and run all over the place at night.

I looked out the entrance and couldn't see a hundred yards in front of me. We seemed to be an island in a sea of smoke. The guard was increased; this was the time of day when most of the attacks came. Soon it was dark. There was nothing to do, so I went back in to catch a nap.

I was awakened by the noise of the entrance of the ration party. Now that the time had come, I was afraid to leave this safe house. I could understand now why the men never liked to go outside. We said the usual "good lucks," shook hands all around and stepped out into the darkness. The Germans had just finished a barrage, so this was the best time to leave.

Most of the men had loads of salvage on the return trip, but there was nothing for me to carry. As we were leaving the town, we heard some machine-gun fire. Looking back, I could see the faces of the men behind me reflecting the light of flares. There was mortar fire, but none came near us. I was glad I had changed my helmet; we were certainly visible to British snipers.

It had rained during the day but the sky was clear now. We kept moving, hugging the walls. In the distance the flashes of our big guns lit the sky at intervals. When we passed the spot where we had hit the dirt the previous night, the captain dropped back and showed me where a shell had landed right in the path. "It came only a few yards from the last man," he said.

The captain walked quietly beside me. Then he asked: "Do you get this kind of training in America?" The big guns were splashing the sky with angry dabs of flame. I looked back at the town, still lit by the flares, listened to the mortar shells exploding and the machine guns playing, studied the valley that the Americans had so appropriately named the Valley of the Purple Heart, and turned back to the captain.

"They didn't when I was there," I said, shaking my head, "but I sure hope they do now."

"I hate this apologizing Business."—*Pvt. Thomas Flannery.*

SECRET WEAPONS FOR THE INVASION OF GERMANY

By Sgt. RALPH STEIN

OLD TOWN INVASION BARGE, SUBMERSIBLE, MARK VII, SECTION 8 (WITH PARASOL AND BANJO)

OUR simple-hearted Nazi coast sentry thinks that he sees only romantic couples, spending Sunday afternoon in canoes. But beneath the surface our invading troops are lurking, well supplied with Spam for the fight that looms ahead and studying their comic books as the Zero Hour draws near. TECHNICAL DATA: Notice the young lady, or frail, in the stern of the canoe. She steers the barge with that innocent hand which she trails so languidly in the water and conceals with her distracting legs, or hockeys, the trap door in the floor of the canoe which serves the attacking force as an exit from the barge.

TRACTION REDUCER, BOOT M13, OR PRATT-FALL INDUCER

THIS two-man motorized dignity destroyer features a pair of automatic hands which pick bananas very rapidly, dropping the peels in the path of advancing enemy infantry. Rest of the banana goes into GI pudding which is used as a devastating booby trap. Automatic hands can also be used to snap fingers under the noses of enemy officers and make other insulting gestures.

HERE is our secret bottle weapon which is used to float troops in battle equipment to Germany by the Gulf Stream, if it happens to be going that way.

KNACKWURST AND SAUERKRAUT PROJECTOR, OLFACTORY

TRACTOR at left carries an engine-driven fan which forces the odor of knackwurst and sauerkraut, cooking on gas range, through the projector tube. Drool sergeant at projector controls can elevate or depress tube through an arc of 70 degrees. Drool meter under Nazi's chin registers excitation of salivary gland. If victim doesn't drool enough, put some more kraut in the pot. METHOD OF USE: The enemy follows the smell of the knackwurst and kraut and he is yours. Then you don't let him eat it.

WENCH MORTAR

THESE weapons create confusion by dropping tasty babes or reasonably exact facsimiles upon installations. SERVICE OF THE PIECE: Tube should be swabbed often with perfume, preferably Chanel No. 5.

PARACOOK, PTOMAINE

THIS cruel weapon of invasion is used only under extreme provocation. Cooks and accomplices armed with copies of the "Army Cook's Field Manual" are dropped behind the enemy's line to cook for him. No special training necessary. Supplies of dried eggs and creamed beef on toast may also be dropped but only as a desperate last resort.

INCENDIARY, PEDAL M1922 OR HOT FOOT

THIS is a light, mobile, single-seat infantry co-operation weapon, which can also be used to illuminate GI crap games at night when the invasion is over. METHOD OF OPERATION: The bewildered Nazi is chased until exhaustion. Then the embracing ring, or hugger, clamps over his head, pinning his arms to his side while the automatic hand appears with a lighted match, applying a hot foot in the customary manner. When a storm trooper or OBERFELDWEBEL is bagged, the weapon applies the blowtorch with satisfactory results. How do the matches get stuck in the boots of the Nazis? They are placed there weeks before the invasion by fifth-columnists disguised as poor but honest shoe-shine boys.

STAGING AREA

By Pvt. ALAN SURGAL

Sketches by Sgt. Howard J. Brodie

At a Port of Embarkation Staging Camp—It is 0700. You hitch your field bag forward where it cuts into your shoulders and stumble stiffly out of the curtained coach, still wiping the hot dusty sleep from your eyes.

You stare at the vast cindered expanse, and a squadron of butterflies spills into a soft-shoe power dive in your stomach.

You stand nervously waiting for directions, and they're not long in coming.

"Troops will form at the rear of the train in a column of threes," booms a bodyless voice through an invisible amplifier.

You scramble to obey, and the butterflies level off a little.

You look at your buddy, Florida, and he grins back at you. You start to say something, but the voice without a body breaks in again.

"You are now at a classified address," it explains. "You will send no letters or telegrams, and you will not be permitted to telephone until you have specific instructions."

Censorship! You've heard about it, and now it's here. You feel a momentary exhilaration and then a sudden isolation. You think of a dozen messages that suddenly seem desperately urgent, but you can't send them. Not for the duration and six you can't.

Even Florida is quiet.

Then for the first time you notice your officers, especially your platoon commander. Dressed in regulation GIs, scuffing his unpolished combat shoes on the cindered siding, he looks inches smaller than in his tailored pinks. And a lot more nervous. You're suddenly liking him better than you ever have before.

He steps back, bawls "Battery atten-tion!" and you stiffen into position.

"Forward march!"

The morning echoes abruptly with the cadenced crunch of GI shoes on cinder. Somewhere in the rear a band strikes up, and you're off to your last camp in the States.

It is 0900.

You're in your barracks now, and you're snatching a little bunk fatigue. You've captured yourself a lower and Florida is on top.

At first you both waited uneasily for someone to bark you out into some detail or formation, but no one has and it doesn't look as if anybody intends to. So you've settled yourself comfortably, and you're quietly thinking.

"Wonder where we're going from here, Florida?" you ask idly.

"Wonder if they give any passes?" he says, completely ignoring your question.

You notice a name carved on the board above your head.

"Pfc. C. E. Hollis," you read aloud.

"I wonder what Pfc. Hollis is doing right now," you add meditatively.

"Don't get corny," Florida replies.

You settle back again with your thoughts, but after a moment they're sharply interrupted by the staccato bark of your platoon sergeant.

"Okay, boys! Off and on! Hit the deck!"

"What is it this time?" you ask, propping yourself on your elbow.

"Show-down inspection."

"*Show-down* inspection?" you repeat incredulously. "Why, we had 12 of those at the other camp!"

"See the chaplain," snaps the sergeant.

You pause, transfixed, staring vacantly past him.

"Funny," you think to yourself. "That's not a bad idea—now."

It is 1300.

You've had your clothing inspection, and you're on your way back from chow.

By now you've looked over the camp, and you're impressed most by its impermanence. Not the buildings so much, though even they seem less stable than the ones at the other camps. Mostly it's the people.

Ever since you knew for certain that you were

going overseas, you've somehow resented the cadre at the other processing camps. Jaunty noncoms with colorful shoulder insignia preparing you for something they may never undergo themselves.

But here it's different. Here everybody seems to be going. Everybody's a transient. Here, literally, everybody is in the same boat. And somehow it makes you feel a lot better.

It is 1500.

"Christ, Florida, did you ever see so many GIs in one place before?"

You're gathered in a huge commons for what they call a general orientation meeting. A salt-water bull session. All the GIs in the world seem to be here.

You listen politely through the speeches of the Army Emergency Relief officer and the Red Cross man, and you're impressed when the chaplain tells you to buddy up with God now and not to wait until you get foxhole religion.

But you're eagerly attentive when the Military Intelligence officer steps forward and starts to talk about "The Boat."

"The Boat!" It's been only a stabbing little flanking thought until now, but now it's ripped through to the front-center of your consciousness.

The MI officer is a breezy, good-humored fellow with a slight Bronx inflection, and you like him immediately. He starts out by telling a few GI yarns right out of "Private Hargrove," but you don't mind because he tells them well.

And when he begins to talk in earnest about the boat, you get the secure feeling that he's not reading from any prepared script. You listen closely, and you learn plenty.

You learn, for example, that you will mess only twice a day aboard ship; that water is scarce; that fire and panic are more dangerous than submarines. And, above all, you learn that the greatest menace to your safety is *you*. You and your big fat mouth.

You can see everybody's impressed.

You turn to Florida, who's looking unnaturally solemn.

"What's on your mind?" you ask sympathetically.

"Chow," he snaps without hesitation. "I'm hungry."

You can see everybody's impressed.

It is 2300.

"Lights out," and you're lying quietly in bed, thinking.

It's been a full evening, and you've written your first censored letter and made your first restricted telephone call. You've sneaked off for a lonesome walk in the nearby fields, drinking in your last few glimpses of American landscape, your last few draughts of American air. You've idled back to the barracks and continued guessing with the boys, trying to decide on your overseas destination. You've dropped a fast deuce in a friendly crap game, and before you know it, the evening's spent.

Now it's "lights out," and you're lying quietly in bed, thinking.

YUGOSLAV DIARY

By Sgt. WALTER BERNSTEIN

Sketches by Sgt. Howard J. Brodie

TUESDAY

SOMEWHERE IN YUGOSLAVIA—The route into the interior is closed, so I must remain here for a while. The Yugoslav front is composed of patches rather than any sort of line. The Partisans have freed large chunks of territory and these are usually connected by narrow strips, along which couriers can be sent. A year ago the liberated territory consisted of little islands in a German sea; now the situation is being reversed. But sometimes the Germans close the corridors between the masses of liberated territory. That is the case now, and it is necessary to wait until a new route is found.

I am staying at the headquarters of the newspaper, *Free Dalmatia,* in an old stone house on the edge of an old stone village halfway up a mountain. The mountain itself is stone, or seems to be. The trees grow fugitively between the rocks and there are stones everywhere. From the village you can look across a valley to another mountain, and over the top of that you can see another and another. Beyond the first mountain are the Germans.

The paper is a hand-set, six-page weekly, distributed throughout Dalmatia (the section of Yugoslavia along the Adriatic coast) by a committee of AVNOJ, the congress of the new Yugoslavia.

Since the Germans at present occupy most of Dalmatia, the paper has to be circulated secretly. It is an indication of Partisan unity and organization that there is probably less warfare incident to the weekly distribution of their several thousand papers in occupied territory than there is every day with the *Chicago Tribune.*

The paper is run by an organization of some 15 people: intellectuals, printers, stenographers, a cook, a handyman. They live, eat and work together, and most of them have seen action as fighters at one time or another. There are five women: the cook and her assistant, two girls who do stenography and technical work, and an elderly woman who works in the printing department with her son. The editorial staff is composed of an ex-lawyer, a young architect, a couple of students, an ex-professor, a white-collar worker and a poet. Their press is an ancient foot-pumped affair that used to print prayer books somewhere in Dalmatia. It can turn out only one page a day, and by now the letters are so worn that sometimes it is hard to make them out. Despite this, the staff manages to print other pamphlets when necessary, turn out a mimeographed news bulletin every other day and monitor radio news for the provincial committee, the staff of the nearby division and other interested parties.

The only one who speaks English on the newspaper is the lawyer, a thin, sunburned man with glasses. He speaks quite well, although bookishly. "Our paper is small," he says, "but it is much perused." His lungs are not good and he must rest every day after lunch. Before joining the staff he was military judge for Southern Dalmatia, and sometimes he talks about the trials he conducted. "We were very lenient with the traitors," he says. "Only those who pillaged with the fascists were shot." He tells of two Ustachi (Croatian fascists) who were captured by the Partisans. They had been Ustachi for only a short time and had not taken part in the usual looting and torturing, so they were freed and told to return home. "They wept when we allowed them free," the lawyer said. "Everyone wept, I also."

Each morning they gather around the public address system and listen intently to the news broadcast.

WEDNESDAY

Today there is ice by the well where everyone washes in the morning. It is technically spring, but you would never know it here. The wind whips around the mountain and it is very cold. There is a radio news broadcast in Croatian from London every morning at 0700, and by 0630 the people have gathered around the public address system which the staff has rigged up outside the house. They come from the village and the units around the village, and they wait patiently in the cold. They are mostly fighters from the division: tough, capable men, women with grenades hanging from their belts, even little boys who act as ammunition carriers. This morning there are also two old men on donkeys and an old woman seated on the steps, sewing a patch on a pair of pants. One of the old men wears a felt hat with a red star on it. They listen intently to the news, occasionally making comments. When it is over, they drift quietly away.

The staff of *Free Dalmatia* takes its meals in the attic of the stone house, where there is a long bare table and a small stove. The food is simple and inadequate. There is usually only one dish to a meal, but the staff is used to that. Some of the food is American, since the village is close enough to the sea to receive a tiny part of the scanty supplies the Allies are sending to the Partisans. They are very grateful for what help they do get.

For breakfast there is bread and tea. The bread is hot from the oven, with a heavy, sweet-smelling wetness. The tea is eaten with a spoon, like soup. After breakfast everyone goes to his job, and I wander through the village. It is a poor little village, very old and built on a slant, with the houses jumbled together and narrow dirt paths winding crookedly about. There are a few skinny chickens scrabbling in the dirt and three lean dogs that stare with mad eyes. On the walls of all the houses are slogans: "Long Live the Army of Liberation," "Long Live Free Yugoslavia," "Long Live Marshal Tito."

Supper consists of a plateful of string beans with pieces of Vienna sausage. There is also a large can of chowchow (mixed pickles in mustard sauce). The Partisans need chowchow like they need a hole in the head, but they regard it as simply some peculiar American dish and eat it. After supper everyone sits around and sings. The songs come naturally; they are beautiful songs, simple and immediate. There is one song about their rifles, and a song about one of their national heroes killed in battle, and one addressed to Marshal Tito by the girls in which they ask "When will you send the boys home?" and Tito answers "It is not yet time, it is not yet time."

In the evening the staff also listens to the radio. There are Croatian broadcasts from London and Moscow every night and occasionally one from New York. American broadcasts seem to be the least popular, because the broadcasters do not seem to have much of an idea of what is really happening in Yugoslavia. Everyone here is very interested in America, although many of the people's ideas about the States come from the movies.

They are extremely interested in the present status of gangsters and Indians. One of the students on the staff of the paper wants to know if it is true about the installment plan. The others are also interested in more basic matters, such as the attitude of our people toward the war, our political situation, our educational system and what has happened to Laurel and Hardy.

THURSDAY

This morning, right after breakfast, there was the drone of planes, and then a whole group of Liberators came over. There must have been 70 of them, heading north. They were very high, flying a beautiful, tight, precise formation, not fast but with a heavy deliberate purposefulness. Everyone in the village ran out to watch, running around and pointing up at the planes and cheering them on. That name "Liberator" really means something here.

In the afternoon one of Yugoslavia's champion soccer players came over to give the staff some material on the relation between sport and the present struggle. His name is Matosic. Big and athletic-looking, he played on the all-Yugoslav team against England before the war.

All day there has been the muffled sound of gunfire from beyond the mountain. The division is in contact with the Germans. The poet went to headquarters early in the day and everyone wonders if he has managed to get in the fight.

There was much excitement at dinner. Two friends whom the staff had thought were dead showed up. They had been in a concentration camp for three years, and finally escaped and made their way to the Partisans. One of them is a man of 27 and the other is 35, but they look much older. The younger man did most of the talking; the other was quiet and seemed almost a little punchy. He kept touching the younger man, putting his head on his shoulder as if for support. The younger man talked

The younger man talked between mouthfuls. The other one kept leaning on his shoulder as if for support.

between mouthfuls of food. He ate delicately, almost shyly, arranging the food carefully with his fork before lifting it to his mouth, then chewing it with great thoroughness. The others opened a can of peaches especially for the two: peaches are like ammunition, and the whole room seemed to eat the fruit with the two men, slowly and with a quiet, enormous enjoyment.

The two of them had been put to work by the Germans in a factory at Wiener Neustadt, the big industrial center near Vienna. The younger man spoke of the conditions there, the lack of food and the great devastation caused by American bombers. But he said there were no signs of an internal crack-up, and little organized sabotage in the factories. The German plan is to fill the plants with different nationalities and keep them suspicious of each other, so that no one ever feels he can trust anyone else. The younger man had also been in the notorious Ustachi camp at Jasenovac in Croatia. This is the camp that is known for burning men alive; its record is 1,500 in one night. While he was talking, the handyman came over and sat down. He had been sent to Jasenovac but escaped. He was a Sephardic Jew from Bosnia, and he still spoke a kind of bastard Spanish. The Germans murdered his father, mother, wife and three-year-old child.

The route is still closed.

FRIDAY
There was a little snow this morning, but it melted when the sun came out. The countryside looks as though a glacier had just retreated. The mountains are thrown up in spasms and the rocks seem torn apart. The people are as hard as the country, but very impressive. They have an immense dignity; they have transformed their fight against the Germans into a struggle to build a new country, and they have a deep pride in what they are building. There seems to be a complete democracy in their army. It is not merely that the officer sits down with his men; it is that they each have an equal share in the present and the future, and they recognize this equality. There seems to be a complete understanding that each is serving according to his capacity. There is practically no one in the army who has not seen action, either at the front or in the underground. There are no soft jobs and no privileges except those that have been earned. The discipline is very high. It is not parade-ground discipline but comes from a knowledge and belief in what they are fighting for. There is also much saluting. Everyone salutes everyone else, regardless of his rank. And all the Partisans have a simple,

understandable attitude toward the future: only those who have fought deserve to share in it.

There was a show of photographs at dinner; the two girls passed around pictures of themselves before the war. They became very coy at this point. The pictures were conventional poses taken at the seashore and in the park. The girls looked modern and pretty in their dresses, and very feminine. One of them is divorced; she has a three-year-old daughter whom she hasn't seen in a year and a half. The other has been married for six months to the secretary of the provincial committee. She gets to see him once in a while. She shows his picture in civilian clothes—a young, good-looking boy who looks as though he were just out of college.

The poet returned tonight. He was in the battle. Only three Partisans had been killed and thirty Germans taken prisoner. The Partisan method of dealing with prisoners is simple enough. If there is proof that they have been pillaging and torturing, they are shot. The rest are offered the opportunity of joining the Partisans. If they refuse they are put to work and held for exchange. In this batch, the poet said, there was only one who wanted to join. The rest wished to be exchanged and fight again, except three Austrians who wanted to be sent to Africa. The Partisans know who has been looting. The intelligence of a people's army is usually good, since its forces are everywhere.

The poet is a tall young man with a mop of black hair. The others always refer to him as "our poet." He had a book of poetry published before the war and everyone says he is a good poet. The only thing they regret is that he is not much interested in world affairs. "He lives in the realm of the esthetic," the lawyer says. The poet is an old Partisan, however, having joined more than two years ago, and he has fought through several offensives.

Everyone listens closely while he tells about the battle. One of the Partisan dead is a woman fighter, who had also been in the movement for a long time. They shake their heads when the poet tells about her, and say she will be missed. They are hardened to violent death but will never be used to it. Afterward they kid the poet about his lack of interest in what has been happening in the world while he has been away. "You are only interested in poetry," the lawyer says. "I am for a free federal Yugoslavia," the poet answers. There is no argument after that.

SATURDAY
Talked this afternoon with the girl secretary of the Anti-Fascist Youth Congress, to be held some-

where in liberated territory later this month. The Partisans expect delegates from all the Balkan countries and even the Soviet Union. This will be their second congress; the first was held two years ago. The secretary explains that many of the delegates who were at the first congress will not be at this one; they have been killed fighting. The secretary is young and pleasantly attractive. She is small, has long brown hair and looks like one of the more intelligent co-eds at a state university. She is also something of a hero, the lawyer says. During one of the offensives she held a hill alone with a machine gun against repeated German counterattacks.

At dinner there are three Slovenian performers, who have been going from brigade to brigade, giving shows. One used to be an actor, the second a theater director and the third was director of the opera in the city of Ljublana. They all fought through the early German offensives, but now they are doing cultural work. The opera director is remaining here for a few days to mimeograph a book of Partisan songs.

For dessert tonight there was an air raid. About 30 German planes came over, looking for a village on the other side of the mountain, where there is some important stuff. They dropped flares and lit up the whole sky. Everyone came pouring out of the village to watch. There are some fighter detachments in the village and they came out on the double, fanning into position on the mountain. One of their officers is a woman and she kept yelling orders in a high firm voice. There was some ack-ack, but not much. The tracers shot into the sky like fireworks and you could hear the dull boom of the bombs as they dropped on the other side. The raid lasted about 20 minutes. Then the planes went away and the firing stopped and the flares died out slowly, returning the sky to the night.

SUNDAY

The poet went across the mountain today and came back with the information that the planes had hit only a few houses and the left wing of a hospital. Only a few people were killed and no damage done to the important matériel. One of the dead was a friend of several of the staff here and they are going to her funeral today.

All day listening to the radio. There is a piano recital from Moscow, opera from Italy, a talk from Berlin on the senselessness of aerial warfare, an RAF dance band from London, and a talk from America addressed to the people of Europe. Everyone thought the American talk a little out of the world, because it seriously discussed the question

of bombing Rome and the Montecassino Abbey as if there were two sides to the question. To the people who are doing the fighting, there is no debate on whether or not to bomb places where there are German soldiers.

There is much admiration and friendship for America among these people, and they still visualize us as the great, young, uncorrupted nation. Most of them would like to visit the States after the war, and they ask many questions. They are amazed that there are houses in America as poor as the one they are in now and want to know if there are beggars on the streets.

The old woman covered the mine and sat down to wait.

The poet also returned with a story that gives some indication of part of a people's war. One of the old women from a nearby village was walking along a road when she saw a Partisan mine that had been planted but insufficiently camouflaged. She covered it up herself and then sat down at a safe distance to watch. After a while a German scout car came along, passed over the mine and blew up. The old woman got up, walked back to Partisan headquarters, told them what had happened and then gave them a good bawling out for permitting such sloppy work.

Tonight the staff had the weekly political meeting. Everyone was present, including the cooks, and they all discussed world events and the present necessities of their new Yugoslav state. Afterward they sat around and sang and there was some spontaneous dancing, much like our square dances.

No news about the route being open.

Need a bath.

MONDAY

The paper came out today. It contains articles about the coming Youth Congress, the Russian offensive, the air war on Germany, the decisions of AVNOJ, developments in the Partisan campaign and accounts of new German atrocities. There are also articles on what is happening. politically outside of Yugoslavia.

There are reports that the Germans are increasing their terror in occupied regions, before the Red Army arrives. It is impossible for Americans to realize the extent of this calculated, sub-human slaughter. The stories make you sick when you hear them. The amount of suffering is beyond belief, and this is one reason why these people have no respect for those who ran to safety. You can only understand the people who have been under the Germans if you realize what they have suffered. That suffering has made the people of Yugoslavia, at least, bitterly definite that only those who have suffered and fought will share the victory.

At dinner there is a hot scientific discussion about when light becomes heat. There is also a discussion about modern art and an argument between the poet and the architect on the relative merits of liberal and classical education. They are all extremely well-informed and highly intelligent. They kid the printer about the fact that he was so well-paid before the war; they accuse him of having eight pairs of pajamas and feeding white bread to his dog. He protests. The lawyer quotes the Gettysburg address and the Declaration of Independence; he is very happy when I tell him I was born in the States. "Now you can be president!" he says. "Otherwise you can only be vice president." There is excitement over the report that the British have closed their eastern coast. The second front here is more than a problem in logistics.

There is much static over the radio tonight, and then suddenly there is a blast of music and the unctuous voice of a real American announcer introducing the Original Dixieland Band. Then the music comes, blatant and foolish, the corn blaring without shame. Everyone smiles politely, but it is wonderful, heavy with rhythm and nostalgia. It is a program for the troops overseas and there is the announcer again, patronizing the soldiers, talking to them man to man. He is on a different planet, a million miles away; he has no relation to this room, these people, this war. But the music is friendly; after a while the others like the music, humming the trite tune, tapping out the rhythm with their feet. And then it is over and there is the announcer, and the coaxed, artificial applause, and the new wartime commercial to sell you-fellows-overseas. And the studio orchestra fading softly out; and the room back to normal, the people concerned, interested, turning the dial for news; and the poster on the wall saying boldly in a flash of red: "Together in the Fight Against Fascism."

Tomorrow they think there may be a route open. The Germans have begun a new local offensive, but there is a way through the mountains.

It looks like rain.

"You're sure you are not just trying to get out of a detail?"—*Sgt. Ralph Stein.*

"Frankly, fellows, I need the extra dough."
—*Cpl. Hugh Kennedy.*

A SACK OF MAIL

By Cpl. PAUL E. DEUTSCHMANN

Sketch by Sgt. Frank Brandt

SOMEWHERE IN SARDINIA—Mail call is one of the most important things in a GI's life, I was reading the other day. It's good for that ethereal something that USO hostesses, advertising copywriters and sundry other civilians back home call morale. With the correspondents some GIs have, though, no mail is good mail. Leave us look at some of these morale-boosters.

FIDGETY-FILLY TYPE

"Snookie, dear—I drove out to Petter's Perch the other night, along the Old Mill Road. You remember, don't you, dear? The moon was bright and the stars twinkled just like when you were there with me, and it made me feel so-o-o romantic!

"Some girls complain about the man shortage. But not me! Last night three fellows took me to the movies, and afterwards they took turns with me out on the back porch—dancing. But don't worry, dear, they were all servicemen. I won't go out with a man except in uniform. One of them, Casper Clutchem, who is sorta blond and cute and a Marine sergeant, says for me to tell you 'the situation is under control.' He is *awful* strong.

"Guess what we were drinking? Those potent daiquiris. They really make me forget myself—almost.

"And, did I tell you? Casper is stationed just outside of town and has promised to come see me real often. I couldn't very well refuse him because he said he was leaving for overseas almost any month now. I believe in doing my bit to help the servicemen because, after all, some of them are so far from home and don't know a soul in town."

HOME-GUARD TYPE

"Dear Corp—I am back in Dayton for another furlough and I am looking after Lulu, just like you asked me to. She's really a wonderful gal and a smooth dancer. And if she weren't your wife I could really go for her myself. Do you realize, I've gotten to know Lulu better than you do—almost! And boy, can she hold her likker!

"We had dinner at the Cove tonight and are now back at your apartment. It is just midnight, and while Lulu is slipping into something more *comfortable*, I thought I'd drop you a line. Ha ha, old man, I'm only kidding."

MAN-OF-AFFAIRS TYPE

"I've been doing swell at the office. Just got the Whatsis Soap and Whoozis Hosiery account. That's $4,000,000 billing besides the pleasure I get from interviewing models for the 'leg art' pictures. But it's nothing like the swell job you boys are doing over there. I wish I were in there with you, but——

"Give 'em hell for me, old fellow! They asked for it—and we're just the guys to give it to them. I'm buying War Bonds like an insane stamp collector. I really wish I were out in the foxholes with you, but——"

CIVILIAN BRASS-HAT TYPE

"Dear Bill—All of us here at the Old Company, from the office staff up to me, are thinking of you boys in the service and doing our part to help you fellas. We're all buying War Bonds and cutting down on meat and butter—and some of the girls in the office are even rolling bandages on Saturday afternoons, when they aren't working.

"Rationing is pretty grim now. Steaks only twice a week and no more cherries in cherry cokes. But we don't mind because the papers say that you fellows overseas are getting all the good things—and you certainly deserve them.

"Yes sir, no one can say that the Old Company is not well represented in the foxholes and trenches of our fighting fronts all over the globe. Rollie is a warrant officer at Camp Dix, N. J., and Jim is at the Brooklyn Navy Yard, and Harry is a chauffeur to a Marine colonel in Philadelphia. Van is way down in Texas and Charlie is a quartermaster clerk in Georgia and you're in the Infantry in Italy. Give 'em hell, boy."

OH-YOU-DEVIL TYPE

"You guys over there in Italy must be having a big time with all those little dark-eyed signorinas. Do they wear those grass skirts like Dorothy Lamour?"

LOCAL-BOY-MAKES-GOOD TYPE

"Your cousin Herman is now a technical sergeant and he has only been in the Army five months. I can't understand why you're still a corporal. Are your officers mad at you?"

ALL-IN-THIS-TOGETHER TYPE

"Dear Pal—Things are really getting rugged now at good old Camp Kilmer. I can only get off every other week end. We went out on bivouac last week and, boy, was it rough! We slept in pup tents for three nights—right on the ground.

"Last week I was awarded the Good Conduct Ribbon at a special ceremony. You might not hear from me for a while, as I am expecting to be shipped out any day now—to North Carolina.

"By the way—what is this Spam we hear so much about?"

THE LEGION OF THE UNCOUTH

By S/Sgt. THOMAS P. ASHLOCK

Australia

The pages of the magazines back home
That feature stuff of war—the march of men,
The awesome crawl of tanks, the flight of planes—
Have shown a tiresome lot of "glamor Yanks,"
With trousers razor-creased and shirts that still
Retain the sheen of new-spun factory cloth;
With ties adjusted right, and shoes, the gleam
Of which will blind. Too much of new-blown rank,
With chevrons bright and neatly sewn on sleeves
Of sarge or corp; and when I view those lads,
So sartorially complete and nice, I think
Of Hollywood, with extras dressed to fit
A part in some stage scene, instead of soldiers
Girt for deadly, bloody, filthy war.

From the Stevens in Chicago town,
To our sun-blistered, bug-infested post,
Is a far, unholy cry—and the difference
Much the same as that which lies between
My lady's boudoir and a stable stall:
For here we boys are not—oh, really not
The photogenic type! Our hair grows long,
We seldom shave; Svengali would be proud

To flaunt the beards that some of us have grown.
Our pants are frayed and bleached and baggy-kneed;
We wear no shirts—and as for ties,—say, tell
Us, please—what is a tie?
And it's a certain sign
You're "tropo," if you start to shine your shoes!

We're a motley, rugged, crumby lot,
No subjects for a Sunday supplement:
But somehow, I don't think a man of us,
Deep down within his heart, would trade his place
With fortune's darlings in the Stevens lounge.
We're "in" the thing, you see—not quite as much
But something like—our buddies at Bataan,
Corregidor, the Solomons, and Wake;
And because we walk in shabbiness—unkempt,
Ungroomed—and live with pests, and breathe red dust
And thirst and bake in searing heat, and drown
In tropic rains,—like them—we're fiercely proud.
Let others have the dress parade, the show,
The full-page spread in magazines. We like
Our role—the real, the earnest, cussin' sweatin'
Dirty, ugly role of men *at* war!

THE DEAD END KIDS

BY SGT. DAVE RICHARDSON

BEHIND JAPANESE LINES IN NORTHERN BURMA—
Things were a little too quiet, even for a Sunday.
After all, there should have been some fireworks by
now, considering that part of the Jap 18th Division
was dug in on one side of the muddy 40-foot-wide
Nambyu River and our unit of Merrill's Marauders
was on the other.

"Looks to me," observed a BAR man as he
stripped his gun for cleaning, "like the lull before
the storm. The Japs won't take this lying down." He
didn't know how right he was.

The Marauders had just completed a 75-mile end
run around enemy positions in the Hukawng Valley and now our unit was only 200 yards from
Walawbum. We had met only small resistance from
Jap patrols during our march. But surely the Japs
would stand and fight us here. The native village
of Walawbum was the bottleneck through which
all supplies had to flow to their front-line troops,
15 miles to the north.

Across the river from us was a pretty tough bunch
of Japs. We could hear their trucks pulling up, and
every once in a while we could spot a few of them
for a fleeting instant as we moved through the
dense jungle. These were the Japs who had smashed
their way into Singapore two years before and now
had succeeded in slowing the Chinese drive down
this valley to a measly 10-mile gain in the last
month. They were fighting a stubborn delaying action from well-chosen positions, falling back from
foxhole to foxhole, pillbox to pillbox.

On our side of the river were some Marauders
known as the Dead End Kids. This was an appropriate nickname for this unit of Brig. Gen. Frank D.
Merrill's volunteer American raiders. They had already fought the Japs in the jungles of Guadalcanal, New Guinea and New Georgia. They had
joined the Marauders after President Roosevelt had
issued a call to their outfits for volunteers for an
"extremely hazardous" jungle-fighting mission in
another theater.

"Most of us guys volunteered," one of them explained, "because we figured we might get back to
the States for training first. We had all been overseas 18 to 24 months at that time and we wanted
to get home. Don't get the idea that we volunteered just because we were itching to fight the
Japs again."

I would have believed that statement if I hadn't

heard Brig. Gen. Merrill say, a few hours earlier,
that the Dead End Kids had been begging all day
for permission to attack Walawbum. And if I hadn't
come to know them in training camp.

The Dead End Kids wound up in India for training instead of in the States. At Christmastime they
went AWOL in droves, popping up in several Indian cities to spend wads of dough that had been
useless during their months in the Pacific jungles.
When they returned to camp, broke but happy,
they were reduced to privates. But they didn't give
a damn.

They hated the GI routine of garrison life—standing formations and inspections, shooting on the
ranges and going on field problems. They broke the
monotony by disappearing alone into the woods
and shooting deer, then bringing back the venison
for a change of chow.

On training problems with other Marauder units,
most of whom were proud of their preparation for
combat in the jungles of Panama, Trinidad or
Puerto Rico, the Dead End Kids confused and har-
assed their make-believe enemy with screwball tac-
tics they had picked up while fighting the Japs. At
night they would sit around their tents and bitch
about "parade-ground soldiering" or reminisce about
their fighting exploits.

"Combat," as one of them put it, "seems to se-
duce a guy. He's scared as hell while he's in it, but
get him back in garrison and he'll start longing for
those foxholes and shellings and bombings."

This Sunday afternoon the Dead End Kids had
patrols out across the river to the north and south
of Walawbum. As the patrols returned, they reported that the Japs were digging artillery and
mortars into position and bringing up truckloads
of men and ammunition from the south.

But the night was just as peaceful as the day had
been. Next morning at 0930 hours, Sgt. Andrew B.
Pung of Malden, Mass., a mortar observer, shinnied
up a tree to a perch 40 feet above the river from
which he could look down across a grassy clearing
on the other bank.

Pung had a walkie-talkie radio with him. Soon
he reported seeing some telephone wires and several emplacements at the edge of the grassy clearing. Then his routine report changed to an excited
one. He forgot all about radio etiquette.

"Listen," he blurted into the microphone, "there's

a bunch of Japs coming out of the jungle and into this grass across the river. A big bunch. Get ready for an attack. I'll tell you when they're near enough to open fire."

The Dead End Kids jumped into their holes all along the riverbank. Bullets were clicked into chambers and machine-gun bolts pulled back twice to cock them. Pung sent firing data to the mortars as crews ripped open shell cases. Minutes ticked by. There was a tense silence.

"Give it to 'em," yelled Pung from his perch. The Japs had crossed the clearing to within 35 yards of the opposite riverbank. They were now in plain sight. Machine guns, BARs, mortars and rifles opened up in a deafening deluge of fire. Shrieks and yells came back from the field. Then the Japs began returning the fire. Their 90-mm mortar shells soared over the river and burst in trees behind the Dead End Kids. Shrapnel and bullets hummed through the brush.

Up in the tree some of the lead knocked off Pung's canteen and splattered all around him. He dropped the walkie-talkie and shinnied down.

The Dead End Kids were dug in on a bluff along the riverbank, a couple of dozen feet higher than the grassy clearing on the opposite bank where the Japs were advancing in spread-out skirmisher formation. This high ground was natural cover; the Japs were firing into the bluff or high over the Marauders' heads. The Americans just lay in their holes and blasted away.

Wave after wave of Japs poured out of the jungle and into the clearing, running and diving and creeping and crawling. Many of them carried machine guns and ammunition boxes. Some, probably the officers and noncoms, yelled "Susume! Susume!" which means "advance." Others shrieked "Banzai," the familiar battle cry.

In a few minutes Jap bodies lay sprawled on the field in little bunches. The Dead End Kids could hear the wounded crying and moaning. But the Japs kept coming—at least a company of them.

The Dead End Kids were happy. They yelled at their machine gunners and BAR men to "Mow down that bunch over there, boy!" and then shouted "Atta boy," as they concentrated their rifle fire on single targets. Pfc. George Fisher Jr. of Napoleon, Ohio, spit a gob of tobacco juice every time his M1 got a Jap.

"Those little bastards must think we're amateurs at this jungle-fighting stuff," grinned 1st Lt. Victor J. (Abie) Weingartner of St. Albans, N. Y., commanding the platoon in the center of the American positions along the riverbank. "Banzai charges might have terrified the civilians in Singapore, but they're nothing but good, moving target practice for us."

Lt. Weingartner was considered one of the most daring leaders of Dead End Kid patrols. Characteristically, he insisted on wearing into action the same dirty mechanic's cap that brought him through New Georgia unscathed; he willingly paid a $100 fine for not wearing a helmet at the last showdown inspection before the Marauders started their 200-mile march into battle.

Half an hour after the Jap attack began, it halted abruptly. But the Dead End Kids knew that the Japs would try again. Almost as soon as the attack ended, Jap artillery boomed several hundred yards back in the jungle. The shells whistled overhead and landed a half-mile behind the Americans, near a rice paddy. This field had been used in the previous two days as a landing area for Piper Cubs evacuating a few wounded, and as a dropping area for transport planes supplying the Marauders with rations and ammunition. Jap mortars threw a few shells into our positions the rest of the morning.

In the afternoon the good news came that another unit of Marauders had thrown a road block on the main enemy supply route from Walawbum to the front. With Walawbum threatened by the Dead End Kids' position and with the supply route blocked, the stubborn Jap defenses 15 miles northward had collapsed. As the Japs streamed back to reinforce the Walawbum garrison, the Chinese began driving through to relieve the Marauders and make a large-scale attack. As a hit-and-run raider outfit, the Marauders were supposed to keep their positions only until relieved by Chinese divisions with the men and large weapons needed to do the main attacking. The Chinese were expected within 24 hours.

But a lot could happen in 24 hours. The Dead End Kids cleaned their guns, opened more ammunition and placed men every three or four feet along the riverbank. While they worked they could hear the Japs digging, driving up more trucks full of men and ammunition and wheeling in their artillery closer.

At 1645 hours the broiling Burma sun had sunk low in the sky. It glared into the faces of the Dead End Kids as they kept their eyes focused on the field across the river. The attack would have to come from the field again because the terrain was unsuitable at other places along the river, where the banks were too high or the jungle too dense for a field of fire. And it came. Two Jap heavy machine guns hammered away like woodpeckers from the flanks of the field. Artillery and mortar fire increased. Knee mortars started clicking out grenades at close range.

The Japs really attacked this time. They came in waves that were wider and more frequent than in the first attack. And they had better support from weapons of all kinds, placed nearer the river. In each wave were several two-man teams lugging heavy machine guns. As soon as one team was hit, another ran out and grabbed its gun, only to die within a few steps. Then another.

Again the machine gunners and BAR men did most of the killing for the Marauders. They raked each wave with fire. But the Japs surged on across the field until they fell. A few of them even reached the river before they were hit, but nobody crossed. This time there was at least a battalion of Japs attacking the Dead End Kids.

And this time the Japs were more accurate with their fire. Bullets sped only a few feet over the Americans' heads. Practically every leaf and every tree were marked by the fire. Some of the stuff barely cleared the bank and did some damage. Bullets smashed two BAR magazines on the bank of the foxhole where T-5 Bernard Strasbaugh of Lewisburg, Kans., was stretched. Another bullet nicked his helmet. Strasbaugh was in the center of the attack, firing as fast as he could shove magazines into his weapon. When he spotted five Japs in a group running toward a dropped machine gun, he stood up, riddled them with fire and flopped down again. He hit the ground just soon enough to escape a burst of fire.

"All a guy has to do to get a Purple Heart here is stand up for 10 seconds," he muttered.

Pfc. Clayton E. Hall of Strawn, Tex., had a close call at his machine gun on the right flank. A knee-mortar shell burst only three yards in front of him. Then two bullets pierced the water jacket on his gun. With his machine-gun corporal, Joseph Diorio of Cleveland, Ohio, Hall managed to keep the gun going by pouring water into the jacket from every available canteen. He burned his hands on the red-hot jacket doing it, but the gun fired 4,000 rounds in 45 minutes.

Back at the Dead End Kids' CP, Maj. L. L. Lew of Baker, Oreg., the unit commander, received a message saying that the Chinese would relieve his unit around midnight. It was then 1730 hours.

The Dead End Kids were running low on ammunition. Men started shouting back and forth above the din: "Hey, you got a spare clip of M1?" From the left flank came a request for every available hand grenade. A unit there, commanded by Maj. Edwin J. Briggs of La Grande, Oreg., was being attacked by Japs who had infiltrated through the jungles from the south.

As ammunition ran out, the tension increased. Dusk turned to darkness, but the Japs still fired furiously and attacked fanatically. Their bullet-riddled bodies littered the field from the edge of the jungle to the river. The wounded screamed.

Then, as suddenly as the morning attack had ceased, the dusk battle halted. Both sides stopped firing. The silence was broken by a Dead End Kid who rose to his feet on the river bank, cupped his hands to his mouth and yelled:

"Come on, you little bastards. Come and get your lead!"

A Jap yelled back. The tension was broken. To a man, the Dead End Kids scrambled to their feet, stood along the riverbank and shouted cuss words at the Japs. From the other bank came only a few bursts of light machine-gun fire. The Japs, too, must have run out of ammunition.

Now they removed their wounded from the field in the dark. The Americans could hear the wooden sound of litters being carried through the brush and the terrifying cries of the wounded as they disappeared in the jungle.

Among the Dead End Kids, thanks to the natural protection of the high riverbank and to the dug-in emplacements, there had been only three casualties all day. But several pack mules, which carried mortars, radios and ammunition, had been wounded or killed by mortar shells.

The little remaining ammunition was doled out equally. A patrol from Maj. Briggs' outfit south of the Dead End Kids brought up some more BAR and machine-gun ammunition.

At 2000 hours T/Sgt. Jim Ballard of Spokane, Wash., chief of the unit radio section, entered the perimeter, leading a mule pack train loaded with all kinds of ammunition. He had tried to contact Brig. Gen. Merrill's CP early in the attack, but couldn't get it on the radio. So he had taken Maj. Lew's message requesting more ammunition and run back four miles to another Marauder unit, over a dark trail flanked by Jap patrols and through Jap shelling part of the way. He brought back the ammunition mule train through an even more severe shelling.

The hours dragged on and a heavy fog set in. A few Japs had sneaked across the river and were booby-trapping trails in the vicinity. Across the river the Japs seemed to be getting reinforcements and ammunition again for another attack.

While some of the men peered through the mist at the field across the river, others dozed off in their foxholes, with their heads propped on horseshoe-type packs. The Dead End Kids weren't cocky or swaggering tonight; they were exhausted from the tension of the two attacks.

Finally the expected message came: "Withdraw at 0200 hours to join Marauder CP. Chinese are taking over your position."

The weary Dead End Kids put on their packs and moved silently Indian-file out of their perimeter with their pack mules.

A little way down the trail another column passed the Americans, going in the opposite direction. It was the Chinese.

"*Megwaw, ting hao!*" they grinned as they plodded past the Dead End Kids. They meant: "Americans are okay." A Chinese divisional commander later put it another way: "Your unit," he said, "made it possible for us to gain more ground in one week than we covered all last month."

One of the Dead End Kids, after returning the Chinese greeting, turned and said to the man behind him: "You know, I could almost kiss those guys, they look so good to me now." He wasn't the only one who felt that way.

Next morning an official report reached Merrill's Marauders that one of their units, as the first American infantrymen to fight a battle on the continent of Asia, had left 800 Japanese dead on the field near Walawbum.

Hearing this, a cocky, swaggering bunch of Americans swung along the jungle trail toward an area where they could rest for two days before going on another mission behind Jap lines. The Dead End Kids were back in their element.

The Dead End Kids scrambled to their feet and cursed the Japs. From across the river came only a few bursts of fire. The Japs, too, had run out of ammunition.

Sketch by Cpl. Ruge

HOW TO GET LOST IN A JUNGLE

By Sgt. JOE McCARTHY

Find some monkey who knows the neighborhood. Watch what he eats. Then follow his example.

EVERYBODY in the Army seems to be writing handy pocket guides these days telling you How to Keep from Getting Lost in a Jungle. These books are all right but a lot of my friends are not reading them. In the first place, my friends never read anything, anyway, except beer bottle labels and the *Daily Racing Form*. In the second place, my friends are all goldbrickers and they don't want handy pocket guides that tell them how to keep from getting lost. All they want is to *get* lost, as soon as possible.

"The thicker the jungle the better," one of them remarked the other day, squeezing himself into the barrel of his M1 when the first sergeant approached to select a detail.

So my friends have requested, through channels, that I write a piece about How to Get Lost in a Jungle. They couldn't have picked a better man.

I happen to be an expert on getting lost. I spent most of the Carolina Maneuvers in 1941 at the top of the center pole in my pyramidal tent, where nobody could find me when there was a truck to be unloaded. As a matter of fact, I would have beaten Shipwreck Kelly's old record one week but a cer-

tain corporal, who shall be nameless, set the tent on fire and smoked me out.

I also happen to be an expert on jungles. I spent most of my summers as a youngster in a jungle near the Gillette razor blade factory in South Boston, Mass.

The first thing to remember if you want to get lost in a jungle is not to lose your head. There are a lot of head hunters in the jungles. If you put your head down somewhere for a minute while you are washing your feet or pressing your pants, a head hunter is liable to pick it up and walk off with it.

And don't be afraid of a jungle. A lot of soldiers get nervous when they find themselves in a jungle and notice that it has no traffic lights or sewers. But the jungle is really your friend. It provides heaps and heaps of food which can be found in the form of animals and plants. It also provides malaria mosquitoes, leeches, snakes, crocodiles and nettles but there is no need to go into that now. However, you will be glad to learn that you have much less chance of catching poison ivy in the average jungle than you have around Lake Winnepesaukee, New Hampshire. Here is another bit of good news about jungles: it hardly ever snows there, so the chances are you won't be liable to slip on an icy sidewalk and hurt yourself.

I see that the T-5 down there in the fifth row with the Good Conduct ribbon and the whistle has a question. Would you mind speaking a little louder, bully? You say you want to know what kinds of food in the jungle are safe to eat?

Well, my fine chowhound, my advice to you is to make the acquaintanceship of some young monkey about your own age who knows the neighborhood. Just watch what he eats. Then follow his example and you'll make out okay. But be careful about the kind of monkey he is before you start associating with him. Be sure he doesn't drink too much or run around with loose women. Many a careless GI in the jungle has been led to rack and ruin by hanging out with the wrong type of monkey.

Now let me see, where was I?

Oh, yes. The best way to get lost in a jungle is to get rid of your compass. I wouldn't recommend this, however, because the supply sergeant may get nasty and swear out a statement of charges to be deducted from your next month's pay. Pawning the compass wouldn't do either. You might get grabbed for hocking government property and sent to Leavenworth to cool off for a few years. But then again, if you want to look at the bright side of it, Leavenworth is an excellent place to get lost in, too. Even better than a jungle because it has no malaria mosquitoes.

I find the best way to get lost is to ask directions from an MP. Simply go where he tells you to go and, in no time at all, you won't have the slightest idea of where you are.

But be careful about crossing state lines. Even though we are at war, don't forget that they are still able to get you for violations of the Mann Act.

That covers about everything except malaria mosquitoes and the natives. The best remedy for mosquitoes is to burn punks. This is getting rather difficult to do now because most of the punks in the Army have either gone to OCS or have been released under the 38-year-old law.

There is no need to try to cover the natives. They have been walking around without clothes all their lives so you can't expect them to do anything different.

In closing, I suggest that you bring this page with you next time you feel like getting lost in a jungle. It might come in handy to light a fire with.

PIN-UPS

DEAR YANK:

We boys do not approve of your very indecent portrayal of the spicy looking female in a recent edition of our much-loved and eagerly read YANK. It seems the intelligent-looking Irene Manning would never pose for such a suggestive-looking picture. We may seem old-fashioned, but sending YANK home to wives and sweethearts with such a seductive-looking picture, we feel compelled to make an apology for this issue.

Is this the much publicized "Pin-Up Girl" that the Yankee soldiers so crave? We have our doubts! Miss Manning is well dressed, but the pose—phew! (Hays office please take note.)

Believe it or not, our average age is 23.

Britain —SGT. E. W. O'HARA °

° *Also signed by Cpl. P. Pistocco Jr. and D. E. Clark.*

DEAR YANK:

I don't know who started this idea of pin-ups, but they say that it is supposed to help keep up the morale of the servicemen, or something like that. Here is my idea of the help it is. In the first place, I would say that 24 out of 25 of the men in the service are either married or have a girl at home whom they respect and intend to marry as soon as this war is over. . . . How many of you GIs would like to go home and find the room of your wife or girl friend covered with pictures of a guy stepping out of a bathtub, draped only in a skimpy little towel, or see the walls covered with the pictures of a shorts advertisement or such pictures? None of you would. Then why keep a lot of junk hanging around and kid yourself about keeping up morale? . . .

I would much rather wake up in the morning and see a picture of a P-51 or 39 hanging above my bed or over the picture of my wife, whom I think is the best-looking girl in the world, than of some dame who has been kidded into or highly paid for posing for these pictures.

Myrtle Beach AAF, S. C. —PFC. JOSEPH H. SALING

DEAR YANK:

Sgt. E. W. O'Hara, in a recent letter about pin-ups in YANK, speaks of "suggestiveness" in the "seductive-looking" picture of Miss Irene Manning. For the life of me, I can't see anything suggestive about it. Shouldn't you say that the suggestiveness and the suggestive look come from an "unclean" mind, not from the picture? . . .

Panama —S/SGT. CLIFF CROUCH °

° *Also signed by S/Sgt. Raymond Cox.*

DEAR YANK:

. . . Don't slam our pin-ups. If I had a wife I would make sure her picture was up, but Irene Manning will do until that big day.

Fleet Post Office —s1c. R. C. WALTERS

DEAR YANK:

. . . Maybe if some of those panty-waists had to be stuck out some place where there were no white women and few native women for a year and a half, as we were, they would appreciate even a picture of our gals back home. The good sergeant [and the other two signers of his letter] alibi that perhaps they are old-fashioned and go so far as to apologize for the mag [when sending it home]. . . . They must be dead from the neck up—and down. They can take their apology and jam it and cram it. And Pfc. Joseph H. Saling isn't he just too too? We suggest that when the next issue of YANK hits the PX these little boys refrain from buying it, as it is too rugged a mag for them to be reading. Perhaps later, when they grow up. We nasty old Engineers still appreciate YANK *with* its pin-ups.

Alaska —T-5 CHET STRAIGHT °

° *Also signed by T-5s F. A. Wallbaum and Cooper Dunn and Pfcs. Robert Ross, Lloyd W. Finley and Elom Calden.*

DEAR YANK:

. . . I can't understand why you would even publish such a letter. In my opinion Sgt. O'Hara owes Miss Manning an apology for his rude description of her picture. I have that picture over my locker and like it very much. I suggest Sgt. O'Hara go out and learn the facts of life from someone who has been around. Also, the boys in my platoon agree with me that he should be examined for Sec. 8. Keep the pin-up pictures coming. We like them.

Camp McCain, Miss. —CPL. JOHN R. CREICH

DEAR YANK:

Why we GIs over here in the Pacific have to read your tripe and drivel about the Wacs beats me. Who in the hell cares about these dimpled GIs who are supposed to be soldiers? All I have ever heard of them doing is peeling spuds, clerking in the office, driving a truck or tractor or puttering around in a photo lab. Yet all the stories written about our dears tell how overworked they are. I correspond regularly with a close relative of mine who is a Wac, and all she writes about is the dances, picnics, swimming parties and bars she has attended. Are these janes in the Army for the same reasons we are, or just to see how many dates they can get? We would like them a hell of a lot better, and respect them more, if they did their part in some defense plant or at home, where they belong. So please let up on the cock and bull and feminine propaganda. It's sickening to read about some doll who has made the supreme sacrifice of giving up her lace-trimmed undies for ODs.

New Hebrides —SGT. BOB BOWIE

DEAR YANK:

I was disgusted when I opened the pages of a recent YANK and saw some silly female in GI clothes. I detest the Wacs very thoroughly and I hope I never meet one. That is also the opinion of all my buddies.

New Zealand —PVT. WILLIAM J. ROBINSON

WACS HIT BACK

DEAR YANK:

After reading the letters of Sgt. Bob Bowie and Pvt. William Robinson [in a February issue] I think it is about time the Wacs had their say. Their stubborn, prejudiced attitude makes many of us wonder if it is really worth it all. . . . There are many heartbreaking stories behind many of our enlistees, stories that have not been published and will never be known, and there is a wealth of patriotism and sincere motives to be found in these girls.

Fort Crook, Nebr. —PVT. CAROL J. SWAN

DEAR YANK:

. . . After reading Sgt. Bowie's disgusting opinion of the Wacs I must say that I think he's one hell of an American.

Indiantown Gap, Pa. —PVT. HELEN LONDON

DEAR YANK:

Hell hath no fury like a Wac criticized. . . . Many of these frilly females Sgt. Bowie blows his top about are a lot closer to action than a smug soldier who apparently has enough time to sit at his desk in the New Hebrides and write letters critical of the Wacs.

Fort Sheridan, Ill. —PFC. MILDRED MC GLAMERY

DEAR YANK:

. . . We have *not* given up lace-trimmed undies; most of us still wear civilian underwear. And, incidentally, I'll bet two months' pay that Sgt. Bowie was drafted. At least we all know we did not have to be forced to serve our country. We volunteered.

Selman Field, La. —WAC PRIVATE

DEAR YANK:

. . . As for sacrificing lace-trimmed undies for ODs, most of us didn't have any like that to sacrifice, as the majority of the Wacs were working girls.

Boston, Mass. —CPL. SOPHIE WOITEL °

° *Also signed by Pvt. Sybil Watson.*

DEAR YANK:

. . . To doff lace-trimmed panties and don ODs takes far more courage than it does to shoot a Jap through the heart.

Great Falls AAB, Mont. —1ST/SGT. EDITH F. KROUSE

DEAR YANK:

. . . Thanks for the bouquets, boys. Go right on sticking the knife in our backs. . . . When it's all over we'll go back to our lace-trimmed undies and to the kind of men who used their anger on something besides the Wacs.

ASTP, Madison, Wis. —T-4 JANE NUGENT

DEAR YANK:

. . . Thorns to Pvt. Robinson and to Sgt. Bowie. Without the roses.

Freeman Field, Ind. —CPL. FRANCES CLOUGH °

° *Also signed by Cpls. Adelaid J. Swett, Nora F. Fields and Beatrice Schweitzer and Sgt. Adelaide Bishop.*

DEAR YANK:

About five months ago—while winding up 3½ years in the Pacific—I wrote to your magazine an article about how much I detested the Wacs. But now I realize what a first-class heel I was. . . . My narrow-minded opinion has changed entirely, and I am very proud of those gallant American women. . . What this country needs is more of those wonderful girls. . . . Please print this, as I got quite a few letters from Wacs after they read my last article, and every one of them wrote such nice letters and wished my buddies and me the best of luck. I felt more ashamed than I have ever been before.

—PVT. WM. J. ROBINSON

Letterman General Hospital, Calif.

"MORE SHOOTIN' "

DEAR YANK:

A recent article described an incident in which a new replacement asked a fellow GI how to load his M1; this during the heat of battle with the enemy 10 yards away. Is it any wonder? I've been knocking around this Army for 24 months—14 months overseas—and have yet to learn how to load an M1 and jive it. I've never been taught to handle anything but the '03, but when action was imminent in the Aleutians I was handed an M1, a rifle I knew little about.

Ever since my induction I've been rushed through training so damned fast that I'm still wondering what the Army is all about. Six-week training took me to POE. Now that I'm in the States we're being rushed through training again. Hell! What this Army needs in training is "more shootin' and less salutin'" and more time to do it in.

Camp Shelby, Miss. —PVT. JOHN GRAHAM

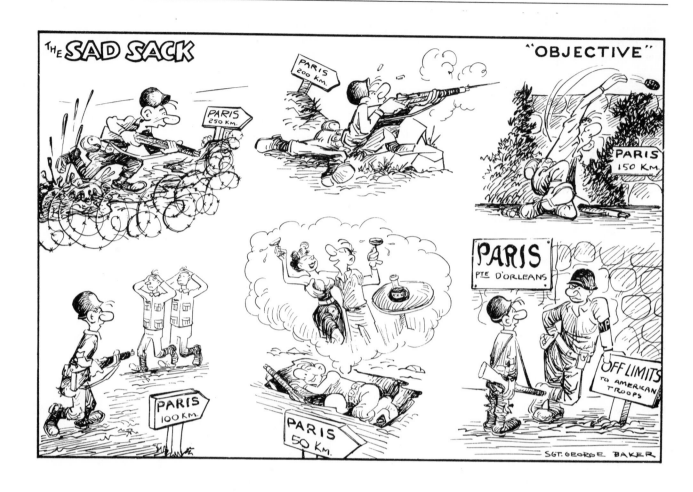

Pvt. Greengroin and the Articles of War

By Sgt. Harry Brown
Yank Staff Liar

Pvt. Artie Greengroin is a character. We ran into him at a USO blackout the other night when we tried to put our arm around him, thinking he was a girl named Edna. Artie is something Damon Runyon might dream up after a platter of rarebit, only worse. He spent his adolescence and early manhood in the fourth grade of a little red schoolhouse in Bread Poultice, Conn. "I had a crutch on the teacher," he says. "She was a darb, that doll. And I was olden for my years."

Before the war Artie drove a hearse in Brooklyn, a job he didn't like much. "I had a stiff neck all the time," he says. "Get what I mean?" In the Army he is attached to the horse cavalry, and his work is such that he is forbidden to leave the post without bathing. Unfortunately, he and water aren't on speaking terms, except for an oc-

casional "Blub!" from Artie, so he spends most of his time on the post.

"I'm glad I got to hang around," Artie says, a flush of pride hovering around his large ears. "I got me a new hobby now. Reading. I read all the time, all the time."

His reading is what really makes Artie a character, because the only book he reads is called "A Manual For Courts-Martial, U.S. Army, 1928." Artie is nuts, to slip into the vernacular, about the Articles of War. To him they're Shakespeare and the Bible and Fanny Hill all rolled together.

"It's like this," Artie says. "They're so beautifully put, I could go on reading them forever." At this point he usually opens the book. "Listen to this," he says. "'The word *officer* shall be construed to refer to a commissioned officer'. Ain't that neatly put? Ain't that succinct? It's got no waste

woids, no frills. Gleeps, it's exciting."

Of course, Artie has his favorite articles. "I like especially the one where it says you can't punish a man by tattooing him," he says. "And the one about false mustard is pretty sharp, too."

Artie doesn't much care where he goes in the Army, as long as he can take a copy of the Articles of War with him.

After the war is another matter. Artie swears he won't go back to driving the hearse, and he doesn't think he's got enough in his noggin to be a lawyer. "The Articles of War is dead pigeons to a civilian," he says. "I won't take them back with me. Just put me down as a fan of the Articles, thass all. Just a fan. Maybe after the war I'll go back to the Fourth Grade and look up my ole teacher. Honest to God, I really tooken to that tomato."

FIRST EPISTLE TO THE SELECTEES

ACCORDING TO PFC. HAROLD FLEMING

LO, ALL ye miserable sinners, entering through the Gate of Induction *into* the Land of Khaki, hearken unto my words; for I *have* dwelt in this land for many months and mine eyes have witnessed all manner of folly and *woe.*

2 Verily have I tasted of the bitter Fruit of TS *and* drained the dregs of the Cup of Snafu:

3 Gird up thy loins, my son, and take *up* the olive drab; but act slowly and with exceeding care and hearken first to the counsel of a wiser and sadder man than thou:

4 Beware thou the Sergeant *who* is called First; he hath a pleased and foolish look but he concealeth a serpent in his heart.

5 Avoid *him* when he speaketh low and his lips smileth; he smileth not for thee; his heart rejoiceth at *the* sight of thy youth and thine ignorance.

6 He will smile and smile and work all manner of evil against thee. A wise man shuns the orderly room, but the fool *shall* dwell in the kitchen forever.

7 Unto all things there is a time: there is a time to speak and a time to be silent: be thou like unto stone in the *presence* of thy superiors, and keep thy tongue still when they shall call for volunteers.

8 The wise man searcheth out the easy details, but only a fool sticketh out *his* neck.

9 Look thou with disfavor upon the newly made corporal; he prizeth *much* his stripes and is proud and foolish; he laugheth and joketh much with the older noncoms and looketh *upon* the private with a frown.

10 He would fain go to OCS, but he is not qualified.

11 Know thou that the Sergeant of the Mess is a man of many moods: when *he* looketh pleased and his words are like honey, the wise KP seeketh him out and praiseth his chow and laugheth much at his jests:

12 But when he moveth with great haste and the sweat standeth *on* his brow *and* he *curseth* under his breath, make thyself scarce; for he will fall like a whirlwind upon the idle and the goldbrick shall know his wrath.

13 The Supply Sergeant is a lazy man *and* worketh not; but he is the keeper of many good things: if thou wouldst wear well-fitting raiment and avoid the statement of charges, *make* him thy friend.

14 He prizeth drunkenness *above* all things.

15 He careth not for praise or flattery, but lend him *thy* lucre and thy liquor and he will love thee.

16 Hell hath no fury like a Shavetail scorned: he walketh with a swagger and regardeth the enlisted man with a raised eyebrow; he looketh upon his bars with exceeding pleasure *and* loveth a salute mightily.

17 Act thou lowly unto him and call him sir and he will love thee.

18 Damned *be* he who standeth first in the line of chow and shortstoppeth the dessert and cincheth the coffee.

19 He taketh from the meat dish with a heavy hand and leaveth thee the bony *part.*

20 He is thrice cursed, and all *people,* even unto the pfcs, will revile him and spit upon him: *for* his name is called Chow Hound, and he is an abomination.

21 Know thou the Big Operator, but trust him not: he *worketh* always upon a deal and he speaketh confidentially.

22 He knoweth many women and goeth into town every night; he borroweth all thy money; yea, even *unto* thy ration check.

23 He promiseth to fix thee up, but doth *it* not.

24 Beware thou the Old Man, for he will make *thee* sweat; when he approacheth, look thou on the ball; he loveth to chew upon thy posterior.

25 Keep thou out of his sight and let him not *know* thee by name: for he who arouseth the wrath of the Old Man shall *go* many times unto the chaplain. *Selah.*

"It's from the old man. He says we're due for typhoid booster shots."—*Cpl. Fred Schwab.*

PALESTINE EXPRESS

By Pvt. IRWIN SHAW

TEL AVIV, PALESTINE—The train for Palestine pulled out of Cairo station slowly, to the accompaniment of wailing shrieks from the platform peddlers selling lemonade, cold coffee, pornographic literature, grapes, old copies of *Life* and flat Arab bread.

The train was long and crowded, and it had seen better days. It had been standing in the wild Egyptian sun all morning and part of the afternoon, and it had a very interesting smell.

It carried Englishmen, Scots, Welshmen, Palestinians, Indians, New Zealanders, South Africans, Australians, Americans, French, Senussi, Bantus, Senegalese; it carried Egyptian civilians, Arab civilians, Palestinian civilians; it carried generals, colonels, lieutenants, sergeants and privates—and it carried bugs. The generals and lieutenants it carried first class. The sergeants it carried second class. The privates it carried third class. The bugs it carried all classes.

It didn't travel fast. A good, strong man in the prime of life, who did not smoke too much, could have jumped out and trotted beside it without too much trouble from Cairo to Lydda. It stopped as often as a woman in a bargain basement. It stopped for coal, it stopped for water, it stopped every time a barge appeared somewhere on one of the hundreds of canals we crossed, it stopped every time the tracks ran near two palm trees growing within 50 yards of each other, for that constitutes a settlement in this part of the world.

When it stopped, hundreds of Egyptians of all ages would spring up, selling pale round watermelons, dirty bunches of grapes, hard-boiled eggs, tomatoes and warm lemon soda right out of the Nile. The merchandising was carried on in hurried shrill yells, like a girls' dormitory after lights out, and your salesman was likely to disappear suddenly in mid-purchase as the local policeman came into view, snapping a long bullwhip over slow calves and buttocks.

The third-class cars were built by firm believers in the Spartan life for the common man. They spurned straw, spurned springs, spurned leather. Everything was made out of good solid wood, at stern right angles with more good solid wood. Every seat was taken and there were packs, rifles, musette bags and piles of canned apricots all over the aisles.

Native women squatted alongside the tracks do-ing their washing in canal water that had been there since St. Paul; brown boys splashed and waved at us; water buffaloes, blinded by straw hats tied over their eyes, went round and round endlessly, drawing water up to the field.

In my end of the car there was a general confusion of British Tank Corps men, returning to their units from the hospital in Cairo, and six Indians who made themselves very much at home, setting up camp in all available space and preparing and eating their native dishes from 3 P.M. until bedtime. Across the aisle were two very tanned South Africans in shorts, who looked disapprovingly on the whole thing and conversed coldly in Afrikaans as we chugged past Suez.

By nightfall, despite the immense quantities of watermelon and lemon soda that had been consumed, there was an air of deep hunger hanging over the car, and when the word was passed around that at the next station there was a NAAFI (British Post Exchange) where we would be fed, there was a determined rush to get out Dixies and tin cups. The British soldier would no more think of going any place without his Dixie and tin cup than he would think of appearing without pants in Piccadilly Circus.

I had neither mess tin nor cup and was mournfully admiring British foresight when a little middle-aged Tommy on my right, who had spent the whole afternoon silently and religiously reading a magazine called *Gen,* perusing advertisements and fiction page by page without partiality, quietly offered me a mess tin.

There was a great combing of hair in the tradition that the Briton dresses for dinner no matter where the meal finds him, and thousands of us started leaping off the train before it had fully stopped. We lined up and were served sandwiches, cakes and good hot strong tea by Egyptians in elegant white cotton gloves.

"There's beer at the other end of the station," reported a British sailor. "Ruppert's. Half a crown a can." There was no movement toward the other end of the station.

On the train was a party of sailors who had just come back from Sicily and were feeling good about it. They had manned the landing barges in the invasion and said it hadn't been bad. "We only had two boat rides," they said. "Boat rides" meant bringing in troops under fire. "It was just like the movies," one of them said. "They kept firing at us and the water kept shooting up all around, but they never hit us."

One of them had been at the Brooklyn Navy Yard for six months during the war while the ship he was on was being repaired. "Oh, it's a lovely city, Brooklyn," he sighed. "And I had a lovely girl in Jamaica. It took me an hour in the subway each way, but it was worth it. A lovely city, but I couldn't live there. The pace is too fast for me. I'd be worn out in a year."

While everybody settled down for the night, I foolishly sat on the open platform, smoking and watching the desert roll by in the starlight. When I went in to go to sleep, I discovered that the Indians had spread a little more, and there was no place to sit, stand or lie inside. Everyone else seemed to be asleep and the car was full of snores and the rich smell of many soldiers who had traveled far in a hot climate with no water available. Only the two South Africans remained awake, staring coldly out through the closed windows at the desert.

I went into the next car. Luckily one of the sailors had rolled off the bench on a turn and remained where he was on the floor, too lazy to move. So I curled myself among the arms, legs, snores and sleepy cries of love and battle in the crowded car and tried to sleep.

When I awoke at 4 A.M. we were in Palestine. As I sat there watching the first orange streaks over the little dark tree-crested hills, the two South Africans came out. We began to talk. They had just come from near Tripoli after 2½ years in the desert, fighting most of the time. This was their first leave, 21 days, and they had flown down to Cairo and were on their way to Tel Aviv.

One of them had suggested getting a truck ride up to Tel Aviv, but the other had said: "No. We are on a holiday. Let's spend some money and be comfortable. Let's take the train." They chuckled sourly as they told me.

"Third class," one of them said. "Why, in South Africa we wouldn't send cows to market in these trains. How about in America?"

I told him that I guessed we wouldn't send cows to market in America in these trains, either.

"Third class," the other said. "Why, before the war, any place I went I would only stay in the best hotel in town."

"And in Cairo," the first one said, "any restaurant with a tablecloth is out of bounds to other ranks. I've had it. I've had this war. I volunteered and I fought for 2½ years and we were among the first to get into Tripoli. I've heard a lot of bullets go by. I've been dive-bombed and I've gone without water and I was perfectly satisfied. But this train ride finishes me. I've had this war, and they can have it back any time they want."

And he went inside to think about the pretty girls on the beach at Tel Aviv.

I sat on the platform and watched the morning sun break over the hills and light the orange groves and vineyards.

A little later the train stopped and we got off to take the bus to Tel Aviv. On the bus I met a lieutenant, a friend of mine, who had also come down by train. He looked very tired.

"What's the matter?" I asked

"That damned first class," he said. "No room to lie down. You sit up all night. Next time I take this blasted ride, I'm taking my bars off and traveling third."

Behind me I heard a wild, snorting sound. It was the South Africans, laughing.

THE SWEETHEART OF COMPANY D

By Pvt. WILLIAM SAROYAN

THERE is something in the heart of street dogs which draws them close to men, and there is probably no camp or post of the Army which does not have at least one dog, whether the post is in a Far Western desolation or in a suburb of New York, as my post is.

Our Company D has one of these dogs. He is called Shorty by some of the men, Short End by others and Short Arm by still others. Shorty is small, lazy and given to a bitter attitude toward civilians, including children. Somewhere in Shorty's family is a dachshund, as Shorty has the lines of such a dog, but not the hair.

The theory of the men of Company D is that Shorty spends the greater part of his time dreaming of women—or at any rate women dogs. He doesn't come across such creatures very often; he doesn't come across any kind of dog very often. Whenever he does, male or female, Shorty goes to work and gives the matter a stab, so to speak. It is a half-hearted stab, with Shorty more bored than fascinated and not the least bit sure of what he is trying to do, or whether or not he isn't making a fool of himself.

Now and then Shorty will be discovered in the middle of the street, dreaming of love or whatever it is, while two or three trucks stand by discreetly waiting for him to make up his mind. Shorty may have come into the world thoughtlessly, but it is not likely that he will leave any children standing around. He is either too tired, too troubled or too old, even though he is probably not more than 2.

I have observed that Shorty makes himself available to any man in uniform, bar none, and while our post is made up mostly of men of talent, Shorty is not above giving himself over to the affections of a man of practically no talent at all, such as our top sergeant, who was not in civilian life the famous man he is now. Our top sergeant may be a genius, the same as all the rest of us: Two-Teeth Gonzalez, Bicycle Wilkinson, Henry the One Hundred and Fifty-first Million and all the others. He probably deserves a story all to himself, but somebody else will have to write that story, as I want to write sonnets. (That is, if I ever learn to spell.)

My hero is Shorty, not our first sergeant. The sergeant is his mother's hero, I suppose, and I wish to God she'd never let him out of the house. If he thinks getting me to do KP is the way we are going to bring the war to a satisfactory conclusion, I believe his education has been neglected. That is not the way to do it. Give me a map of the world, a pointer and a good-sized audience and I believe I can figure the whole thing out in not more than an afternoon. The idea that generals are the only kind of Army personnel capable of figuring out ways and means and all that stuff is unsound. For every general there ought to be one private on the ground floor. As it is, half the time I don't know what is being done, what the idea is, or anything else. The result is that I must go out into the yard and whistle for Shorty, who instead of leaping to his feet and running to me opens his eyes and waits for me to run to him.

Shorty knows me all right, but what kind of planning can you do with a dog, and a sleepy one at that—a day-dreamer, an escapist, a lover of peace, an enemy of children in sailor suits? I don't know who the chaplain of Company D is, but for my money he can pack up and go to some other post, because Shorty is doing the same work and sending in no reports to anybody. He is a quiet creature, he is patient, he will listen to reason or anything else, and he will get up after a half hour of heart-to-heart talk and slowly wag his tail. He will wag thoughtfully, with effort, and unless you are blind, you will know what advice he is giving you after carefully considering your case.

Now, there was the celebrated case of Warty Walter, the Genius from Jersey, who had a secret weapon all worked out in his head which he believed could finish the war in two weeks. Warty mentioned this weapon to our top sergeant only to hear the man say, "You do what I say, Warty, or you're going to hear otherwise."

Warty went out into the yard to Shorty and unburdened his heart, whereupon Shorty got to his feet, stretched his body until it hurt, wagged his tail three times, kissed Warty on the hand, turned and began wending his way across the street where a girl of 6 in a sailor suit was looking at a movie billboard. That was the end of Warty's secret weapon. The following day he got his orders to go to Louisiana, took Shorty in his arms to say goodbye, and the war is still going on—a good three months after Warty got his idea for the secret weapon. Our top sergeant said, "If it's a secret, what the hell are you coming to me about it for? Keep it a secret."

Not every man at our post is as brilliant or as sincere as Warty, but I can think of no man who is not as devoted to Shorty. No girl of the USO has done Army morale as much good as Shorty. He may not be a dancing dog, but he's got eyes and many a man's seen a lot of understanding in those brooding eyes—many and many a man.

As for the little girl in the sailor suit, she turned and ran, so that Shorty, not knowing what else to do, went up to a second lieutenant and bit him. The following day there was a notice on the bulletin board saying: "Yesterday an enlisted man was bitten by a dog who might or might not have had rabies. Therefore, in the future, any man caught without his dog tags will be given extra duty." This of course was a subtle way of saying that Shorty had rabies, a lie if I ever heard one.

The basic failing of Shorty, if he must be given a failing, is his love of comfort, his passion for food and his devotion to sleep or The Dream. Shorty probably does not know this is 1943. I doubt very much if he knows there is a war going on, and I am convinced he does not know that the men of Company D are soldiers. I believe he has some vague notion we are orphans.

Shorty eats too much and never does calisthenics. He has seen a lot of men come and go. He has loved them all, and they have all loved him. I have seen big men with barracks bags over their shoulders bend down to whisper good-bye to the sweetheart of Company D, get up with misty eyes, swing up into the truck and wave to the little fellow standing there in a stupor. And I have heard them, as the truck has bounced out of the yard on its way to the war, holler out—not to me or to our top sergeant, but to Shorty: "So long, pal! See you after the war!"

I don't think they will see Shorty after the war. I think he will lie down and die of a broken heart once the boys take off their uniforms. Shorty lives to watch them stand reveille and retreat. All that stuff will stop after the war and Shorty will be out in the cold, just another dog of the streets, without honor, without importance—lonely, unfed, despised and unwanted.

That is why I have written this tribute to him.

"I understand he and the mess Sergeant had a little spat."
—*Pvt. Walter Mansfield.*

OVER THE HILL

By Sgt. RAY DUNCAN

It was almost exactly 1530 hours when Walt Durkee went over the hill. The adjutant, in the orderly room, glanced up at the clock and noted the time.

"Looks like your new man is taking off," he observed to Snell. The duty sergeant glanced out the window. "Who, Durkee? No, he ain't takin' off. He's policin' up the area. Nobody ever goes over the hill from this camp."

Which was exactly what the sergeant had been telling Walt Durkee.

"Welcome to Desert Hole Army Air Base," Snell had said. "We hope you'll like it here." And he had waved his hand at the sage-dotted desert that stretched far away to the hills.

"No," Walt Durkee said, "I don't like it here. I've been in camps like this before. Don't be surprised if I go over the hill."

Sgt. Snell glanced sharply at the new man, an odd light in his eye. "Oh no, you won't go over the hill. Funny thing, nobody ever goes over the hill from this camp."

"No?"

"No. You will be assigned general duty. Your first duty will be to police up the area." Again the sergeant waved his arm at the desert around them, and handed Walt a little brown sack.

After two hours of policing up Walt found three small bones and a dried-up rattlesnake skin. "I sure would like a glass of beer," he thought. "I would like very much to sit under a tree somewhere." It was then 1100 and time for a break. He began to work away from the orderly room, so he could lie down for a while with his head in the shade of a sagebrush.

But as soon as he was settled and beginning to drowse in the desert silence, Walt heard a sharp click as the orderly-room door opened half a mile away.

"All right, all right," said the duty sergeant. "Let's get on the ball out there, Pvt. Durkee."

Durkee roused himself. "Yeah," he muttered, "okay, you loud-mouthed orderly-room jerk."

"I heard that!" rang Sgt. Snell's angry voice across the desert.

At noon chow Walt Durkee picked up extra sandwiches and fruit. "I sure would like to see a tree," he kept thinking as he resumed his policing-up duties. "See a tree, see a tree," something sang in his ear, "over the hill and see a tree."

He kept drifting farther from the orderly room,

pretending to pick up cigarette butts. After three or four miles he dropped pretense and strode boldly toward the hills in the east, toward his home in New Hampshire.

"Look," said the adjutant, "look at that man Durkee now. He's definitely taking off. Aren't you going to say anything to him?"

"No. Not yet." Snell came to the window. "But don't tell the Old Man about this. He promised me another stripe on the first of the month if none of my men went AWOL. He's proud of our record."

All that night Walt walked toward the east. He lay down by a big sagebrush just before dawn, but after a few hours he wakened suddenly. Someone was calling his name.

"Here!" cried Durkee instinctively, sitting up.

"Okay," came the voice of the duty sergeant across the wasteland. "Just taking roll call. Carry on!" Walt heard the faint far-off slam of the door.

"I'm afraid," said the adjutant three mornings later, "that we'll have to mark your man AWOL. He didn't answer roll call for today."

"But sir," argued Snell, "it's windy today. You can see him for yourself, heading for those mountains to the east. After all, you can't count a man AWOL when he's in plain sight. They'd laugh you out of courts martial!"

"We've argued this out a hundred times, Snell, every time one of your men takes off. But I'll check regulations again."

"Can't we put him on special-duty status for a while, till after the first of the month? Let's say he's a weather observer on special duty. It's not like we didn't know where he was."

Walt Durkee's food was beginning to run low, but he wouldn't give up. He could see the hill he was going over, looming closer and closer, as he plodded along a dimly marked trail leading east. The orderly room now was only a speck in the distance.

"No," said the adjutant firmly on the following Monday, "I certainly will not permit the use of binoculars. As soon as he can't be seen with the naked eye, he's AWOL."

"Everything's gotta be just *so* with you," muttered Snell. "Anyhow I think he'll be startin' back soon. I had the observation plane drop a little more food."

"Well, I took him off special duty this morning.

I had to. The Old Man was beginning to wonder, I think. Durkee's now carried as detached service."

Sgt. Snell grabbed the binoculars. "Look!" he cried, "I think he's turned around at last. We can put him back on squadron-area duty as of tomorrow's morning report!"

When Pvt. Walt Durkee staggered into the orderly room about eight days later, he kept trying to lick his swollen lips with a dry tongue. "I've come to give myself up," he gasped.

"Did you finish policin' up?" asked Snell, now a staff sergeant. He glanced out across the desert. "Looks pretty good. Now why don't you get back to the barracks before the Old Man catches you in that ragged uniform."

"I was AWOL," muttered Durkee, "I was over the hill—I mean——"

"You mean you got lost," said the staff sergeant, shoving him toward the barracks. "Nobody ever goes over the hill from this camp."

THE POET'S CORNERED

LITANY FOR HOMESICK MEN

By Cpl. Hargis Westerfield
New Guinea

A litany for all men homesick:
For all men crying sick
In all camps over all America
And too far away across the waters
For even the furloughs we yearn about,
In a circle under the one dim bulb
In the barracks.

A litany for all men:
Those who dream at night of home
Before battle-dawn and the bombers rising;
And those with too much time to think
Here in the humdrum barracks,
Training finished and waiting for shipment,
With MPs at the gates; and those
Behind electric wires with the jaded guards.
Japanese or German, hoping to shoot
When they cross the dead line.

A litany of all our longings,
Walled in overweight khaki
Or turreted in the nauseous tanks
Bolted down for the break-through.

A litany of yearnings:
For the town we came from, Joe's place on the corner
And beer and chili and Cincinnati Dutch accents;
For the sickish ozone of the 6 o'clock rush
In the subway; or the Polish cry
Of the El conductor in Chicago; for the thick steaks
Of a little restaurant in DuBois, Pennsylvania;
Or the sleepy streets of Georgetown, Kentucky,
Walking into stone-walled blue-grass meadows;
For Memphis and the great bluff on the Mississippi·
And the high woods of the Arkansas shore
After sunset.

A litany for all·homes we lived in:
For the tall apartments in Yonkers with zig-zagged
Fire escapes, and round and rich with the Yiddish voices;
For the cabin in a Kentucky cove, puncheon-floored
And with a Spanish rifle won from another war
Gracing the mantelpiece; for the tall-gabled
Brick villa in the wide-lawned suburb.
For my own home, small weathered white cottage
On a quiet street in Bloomington, Indiana,
And a robin nesting under the front-porch eaves,
And a rabbit in the garden thinking it his right
To lop my tomato plants, and a great black table
With a line of my books on it, and Peggy my wife
To walk with on the back lawn among limestone walls
With twilight coming on.

A litany for all of us;
O words that bring back our homes for a space
And give us a quiet place for worship,

And peace in our hearts, after the cursing camp.
Home will always be with us, whether or not
We ever see it again, a picture in our brain,
Colors and odors and sounds half remembered.

When hate of an unseen enemy cannot hold us,
This homesick litany will lead us into battle;
For the homes we lived in once long ago
Are strength on the march and a steady grip
On the killing tools and a tried hand
On the poised trench mortar.

ARMY CHAPEL

By Pvt. Darrell Bartee
Camp Crowder, Mo.

The doors stand open for the files of men
Whose step is lighter at the Sunday dawn.
These are the ones who yesterday had been
All fierce and heavy with their weapons on.
They are the grimmest worshippers of all
Who come to sing the quiet songs today,
Who have the strident marches to recall
And who have knelt to fire, but not to pray.
Just what the troubled heart will call its own
And will remember from this steepled place,
If fully felt, but not precisely known,
And written only on the soldier's face.
It is a search for rightness, little more—
The strangest, strongest weapon of the war.

BUNA BEACH

By Pfc. Keith B. Campbell
AAFTAC, Orlando, Fla.

(On seeing a picture of three dead American soldiers on Buna Beach, see page 246)

Perhaps they struggled with geography
When they were boys, lisping the sinewy names
Of far-off lands they never hoped to see,
With thoughts intent upon their outdoor games;
The wild halloos and shouts of after-school,
A rag-tailed kite against a gray March sky,
And boyish laughter ringing "April Fool!"
When someone took their bait.

    Well, here they lie,
Three lads on Buna Beach, grotesquely laid
In the informal pose of sudden death;
While we, who live secure because they paid
In currency compounded of their breath,
Would hesitate and ponder on a scheme
To bargain interest to preserve their dream.

OBITUARY

BY S/SGT. FRANKLIN M. WILLMENT

Camp Gordon Johnston, Fla.

Under a friendly tavern spigot
Lay out my grave and write my ticket.
My life was raw but always cricket
And Bacchus my partner and guide.

This be the verse that you grave for me:
"Here lies a GI where he longs to be
With a flask on his hip and a blonde on his knee
And a quart of shellac in his hide."

TRAVEL NOTE

BY SGT. JACK N. CARL

Southwest Pacific

From London to Tahiti,
From Attu to Port of Spain,
From Bougainville to Martinique,
You'll hear a new refrain;
From Frisco to Pearl Harbor
The legend will appear
That during World War No. 2
Mrs. Roosevelt slept here.

ON THE MARCH

BY PVT. EDMUND M. ZASLOW

San Angelo AAF, Tex.

After the seventh mile the men
    Prefer the chanting of the shoes
To singing thrice-sung songs again—
    Too little breath to lose.

A mental song does just as fine
    To add some voltage to the chaste
Cadence of our marching line,
    And gives each man his taste.

Pete in the second section, last
    Platoon, squad number five,
Is beating him a rhythmic feast
    Of Dixieland jive.

Out front the right guide steps alone,
    Pivot of the column's tread,
Drawing strains of Mendelssohn
    From fiddles in his head.

Old homely hymns, tart ballads, blues,
    Songs of all times and recent date
Sung to the chanting of our shoes—
    Silent conglomerate!

And there's a private music lingers
    In the helmet of many a rover,
Of houses to be built, and fingers
    Ringed, when this is over.

IN MEMORIAM

(Freeman Nimhauser, killed in action)

BY PVT. JOHN E. BROWN

ASTP, Atlanta, Ga.

From pen to rifle
It was a long way,
From Greenwich Village to New Guinea
Yet it was the same.

Mourn for the dead who died in vain,
But not for him.

When the poems gave out,
When it wasn't enough
To sing of freedom,
He fought for what he wrote for,
He died for what he lived for.

Mourn for the dead who died in vain,
But fight for him.

NIGHT MARCH

BY PVT. JOHN ROLFE

Buckley Field, Colo.

Light, through the open doorway, brushed a feeble
    gleam
Of yellow on the night, and the boy stood
Square in its beam, shock-haired, bowlegged, dirty fist
    in mouth—
A stout, small silhouette against the glow—
Staring upon the road.

Clearly he heard
Through the soft cushion of the star-hung dark
The swift unending whisper of their tread, the rush
And pad of hurried feet, a hushed unease
Much like the rumoring of hidden leaves
Portending storm.

Clearly he saw
Their blackened shape against the lighter night—
The lurching packs, the forward-pressing file
Flung like a rack of angry summer clouds
On the horizon. And the boy felt
Quicken within himself the smoky thrill,
The formless, fearful joy that always came
When the sky cracked and blazed and the maniac wind
Beat like a flail upon the stubborn trees.

Not a star blinked
In all that quiet night, yet the boy knew
That on the dusty red-clay road which ran
Before the farm a storm was being born.
How great a wind would rise, how many towers
Would topple, Caesar's thrones and fasces fall,
How many hollow eagles overturn,
No barefoot farmer's boy might even dream.
    Nor yet might they,
Whose silent, purposeful columns in the dark
Were shaping fury that would shake the world.

ARKANSAS

Gov. Adkins said he would sponsor legislation to outlaw horse and dog racing in Arkansas. At Little Rock, a Circuit Court jury acquitted 18-year-old William Browning, Catholic High athlete, in the bludgeon slaying of his mother last September. Fire destroyed Harrison's High School. At Monticello, the Allen Hotel and three other business buildings burned. Twenty-three carloads of lumber, oil and other war material burned after the Rock Island freight train was derailed near El Dorado.

CALIFORNIA

After a heated controversy, the State Board of Agriculture passed a resolution declaring that Japanese-Americans should not be barred from farming when the Government approves their return from relocation camps. At San Francisco, Gilbert Anson, 19-year-old merchant seaman, was under indictment for bringing nine uncensored letters from the war area for posting in the U.S. A $325,000 community-hospital was to be built at Marysville. A general-alarm fire forced 50 persons to flee from the Pendergast Apartments in Sacramento. Women outnumbered men 2-1 on the Superior Court jury list in San Diego.

CONNECTICUT

Hartford firemen organized a union but promised Mayor Mortensen they would never strike. Carlo DeCaro, 19, of Thompsonville was sentenced to die the week of May 4 for the fatal shooting of Salvatore Bonelli, 62, also of Thompsonville. When the New Britain *Herald* declined to accept additional subscriptions because of the paper shortage, Mayor Quigley induced his friends to contribute their papers so he could send them to servicemen. An 11-pound eight-ounce boy 22 inches long, the biggest baby born in Waterbury Hospital this year, is the 13th child born to Mr. and Mrs. Donald Birdsall of Water-

News From Home

•

What goes on in your own home state

town. A five-alarm fire swept the Persky Block in New Haven, causing $500,000 damage.

DELAWARE

WO Carl Moulinie of Fort Miles was sentenced by a Georgetown court to 18 months for shooting to death his close friend, WO John Worthington, in the latter's Rehoboth Beach home; the state charged the shooting occurred after a quarrel in which Worthington accused his wife of intimacies with Moulinie. In Wilmington, the Walnut Street Christian Association building was remodeled to accommodate 50 war workers. The Rev. Lewis Uhlendorff, pastor of Jerman Chapel in Smyrna, became an Army chaplain. Josiah Messick, Seaford's oldest citizen, died at 94.

DISTRICT OF COLUMBIA

Washington police arrested Benjamin Corvelle, a taxi driver, for authorities in Arlington, Va., where he was accused of beating a 20-year-old wounded war veteran who was unable to pay an $8 fare demanded by Corvelle. A two-alarm fire did $50,000 damage in the Kay Jewelry Co. store at 409 Seventh Street, N. W. The Columbia Typographical Union struck for one day, crippling the capital's four daily newspapers. Jack Hodges, a hotel bellhop, rejected two nickels offered him as a reward for recovering a wallet and $8,800.

FLORIDA

Secretary of State Gray estimated 200,000 Florida servicemen and women would be eligible to vote in the state primaries next May; requests for ballots should be addressed to the secretary

of state. Pensacola had its first snow in 44 years. A four-day cold wave swept the state and spoiled 5,000 carloads of fresh vegetables of an estimated value of 5 million dollars. A record crowd of 9,517 bet $443,953 on the opening day of the season at Tropical Park. While waiting in her car for her husband to return from hunting, Mrs. M. R. Gray of Ocala shot a 13-point buck, the largest deer killed in six years in Ocala National Forest. A gasoline shortage halted 50 percent of Key West's motor vehicles.

ILLINOIS

Illinois license plates this year have cream-colored numerals on brown fiber plates. Chicago had 165 murders last year, of which 28 were unsolved. The 1943 income from farm crops totaled $770,171,000, the highest since 1919. Cornelius Warmerdam, the only pole vaulter to clear 15 feet, was assigned to the Navy Pre-Flight School at Monmouth College. Pulaski's Postmaster Reeves retired. Died: Mr. and Mrs. George Dailey, 89, on the same day, at Farmington; Chief William Williams, 106, Indian scout for Gen. Custer, at Quincy.

INDIANA

The Indianapolis City Council voted to rename the municipal airport in honor of Col. M. Weir Cook, who was killed in the Pacific area last March. A break in an oil pipe line at Lebanon caused a fire visible for miles. St. John's Hospital at Anderson was given an "iron-lung" respirator by the VFW Order of the Purple Heart and Disabled Veterans of CIO Locals 662 and 663. Fire destroyed the Central Cut Rate drug store at Franklin. At Indianapolis, Albert Evans, 66-year-old watchman at the C. D. Kenny Grocery Co., shot and killed one burglar, wounded a second and captured a third.

IOWA

Humboldt's churches and schools were closed for two weeks to combat the flu epidemic. With Dr. D. W. Harman ill with pneumonia in a Council Bluffs hospital, Glenwood was left without a physician when Dr. J. M. Donelan died. At Manchester, a steam boiler broke down in Ray Solberg's greenhouse, causing $3,000 worth of flowers to freeze. William H. (Billy) Bare, 63, was found shot to death in his filling station at Pleasantville. Conservation officials were baffled because only 200 of the customary 3,000 bats had returned to hibernate in Bat Cave, Maquoketa Caves State Park.

KANSAS

Thomas Kaster, Kansas City jeweler, shot to death a burglar who had wakened him while he slept in the rear of his store; the same thing happened seven years ago. Hugoton plans to build a high-school stadium this year. Parsons expects to erect a 100-room hotel after the war. The Manhattan courthouse clock was out of order and it seemed likely to remain so as it will cost $800 for repairs or $4,000 for a new clock. Baker University planned a new gym to replace Taylor Hall, destroyed by fire. At Topeka, Ernest Hoefgen confessed that he killed Bruce Smoll, missing Kansas State College student, because Smoll recognized him as a fugitive after Hoefgen gave the student a lift near Peabody last September.

KENTUCKY

Thomas Robinson Jr. received the death sentence in Federal Court at Louisville for the kidnaping in 1934 of Mrs. Alice Stoll. Gov. Simeon Willis, inaugurated the 49th governor of Kentucky, heads the first completely Republican state administration since 1919. Paducah's flood wall was almost completed. McCracken County voted "wet" at a local-option election. Somerset citizens organized a committee to demand better fire protection after the city's worst fire in 25 years caused $100,000 damage in the business district. Newport's City Manager Morlidge banned bingo.

MASSACHUSETTS

Miss Ruth Dondero of Weymouth was awarded $4,501 for the loss of her sense of taste as a result of injuries in an auto accident. Quincy's Supt. of Schools Muir resigned. Denis Delaney of Lawrence was named collector of internal revenue for the state. The Rev. A. B. Crossman, pastor of Worcester's Lincoln Square Baptist Church, demanded a "house cleaning" of the City License Commission after it failed to revoke licenses of three restaurants involved in gambling-case convictions. Elmer Rice of Melrose donated 15 tons of letters—his business correspondence for the last 32 years—to the paper-salvage drive. Fires in the same week destroyed the YMCA and the old Corser Building on High Street in Holyoke.

MICHIGAN

Detroit police arrested six men and a woman after finding ration coupons for 2½ million dollars worth of gasoline and a complete set of burglar tools in their apartment. An anonymous soldier stationed in Australia sent $27 to Mrs. D.

Knox-Hanna in Caro, with the explanation that he had stolen the money from her husband nine years ago during the Kerns Hotel fire in Lansing in which her husband perished. Workmen insulating the Homer Harper house in Hudson found five quarts of 25-year-old Scotch under the attic floor. The Flint CIO Council bought the Industrial Bank Building for $100,000.

MINNESOTA

Twenty-three Minnesota hunters were killed and 67 injured during 1943. Streetcar service in Minneapolis and St. Paul was curtailed because crewmen refused to work overtime. Declaring that ghosts played their piano and emitted nightly groans, the Clarence Ruud family moved from a house in Crookston. John Recko and Joseph Mondou, Duluth meat dealers, got two years each plus $500 fines for violating rationing and price-ceiling regulations. At Minneapolis, the names of 12 Bay View High students who have died in this war were inscribed on an honor roll which was unveiled at the school.

MISSISSIPPI

Fire destroyed the high school at McComb. Trusties in Hinds County Jail at Jackson foiled an attempted escape by death-cell inmates by aiding jailer E. H. Currie, who was attacked when he brought food to the prisoners. Died: Dr. J. L. Cooper, Meridian dentist, after falling from a tree; George Brannon, 65, owner of the Jackson baseball club for 22 years. Meridian High was defeated by Boys' High of Atlanta, Ga., 13 to 0, in the annual Blue and Gray football game played at Montgomery, Ala.

MISSOURI

A new law is now in effect in Missouri, requiring applicants for marriage licenses to have blood tests. J. Fred Koenig, St. Louis Republican member of the State Constitutional Convention, was arrested in a drive against black-market whisky. Twelve members of the L. F. Van Countren family in Columbia, including three Wacs, were in the armed forces. At St. Louis, ex-Mayor Dickmann was named postmaster to succeed the late W. Rufus Jackson. A Caesarean operation performed at Providence Hospital, Kansas City, saved the life of a baby girl delivered 10 minutes after her mother died.

NEBRASKA

In a state-wide straw vote conducted by the Omaha *World-Herald*, New York's Gov. Dewey led Wendell Willkie 2 to 1 for the Republican presidential nomination. Owing to draught, the winter wheat crop was in the worst condition in 30 years except for 1939. A $50,000 fire destroyed Omaha's Chermont ballroom. An appeal to the Supreme Court stayed for six months the execution of Joseph MacAvoy, former sergeant at the Harvard Air Base, for the slaying last August of 16-year-old Anna Milroy of Sutton.

NEW HAMPSHIRE

Whitefield considered using the Town Hall for movies after fire destroyed the Stoughton Block, including the town's only theater. James Sheein, an employee at the Whiting mill at Wilton, chopped free several mallard ducks frozen in the ice on Whiting's Pond. When Officer Romeo Fournier found the door of L. E. Hildreth's radio

YACHT CLUB FIRE. Firemen fight the blaze that destroyed the building and marine equipment of the Milwaukee Yacht Club, causing $50,000 damage.

store in Laconia unlocked and couldn't secure it properly, he finally fastened it with a pair of handcuffs. Fires destroyed the Robertson Motor Co. in Keene, the Green Gables Inn in Bradford and the Wilson Beef Co. warehouse in Concord.

NEW MEXICO

The driver of a Greyhound bus and one passenger were killed in a wreck near Capulin. Hobbs police shot a pack of stray dogs after they attacked and seriously wounded 11-year-old Jimmy Evans. Nearly 1,700 A & M alumni are in the armed forces. William (Uncle Bill) Washington, Carlsbad rancher for 60 years, died at his home at 90. At Albuquerque, a 66-mph gale tore tiles from roofs and uprooted trees. The Rev. George Culleney of Arkansas was appointed canon of St. John's Episcopal Cathedral, Albuquerque.

NEW YORK

On his 50th birthday conductor Artur Rodzinski received from the directors of New York City's Philharmonic-Symphony Society a pedigreed Guernsey cow named Tulip for his Stockbridge (Mass.) farm. At Buffalo, Owen Bugman, a war-plant worker, faced manslaughter charges in the death of Pfc. Edward Raslawski after a tavern fight that started when Bugman and his friends allegedly greeted one another with "Heil Hitler." Roger Huntington, 54, former mayor of Waterville, died at Utica. Mayor Kennedy announced that emergency calls for coal by Syracuse residents will be checked by police. The Rev. Edward Welles of Alexandria, Va., became dean of St. Paul's Cathedral in Buffalo.

OHIO

Two burglars tied up a porter in the offices of the Cleveland Hockey Club, broke open two safes and escaped with $37,000. Two Youngstown firemen were injured when struck by a car while they were fighting a $50,000 fire in the large

HERO'S SON. James Patrick Deveraux, 10-year-old son of Lt. Col. James F. Deveraux who led the heroic Marine defense of Wake Island, gets a letter from his father now in Jap prison camp in Shanghai.

business building on the northwest corner of the square in Hubbard. At Columbus, it was announced that Atty. Gen. Herbert's campaign for governor will be managed by Milo Warner, former national commander of the American Legion. County and city tank trucks were commandeered to haul water for livestock on drought-stricken farms in Washington County.

OKLAHOMA

El Reno's Main Street was swept by a $100,000 fire that destroyed five buildings, including that of Rector's Hardware Co., and damaged five others. Wielding clubs and hurling rocks, 18 girls in the detention building of the Oklahoma Industrial School at Tecumseh held guards at bay for two days. The Alvin Hotel in Tulsa was reopened to soldiers, after being out of bounds since last September. At Oklahoma City, the safe of the Veazey drug store was robbed of $1,100.

PENNSYLVANIA

The state extended whisky rationing for six weeks and reduced the amount each customer may purchase to one-fifth of a gallon. The Civil Aeronautics Board halted commercial traffic at the Philadelphia Municipal Airport for military and safety reasons. Allentown's Police Chief Yohe resigned to accept a position with the

Pennsylvania Power and Light Co. A three-alarm fire, in which one fireman died, destroyed a six-story University of Scranton building used by classes of aviation cadets. Mrs. Anna Freed of Pittsburgh named her baby George in honor of a taxi driver who delivered the infant after arriving too late to drive Mrs. Freed to the hospital.

RHODE ISLAND

A war monument was unveiled in Woonsocket honoring 670 servicemen and women of the North End. Everett McCurdy, who rescued three children from a burning building, was made a life member of the Conimicut Fire Company. Hartley Roberts succeeded Harry Slide as chairman of the Republican City Committee in Providence. Warwick city officials prepared to enforce an ordinance requiring all houses to bear numbers. Mayor McCoy said that 40 percent of Pawtucket's municipal employees are members of the armed forces.

SOUTH CAROLINA

Firemen rescued R. W. Griffin from his photographic shop when the Todd Block burned in Laurens. President Green of Coker College, Hartsville, resigned to become editor of the Durham (N. C.) *Morning Herald*. Columbia's City Council favored the closing of nonessential businesses on Sunday. S. M. (Zip) Hanna succeeded Ab Wallace as director of physical education at the Columbia YMCA. Mr. and Mrs. T. H. Edwards and their daughter Margaret of Florence were killed in an auto crash.

SOUTH DAKOTA

Lane McComb, 15, of Highmore lost an eye, thumb and finger in the explosion of a souvenir German shell sent him by his cousin, who fought in Tunisia. Miss Alberta Caille, head librarian at the Sioux Falls Public Library for 28 years, resigned. Mrs. Dorothy Salnave, a soldier's wife, won a $200 judgment against a Sioux Falls hotel accused of overcharging her. The South Dakota Civil Air Patrol of 373 members was flying mail and critical supplies 2,400 miles daily. Albert Nelson, Wakonda night watchman, got six years for stealing rum and money from a pool hall.

TENNESSEE

U. S. Senator McKellar asked Gov. Cooper to call a special session of the Legislature to suspend the state poll-tax law as a prerequisite for soldiers voting. The state paid a $1,000 reward to J. E. Storrs, Nashville policeman, for evidence leading to the conviction of Charles Coley in the 1939 slaying of Marian Ellis, 12-year-old Nashville girl. The Bijou Theater in Chattanooga was destroyed in a three-alarm fire. Joseph Meador, a Memphis coal salesman, was held for the grand jury after admitting he took six cases of whisky into dry Haywood County.

TEXAS

Capt. E. T. Dawson, chief state game warden in the Houston area, reported that thousands of wild ducks alighting on Skull Creek in Colorado County churned up the water and killed all the fish for several miles. Thieves broke into three Houston jewelry stores on Travis, Preston and Capitol Streets the same night and took jewelry worth $1,300. A $200,000 fire damaged Reed's Department Store in Henderson. The tempera-

INGENUITY. Michael Horan of Brighton, Mass., invented this pasting, rolling paperhanging machine that hardly even needs a one-armed paperhanger.

ture in Fort Worth registered 14 degrees above zero, the lowest recorded there on a December day in 19 years. W. A. Strange, Elvis Lively and C. A. Hindon, all of Crockett, were killed when their truck was struck by an IGN train.

UTAH

After the Emery School Board closed Castle Dale High because of the teacher shortage and the difficulty of making building repairs, some students protested by refusing to attend classes at Ferron and Huntington. Hiring of employees for the 180-million-dollar Geneva steel plant near Provo was started. President Cowles said that the University of Utah's enrollment had dropped 34 percent since the war started. Clearfield, formerly served by the Layton Fire Department, bought a 500-gallon pumper truck. Ration-book registration showed Logan's population to be 11,577, a decline of 1,200 in a year.

VIRGINIA

Norfolk jewelers reported that men's wedding rings were selling unusually well. Lynchburg's city auto-license plates for 1944 had a new color scheme—black letters and numerals on yellow. Prostitution in Roanoke was declared to be "wide open" by Dr. Geringer, director of the city's venereal-disease clinic. Duck hunting was spoiled when ice covered Princess Anne County's famous Back Bay. Hunters bagged 65 turkeys during a season of one week in the state forests in Buckingham and Appomattox Counties. Twenty-eight candidates, the smallest class in 30 years, took the state bar exam; 11 men and one woman passed.

WASHINGTON

The Douglas County Fair, canceled since the war started, may be held again this year. Harry Cobain, Castle Rock Junior High principal for

WAR HAT. They could always make a hat out of anything and since the war that's truer than ever. Film actress Jane Wyatt models this one for a Los Angeles show. It's made of newspaper and twine.

eight years, was named county superintendent at Longview to succeed Clare Mendenhall, who took a position in the Bremerton school system. The Foster Building in downtown Chehalis was purchased by C. A. Moore. Working in the Associated Shipyards at Seattle, Mrs. June Schults and Mrs. Sandra San Juan, who had never seen each other before, discovered they were orphaned sisters. Jerry and Allen, 4 and 7, of Bellingham drowned after breaking through the ice on a lake near Lynden.

WISCONSIN

Fire Chief Burroughs was accused of refusing aid from the Fond du Lac Fire Department when fire in Ripon destroyed the First National Bank. The Eau Claire Ordnance Plant was expected to be converted this spring for synthetic-rubber production. When a dog broke through the ice on Fox River at Oshkosh, Harold Parsons swung hand-over-hand along girders of the bridge and rescued the animal by getting a scissors hold on its neck with his legs. Alumni of Milwaukee's South Division High celebrated the school's 50th birthday with a party. Paul Weiss was fined a dollar in Milwaukee for driving through a funeral procession, then thumbing his nose at the hearse driver and mourners.

TELL IT TO THE CHAPLAIN

By Cpl. GRANT ROBBINS

China

"Look," said the first sergeant. "Why don't you just tell it to the chaplain?"

I gave him the look I'd give to a two-headed thing pickled in a bottle, then I turned and walked out. When one has been in the Army for two years, at home and abroad, he becomes a little tired of the so-called GI slang, the oft-repeated phrase picked up in boot camp by a stunned civilian mind and dropped immediately thereafter—unless the mind remains stunned, as in the case of 1st Sgt. Stein.

I had gone into the orderly room because my name was not on a new rating list. My sad story has such a long background of pyramided woes that I shall not go into it more than to say that only a good heart-to-heart talk with someone would straighten me out.

All right, I decided, I *would* see the chaplain.

Of course that interview required considerable preparation, like finding out which chaplain in camp had the highest rank, investigating the CO's religion and memorizing a few chosen texts from my Gideon Bible. It doesn't hurt to talk their language.

The following day I stood before the door of a chaplain dressed neatly in patched fatigues to give the impression of a poor but honest homespun GI.

"Hello," he said, eying me suspiciously as I closed in on his desk. "Have a cigarette." That wasn't on the schedule, but I sprung a text on him anyway.

"Chaplain," I began, "I was greatly inspired by the sermon you gave on the parable of the loaves and fishes at No. 4 mess hall last Sunday at 2 P.M. Right now I am badly in need of a rod and a staff to comfort me, and I hoped that you might show me how to find a place beside the still waters."

The chaplain winced. "What have they done to you now?" he asked. "And kindly make it short."

I sat down and let him have it straight. I went back to the very first—the double stretch of infantry training; the misassignment to mechanics school; the lost records and the three solid months of KP; the transfer to an outfit that didn't need men of any classification but guards; all ratings filled by men ahead of me; no furlough; one small stripe thrown to me like a bone to a starving dog, then held in that rank for eight long hideous months. When the torrent had subsided I sat back and searched the face of the chaplain for a reaction. He gazed at his feet and shook his head slowly.

"I just can't understand the Army," he said. "Now, take me for example. You may think that I am doing pretty well, but I'll tell you appearances are deceiving. After five country churches with an average salary of $10 a week, I finally get settled in a good town with a good congregation. And then, of course, I leave it to become a chaplain. Where do they put me first thing? Out on a sand-blown camp in the desert with a tent to preach in and a bunch of tank men who have no more inclination toward religion than an equal number of Hottentots. Then the wind blows the tent away."

I said that that was too bad.

"That was only the beginning," he continued. "Shortly after I experienced a slight success in bringing some of the boys into the fold, they put another chaplain over me."

He went on and on, from one misfortune to another, and as his story developed one could easily see that he and Fate were at odds, and that it was getting to be too much for him. Tears trickled down his cheeks and splashed off the bars on his collar.

Since passes were issued now only on Sundays his congregation had suffered a heart-breaking drop in attendance. And he had been ousted from his warm office to make room for the Red Cross. When he protested to the commanding general he was mistaken for a mess officer and installed in a cubbyhole, just off the mess kitchen, where from 0600 to 2100 came a heavy odor of frying Spam.

"And to top it all," he said, "I have not received a promotion in 18 months."

I couldn't stand it any longer. I reached across the table, patted him on the shoulder and said: "Keep your chin up, sir. I'm sure things will work out in the long run."

He smiled miserably and thanked me. I tiptoed quietly out the door, leaving him in his grief.

"Gorman would like to know if he can take his finger out of the leak now, Sir."—*Pfc. Joe Kramer.*

SUPERMAN AND THE ARMY

BY PFC. HAROLD D. SCHWARTZ

Britain

WITH bankers in banks, with children in the streets, with housewives, cops and undertakers, even with generals, the most vital question today is: "Where is Superman?" "If only Superman would come and end this war." "If only he would join the Army, the war would be over in no time."

Poor, dear, innocent people. They must never know. Never.

I was standing in line, the first line in my military career. It was at Fort Dix near New York City. I got to talking to this guy in front of me—a nice guy. He said his name was Clark Kent. He looked sort of fat, wore glasses and had nice curly hair. He had, to put it mildly, a strange taste in clothes. He wore a blue cape draped over his shoulders and under his clothes, as we later discovered when we stripped in the dressing room, he wore long red underwear. Some of the other guys slapped their wrists when they piped the red long Johns. In the raw he looked kind of big in the biceps. Glands most likely.

We got talking with Kent. You know how it is, sweating out a line; you talk to anyone who'll listen. He told me he was a newspaperman. Worked on a rag called the *Globe*. Told me all about his girl Lois. She sounded like a dope to me, but I didn't say anything. He had damn good eyesight. In fact, he could read even the watermark on the eye chart. He was put in 1-A. I didn't do so good, either. I was put in 1-A, too.

I don't have to tell you what the next few days were like. We learned to police grounds, tear cigarettes GI style and eat bologna.

When we filed in for our IQs, it was around midnight. Kent sat next to me. We got the signal to start, and I just about finished wetting the pencil with my tongue when this guy leaned back in his chair and said, "Finished."

They wanted to court-martial him right there for cheating, but they gave him the benefit of the doubt and marked him 110.

Next morning bright and early we marched in to be classified. Then it all came out: It seems this guy was *Superman*.

"Never mind your nicknames," said the interviewer. "What's your real name? Clark Kent, huh? Whatcha do as a civilian? Newspaper, huh? Can you type?"

"Listen," said Kent, "I volunteered for the Infantry. Look." And quick as a flash, in fact quicker,

he was down to his red underwear. He picked up the building we were in and flew all over the state, pointing out all the spots of interest.

"Or maybe," panted Kent, "I could get in the Armored Command, as a tank. Look." And he went zooming down the road through woods, knocking down trees and plowing through barns and latrines. Then he stood in the middle of the rifle range, bullets bouncing off him like ping-pong balls.

The interviewer looked bored. "Got any hobbies?"

"I'm a crime buster."

"Reads *Detective Stories*," wrote the interviewer.

"Listen," said Kent, a wild gleam in his eye, "maybe I could be a fighter plane. Think of the money you'd save. I'd be both plane and pilot." And up he went into the air. Looped, rolled, what have you. And fast. He grabbed a passing P-38 and pulled it backward, "Well, how's that?" asked Superman when he came back.

The interviewer took a drag on his cigarette and looked unhappy. "Listen, wise guy," he said. "We don't like rookies coming in here and telling us how to run things. We have plenty of good fighting men, our equipment is the best, but we don't have enough clerks. So that's what you're gonna be."

"Have a heart," pleaded Superman. "Make me an MP, anything, but gimme action."

"Next," yelled the interviewer.

That was a long time ago. The other day I got a letter from Kent. He's working at Camp Dix with a chaplain. He runs a mimeograph machine, turns out a daily sheet about the post chapels and he's sweating out pfc. Damn nice guy.

"He says for you to take the marbles out of your mouth."
—PVT. *Thomas Flannery.*

WHAT'S YOUR PROBLEM?

NAVY NUMERALS

Dear YANK:

A lot of Navy men I see have little numerals, like "1" and "2," pinned on their campaign ribbons. I think they signify the number of engagements the wearer has participated in, but my buddies aren't so sure I know what I'm talking about. Am I right?

Hawaii   —JOE CURTIS S1c

You're wrong. Those numerals refer to the kinds of service the wearer has performed. The Navy has four kinds of service: escort, submarine, amphibian and patrol. If a sailor served on an escorting destroyer during a specific campaign and his destroyer was also engaged in amphibian landings, the numeral "2" on his ribbon would show that he had performed two kinds of service. Incidentally, you won't be seeing them any more; the Navy has decided to eliminate their use.

MEDICAL OPERATIONS

Dear YANK:

Just before I got into the Army I thought I needed an operation, but my doctor told me not to have one because it would have after-effects worse than the ailment itself. Now the Army tells me I must have the operation, and when I protested, the Army doctor said I could be court-martialed for refusing. I don't think I should have any operation I don't need, and I want to know whether it is true that I can be court-martialed if I refuse?

Hawaii   —PFC. FRANK G. PENDALL

Yes. AR 600-10 (2-e-9) states that refusal to submit to a dental or medical operation in time of war may result in court martial. If you really doubt the necessity of an operation, the matter will be referred to a three-man medical board, which decides whether the operation is necessary in order for you "to perform properly" your military duties. If they say operation, operation it is; and if you still say no, you may be tried by court martial.

REFUSING A DISCHARGE

Dear YANK:

What's my problem? Here it is. I was drafted in 1942 with a bad ankle. I was discharged with a CDD five months later. After being a civilian for only two months, I was drafted again. Now the Army wants to discharge me again; I have recently rejected two CDDs but I am up for a third, and this time the Army doctor tells me I won't be able to do anything about it and that I will have to ac-

cept the discharge. But that's pretty damned dumb. If I am released I will be drafted right away again, and I don't mind saying I'm pretty sick and tired of going through induction stations.

How can I stay in the Army, YANK, and save myself a lot of mess and bother?

Panama   —CPL. ANTON LACHENBRUCH

If the Army doesn't want you, you're out. Your draft board might try to reinduct you into the Army, of course, but our guess is that it won't. Army physical standards today are probably at rock-bottom, and if Uncle Sam can't use you now, you almost certainly will be let alone from here on in. Incidentally, that must be one helluva bad ankle you've got.

FATHER AND SON

Dear YANK:

I've a problem that even Mr. Anthony couldn't solve. He wrote me and said to go and see my chaplain. Well, sir, it's this way. I met a girl in the States in 1939. She was living with a fellow, not legally married. In 1940 she gave birth to a baby boy, my son. But as I wasn't at her side, she gave the baby this fellow's name. Later he died. I was away at that time, too, and couldn't get back to her. Later she married, legally, another fellow. Then in 1942 this man committed an FBI crime. He's now serving his second year of a possible 10-year sentence. I've written to her, and she's willing to cooperate in any way to have my son's name changed to mine as I'm helping with his support. I'm still not married to my son's mother, and at this time she is living with yet another fellow and by September will give birth to his baby. Isn't there some way I can give my son my name without having to marry his mommy?

Britain   —SGT. M. C. H.

In most states it is possible to change an official birth record to show the name of a child's real father. You did not mention the state in which your son was born, but if you tell your legal assistance officer he will be able to inform you just how to apply to the proper state authorities to get your son's record corrected.

RETURN TO OVERSEAS

Dear YANK:

I am 38 years old. They told me, when I was over in North Africa last summer, that I could get out of the Army if I applied for discharge before Aug. 1. I fulfilled all the requirements and eventually found myself hanging on the rail of a transport sailing for home. Well, YANK, when I saw Liberty's statue in New York Harbor—and I know this sounds corny—I got to regretting I was gonna be a civilian. And that's what I told my new CO; I told him I wanted to withdraw my application for discharge. He blew up like an ammunition dump. When the smoke cleared, I found out that he had orders fixed up for me to be shipped right back to the North African Theater—to my old command! At this very moment I'm looking at the transport that is probably going to take me back across the Atlantic. But what I'd like to know is, can this CO *legally* do this to me?

Port of Embarkation   —S/SGT. JOE MORTON

He sure can. Ours is the sad duty to refer you to Sec. IV, WD Cir. No. 10, 6 Jan. 1944. Subparagraph 2 says that any man 38 years old serving overseas who has asked for a withdrawal of his approved application for discharge after he has already been returned to the States will be packed off in the first shipment heading back to his old command. One of the reasons for this circular, the Army says, is that some GIs were using the over-38 discharge rule, not as a way to get out of the Army, but simply as a pretext to get back to the States.

LOST TEETH

Dear YANK:

Does a GI have to sign a statement of charges if he loses the set of false teeth issued to him by the Army? Some guys say you do, and I'm worried. While we were crossing on the ship I was put on a detail as a sort of "bucket brigade" member who passes cardboard cases down to the galley below. One wise guy threw a box at my chest and the jolt bounced my false teeth into the Pacific. It wasn't my fault, and I'll be one damned sore dogface if I am expected to pay for them.

Australia   —PVT. DOMINICK ATRELLIA

False teeth are not considered "property" in the usual sense of the word, and the Judge Advocate General has ruled that a GI who accidentally loses his dentures does not have to pay for them on a statement of charges.

ALLOTMENT MUDDLE

Dear YANK:

I have been overseas since June 1942. My pay was stopped in October 1942 because my mother was supposed to have been overpaid by the Office of Dependency Benefits. Since then I have had a few partial payments amounting to about $200.

Now the ODB has cut off my mother's allotment entirely. They have also cut off my 6-year-old son's allotment. My mother is 68 and in very poor health. I can't understand why I get no pay and why the allotments were cut off. I've tried writing to the ODB and seeing my first sergeant, but it doesn't do any good. What can I do to get some money?

Italy   —NAME WITHHELD

You'd better get used to living on partial payments, brother; you owe the ODB a wad of dough. ODB's records show that your mother has been overpaid to the tune of $1,292. Here are the facts:

In May 1942 you made a Class E (voluntary) allotment of $25 a month to your mother. Later that month you discontinued that allotment and set up one for $45. Your orderly room failed to notify ODB about your discontinuing the $25 allotment, so ODB paid both amounts through September 1943, at which time the $45 allotment was stopped. The $25 check kept on going to your mother until January 1944. A third Class E allotment, based on an incorrect serial number, was also paid to your mother from October 1942 to September 1943. Total overpayment: $1,760.

You made out still another Class E allotment in June 1942 for $18 a month. The ODB never paid this one, however, so in theory at least they owe you $468. After this is deducted from the overpayments, you still owe ODB $1,292.

In January 1943 you applied for a Class F (family) allotment for your mother and son, retroactive to June 1942. This allotment was granted, costing you $27 a month back to June 1942, so that for over a year your mother received almost $200 a month in allotments. The ODB says that your wife, who you say died in 1941, is very much alive and has applied for a family allowance, claiming that your son lives with her. Your mother contends that the boy is with her. Both claims are being investigated now.

Don't worry, though. Money isn't everything.

TIRE RETREADERS

Dear YANK:

I am going nuts retreading tires. I am getting stale and despondent. Only YANK can help me. You see, I have always wanted to get into the Infantry, and when I heard about that new *WD Cir. 132* making it practically mandatory for COs to approve any GI's request for transfer into the Infantry I rocketed over to the Old Man here. Smiling blissfully, I told him to get me outa this unit pronto. Shocked, I heard him say he wouldn't let me transfer, and yet with my own eyes I had read in that circular where only the War Department could say "no" on such a deal. YANK, it's up to you now.

Aberdeen Proving Grounds, Md.   —PVT. F. L. H.

Sorry, but we have to fail you. WD Memo. W615-44 (29 May 1944) lists tire rebuilders among the specialists who "are and have been for an extended period of time critically needed by the Army." The memorandum goes on to say that such critically needed specialists "may not volunteer for assignment and duty in the Infantry" under the provisions of Cir. 132.

FALL OUT FOR AN INTERVIEW

By Sgt. RAY DUNCAN

I'M KEEPING a scrapbook of newspaper stories about movie stars in the service. I suppose the rest of you soldiers are doing the same thing. If you can bear to part with any of your clippings about Hollywood men in uniform, I certainly would like to buy them from you. Or maybe we could trade duplicates.

The newspapers are doing an excellent job of covering film actor-soldiers. Only trouble with this kind of reporting is that there's not enough of it. It would be nice if similar stories could be done about all of our servicemen.

Surely there are enough good writers in this country to cover the activities of every GI in full glamorous detail.

Take for instance Floyd Pringle. He used to be pin boy at the Sportland Bowling Alley in Little Ditch, Ohio. When Floyd was drafted there should have been a story like this in all the papers:

LITTLE DITCH, OHIO, Feb. 21—He used to set 'em up for the Sportland bowlers—now he'll mow 'em down for the United Nations!

Into the greatest match of his career today went pale, slender Floyd Pringle. The idol of thousands of Little Ditch bowlers joined the United States Army!

Grinning happily as he reported for induction, Pringle appeared pleased when informed that he had been selected for 13 weeks of basic training.

The famed pin boy did not apply for a commission. He stated simply that he wished to serve in the ranks with the ordinary soldiers.

Flashing the famous Pringle grin that thrilled thousands in Little Ditch, he said: "Anybody who can dodge bowling balls can dodge Nazi bullets!"

Floyd Pringle awaited his turn in line at the induction station, just like everyone else. Everybody said he was a "regular guy" and a "swell fellow," and the examining doctor declared he was a "splendid physical specimen."

Think of the boost to Army morale if every GI hit the metropolitan press with a story like that!

Now suppose that our hero comes home on furlough from foreign service. Still following the model of the write-ups about the movie stars, the press would flash a story like this over the wires:

LITTLE DITCH, OHIO, Dec. 19—Back from the battle front today came Pvt. Floyd Pringle, his face drawn and a little haggard beneath its rich overseas tan.

The celebrated pin boy from this tiny Ohio town has been on a dangerous ammunition-supply mission in a combat zone, the nature of which cannot be disclosed.

(This is an example of tactful handling of material by a skillful newspaper writer. What Floyd actually told reporters was this: "I am a basic in a gun crew and I have to carry the shells from the truck and make a pile on the ground. We never saw no action. We had a dry run every day, and the rest of the time we set on our dead hams." . . . Now go on with the news story.)

Pvt. Pringle received an ovation when he arrived at the Little Ditch station. Women on the street stared at him in frank admiration, and several girls made low whistling noises.

The Pringle charm, which brightened Sportland alleys for so long, has not been dimmed by the strenuous army training which Pringle endured without complaint.

Pringle has been on a dangerous combat mission in a war zone. He goes on all the marches with the men in his crew and insists on sharing every hardship equally with the others.

Reports from the fighting front are that Pvt. Floyd Pringle is a "swell fellow" and a "regular guy," just as common and unaffected as any man in the dangerous combat war zone.

Remember, a glamorous soldier is a good soldier. Why be content with your name on a billboard honor roll in a vacant lot? Why not sit down right now and cut a stencil, to be run off and mailed to every editor in the land, urging the full glamor treatment for all of our boys in the service?

"I'd like a little fatherly advice, Sir."—Cpl. Ernest Maxwell.

NOTES FROM A BURMA DIARY

BY SGT. DAVE RICHARDSON

BEHIND JAPANESE LINES IN NORTHERN BURMA—Odds and ends from the battered diary of a footsore YANK correspondent after his first 500 miles of marching and Jap-hunting with Merrill's Marauders:

Volunteer. One of the Marauder mules balked at the bottom of every rugged Burma hill. The driver had to coax, cajole, cuss and tug at his animal constantly. Finally on one hill the mule stopped dead and lay down. That was the last straw.

"Get up, you sonuvabitch," cracked the driver, who had answered President Roosevelt's call to join the volunteer Marauders. "You volunteered for this mission, too."

Unwelcome Visitor. When the Marauders reached the rugged hill country of the Mogaung Valley, their columns started to string out as pack mules tumbled off ridges and bogged down in muddy ravines. Frequent messages were passed verbally from man to man up the column to keep the point platoon posted on the progress of the rear.

Usually these messages were "The column is broken behind the —th platoon" or "Lost contact with the pack train." Occasionally, however, the wording was varied, with confusion the usual result.

One rainy night, on a forced march through enemy-infested jungles, a message was passed up the line. "There's a gap in the column" was the way it started. But when it reached the front, it had changed to "There's a Jap in the column."

The front, unperturbed, sent back word to throw him out.

They Satisfy. In an enemy supply dump we found packs of Silver City cigarettes that showed the Jap flair for imitation. The packs were similar in size and design to those of popular U. S. brands. According to the English wording on each pack, they were manufactured by the "Eastern Virginia Tobacco Company." And there was a familiar ring to the blurb: "Silver City cigarettes are a blend of the finest Turkish, American and domestic tobaccos, manufactured by expert craftsmen and guaranteed to satisfy the most exquisite of smokers."

Books of the Month. For weeks the Marauders hadn't seen a piece of mail or a scrap of reading matter. Every time transport planes roared over to drop rations and ammunition by parachute, the men sweated out a few books or magazines. Then one wonderful day after an attack on the main Jap supply route near Laban, the unit I was with finally received manna from the sky—an airdrop of books. Not many—just one book to a platoon. Eagerly we scanned the titles.

They were a "Pocket Book of Etiquette," "Children's Book of Wild Animals," "Boy Scout Handbook" and—last but not least—a "Rhyming Dictionary of Poetic Words and Phrases."

Poets: 1 Quick, 1 Dead. Speaking of poetry, they say that when a GI starts composing verses he's been in the jungle too long. The Marauders and the Japs they fought each had at least one jungle-happy poet laureate among them.

Representing the Marauders was T-5 Stanley L. Benson, a gun-repair man. Here's his first effort as a poet:

> *Four thousand dead Japs behind us—*
> *A hell of a stinking mess.*
> *The live ones now around us*
> *Soon will join the rest.*
>
> *When Tojo gave his orders*
> *To kill us one by one,*
> *He didn't know Merrill's Marauders*
> *Would sink the Rising Sun.*

(Benson took a slight poetic license in his first line. The Marauders were credited with killing 2,000 Japs in six weeks.)

The Japs' weapon in this battle of poets was a hymn of conquest found on the bullet-riddled body of a dead Son of Heaven. It doesn't rhyme in English, but it still possesses undoubted literary merit:

With the blood-stained flag of the Rising Sun,
I'd like to conquer the world.
As I spit on the Great Wall of China,
A multi-hued rainbow rises above the Gobi Desert.

On the Ganges River at the foot of majestic
  Himalaya Mountains,
Sons of Nippon look for some crocodiles.

Today we're in Berlin,
Tomorrow in Moscow,
Home of snowbound Siberia.

As the fog lifts we see the City of London,
Rising high, as the ceremonial fish of Boys' Day does.

Now we're in Chicago, once terrorized by gangsters,
Where our grandchildren pay homage to our memorial
  monument.

Oh, governor general of Australia and South America,
Only in Japan sweet odor of fragrant blossoms per-
meates.

When I die I'll call together all the devils
And wrestle them in a three-inch rivulet.

I've set my mind on making my home in Singapore,
For there my darling awaits my return.

Mail Call. For security reasons the Marauders could neither write nor receive mail while behind enemy lines. After two months of marching and fighting, however, they were pulled back for a rest and got that long-awaited mail drop and a chance to write V-mail replies.

In a stack of letters from the gal back home, S/Sgt. Luther S. Player of Darlington, S. C., came across this remark: "I'll bet you're seeing plenty of action." Player's unit had been cut off for 10 days while the Japs shelled and counterattacked constantly. He answered his gal's letter as fully as censorship would permit. "Baby," he wrote, "you ain't kiddin'."

T/Sgt. Joe Diskin of Hoboken, N. J., received a letter from a pal who didn't know Diskin was overseas. Joe is a veteran of the first World War who's been in the Regular Army for 27 years and was sent back to the States from Pearl Harbor as "unfit for foreign service" because of 1918 wounds and age. His pal's letter read: "I am in Italy and have been in action. Believe me, this war is too tough for you old guys. No wonder you're back in the States." Diskin had just led his platoon against a fierce Jap counterattack. His reply is not for publication in YANK's sacred pages.

MENU FOR TOMORROW (AND THE NEXT DAY)

(Ham and Eggs in Cans Prepared for Army. —Newspaper headline.)

Fried eggs, farewell,
  With your rasher of bacon;
You're shot all to hell
  Unless I'm mistaken.

For eggs and ham
  In a can, like a bomblet,
Means eggs that are scram—
  Bled or ham in an omelette.
LT. RICHARD ARMOUR
FORT TOTTEN, N. Y.

AGE BEFORE BEAUTY

One of the effects of Australia's "austerity" program is a ruling that chorus girls must be more than 45 years old. Younger women are being drafted into war work.—News Item.

If chorus girls of forty-five
  Cavort upon the platforms
Of every honky-tonk and dive
  And flaunt their all-too-fat
    forms
While younger gals conceal their
    charms
  In denim or in khaki,
I tell you, gentlemen at arms,
  Old Sherman wasn't wacky.
LT. RICHARD ARMOUR
ANTIAIRCRAFT ARTILLERY

LINES TO A SETTING-UPPER

Make us raise our arms to thrust,
  Make us sideward wend,
Twist our necks or finger flex,
  But nix on deep knee bend.

Exercise our trunks at will,
  Ligaments will mend.
Straddle hop is bad, but stop
  Before the deep knee bend.

Make us stretch and leap and
    stoop,
  We're right with you, friend,
But to thrive and keep alive,
  Forget the deep knee bend.
LT. RICHARD ARMOUR

PRIVATE PROPERTY

Noncoms have their chevrons,
  Lieutenants have their bars,
Colonels have their eagles,
  Generals their stars.

What, then, has the private
  Fastened to his arm,
Or resting on the shoulder
  Of his uniform?

Only this (but tell me,
  Who'd not like the same?):
On his arm or shoulder,
  One delicious dame.
—LT. RICHARD ARMOUR
Antiaircraft Artillery

Paratroopers are tough guys who tell tough stories about themselves. This is one they tell in Britain. And who are we to doubt it?

By Sgt. ANDREW A. ROONEY
Britain

YEAH, them six holes up there is what the paratroopers left. Tough? They was plenty tough. Here six weeks before they pulled out. One of 'em's name was Marcetti. Toughest guy I ever see. Damn, he was tough! Marcetti used to be a rigger in a steel mill at Pittsburgh, and when he come into the Army they made an engineer out of him. Sent him to Belvoir and taught him how to make bridges out of them little boats and how to dig. If there was anything Marcetti didn't want to know how to do, it was dig.

They kept him at Belvoir till they found out they'd got the wrong guy to teach digging to. He used to give half his month's pay to a guy named O'Hara to pull his KP for him, and the other half he'd spend on Scotch up to Washington. Hell of a guy he was; sergeants couldn't do nothing but put him in the guardhouse when he popped off. Too good a man for the guardhouse, Marcetti was, and them officers of his knew it.

After they had him about six months they decided they better get someone else to do their

Too Good for the GUARDHOUSE

engineering, so they sent him to Paratroop School where he'd been trying to get since they got him. It wasn't so much they let him go where he wanted but they sure'n hell didn't want him, and the Army just don't send nobody back to a Pittsburgh steel company.

Marcetti got hooked up with this rugged Paratroop outfit—one of the first. Hand-picked, them boys was, back in the days when you hadda be able to lick hell out of three marines before they'd let you in.

They wasn't having no more trouble with him like they was having at Belvoir. He didn't get drunk much, and he begin listening because he figured them babies in the paratroops knew more about stuff than he did. At Belvoir he'd always guessed he could dig as good a hole as the next man without a sergeant telling him how.

Well, hell, first thing you know this Marcetti gets to be the demolition expert of the outfit. Goes to demolition school and learns everything there is to know about blowing things up. Before long the outfit moves over here, and they're the babies that's going to drop right out of the ETO onto Jerry some day when he's still tryin' to figure out what day he's going to get dropped on.

Them six holes is a story. At night Marcetti, Hannock, Taragan and the rest would be sitting around here playing poker for what they had. Marcetti would get restless, and without saying much he'd get up and wander into that little room at the end he had to himself. He'd start taking down all them bottles of stuff he had on the wall.

Damn, he had a pile of the stuff. TNT, nitro, dynamite, everything. Had enough to blow this whole ETO to hell and gone. Under his sack Marcetti kept a hack saw, a bunch of them heavy English beer bottles and three pieces of pipe that run the length of his bed. He'd saw himself off a foot or so of pipe, then he'd come back out here and, talkin' natural all the time, he'd smash himself up about six or eight of them beer bottles in a bucket. He'd go back to his room with the bucket of glass, and pretty soon you'd hear that sound like coal running down a chute when he poured the glass into a hunk of pipe.

Marcetti'd come out of his room with his pipe in one hand and a fuse in the other. He'd sit down with the boys again for a while, talking just like he was knitting a sock as he put the fuse into the moxie he'd packed into that length of pipe.

When he was satisfied with the job he'd lean back in his chair, finish what he was talking about and then wander out. In five minutes he'd be back in his chair, sitting there talking and smiling.

All of a sudden all hell would break loose. The whole damn hut would shake, and the rivets holding them corrugated-roof pieces together would snap off, a few of 'em. For 30 seconds you couldn't think what was happening for the noise of stones and dirt rattling down on the roof.

You shoulda seen the trees out here at the side. You can still see the scars on 'em. Big hunks of broken bottle stuck into them trees from all angles, and out in the field here there was a hole blown deep enough to bury a horse.

After looking around to see how Marcetti's concoction worked that time, the boys would go back to the hut and start playing cards again. In a few minutes this here meek little shavetail from the provost marshal's office would pull up in a jeep outside. He'd come every time, and I knew he hated to come in that hut worse'n anything in the world. It didn't bother Marcetti and this Paratroop outfit none. Nobody who wasn't a paratrooper bothered them guys none.

This second louey would knock on the door real light and then come into the hut. He'd stand there looking pretty helpless with a .45 on his hip and try to make the boys look up from the game by slamming the door. Hell, everybody that come in there slammed the door.

"Look, you fellows," he'd always say. "I asked you not to pull that stunt any more," he'd say. "Cut it out, will you?" he'd say, pleading. Hell, it was funny. There wasn't anything he could do because no one give a damn. They knew where they was headed for, and what anyone but their CO told them didn't carry no weight.

ONE day they brought some new boys in. Fellows up from an Infantry outfit. They'd been through a pretty rugged course, but they wasn't paratroopers. They'd got most of their training back in the States, and they was pretty cocky. Always showing these paratroopers how they learned it.

Things didn't go too well between 'em, and the CO decided something hadda be done. He gets Marcetti to fix up a bunch of tear-gas bombs under the sacks of a couple of these new joes. They was in here then, and Marcetti and his bunch was over in the bigger hut next door.

That night the Infantry boys come in after a speed march, pretty rugged they was, and a couple of 'em flops down on these sacks with the tear gas underneath. Boy, you shoulda been around. The bombs go off, and the hut starts filling with gas. The boys think they've been hit direct with HE.

They come hollering and screaming out of this hut like wild Indians. Marcetti is over there in the next hut, not even watching—just laying on his bunk, looking up at the ceiling and smiling.

This new crowd finally catches on. They get pretty mad but take it good. Can't get back into their hut, though. All their stuff is in there, and a man can't go near the place for the gas.

This shavetail from the provost marshal's office comes along to find out what all the excitement's about. It's getting dark, and he begins to worry about the lights in the hut. Doors and windows are wide open, and there'd been plenty of damn Germans around them nights.

Marcetti hears what's up and comes out of his hut. The louey looks at him pained and helpless like. He knows damn well who set them tear-gas bombs off.

"Can I do anything for ya, lootenant?" Marcetti asks, real casual.

"Well," says the lootenant, "I gotta get them lights out some way. If you'd put your gas mask on and put them lights out I'd be much obliged to ya, sergeant."

Marcetti disappears into his hut just like he's going in to get his mask like the lootenant said.

Well, the funny thing is that Marcetti does come out with his mask—last thing anyone expects to see him do. But on his hip he's strapped his .45.

He flips his hat between his legs like they taught him at Belvoir and starts fixing the straps on his gas mask. He gets his mask on, puts his hat on his head, waves at the louey and starts towards the hut. Marcetti is smiling sure as hell behind that mask, but you can't see it.

About 20 feet from the door of the hut he stops, pulls out his .45 and starts aiming. Everyone's expecting something from Marcetti but not this. He just plugs away six times at them lights hangin' there from the ceiling of the hut, knocks 'em clear out and then calmly walks back towards the louey.

Marcetti pulls off his gas mask. "There you are, sir," he says to the louey and walks back into his hut and lays down.

That's how them six holes got up there. Marcetti. Sorta sorry to see them paratroopers go, but damn! they was tough.

SPORTS: EX-PRISONER TELLS OF SPORTS IN JAP CONCENTRATION CAMP

By Sgt. DAN POLIER

LATE one afternoon in 1942 at the Japanese concentration camp at Santo Tomas University, Manila, the imprisoned Americans gathered around the playing field to watch a soccer game between the American and British men. Suddenly there was a big commotion at the gate. The Jap guards, who had been leaning on their rifles watching the game, popped to attention and presented arms. A whole company of Jap soldiers marched onto the field and proceeded to drill alongside the soccer players.

"We were so stunned at first we didn't know what to do," said Royal Arch Gunnison of the Mutual Broadcasting System, who returned on the *Gripsholm* after spending almost two years behind barbed wire at Manila and Shanghai. "But we decided we had to save face. You know how important that is out there. So we continued to play. The Jap officer deliberately marched his company as close to us as he could. In fact, he got so close that the soccer ball got tangled up in the feet of his men. You never saw such confusion. The Japs were stumbling and falling over each other. Then to make things worse, this officer gave the command: to the rear march. Honestly, it was just like a Bob Hope comedy, only funnier.

"You know how the Jap carries his helmet on his back. Well, when these guys started bumping into each other their helmets fell off, and every time one tried to pick up his helmet he would pick up the soccer ball instead. Finally the officer saw he was losing more face than we were, so he marched his men off the field. We were afraid of how the Japs might take that embarrassment, so we quit playing. When we stopped the Americans were leading. It was the first time we had beaten the British. But they kept insisting we had to bring in Jap ringers to do it.

"That incident might sound funny to you, but actually it was serious business. If we had laughed, as most of us wanted to, they would have punished us severely. The Jap humiliates easily.

"They were always doing things like that if they thought we were enjoying ourselves too much. Sometimes they would come out to a softball game and pick four or five men from each team and cart them off somewhere to dig ditches until the game was over."

Gunnison continued:

"Sports were practically our only form of entertainment at Santo Tomas. Everybody from the little children to the women played some sort of game. We even built special fields for them. We held our own Golden Gloves boxing tournament and one for the children, too. The Japs let us organize softball leagues, and we had 30 teams playing. Each community in the camp had its own team. Some of the names were funny, like East Shanty Town, Frog Bottom, Room 13 (that room had about 30 fellows crammed into it), the Manila Polo Club and the Pan-American Airways. They were divided into the American and National League and, of course, we had our own World Series. As I remember it, the Pan-Americans won the series.

"Speaking of the World Series, we got full reports on the 1942 series through our underground system in Manila. The people on the outside would pick up the game on the short wave and slip us the batteries and inning-by-inning scores through the fence. Somebody put up a blackboard behind the lost-and-found department and kept it up to date. The Japs never did catch on. They thought it was the score of one of the games we were playing.

"As far as I know we played the Japanese in the first softball game between enemy teams in this war. The captain of the guard at the Shanghai camp was nuts about softball, and he watched us play every time he had the opportunity. One day he came over to me and said: 'Hey, *Gun San,* someday we play softball?'

"We stalled and tried to prevent the game, because we knew so many things could go wrong. But he kept insisting, so the game was scheduled. Everybody turned out including all the big shots from the Embassy and the Army.

"Before the game started we noticed that the Jap pitcher was warming up with an overhand delivery. Since I was one of the prison committeemen, the fellows said it was my duty to go over and tell him this was a softball game not baseball. I got the interpreter and we both tried to show the pitcher how to throw the ball with an underhand motion. He tried it once or twice and then said in Japanese: 'The hell with it.'

"As it turned out it didn't make any difference whether this Jap threw overhanded or not. We walloped the daylights out of him and scored 27 runs in the first inning. After the inning was over I got the team together and told them we had better throw the game and let the Japs save face.

"Well, it got so funny that everybody on the side lines, except the Japs of course, nearly choked while trying to keep from laughing. We dropped balls, muffed easy grounders and stumbled all over ourselves. But they still couldn't make it an even ball game. We even tried applauding every time one of them hit the ball or scored a run. We only applauded twice, though, because after the seventh inning the score was 28 to 2.

"Then the captain of the guard called time. He came over to me and said: 'Hey, *Gun San*, I think more better we do not keep score. I think more better we play for sportsmanship.' That saved face for everybody including the umpire who was a Dutchman. This Dutchman was sweating plenty. He knew if he called a close one wrong, the Japs would ask his name, number and nationality, and when they discovered he was Dutch they would give him hell. The Japs really hate the Dutch.

"That softball game was practically the only contact in sports we had with the Japanese except for a wrestling match. We had a big fellow with us, a guy named Chris Bell, who was 6 feet 2 and the rocky sort. He used to be a lumberman in Shanghai. The Jap guards were having a wrestling tournament at the guardhouse and they wanted Bell to come down and wrestle one of those huge *sumo* men. These *sumos* weigh about 300 pounds and are very agile. We tried to duck the challenge, but it was no use. They insisted. Anyway, Bell said he would like to take them on. We went to the guardhouse with him fully prepared to bring away the little pieces. But darned if they could pin him. He threw the *sumos* all over the mat. In fact, it became so one-sided that Bell had to make it look good and let them save face.

"After that the Japs always treated Bell with respect. Every time they saw him they would pat him on the back and say: 'Bell, you plenty big man.'"

NUDGE IN REAR CAME TOO SOON, SO HE BOMBED WRONG TARGET IN CHINA By Sgt. MARION HARGROVE

SOMEWHERE IN CHINA—This story has been held back for a while because the fellow was mighty sensitive about it, and he happens to be a tech sergeant, 6 feet 2 and weighing 200 pounds. He's cooled off a little, so now it can be told.

The tech sergeant is Karl May of Yakima, Wash., an aerial engineer and gunner in one of the local Mitchell B-25 bombers. The tale goes back to the time when he was still a buck private, working as an armorer in his squadron and bucking like hell for a job on a combat crew.

They finally let him go on a few missions to try him out. He got along fine until his third trip. That was the raid on the big Jap base at Hankow, former Chinese capital, on the Yangtze.

There were two minor defects that day in the bomber to which May was assigned: there were no racks in the ship for fragmentation bombs and the interphones were temporarily out of commission.

Well, they were working the thing out all right without fragracks or interphones. They had Pvt. May squatting by the photo hole with a stack of frag bombs and the understanding that when the turret gunner nudged him in the behind he was to cut loose with all he had.

It happened that the bomber had a passenger that day—maybe an observer from Washington, maybe a newspaperman, maybe just a sightseer.

This worthy person grew unaccustomedly chilly, saw that the draft came from the open photo hole and decided to ask the private beside it to close it. The private—yep, it was May—had his back turned, so the passenger sought to attract his attention with a gentle nudge in the rear.

Pvt. May reacted like the eager beaver he was. He held one frag bomb over the hole and let it drop. Then he turned another loose into thin air. He was preparing to drop every bomb in the ship—until he was rudely and violently stopped. To May's dismay he learned 1) that the ship was nowhere near Hankow, 2) that he had been given no signal and 3) that he had just wasted a couple of hundred dollars' worth of U. S. high explosives.

The mission proceeded to Hankow, where May dropped the rest of his bombs through the photo hole, an armful at a time. But his heart was heavy at the thought of having goofed off.

When the plane returned to its base, there was an intelligence report from the Chinese Army waiting for it. According to this report, two bombs dropped on a Japanese barge on the Yangtze had scored direct hits, sinking the barge and drowning 160 Japanese soldiers.

T/Sgt. May never tells the story himself and he gets mad when he hears anyone else tell it. Only those who've seen the records will believe it.

FIFTY MISSIONS

By Pvt. JOSEPH DEVER

YANK Short-Story Contest Winner

I AM on my way to see my girl in Boston, and it has been a long time. It has been 26 months since I said good-bye to her in Boston.

Fifty missions always seemed incredible to me. How could anyone ever come back to the States after 50 missions? How could anyone step off a DC-4 in East Boston and quietly take a taxicab to the Hotel Statler after having been over Europe 50 times?

I'm doing it, though; I'm home in Boston. And I'm not being sentimental when I say that it's damned good to be here.

I'm just like them now; I mean the gunners I knew at armament school—the exotic GIs with 50 missions, with their wings, their rainbow service ribbons, their medals and the quiet, easy way they had about them. They'd say: "You'll get your chance, kid." "Yeah, it's kinda rough up there." I wanted some day to be wordless, humble and friendly with other eager kids the way the gunners were with me. How far away it all seemed then: 50 missions, the ribbons and the quiet, easy manner.

And now I'm riding through East Boston; I'm just like they were. I know a hell of a lot of things, but I would rather turn my face away and ask about your brother John who is in the ASTP. I know what flak is now. I know how a gunner can make a chapel out of the Sperry lower ball; I know that he can pray with rich eloquence. I know what the enemy looks like. There is also, of course, the blood fleck, the mother-mercy-calling and the blubbering, steel-given death of the nice guys who were hilariously drunk with you just a few nights before.

And now I'm looking at Boston. My taxi driver is a maniac at the wheel, as all taxi drivers are. He is doing 47 miles an hour through this big-city street. On a street in Berlin he would listen for the menacing wail of the air-raid sirens.

"This is it," the Boston taxi driver says.

I get out, I pay him, I walk into a beautiful, thick-rugged Boston hotel, and I get a room.

It is a room on the seventh floor. My stuff is all unpacked, and I stand by a window looking out. I stand looking out at downtown Boston, and I see only the white face of a nun.

My girl Jane is a nun now. We were going to be married, but something struck her, some kind of spiritual ack-ack, I guess. And now she's gone off and become a nun.

She's here in Boston now, in some kind of a cloister, and I'm on my way to see her. I figured the 50 missions wouldn't let me see her again, I was almost sure of it, but here I am in Boston looking out a window.

The Copley Plaza is over that way. And on the other side of it, about four stories high and facing Copley Square and the Boston Public Library, there is a little marble balcony. The night of my college senior prom I threw highball glasses into the square. I liked to hear the tinkling clatter of the glass against the cobbles, and I wanted to do it again and again.

"Jay, come inside," was all Jane had said.

I went inside; I loved her greatly, more than even the sound of breaking glass, and I always did what she said.

And over there to the right is Beacon Hill. We liked that place very much. When I was a feather merchant, Jane and I used to walk all over it in the blackout. We knew all the places—the quaint, cobbled, snaky alleys, the huddled coffee nooks, the little barny theaters where you could see Philip Barry's plays for 20 cents, the H. M. Pulham doorways with the white marble steps and the shiny brass door plates. We used to sit in those doorways at midnight, on our way home; I used to kiss her there a lot. We'd pretend we were locked out, and sometimes we'd yell loudly for Nana or Jeeves. If anybody came to the door we'd jump to our feet and run like scared rabbits all the way down the hill to the Charles Street elevated station.

And there, across the Charles River, is Cambridge. That's where I used to live; that's where Jane lived. Our playground's there, too.

In the summertime Jane and I worked on the playground. She was my boss, and Christ, did we have a time. There was a big brick schoolhouse called the Peary. There was a playground in back of it, a sun-baked macadam rectangle, and there were kids from the stinking Cambridge tenements.

She wouldn't say a thing when I'd come in, maybe an hour and a half late. Sometimes she'd pretend she was peeved and go on with her jigsaw project. She'd sit there in the sun wearing a colossal straw bonnet, and she'd prattle merrily but exclusively to the little girls who were gathered busily about her feet.

I'd keep teasing her. I'd hit a softball out to my outfielders from a place right near her; I'd make the ball roll right over to her sometimes and in retrieving it I'd get myself all tangled up in her and the jigsaw plywood animals she and the girls were making. After a while she would burst out laughing and come after me with a bat, a shrill chorus of girl voices urging her on.

It was on the playground that I really became infected with the planes. The P-38s would go over at about 8,000, and I'd stand down there by shortstop and crane my neck until the planes were little silver winks way out to the west.

I never knew about Jane leaving me then, but I did know that someday I was going to be up there in a plane.

About 4:30 in the afternoon we'd quit for the day and lock up. That was when Jane and I played our own little game. I'd go in the front door of the school and she'd go in the back. We'd both slam the doors and run quickly towards each other.

I'd take her in my arms, then I'd kiss her hair, her eyes, her lips and the very tip of her nose. I'd hold her close in my arms and we'd talk about being married and having a place of our own; we'd wonder what our children would look like and if they'd be scampering off to a playground like the Peary every day.

Then the kids would start banging on the door and hollering for us to come out. We'd kiss a few times more and walk innocently out to them. They used to escort us part of the way home, and they never said a thing about the kissing, even though they knew, as all kids know.

That was the way it was. It was a good way to be living and loving. Now it is all changed.

Well, anyway, I am going out to the convent to see her. It is a place called Mission Hill, which is in Roxbury. Roxbury's a part of Boston and only a short ride from the hotel.

A girl who used to double-date with Jane and me wrote to me when I was in England. She said she'd seen Jane and that Jane told her to tell me that if I ever got back to the States I was to be sure and make a visit to the convent. I wrote to the girl and said I would.

I am in a taxi again, riding very fast along Huntington Avenue. The Museum of Fine Arts is on the right. I used to look at the statues of naked women in there when I was a kid.

The taxi climbs up Mission Hill, and the convent is at the top. It is red brick with a red-brick wall around it. It is low and quadrangular, and there are those cylindrical clay shingles all over its roof and on the top of the brick wall.

I ring the front-door bell. You only ring once in a convent because that ring, however slight, is amplified by the silence and the distance that fills the inside of a cloister until the ring becomes something like an echoing clap of thunder.

A little nun lets me in. I ask for Jane. Jane's nun name is Sister Felicitas. I pretend I don't notice, but I see the little nun who let me in eat up the gunner's wings and the service ribbons. I go into the parlor and wait. There is always a large wall clock in this kind of parlor, and it always says: "Wait, wait, wait." It says this over and over again. You hear a door softly open and softly close way off in a cool interminable distance. You know then someone is coming.

Jane comes into the parlor.

She is just as I pictured she'd be. Her face is white, her eyes are sparkling blue pools of goodness and mischief, the backs of her hands have little red and creamy blotches as though she does a lot of dishes and scrubs a lot of floors.

She is all swaddled up as I was afraid she'd be, wound in endless and oppressive reams of black cloth; she wears a tremendous white starched collar and a black veil over her head. But she is my Jane all right, she is my Jane.

She stands in the middle of the room and looks right at me for about a minute.

"Hello, Jane," I say.

She doesn't say a thing. She walks over to me and takes hold of both my hands; she comes up as close to me as a nun ever can and squeezes both my hands until they sting.

She stays close to me that way for what seems a long time; she eases the pressure on my hands and looks strongly at me so I can see that everything is there just as it had always been: all the love and the light and the music are there for me in just the way they used to be, and even though these things are God's now, I can somehow see and know they are still mine, too.

"Oh, Jay," she says, and her eyes are a little wet, "I'm so very, very glad to see you. Let me look at you."

She steps away from me, and I notice that her step, although as light and graceful as ever, is now a swish instead of the swirl that it had once been. A girl has become a nun; an elfin skirt has become a ponderous petticoat.

"My, what a handsome soldier you are! You know, I've never seen you in your uniform before.

And the wings, and the ribbons. Jay, you're really a man now, aren't you!"

"Am I, Jane?" I gulp, fumbling desperately for words. "Wasn't I one before?" I finally ask.

"Of course you were," she says, "but you were a boy's man then, Jay. You're a man's man now. The kind I always knew you'd be. But come, let's sit down."

We sit down in separate, straight-backed wooden chairs. The chairs are cold, unyielding symbols of poverty, chastity and obedience. We sit in them a while and, although she does not come right out and say it, I think she wants me to talk.

But I don't want to talk. I want to be with her, to be near her, to hear her voice and watch her eyes. I want to sit with Sister Felicitas and think about my Jane.

She kind of guesses that I don't want to talk.

She says she likes it here; she has prayed for me night and day; she is happy teaching fourth grade to the little Roxbury urchins; she is proud of me and tells the little kids in her class stories about me all the time; she has read everything in the Cambridge *Clarion* which someone sent her, and she doesn't care if I never utter so much as a syllable about airplanes.

I have not changed greatly, she says; the wonder and the impudence are still in my face; my eyes have a distance in them that wasn't there before; I'm not as loquacious but—"Glory," she says, "things have happened!"

I have had enough of looking at her. I begin to ache for her like when I was across. I begin to want her in my arms, and I know that it is time for me to go.

I say I have to be going. We stand up. She looks at me a while and takes both my hands; she makes them sting again.

"What happens now, Jay?" she asks.

"They're sending me out to Denver as an armament instructor. I don't want to go, but you just go, that's all.

"Well, I guess this is good-bye, Jane," I stammer. "I hope you'll be very happy, kid." She hasn't heard me call her "kid" for a long time.

I turn to go.

"Wait," she says quickly. "Come in the chapel with me, Jay, and we'll say a prayer together. It's down here."

We walk down the hall toward the chapel.

"You can leave me inside," she whispers when we are about to enter the chapel. "You can go out the front door of the chapel and into the street."

She hesitates a little, then she says quietly: "I love you, Jay; I'll always love you and I'll pray for you constantly, all the days of my life."

She turns away swiftly and moves into a pew about three yards from me. She begins to pray.

I kneel down and I pray, too. I tell God I am sorry for not wanting to come back from 50 missions; I thank Him for bringing me back even though I had not wanted to come. I say three Hail Marys. I take a long look at Jane. I genuflect and walk out of the chapel and into the street.

A STRANGER AND ALONE

By Pfc. John Behm

We are the insolent invaders with many uniforms
Who have come to England from far away
Bringing gifts of chewing gum and Chesterfields.

We are the harsh strangers—the vain, hearty foreigners,
The aliens thoughtlessly trampling your calm vineyards.

The slim colored boys send our heavy trucks
Screaming along your narrow roads.
The big tanks rip up the pavings
Of your ancient towns.
The jeeps and weapons carriers
Do fifty-five around your Z-shaped curves.
The half-tracks hold your traffic up for hours.

The countryside rings
With the blare and whirl of our machines.

We are loud and fast and wild and lusty.
We are drunken, proud, hard and potent.
We could drink your island dry if you would let us.
We are the terrible, mischievous warriors
From far away.

We are, I'm afraid,
Just a trifle bestial
For your highly tempered tastes.

But, England,
Understand us!
Though we sneer and boast in the pubs,
Consuming your beer and belittling your glory,
We tremble and are afraid in the streets
Before the blind audience of closed doors.
We are young men whose roots
Have been left far behind
In strange places called Brooklyn and Sacramento and
    Tucson and Thief River Falls and Council Bluffs and
    Cincinnati and Coon Hollow.
We have been torn from the soil where we grew
And flung like exiles across an ocean
To a land we never dreamed of.

We are bewildered and weary,
Lonely to the point of madness,
And if we shout and curse
Through our quiet dreams,
Forgive us.

We are merely looking for a way to go home.

THE BIRTH OF A MISSION

BY SGT. WALTER PETERS

A HEAVY BOMBER STATION, BRITAIN—Two second lieutenants, recent arrivals from the States, walked to the Officers' Club bar and ordered whiskies.

"Make it a double," said one of them.

"Sorry, sir, no whisky is sold during alerts," said the bartender, Cpl. James Mohafdahl of Dayton, Ohio.

"Oh, I see," the other lieutenant mused. "When'd the alert come through?"

"About 15 minutes ago, sir. Right, Dan?" The corporal turned to the other bartender, Pvt. Daniel Costanzo, an ex-cowboy and saloon owner from San Antonio, Tex.

"Yeah, about that long," Costanzo agreed.

The lieutenants smiled. "Well, we may as well get some sleep then," one said. They walked out.

"It's funny," the corporal said, "but I can practically always tell when there's going to be an alert and, better yet, whether the raid'll go through. It's just instinct. That's all. Just instinct. Ask Tiny. He'll tell you."

Tiny was a 6-foot, 260-pound former foundry worker, Pvt. Frederick Tard of Everett, Wash. He was also assigned to the club staff, but that night he was on pass.

"They're a swell lot of boys here," the corporal said. "There's no rank pulling. I've seen lots of them come in fresh from the States, and I've seen lots of them go on their first mission and never come back. There used to be one fellow, a lieutenant. He always used to come in and order a drink and never talk to anybody but me. He'd rather talk to me than to a lot of majors around. He went down on a raid. He always said: 'Corporal, you take care of me. And believe me, I always did."

Another lieutenant walked in and asked for a whisky. Costanzo explained again that no hard liquor was sold during alerts. Beer was okay, though. The lieutenant bought a beer.

The corporal took up where he'd left off. "I don't know whether the lieutenant is a prisoner of war or not. But I'd sure like to meet him again. He was a nice guy. One thing, all these fellows know where to come when they want something. They see me, Jimmy. If it can be gotten, I get it."

A sign on the wall behind the bar read: "MEMBERS OF THE WORLD'S BEST AIR FORCE ARE SERVED AT THIS BAR."

Costanzo looked our way, paused for a moment and said: "We don't sell whisky the night before a raid."

OFFICERS AND THE FO

Beyond a one-lane winding road from the Officers' Club, deep inside a single-story building, was the intelligence room. Large maps of the fighting fronts adorned the walls, and colored markings indicated important enemy targets and other information about them.

Except for the maps, the intelligence room might have passed for a board of directors' office. In the center was a long, well-polished table, surrounded by eight comfortable leather chairs. In the corner was a radio playing soft, slow music transmitted by a British Broadcasting Corporation station. An S-2 first lieutenant relaxed in one of the chairs, his legs slung over its arm. A staff sergeant walked in and out of the room incessantly, always looking very serious, always carrying what appeared to be important documents.

The sergeant walked out of the room, then returned. "The FO is in, sir," he said.

"Okay," replied the lieutenant, "call the colonel."

Three other members of the S-2 staff walked in—Maj. F. J. Donohue, chief of the group's intelligence section, a former Washington (D. C.) lawyer; Capt. Wayne Fitzgerald of Kalamazoo, Mich., the group bombardier, and Capt. Ellis B. Scripture of Greensburg, Ind., the group navigator.

The three men sat down and watched as the sergeant tracked a narrow red tape from the spot on the map that represented the base in Britain to the enemy target that was to be bombed the next morning. The tape followed the exact course as directed by the field order.

Presently a tall, middle-aged man walked in. He was a good-looking guy with a friendly smile. This was Col. John Gerhardt of Chicago, commander of the group. With him was Lt. Col. David T. McKnight of New York, the air executive officer of the group. McKnight was short and had a personality that makes friends quickly.

Each colonel was eating a bar of candy and they offered a bite to everyone in the room. Col. Gerhardt stood before the map and studied it. Then he asked for a copy of the field order. A cat strolled by lazily. Lt. Col. McKnight stroked her back until she lifted her tail and purred. When the field order was brought in, the officers began to study it.

SUPERSTITION AND FATE

The base theater, which also houses the chaplain's office and serves as a church on Sundays, was filled to capacity that night, as it usually is. The sergeant gunners and officers apparently liked the film, because they laughed a lot and occasionally somebody whistled. The picture was "Duke of West Point," featuring Louis Hayward and Joan Fontaine.

Inside the Aero Club, run by the Red Cross, enlisted men were reading home-town newspapers, playing billiards or standing in line by a long counter for an evening snack. A round-faced sergeant with a neat black mustache, Vincent Barbella of Brooklyn, N. Y., was drinking a Coca-Cola and doing a lot of talking. With him was T/Sgt. Harry D. Cooper, a radio gunner from Dayton, Ohio, and T/Sgt. Robert E. Bellora, a top turret gunner from Ellwood City, Pa.

"Tomorrow's my 12-B," Barbella said, then laughed. "To hell with it. I won't call it 12-B. I'm not superstitious. I'll call it straight number 13. I certainly hope we go tomorrow, though," Barbella said. "That will make it about the sixth time I've been trying to make my thirteenth."

Cooper smiled. "You'll make it tomorrow. I'll bet anything on that. The night is clear and the odds are that it'll stay that way until morning."

"It's not the raids that bother me," Barbella said. "It's these damned abortions. People don't realize how much there is to making a raid. They figure all you do is jump in a Fort and up you go. They don't figure that weather out here can change within a half-hour, or that after a guy is up there for a couple of hours, something can go shebang with an engine or the oxygen system, and then you have to turn back."

At an adjoining table a sergeant was reading a newspaper. Barbella turned and read the headlines. "Berlin," he said. "Boy, is the RAF giving them the works now. Boy, would I like to go there. It'd be nice to say I'd been over Berlin."

Bellora spoke up. "For all you know, you may get the chance. You never can tell. That's where they may send us tomorrow, but I doubt it. Tomorrow will make me 21 missions. Hell, it doesn't matter where you go. If it's going to get you, it'll get you over Bremen or over Emden or over Kiel or anywhere. It's all up to fate, I think. But I'm not taking any chances. I think my two .50s have a helluva lot to do with this fate racket."

Enlisted men from the theater filed into the Aero Club when the movie was over. A short, frail sergeant stopped and whispered something in Bar-

bella's ear. Apparently it was some sort of a private joke. Barbella laughed so enthusiastically that he had to stand up.

"What the hell's eating you, man?" Cooper asked in a friendly tone.

"Oh, nothing. Nothing," Barbella replied. "But I'm going to eat somebody's stuff out if we don't go out tomorrow." He laughed again.

DISAPPOINTMENT AND HUNGER

Tall, bespectacled 1st Lt. David B. Henderson, in charge of the base photographic section, walked into the laboratory looking very sad.

"He wouldn't let me go. Said maybe it'd be okay next mission," Henderson said. He had just returned from the S-2 room where he'd asked Maj. Donohue if he could go on the next morning's mission. In civilian life Henderson worked for the Ashland Refining Company in Ashland, Ky. His job on the base was an important one, but you got the impression that he'd be happier as a sergeant gunner.

There was an aroma of fried onions in the laboratory. It came from a room where a couple of staff sergeants were packing film into the combat cameras.

Sgt. David B. Wells of Trona, Calif., walked into the room with a loaf of bread.

"No, sir. It's nothing like this back in the States. If we're hungry, we just scrounge some grub and prepare it right in here. Wish I had a nice piece of steak to go with those onions. A guy gets hungry at this time of night. I always get hungry before missions."

"You ain't kidding, bub," said T/Sgt. Berton Briley of Wilson, Okla. Briley was a musician in civilian life. Now he is a combat photographer.

Lt. Henderson walked into the room and poured some coffee into a large tin cup. "There's nothing like a good hot cup of coffee at night. Too bad I can't go out in the morning."

COMBAT AND COMRADESHIP

There was no electric power that night in one of the squadron areas, so a group of lieutenants sat around inside their flat-roofed quarters and chatted by candlelight.

Four of them—Lt. Robert Sheets of Tacoma, Wash.; Lt. Jack Watson of Indianapolis, Ind.; Lt. Elmer W. Yong of Roachdale, Ind., and Lt. Joseph C. Wheeler of Fresno, Calif.—had joined the squadron only that week. They had been in the Fortress that buzzed the Yankee Stadium in New York during a World Series game in September. Mayor La

Guardia raised an awful stink when that happened. The boys were hauled over the coals for it by their CO when they reported to their field in Maine.

"All of that looks funny now that we're going into actual combat," said one. "It's the first mission that counts. Once I get over the hump on that one I'll gain my bearings. I'm just itching to get that first one in."

A first lieutenant called Hapner, who kept talking about his home town, Hamilton, Ohio, stopped cleaning a carbine.

"I know just how you feel," Hapner said. "You change a lot after about the first five missions. I don't know how to put my finger on it, but you sort of become more human. You become more appreciative of the men you fight with and the men you live with. It's particularly bad when you lose some of the men on your crew, or if one guy finishes his ops ahead of you and then leaves the crew.

"My pilot just finished his ops and he's off combat now. He was a swell guy. He always said that as long as I was doing the navigating and he was holding the stick, we had nothing to worry about. That guy should have gotten the Congressional Medal if anyone ever should.

"Kit Carson went through more hell than anyone I know of, but he never complained. He was a very religious guy and talked about his mother an awful lot. He never talked about himself, though. Except for the way he talked, you'd never get it from him that he was from Texas.

"Kit lost his original crew. They went off without him once and never returned. He was really shook up by it. But would he complain?" Hapner turned as if expecting somebody to say something, then answered his own question. "No, Kit never complained."

"They assigned him as co-pilot on the *Brass Rail*. That's how we got on the same crew. The pilot at that time was Lt. John Johnson. Johnson was married and had a helluva pretty wife in East St. Louis, Ill. On a raid over Kiel, a 20-mm exploded against Johnson's side and killed him. The *Brass Rail* nose-dived about 4,000 feet and everybody in it thought sure they were goners. Ammo boxes and everything else were flying all over the plane. By some miracle, Kit was able to level the ship off. Except for Kit the whole crew would have been goners. He got the DFC for that. I really miss that guy."

The new lieutenants listened carefully. They had met Kit just before he left the squadron, but up to now they hadn't realized what he'd been through. One of the lieutenants said: "He certainly didn't toot his own horn, did he?"

"Well, neither will you after a while," Hapner said. "Combat does something to a man. You'll see."

Hapner began to undress. "Well, guess I'll turn in. It may be a long one tomorrow."

ARMAMENT AND THE MEN

It was 2230, and the weather was still holding up. A long single file of men, almost all of them with torches in their hands, walked out of a Nissen hut. They were the armament men. They talked, but in low tones. Most of the officers and gunners had turned in, and armament men respect sleeping men of the combat crews.

An armament man said: "Maybe we won't have to unload again for a change. It looks too good out tonight, even for English weather."

Two sergeants stopped playing blackjack for a minute and talked about the armament men. Almost everybody else in the hut was in his bunk. The two sergeants were sitting on the lower section of a double bunk. A spotlight hung from the spring of the upper bunk, throwing just enough light on the cards.

"I suppose we ought to turn in," said one. "It may be a tough one tomorrow. When it comes right down to it, these armament guys really have the toughest racket. It must be hell on them to load up and then have to go out and unload when a mission is scrubbed. I hope it isn't scrubbed tomorrow."

From the corner of the room came a loud protesting voice. It was a Southern voice. "Damn that fire. Who the hell wants a fire on at night? It only goes out before you get up, and then we're cold as hell."

"Aw, shut up, you rebel," another voice answered.

The Southern boy complained again. "Well, I don't want to be going on any missions with a cold. Somebody ought to throw water on the fire."

The sergeants who were playing cards stopped the game. One of them spoke up. "You're liable to blow the place up if you throw water into that stove now, boy."

"I don't give a damn," said the Southerner.

DOGS AND THE AAF

It was 0400 and all the combat men were sound asleep. An excited voice bellowed out of the PA system.

"Attention all combat crews! Attention all combat crews! Breakfast until 0445. Breakfast until 0445. Briefing at 0500. Briefing at 0500."

In the kitchen of the combat mess, two cooks were standing by a stove with pans in their hands. They were frying eggs for the men scheduled to fly that morning.

"I don't know why it is," the short cook said, "but about every dog in England seems to have found a home on this base."

"You'll find the same thing on all the bases," the other cook said. "Even the RAF has its share of dogs. Some of them have seen more combat than a lot of guys."

"You know, I was thinking," said the short one, "almost every new crew brings in a dog from the States. Now, if some smart apple of a German spy wanted to figure the Air Force strength in Britain, all he'd have to do is figure how many dogs there are on the bases and then multiply it by 10."

The other cook gave the short one a disgusted look.

"You're as crazy a guy as I've ever met. Who the hell's going to chase all over Britain counting dogs? Besides, you've got to figure how many of these dogs get in the family way as soon as they land here. Trouble with you is, you read too many detective stories."

The short cook grinned. "Aw, I was only thinking," he said and went on frying eggs.

No. 25 and Herky Jerky

Briefing was over. A half-ton truck was rolling along the runway. It was about 0600, but still very dark. The truck turned into a narrow road and stopped at a small shed. Then about six men jumped out and went inside.

About 25 sergeants were cleaning caliber .50s on long benches. Above them were signs reading:

WITHOUT ARMAMENT THERE IS NO NEED
FOR AN AIR FORCE

Lord Trenchard, Marshal of the RAF

Sgt. Barbella was cleaning his guns alongside the top turret gunner on his crew, Dean Hall, a tall, slim boy from New Jersey. Hall and three others from the crew of the *Herky Jerky* were making their 25th mission that morning.

The sergeants carefully enclosed their guns in burlap bags and headed for the hardstand.

A Baby and a Mission

It was five minutes before stations. Capt. Rodney E. Snow Jr. of High Point, N. C., walked over by the tail of the plane and stood there for a moment. It was a ritual with him, just as it is with a lot of other men who are flying in this war.

Snow's bombardier, Lt. George Lindley of Seattle, Wash., was smoking a cigarette and telling the left waist gunner about his baby son. The baby was born on Oct. 16 and Lindley was sweating out a picture that was supposed to be on the way over. The mission didn't seem to bother him, but the absence of the baby's picture did.

In the ground crew's tent, a little off the hardstand, two other men from the *Herky Jerky* were debating whether they'd even get off the ground that morning.

"No. 7 was always my lucky number, and I think this is the seventh time we're trying for this mission. So I guess we'll make it," said the co-pilot. He was a big strapping fellow, Lt. John Merriman of Spokane, Wash. Everybody on the crew razzed him about his large belly and somebody kidded him about being pregnant.

"No, that's what I got for being a chow hound, I guess," Merriman answered, taking it seriously.

Snow called on all the men to get into the plane. Then No. 1 engine was started. No. 2 followed and 3 and 4 began to roar next. The plane taxied up to the edge of the runway and in a few minutes it was airborne. And that was the beginning of the mission.

"No Ma'am, it was neither Bizerte or Attu. It was an upper bunk at Fort Brookings, S. Dak."—*Cpl. F. J. Torbert.*

MESS HALL IN ALASKA

BY SGT. A. N. MALOFF

ALASKA—He stood out by the side of the runway and waited, as he always did. When the weather permitted, the planes would take off in the morning and come back in the afternoon. Or they would take off in the afternoon and come back in the evening. He would always stand by the side of the runway and wait for them to return. Sometimes he would stand a long time, and they would never come back.

He was the only one who came out to watch any more, and the others never understood it. "Joe Buza," they said, "he's nutty. He's plane-nutty." He used to tell them he had to know how many tables to set up in his mess hall, but they laughed at him. He didn't know himself exactly why he wanted to watch, but he was always there. Every day there was a flight he would walk over to Operations and ask when the men were coming back. If it was Kiska, it meant he had to prepare an early lunch; if it was Attu, he would have the KPs set up a few tables in the middle of the afternoon. Then he would walk out to the runway and watch.

He dug his face deeper into his mackinaw, trying to shield the tip of his nose with his collar. He moved around a little to keep from standing still and shoved his back into the wind. The sound of footsteps behind him made him turn around. It was one of the cameramen from the photographic unit at the hangar line.

"You sweating it out, too?"

"Yeah," Joe said. "Will they be coming in soon?"

The man nodded. "In a minute, I guess. There's just one. A fighter. We took a gun out of the nose and put a camera in. Something about one of the boys spotting some Jap ships."

They heard the engine before they saw the plane. It must have been hidden in the fog. Then it circled slowly, dropped its wheels, gently lowered itself onto the ground and taxied down the runway. It pulled up at the end of the field, turned around and moved back to the center again where the mechanics were waiting for it.

The pilot lifted himself out of the cockpit and jumped down. He turned to the cameraman and grinned in satisfaction. "This is it, boy. Just what the doctor ordered. Develop them right away and bring them over. The colonel will want them right away." The pilot started unstrapping his parachute. "Right away," he said again.

Joe walked back to the mess hall. He never used to worry about feeding the men, but it was different now. He didn't like to set up the tables with all the food and watch some of them stay that way— clean and untouched. Some days some of the planes didn't come back, which meant some of the men would never eat again. Those were the days he hated, and he always made the KPs elbow the floor and told the cooks to make hamburgers or a stew so the unused meat wouldn't go to waste.

He kicked open the door to the kitchen and entered. The cooks had already started to prepare supper and the KPs were standing around, smoking and waiting to see whether they could get a couple of hours off. He sat down on a box and picked up the menu for tomorrow. One of the men came over to him. "Sarge," he said, "we set up the mess hall for supper already. Is it okay for us to take off for a couple of hours?" Joe bent his head toward the dining room and looked it over. "Okay, Sherwood. Be back by 4. Don't make me send for you."

He half expected the telephone call that came in the evening. Lt. Johnson of the Operations Room. There was a big flight the next day, starting early. Could he have an early breakfast ready for about 30 or 35 men, early, say about 0430? "Sure, lieutenant, anything. Anything at all. Hot cakes and cereal and—— Yeah, okay, lieutenant. Anything I can do——"

Something was up, something pretty big. He could see that by the way the men ate their chow the next morning, concentrating on every bite they put in their mouths. Maybe it was what that fighter brought in yesterday; he didn't know. There was too much quiet in his mess hall, and the men passed the coffee too promptly. It bothered him. Then they got up and left. Joe liked it that the tables were dirty and the food bowls were mostly empty. That was the way it should be. No waste, and everyone in his place.

At Operations, after the rest of the squadron had eaten breakfast, they told him he could expect the planes back in time for dinner if everything went all right. You couldn't be sure because you never knew how much flak and fighter opposition the men would meet. But dinner looked like a safe bet, maybe even a little earlier.

The clerk at the desk smiled. "Buza, I can't figure you out," he said. "You're like an old maid half the time. Always afraid you'll be missing something. Why don't you relax?"

"It's not that," Joe answered. "It's the tables. I got to get them ready, don't I?"

By the time he reached the mess hall again, the men were just finishing the cleaning. There wasn't so much to do after breakfast—clean off the tables and sweep the floor. Someone would bring out the silverware and the cups, enough for each man; then they would wait until just before the men came to put out the food and coffee. Joe walked over to the pantry and pulled out a pack of paper napkins. He saved them for special occasions, like Christmas dinner or maybe a squadron party sometime, but today was special—more special than other days, because 14 of the big boys took off today, and that was more than usual. He put the napkins under the silverware and made sure the forks were at the left. He lit a cigarette and took a long pull. In another hour or so he would walk out to the field to watch them come in. Another hour at least.

The wail of a siren jerked him to his feet. It took a second before he recognized it; then he ran to the window. A field ambulance tore down the company street, skirted the corner on two wheels and raced for the runway. Everyone seemed to be running. Men streamed out of the hangars and pulled up sharply at the edge of the flying field. A jeep shot out of the headquarters enclosure and dashed toward the fire house. The red light at the head of the control tower started blinking furiously, then

remained on. A plane sitting at the end of the field spun around and pulled itself out of the way.

Joe shoved through the crowd. Then he saw it, limping in out of the fog. He saw it circle slowly and lose altitude. The wings leaned over to one side. The wheels edged into position and the plane started to level off. The engine whined in an unsteady cry and the body quivered with the effort. Painfully the nose tilted downward and as painfully the plane slipped onto the runway, bounced nervously into the air for a few feet, dropped onto the ground and rolled to a stop. It just lay there.

Joe pushed forward with the others. They watched the crew come out of the plane, bunched together as if for protection. The captain punched a finger through the black hole where a .50-caliber had struck. His face was blank and half-believing, tired beyond weariness. The crew stood around him, waiting for him to do something. Then the words poured out as if he couldn't stop them, as if he could tell his story only once and then forget it.

"They caught us. They were waiting for us and they caught us. We were like rats, caught, and we didn't know what hit us. In the fog and in the clouds, that's where they were. Forty, 50, something like that, and they hit us with everything. We didn't have a chance. They bombed us from above and then they passed over us with their machine guns. It happened quick, like I'm telling it. You could see how our men exploded with the ships. Only some exploded. Some burned. We got away. I don't know how. They hit us with everything they had."

He stopped and pulled his lips tight over his teeth. The crowd made room for him, and he passed through it. His crew followed after him, still not talking.

Joe Buza stayed there after everyone had gone. One out of 14! No one was coming back now, but he stayed there and waited. He pecked at the ground with the toe of his shoe. He didn't want to go back just yet, because the others would be eating and he didn't want to see them. Maybe another would return. He propped a cigarette between his lips before he remembered he couldn't smoke there. Overhead the sky was empty and the fog was thick.

But for the KPs clearing away the plates, the dining room was empty. Everyone had eaten. Tables were covered with patches of bread and half-used platters of butter. On the floor was a little pool of water where someone had spilled a cup. He pushed the water with his foot so it would dry quickly.

In the back were the unused tables where the combat crews were supposed to eat. They would have to be cleaned off now, just like the others. Just as if the men had eaten there, even though they hadn't. The floor was clean of crumbs and all the bread was still neatly piled. Joe toppled a pile so it wouldn't look so neat. Tomorrow the men would have hamburgers for dinner because he couldn't waste the meat. He picked up the meat dish.

A KP had been standing behind him. "Sarge," he said, "I think this butter ought to be put away. It's been standing pretty long." Joe looked at him for a minute before he understood. There was a lost mission in his voice. "Soldier, it's not your job to think here," he said. "It's your job to scrub this floor till it's clean enough to kiss." He moved into the kitchen and stopped suddenly. Muttering to himself, he turned, walked to the garbage can and dumped the meat.

"Quick! A tourniquet!"—Pvt. Thomas Flannery.

"Oh, some slip-up somewhere. I imagine we'll be back on regular rations in a day or two."
—Sgt. Douglas Borgstedt.

"Now, before we go any further, is there anyone who doesn't understand what we're doing?"—Pfc. Joseph Kramer.

"Just carry the messages we give you. Never mind the peace propaganda."—Cpl. Louis Jamme.

HOUSES OF ITALY

By Sgt. NEWTON H. FULBRIGHT

WITH THE FIFTH ARMY IN ITALY—The house on the east bank of the Rapido River was a very fine house for a CP. Like all Italian houses, it was built entirely of stone; there was no wood in its construction at all. It was two-storied, and there were many rooms. A room on the ground floor of a strong two-story house, on the side that is as far from Jerry as you can get, always makes a fine company or battalion CP.

There were barrels of *vino* in this house. The men drank the *vino* and slept in the beds and cooked in the large, smoky, messy fireplace, and lived as well as can be expected on the Italian front.

Looking back over the whole Italian campaign, especially the "40 days and 40 nights" on the Rapido River and the high cold hills above Cassino and the celebrated Abbey, I feel that the big, dingy and terribly dirty old houses of Italy have had an epic meaning in the lives of us all.

After I was captured by the Germans at Altavilla, I learned from them how to appreciate a good house. And there is something about a house—aside from its massive stone walls, tile roof and thick braced concrete floors above your head—that is spiritual, emotionally embracing and warm.

Sitting on a bed roll with two or three massive *vino* barrels in an opposite corner, I have enjoyed with our men a particular joviality and comradeship, a sort of high security, while German shells thundered a few short yards away.

"The Tedeschi is a madman," someone may say. "Listen at that—like a mad ol' man coming in the house an' kicking the dogs off the porch an' smashing cooking pots and glass bottles all over the kitchen."

We made a costly attempt to cross the Rapido on Jan. 21. After that we stayed in our houses, and the Jerry stayed in his on the smoothly sloping west side of the river. Occasionally someone at an OP would call down to us in Company M and report that the Jerry had been spotted in a house across the river. Then our mortars out in the yard would get busy. Sgt. Quentin D. Barrington of Hubbard, Tex., or Sgt. Hubert (Cowboy Slim) Simons of Rosenthaul, Tex., would drop a dozen or two HE Heavies through the roof, and the OP would report the Jerry running away and diving into dugouts.

That would make the Jerry sling a few back at us. We would receive a barrage of Screaming

Mimis, or a tank would open up across the river and throw a few fast ones at one of our houses.

"I don't like this," Cpl. Harlan Copeland of Waco, Tex., a member of Cowboy Slim's mortar section, would protest. "Tear down one of the Tedeschi houses and he comes right back and wants to tear one of yours down! Somebody's gonna get hurt if this keeps up."

I remember, in particular, the excitement we had one afternoon.

I had just returned from our 1st Battalion area, up the river toward Cassino, and was standing in the road near our house, looking at a pile of mortar ammunition. The ammunition had come up during the night. Someone who didn't know what he was doing had piled it against a strawstack. A shell could set the strawstack on fire and blow up the whole dump.

I had turned away and taken a few steps when a heavy German shell—the "north of Rome" kind—crashed with a great shattering of earth and flame a few yards in front of me in the yard of the house where Cowboy Slim had his mortars. Instinctively I ducked and turned back toward the strawstack, but at that moment another shell struck it. I jumped up; there were some slit trenches in the field to the left, but just then a shell landed there, too.

"To hell with it!" I yelled, running as fast as I could. I headed for the house, about 70 yards away, where our company CP was located. As I crossed the road a shell crashed into the roof of a shed attached to Cowboy Slim's house. Something as big as a stove cap sailed by my head.

Inside the CP 1st Lt. Robert Hand, company executive officer from Seattle, Wash., stood with a wad of chicken feathers in his hand. Everyone laughed as I came dashing in.

"Barrington and I were preparing supper," said the lieutenant, holding up the chicken feathers, "when they caught us outside."

I looked back, and the strawstack was blazing like a bonfire at a college football rally.

It took a few minutes before the first shell in the mortar ammunition dump went off. Shells burst sporadically after that, sending blazing brands and sparks flying through the air. When the big explosion came about 30 minutes later, it flattened me against the wall.

I stood up, spitting dirt and dust. The others

were looking at me anxiously out of blinking, dust-rimmed eyes. I went out in the yard and looked up at the roof of the house. Nothing but a railway gun dropping one in the upper story could have made such a noise. But the house seemed to be as sound as ever. A charred brand, still smoking, was driven into the wall. A shelter half a few feet away, covering a small pile of ammunition, was on fire.

One of the men ran up and yanked the shelter half off the ammunition. I looked toward the road where the blazing strawstack had been. In its place I saw a crater wide enough to hold a heavy truck. A shed that had stood near the stack was now only a pile of scattered stones.

Telephones began ringing, battalion from regiment, regiment from division. What had happened?

We made a check and reported back: 400 rounds of HE Heavies blown up and one man with a tooth knocked out.

Cpl. Copeland was the casualty. As he dove for safety through a hole in the side of the house, he made the mistake of turning to look back. The next man crashed through, struck Copeland in the mouth with his helmet, and out went the tooth.

An hour later an old grandmother, two other women, two little girls and two little boys came up the road to fill their bottles from the *vino* barrels. The grandmother, whom we called "Mama," saw the chicken feathers first thing and made a dive for the CP.

"Tedeschi!" I shouted. "Tedeschi—boom-boom!"

"Tedeschi, hell!" the old woman shouted back, shaking her head and waving her arms. Her meaning was unmistakable. "The damn Americanos! Americanos!" We rocked with laughter.

And I shall always remember another house, the one we had high up on Mount Cairo with a deep, narrow canyon separating us from the Germans in their houses a few yards higher up the steep, terraced hillside.

This was a three-story house, constructed entirely from flinty mountain stone; the walls were nearly three feet thick, and the floors above were of heavy concrete, supported by iron beams. The forward company CP was located in a tight little room on the ground floor, with a fireplace and one high, narrow window.

It looked out over an abrupt cliff; the tiny blasted roofs of the village of Cairo lay far below, and beyond this, smoky from shells and the belching muzzles of many British and American heavy guns, was the picturelike valley of the Rapido. The yard was encircled by a thick stone wall, waist high. There was a well of clear, clean water at one corner of the house. There were many rooms inside, safe rooms, and at the edge of the yard was another strawstack where the men could get clean straw for their beds.

I had found this place one morning after we had moved into the area in the night to relieve an American battalion that had been holding here for some time. Company K, with possibly 25 men in

As he dove through a hole in the side of the house, he made the mistake of turning to look back.
Cpl. Jack Ruge.

three houses across the canyon, was trying to hold terrain formerly defended by a complete battalion. The nine machine gunners of our 1st Platoon were with them. I entered the house with the idea of bringing up our 2d Platoon to help them out. And this was such a strong house, sitting so ideally on a protruding hump of rock 50 yards above the canyon, that I immediately fell in love with it.

Inside I found an old Italian lying in bed—a virtual bag of bones in a tangle of dirty, ragged quilts and blankets.

In a thin voice he wailed: "I dunno—I'm no good for anything. I'm a sick old man."

"You speak English?" I asked.

"I work in Jersey, New York—in New Haven many years," he said.

Later in the afternoon—assisted by Pfc. Henry Hohensee, a Ganado (Tex.) boy known as the Dutchman and as Eighth Corps, who has a Purple Heart and three Oak Leaf Clusters to his credit—I succeeded in opening up and wiring in the forward CP. Cpl. R. L. Scott of Blue Ridge, Tex., returned to bring up the 10 men who then composed our 2d Platoon.

That night the Dutchman built a roaring fire in the fireplace, and we hung a blanket over the window. The men gathered around and had a roaring bull session until midnight. Two men stood guard in the upper story; the machine guns were trained on the Jerry across the draw.

Early in the evening Cpl. Scott helped the Dutchman brew up a canteen cup of bouillon for the old man in the next room. "They say it's good, else they wouldn't put it in the K rations," said the Dutchman.

The following day was quiet. The Jerry threw rounds intermittently in the draw where the battalion before us had lost 60 men. But he would never get any of us that way—we had learned long ago to keep out of draws.

In the afternoon we heard that the battalion had been suddenly ordered to withdraw to the valley again. The order, as finally acted on by Company K, called for us to withdraw from the houses immediately after dark. We were to proceed by way of a donkey trail that intersected the Terelle road several hundred feet down the almost-vertical face of the mountain.

Company K began the withdrawal shortly after dark, but as the men filed up the draw toward our house, the Germans opened a phony attack against the French, on the ridge above Terelle, over against the right horizon.

The withdrawal was held up at our house; after

we left there would be no one in this sector at all. But a phony attack is nothing but sound and fury, with little or no displacement of troops; as the Jerry on the hillside above remained inactive, Company K continued its withdrawal by way of the trail.

Our 2d Platoon had been designated to withdraw with their weapons by way of the Terelle road. They had scarcely left the house to begin the climb up the terraced slope behind us when German shells began falling all over the place. We ducked inside as three crashed in the yard. Shell fragments leaping across the yawning canyon struck fire from the rocks like a whole battalion of attacking Jerries. The Dutchman and I were alone in the house. Our telephones had been ripped out, so we were isolated. Some 30 minutes later, when the Jerry artillery shifted toward the Terelle road, we ducked out the back door and scurried down the donkey trail to safety.

As we caught up with Company K, which was taking a break where the trail entered the main road, someone drove up in a jeep with an order for them to return to their positions at once.

"We'll blow for a moment," I said to the Dutchman as the company prepared to move out. I threw my roll down and sat on it. Since one cold wet night in November, I've carried a standard roll of six blankets inside two shelter halves. It's plenty heavy but it's always convenient once we reach a stopping place.

We reached the top of the hill ahead of Company K, only to find that the counterattack had played out. A few artillery shells were still falling on the hill, but we were going down again as scheduled.

"Eighth Corps," I said, "to hell with the road!" We were too tired to follow the road anyway. We just slid vertically down the mountain. We knew that the road, winding about in the perambulating style of all mountain roads, would pick us up again. A rain had started to fall, and we sat at the side of the road until the battalion went by, then slid down to the next turn.

At one of the turns we met Cpl. Scott, sloshing along with a wet roll slung over his shoulder. Just as we were doing, he was thinking of the wonderfully warm house we had just left, the roaring fire singing in the fireplace and the gallon can of coffee simmering on the coals. "Dutch," he said, "the old man will die. Nobody to take care of him."

Toward morning the Dutchman and I crawled into the one good room of a blasted house on the slope above the village of Cairo and went to sleep.

MY OLD OUTFIT

By Sgt. MACK MORRISS

They started out together at Fort Jackson back in the States and fought their way across Europe until the faces were no longer familiar and you could count the old men on the fingers of one hand.

MAASTRICHT, HOLLAND—We walked at five-yard intervals on either side of the concrete highway and watched without much interest the Typhoons and P-47s that were strafing something off to the left.

The planes went into long dives and pulled out in tight circles to come back and strafe again. The sound of their machine guns reached us long after they had pulled out of the dives. We glanced occasionally at the ready-made German foxholes, dug by impressed civilians and lining the road every 10 yards. They were chest deep and round, with dirt piled neatly beside them; but every one was smooth on the inside so we knew that Jerry had never used them.

We plodded along past wrecked vehicles and modern homes with well-kept yards, and glanced at the terrain off to our left where the war was. Dutch kids by the side of the road, wearing bright orange bows in their hair or on their jackets, reached for our hands.

"Good-bye," they said. They say that either way, whether you're going or coming, as a greeting or as a farewell.

Hutch was walking behind me.

Hutch is Mack Pierce, a mortar sergeant in F Company. He used to be in A Company, where he was a line sergeant, then an artificer and finally mess sergeant. He was a mess sergeant for 18 months, and then he went over the hill and got busted. He transferred to F Company after that, and they finally gave him three stripes again, but he didn't care. He never did care much for things like that.

This was our anniversary—Hutch's and mine. We had been in the Army four years. We were members of the Tennessee National Guard, inducted Sept. 16, 1940, among the oldest of the "New Army." Today we were moving up to an assembly area where our outfit—the 30th (Old Hickory) Division—would get set for an attack.

It was a bright day, as days go here. The 2d Battalion was two parallel OD lines moving across the brow of a hill up ahead and swinging around the shaded curve behind us. They were leaving Maastricht, a fair-sized town taken two days before. Now

—after France and Belgium and Holland—they were headed for Germany.

I was with Hutch down in F Company because Hutch is the only line soldier left out of the old bunch from the highlands of east Tennessee who came into the Army as Company A. There were about 150 of us then. Now there are only four in the regiment. There's Hutch, down in the 2d Battalion. Then there's Porky Colman, a mess sergeant now; Charlie Grindstaff, still cooking; and Herman O. Parker, still driving a truck. They're all that's left of old A Company.

We started out in the Army at Fort Jackson, S. C., when they were singing the song "I'll Never Smile Again." Lord, we were sentimental about that song. I remember Hilton was just married and was leaving his new wife. Crockett slugged the juke box in the drug store at Columbia; Tommy Dorsey's arrangement came out soft and smooth, and Hilton cried. We were all privates then, going into the Army for a year.

Since then, Hilton's kid brother had become a tail gunner in a Fort and had gone down over France. Hilton got out of the Army and his wife had a baby on the same day. Hilton stayed out of the Army for two years. Now he's in the Navy somewhere. Crockett went from a basic private up to first sergeant and then to OCS. Now he's a first lieutenant in an infantry outfit over here.

Hutch Pierce and I walked up the road. Somebody—a replacement—sang briefly and then stopped. The infantry doesn't sing much, especially moving up. Not after St. Lo and Mortain, they don't sing much. The replacement chanted: "Or you might grow up to be a mule. Now, a mule is an animal with long funny ears."

Hutch and I talked along the way. When we got a break we lit K-ration cigarettes and tried to reconstruct A Company.

It was a picturesque outfit. Those originals were close-knit, clannish and independent as only hill people can be. It was a company with a heart and a soul. Its code was "Independence." Its motto, in our own language, was "take nothin' offen nobody." That was a philosophy that needed tempering. It works better in combat than in garrison. We had our troubles.

I had seen Col. Crumley in London. He's had a desk job there now since his lungs finally took him out of the field into the hospital. He was a first lieutenant when we went to Jackson, then company commander and then battalion commander. We talked about the old company before it broke up. Crumley was hard, but he loved the company. He was a better soldier than any of us, but he was proud of us—a man who lived by our philosophy and tempered it, too. We learned to take a lot, as the infantry does.

It has been three years since Crumley was with us as a company officer, but Hutch said: "When you're out here you appreciate a man like him."

We tried, Hutch and I, to tell each other what little we knew of the men who came in with us. The outfit had deteriorated slowly in the natural process of transfers and discharges, like an eroded hillside gradually falling away.

Harry Nave, the company clerk, went into the Air Forces as a cadet and got killed in training. Lardo Boring went into the Air Forces, too, and the last we heard, he had pulled his missions and was back home. Lardo used to be in the machine-gun section.

Earl Marshall went into the Paratroops, and so did Bill Longmire. Elmer Simerly was in the Airborne Infantry. Bill Potter went to OCS and the last we knew he was in New Guinea. Red Mason was a lieutenant over there somewhere. Ralph Snavely was one of the first to transfer out. He went down to the Southwest Pacific, too. Lucian Garrison went to Italy and got wounded, and so did Capt. Ritts. Ed Mottern was in Iceland for a long time but he's probably over here now.

Hutch had seen Pony Miller on the beach back in June. Pony is a first now, and an executive officer. Hutch said he'd heard that Howard Fair went in with the 1st Division on D-Day. Charles Hurt got his jaw broken on maneuvers just before A Company came overseas, so he stayed in the States.

Doc Sharp was transferred; he's down in the Islands with a jungle-training unit, still letting the cards fall the same as always. Jack Ellis came over with another regiment in the division, but he got wounded and we lost track of him. Fred Davis was a captain in the TDS the last we knew.

A Company came to England with only 12 of the old National Guard bunch still left and just a few of our first and second batches of selectees. Now there's only one line soldier left from the first group of selectees we trained—a boy named J. C. Wright. Wright was wounded some time back, but he rejoined the company later as an acting platoon sergeant. Then they got a new lieutenant, and he and J. C. had an argument. J. C. is platoon guide now.

The outfit came to France on D-plus-9. Three weeks went by before they hit it rough. Then, on July 7, the regiment spearheaded the way across the Vire River and fought down through the hedgerows toward St. Lo.

It was a war foreign to the sage fields and pine thickets of South Carolina. It was a war from one piled-up mass of earth and shrubbery to another, with the Artillery blasting savagely and the infantry moving up 50 yards behind it. Those hedges are old, and the decay has built up at their base to form solid walls. Each one of them was a wall of fire, and the open fields between were plains of fire. The flanking hedges on either side belonged to him who could cover them.

Two of the boys from the hills stopped there. One of them was Bill Whitson, black-haired, with a face so dark that his teeth seemed whiter than they really were. He was built like a god—broad and tall. He lived like a happy devil, untamed and untameable. Whit never took anything very seriously. He moved with the corded grace of a panther, lethal and full of power. He could make the sling of his '03 rifle crack like gunfire when the leather hit the hardness of his hand.

Whit raised his head out of a foxhole and a piece of shrapnel caught him flush in the temple. He died somewhere northeast of St. Lo. Bull Bowers got hit there, too, the same day.

Bull is a big boy, almost pudgy, with round cheeks that are a perpetual cherry red. His name is James, but he's always been called Bull because when his voice changed it came out low, deep and throaty, so that whatever Bull said he said it in a rumble with a drawl.

Bull is easygoing. He never pushes anybody unless somebody pushes him. His make-up is not the make-up of a tough platoon sergeant. Bull's a platoon sergeant who swore softly rather often, but never with very much conviction.

So when they pulled Bull out of the foxhole, after the shrapnel had gone into him, he looked at his legs and then said to nobody in particular, without a great deal of violence and in a slow rumble: "Them gawdam sons o' bitches."

Bull was evacuated. Two days later Dale May left the outfit because of sickness. He had stomach trouble—ulcers or something.

Dale got to be a sergeant right after we came into the Army because he was one of the few men in the outfit with service in the Regulars. He had pulled a hitch at Schofield Barracks, and he told us stories about the Old Army—of afternoons off, tailor-made khaki blouses, white gloves and chrome bayonets, and how he was pulling KP when his discharge papers came through and he could go back to the mainland.

Dale was a tech sergeant when he left A Company. The boys in the kitchen hear he's in a Quartermaster outfit now.

The regiment's objective was the high ground to the west overlooking St. Lo. They took it, so they were a protective screen for the outfits that went into St. Lo itself. Then A Company moved south toward Tessy-sur-Vire.

On July 28, the regiment hit trouble. The next day the 1st Battalion went in to attack near a place called Le Mesnil Opac. There were hedgerows again, and a long slope exposed to observation and heavy fire. One of the men wounded in the action was Pfc. James R. Baines.

We always called him Beans. He had been a tech sergeant but had got busted. When he made platoon sergeant he told one of the boys who got another rocker with him: "Well, they made everybody else, now they made us." That was back in the States. Nobody cared much for stripes back there any more than they do over here now. Too many people on your back, too much worry, too much bother. Beans got hit by shrapnel and was evacuated. The next night Clyde Angel was killed.

Clyde was blond and fair. He talked with the nasal twang of east Tennessee. He was a mess sergeant and before that he had been a cook in the company, just as his brother Monk had been a cook for us before him. There were two other cooks, men who had come to the company later, who were killed with Clyde.

The kitchens were dispersed and everybody was dug in. Charlie Grindstaff said Clyde had the best shelter in the area. He and the other two dug a deep one and covered it with logs and dirt. Then Jerry came over, dropping big-stuff bombs that straddled the shelter. The concussion killed all three of them in the hole. A Company's kitchen was blown to hell. Now Porky uses the battalion h.q. blackout tent for a cook tent.

The next night the regiment made its objective beyond Tessy-sur-Vire and later moved on to relieve elements of the 1st Division near St. Barthelmy. St. Barthelmy is close by Mortain, not far from the base of the Cherbourg peninsula. It was between Mortain and Avranches by the sea that our armor had roared southwest into Brittany after the breakthrough at St. Lo. At St. Barthelmy A Company gave everything it had. It was there that the regiment was hit—hard.

The SS had counterattacked with tanks, and the German artillery was trying to cut through to split our forces in Normandy and Brittany. The Germans hit savagely. They ran over A Company and C Company. The regiment fought like animals with everything that would fire and then fought hand-to-hand with the German infantry that poured in behind the tanks.

Jerry almost made it. The fight went on for four days while the division struggled and gave ground but never broke. Then, on the fifth day, the power was gone and we went back into St. Barthelmy. The SS spearhead was blunted and then broken off. But Bud Hale was gone, and Ed Markland.

Bud was the top kick. He was a little guy with delicate hands and a skin that stretched tight across the cheekbones. His eyes were the eyes of all his family. At home the Hales have eyes that are all alike. Frances, Virginia, Luke, Sara, Bud, Mary, Nell and Sonny—they all have eyes that are their medium of expression. Bud played football at home the year we won the state championship and before. He was the kind of boy who drew people to him. Over here one of the new boys in the kitchen put it right: "We had to take the chow up to the line, and when I could see Bud I felt like the whole company was there."

After the SS ran over the company, Bud was listed as missing in action. So was Markland.

Ed and I were mortar corporals together for a long time, and our anniversary today would have been a great day for him. The division commander came around this morning presenting medals to a few officers and men in the regiment. The general order for the award of the Silver Star included T/Sgt. George Edward Markland "for gallantry in action in France."

The day after Angel was killed Ed's outfit had been held up by fire from a dug-in position. Ed crawled up ahead, "consistently exposed himself to murderous enemy mortar and artillery fire." We adjusted our own artillery on the strongpoint and the attack went on. Ed wasn't here to get in on the little ceremony by the road this morning, but he may catch the later one. A Company doesn't refer to Bud and Ed as MIA but as captured. Jerry got a lot of prisoners that day. Ernest Oaks was hit there, too.

When the SS overran our antitank positions and knocked out four of the guns, Oaks had to be evacuated. He had been in A Company for a long time —part of the triumvirate of Potter, Oaks and Russell. When we came into the Army none of them was 20. They were wild. They laughed and did insane things. Russell—we called him "Reb" although all of us are Southerners—was wide-eyed during our training on the machine gun. The nomenclature delighted him. One day the section sergeant had us naming the parts of the piece and he picked up a tiny pin and asked Reb to identify it.

Reb gazed thoughtfully at the pin.

"That," he said, "is the forward cam lever for the plunger guide on the barrel extension with the swivel pawl."

St. Barthelmy-Mortain was the division's great trial. It was infantry against armor, and the division fought for survival. Col. Frankland, the 1st Battalion's commander, saved his own CP by killing the crew of a German tank with his .45. Parts of five German *Panzer* outfits hit the division, striking along the main highways and the back roads. The division was committed to the last man. The artillery was overrun and fought as infantry. The engineers and cavalry were on the line. Thirty Jerry tanks were destroyed. The engineers got a Mark IV with a bazooka. An AT commander stopped another with a bazooka and killed the crew with a carbine as they tried to get out.

In the fog of the morning of Aug. 7, the regiment and division survived. Our artillery, TDs, rocket-firing planes and armor were thrown in to add strength to a line that was thin. A Company survived.

One battalion of a sister regiment was isolated for three days, cut off on a cliff and blasted mercilessly. When the Germans came forward under a white flag to talk surrender, the battalion said: "Go to hell."

Our 2d Battalion—Hutch's outfit—helped get them out.

Hutch has had the experiences of a line soldier. A machine-gun bullet burned the back of his neck. The blast of Screaming Minnies cartwheeled him off his feet. A little piece of shrapnel cut across the top of his foot, but he didn't bother to have it treated.

Hutch laughed and said: "The damndest thing I've seen in combat happened that day. We went up after the battalion that was lost. There was a goat up there. He was a sorry-looking goat, sort of a dirty gray.

"Well, we were getting artillery, and every time a shell would come in this goat would dive for a foxhole. Then he would raise his head up and if he didn't hear anything he would come out. There were plenty of foxholes and he knew what they were for. He'd do it every time."

We laughed at the picture of a bewhiskered goat in a foxhole. One infantryman said: "Yeah. The reason he beat me into one was because he had four legs and me just two."

A Company had two of our originals left in the line after St. Barthelmy. Now both of them are gone —perhaps to come back to the outfit, perhaps not to come back to it at all.

Both went back with fatigue, with nerves that had stood all they could stand for a while.

One of them left just a few days ago, after a river crossing that stirred up a fight. It was a fight like a dozen others the company has had. But it was one too many for him.

The other one who went back is a twin. He and his brother are identical. There were some of us who had soldiered with them every day and still couldn't tell them apart. They're squat and tow-headed and when they laugh their faces crease into a fan of wrinkles from the outside corners of their eyes. They grinned almost always, but when they got mad their lips quivered and they trembled all over, and we were surprised that they did. Not long before the company left the States, one of them was transferred and the other stayed on alone. But part of him was gone.

Yesterday, in a courtyard, Parker and I lay sprawled on the trailer of his jeep and watched as the infantry went past on the outside lane. It was a patrol coming in. "Hit anything?" somebody asked. A voice answered: "Nuh." The patrol went by silently.

"Was that some of us?" I asked Parker.

"Doggone," said Herman, "I don't know. I don't know anybody in the company any more."